T0327605

RESEARCH IN MARITIME HISTORY
NO. 23

THE GLOBALISATION
OF THE OCEANS:
CONTAINERISATION FROM THE 1950s
TO THE PRESENT

Frank Broeze

International Maritime Economic History Association

St. John's, Newfoundland
2002

ISSN 1188-3928
ISBN 0-9730073-3-8

Back issues of *Research in Maritime History* are available:

Research in Maritime History would like to thank Memorial University of Newfoundland for its generous financial assistance in support of this volume.

PROFESSOR FRANK BROEZE

Table of Contents

i

List of Figures

List of Tables

Abbreviations, Acronyms and Glossary

ACE	Container Consortium in the Europe-East Asia Trade
ACL	Atlantic Container Line
ACT(A)	Associated Container Transportation (Australia)
AECS	Australia Europe Container Service
ANERA	Asia North America Eastbound Rate Agreement
ANL	Australian National Line
ANZECS	Australia New Zealand Europe Container Service
APL	American President Lines
B	Belgium
B&C	British and Commonwealth
BLG	Bremer Lagerhausgesellschaft [Bremen Warehousing Company]
BNSF	Burlington Northern and Santa Fe (US railroad system)
CAROL	Caribbean Overseas Lines
CDS	Construction Differential Subsidies
CEO	Chief Executive Officer
CGM	Compagnie Générale Maritime
CGT	Compagnie Générale Transatlantique
CIY	Containerisation International Yearbook
CMA	Compagnie Maritime d'Affrètement
CMB	Compagnie Maritime Belge
CND	Canada
COSCO	China Overseas Shipping Corporation
CP	Canadian Pacific
CR	Chargeurs Réunis (France)
CRSSI	Council for the Rationalization of the Shipping and Shipbuilding Industries (Japan)
CSAV	Compañia Sud Americana de Vapores (Chile)
CT	Container Terminal
D	Germany
DG	Directorate-General
DPA	Dubai Ports Authority
DSR	Deutsche Schiffsreederei Rostock [German Shipping Company Rostock]
dwt	Deadweight tonnage, a vessel's cargo carrying capacity
EAC	East Asiatic Company (Denmark)
EC	European Commission
ECT	Europe Container Terminus (Rotterdam/Europoort)
EU	European Union

F	France
FEFC	Far Eastern Freight Conference
FESCO	Far Eastern Shipping Company (Vladivostok)
FEU	Forty-feet Equivalent Unit (both a standard container of forty by eight by eight feet and its equivalent volume, e.g. two TEU boxes)
FOC	Flag of Convenience, registration in another state than that of a shipping company's headquarters; mostly for fiscal, financial and/or crewing considerations in order to cut costs
GB	Great Britain
GL	Germanischer Lloyd
GRT	Gross Register Ton
HAL	Holland-America Line
Hapag	Hamburg-Amerikanische Packetfahrtgesellschaft (also known as Hamburg-America Line)
HHLA	Hamburger Hafen- und Lagergesellschaft [Hamburg Port and Warehousing Company]
HMM	Hyundai Merchant Marine
HPH	Hutchison Port Holdings
hub	Central port in a regional system
ICTSI	International Container Terminal Services Inc.
IGA	Inter-Group Agreement
ILA	International Longshoremen's Association
ILO	International Labour Organisation
ILWU	International Longshoremen and Warehousemen Union
Intermodalism	Integrated maritime-railway transport system
IR	International Register (second, alternative, shipping register of a non Flag of Convenience country, conveying similar advantages as a Flag of Convenience registration)
IT	Information Technology
ITF	International Transport Workers' Federation
JESCO	Japan-Europe Shipping Company (trading name for the trans-Siberian container landbridge in the Japan-Europe trade)
K-Line	Kawasaki Kisen Kaisha
KSC	Korea Shipping Corporation
KNSM	Koninklijke Nederlandsche Stoomboot Maatschappij (Netherlands)
LASH	Lighter Aboard Ship, alternative maritime transport system, based on the carriage of barges
Loop	A series of successive ports of call, broadly characterised by a circular pattern; the first port occasionally is identical to the last one
LNG	Liquid Natural Gas
LPG	Liquid Petroleum Gas

M&M	Mechanization and Modernization
MISC	Malaysian International Shipping Corporation
Mitsui OSK	Mitsui Osaka Shosen Kaisha
MOL	Mitsui OSK Lines
MSC	Mediterranean Shipping Corporation (Geneva/Genoa)
MUA	Maritime Union of Australia
NAA	North-Atlantic Agreement
NAFTA	North American Free Trade Agreement
NCDUJ	National Council of Dockworkers' Unions of Japan
NL	Netherlands
NOL	Neptune Orient Lines (Singapore)
NSU	Nederlandse Scheepvaart Unie
NYK	Nippon Yusen Kaisha
OCL	Overseas Container Ltd
ODS	Operation Differential Subsidies
OECD	Organisation for European Cooperation and Development
OOCL	Orient Overseas Container Line
OPEC	Organisation of Petroleum Exporting Countries
OSK	Osaka Shosen Kaisha
OT&T	Ocean Trade and Transport (previously Ocean Steam Ship Company)
P&O	Peninsular and Oriental Steam Navigation Company
P&OCL	[is full name]
PAD	Pacific Australia Direct Line
Panamax	A ship with a width capable of traversing the Panama Canal
Pendulum service	A shipping service covering two or all three of the following trade routes: US East Coast-Europe-East Asia-US West Coast, without traversing the Panama Canal; with integrated railroad connections between the US West Coast and US East Coast, an intermodal round-the-world service may be offered (cf. RTW)
Piggy-back	The carriage of trailers on railway cars
PMA	Pacific Maritime Association
Post-Panamax	A ship that is too wide to traverse the Panama Canal
PSA	Port of Singapore Authority
PNW	Pacific-northern West Coast USA (service)
PSW	Pacific-southern West Coast USA (service)
QD	Quick Despatch (Rotterdam stevedore)
RoRo	Roll-on Roll-off, alternative maritime transport system, based on the carriage of trailers aboard ship
RSA	Republic of South Africa
RTW	Round-the-World (only used for purely maritime services)
S	Sweden
SAECS	Southern Africa-Europe Container Service

SCT	Southampton Container Terminal
Shp	Shaft horsepower
Stack train	Double-decker freight train for the carriage of containers
String	A series of successive ports of call
TAA	Trans-Atlantic Agreement
TACA	Trans-Atlantic Conference Agreement
Terminus	First and/or last port of a service
TEU	Twenty-feet Equivalent Unit (both a standard container of twenty by eight by eight and it equivalent volume; one FEU, for example, equals two TEUs)
TFL	Trans Freight Lines
TGWU	Transport and General Workers' Union
TMM	Transportacíon Marítima Mexicana
TNT	Thomas Nationwide Transport (Australia)
TRIO	Container Consortium in the Europe-East Asia Trade
TPWA	Trans-Pacific Westbound Rate Agreement
UAE	United Arab Emirates
UASC	United Arab Shipping Company
UK	United Kingdom
ULCC	Ultra-large crude carrier (oil tanker of over 350,000 dwt)
UNCLOS	United Nations Convention on the Law of the Sea
UNCTAD	United Nations Conference on Trade and Development
US(A)	United States (of America)
USEC	US East Coast
USSR	Union of Soviet Socialist Republics
USWC	US West Coast
VLCC	Very Large Crude Carrier (250,000-350,000 dwt oil tanker)
VNS	Vereenigde Nederlandsche Scheepvaart Maatschappij (Netherlands)
WTO	World Trade Organisation
YS	Yamashita-Shinnihon

Acknowledgments

This book could not have been written without the inspiration, encouragement and material assistance of many people. Among those who helped bring together maritime studies, documents and other research data from across the globe I express my deepest gratitude to the staff of the Reid Library of the University of Western Australia, especially Mrs. En Kho at its Inter-Library Loan desk, the Library and Information Services of Western Australia, the bibliographical service of the Netherlands Directorate-General of Transport and, last but not least, Ms. Sunita Thillainath, librarian of the Port of Fremantle Authority.

Over the years public-service officers of numerous shipping companies and port authorities were particularly helpful in making material available to me. At the risk of being unjust to other firms, I may single out and thank P&O Nedlloyd and many of its constituent companies, the Compagnie Maritime Belge, Hapag-Lloyd, Sea-Land, American President Lines, Maersk Sealand, Zim Israel and the United Arab Shipping Company. It was several of these companies, too, and none more so than APL, which in most recent times alerted me to the full potential of the internet for the purposes of historical research.

Many colleagues over the years, in the classical scholarly tradition of the generous sharing of documentation and ideas, discussed rougher and finer points of the container revolution with me in academic forums and numerous informal meetings, emails and other means. Among those who helped propel my project forward and maintain its global focus I should like to mention Lars Scholl, Sarah Palmer, David Starkey, Gordon Jackson, David Williams, Peter N. Davies, Adrian Jarvis, Robin Craig, Lewis R. ("Skip") Fischer, James Reveley, Keith Trace, Dr. K.V. Hariharan and, especially singled out for her enthusiasm, Gelina Harlaftis. To all I owe a deep and heartfelt gratitude.

I should also like to express my appreciation for the advice, both in person and by correspondence, from Arthur Donovan, Professor of Maritime History at the US Merchant Marine Academy, Kings Point, New York, whose important book *The Abandoned Ocean. A History of United States Maritime Policy* (co-authored with Andrew Gibson) regrettably arrived too late Down Under for me to be able to consider its rich contents for consideration in this work. But most of my academic debt I owe to Malcolm Tull, Murdoch University (Perth) and Hugo van Driel, Erasmus University (Rotterdam), who, most generously drawing on their own expert knowledge of the modern maritime industries, read and commented on drafts of individual chapters. Needless to say, the responsibility for all flaws of the book remain mine.

Ironically, perhaps the greatest encouragement to write about containerisation came from friends and colleagues without any interest in ships, ports or land transport who increasingly complained they could go nowhere about their business or on vacation "without everywhere seeing those damned boxes of yours!" Some of them became converts, even, as my son did, spotting sea containers through their favourite TV programs.

Last but not least, this book is dedicated to Ulli and Carsten for all their love, inspiration and companionship.

Preface[1]

We are as strategic as Singapore so there's no reason why Malaysia cannot be a hub for shipping routes in the region.[2]

But Singapore does boast something extra – "connectivity." In shipping parlance this refers to the number of global destinations that can be reached by shippers...in the fastest possible time.[3]

When Frank Broeze died in April 2001 his last manuscript was almost ready for publication. His wife, Ulli, asked me to read and proof the manuscript, and so I entered upon my last collaboration with Frank. As always Frank opened up new horizons for me and provided an opportunity to explore a new, exciting and revolutionary chapter of maritime history. The International Maritime Economic History Association, in its series *Research in Maritime History*, generously offered to publish a work that in its vision and analysis stands as a fitting tribute to a great scholar and champion of maritime studies.

Shortly before Frank Broeze died we had a discussion about the on-going impact of containerisation upon the world community. Frank was convinced that the next great area of impact would be the international political arena and briefly mentioned the tension between Malaysia and Singapore that in part focussed on the growth of rival container ports.

In early 2002 the rivalry between the two states caught the attention of the local media. In March, *The Straits Times* noted that Malaysia was planning to develop Senai Airport as a major regional cargo uplift point to be linked by rail and highway to two Malaysian container ports facing Singapore island: Tanjung Pelepas and Pasir Gudang.[4] In April 2002, the Singapore *Sunday Times*

---

[1]My thanks to Peter Reeves of the National University of Singapore for providing newspaper material.

[2]The Malaysian Prime Minister, Dr. Mahathir Mohammed, *The Sunday Times* (Singapore), 17 April 2002.

[3]Michael Fang (transport reporter), in *The Straits Times* (Singapore), 20 April 2002.

[4]*Ibid.*, 7 March 2002.

had a banner headline reading "Johor Gears Up for Port Battle" in which it outlined the development of a political and economic struggle between Malaysia and Singapore for supremacy in the container hub stakes.[5] Later that month, the *Far Eastern Economic Review* had a lengthy article examining the growing political row between the two states, ostensibly based upon Malaysian claims that Singaporean land reclamation was aimed at closing the shipping channels to its potential Malaysian rivals.[6]

The dispute caught my attention because it involved so many of the factors and actors that Frank Broeze covered in this book. It seemed to me that a brief postscript to his work was warranted since the dispute between Singapore and Malaysia highlighted the central points of Frank's history of the "container revolution."

Put briefly, the story of the rivalry between the two countries over the issue of containerisation took shape when Malaysia lured Maersk – the Port of Singapore's (PSA) biggest customer – away from Singapore in 2000. Early in 2002, a second major container company, Taiwan's Evergreen, was also tempted away from Singapore with the offer of a thirty-percent stake in Tanjung Pelepas, handling costs that were thirty to forty percent lower than in Singapore and a haulage joint venture with a Malaysian consortium.[7]

But the luring of Maersk and Evergreen was only one part of the Malaysian plan to create the major regional container hub. Hand-in-hand with attracting these companies (which accounted for some twenty percent of Singapore's container traffic), Malaysia embarked on a major infrastructure programme to link its container ports to its national road, rail and airport network. The Malaysian government has allocated over US $1 billion to build highways and a rail link, to improve container-handling facilities, and to upgrade airport facilities to provide an integrated transport and supply network for the new container ports. A German company, Hochtief Airport GmBh, was contracted to manage Senai Airport and to increase its uplift capacity from 7000 to 100,000 tonnes of cargo by 2008, thereby transforming it into a major transportation hub. In addition, plans were announced to improve the international airline linkages of Kuala Lumpur, and part of the deal with Evergreen was the promise of increased landing rights for its airline, EVA, at both Senai and Kuala Lumpur.[8]

---

[5]*The Sunday Times* (Singapore), 17 April 2002.

[6]*Far Eastern Economic Review*, 18 April 2002.

[7]*The Straits Times* (Singapore), 13 April 2002.

[8]*Far Eastern Economic Review*, 18 April 2002; *The Straits Times* (Singapore), 7 and 19 March, and 2, 4, 10 and 11 April 2002; and *The Sunday Times* (Singapore), 17 March 2002.

Malaysia has learned well. Its plans include a fully-integrated transport system linking port, road, rail and air, and its handling costs are cheaper than those of Singapore. Here the story rests for the moment. Malaysia has put in place all those pieces of the container puzzle that Frank has examined in his story, and the battle for containers has now entered the political arena. Land reclamation, blocked shipping channels and an increasingly bitter rivalry to attract containers has exacerbated already-heightened tensions between two states. Singapore has publicly shrugged off the Malaysian challenge,[9] but it has been warned that it needs to lower the cost of services to shipping and in the longer term "will have to move beyond its traditional role as a port and cargo centre to stay competitive...[and] to develop further all other services required by users of an international maritime centre including intellectual services such as financing, insurance and legal services."[10]

Kenneth McPherson

---

[9]*The Straits Times* (Singapore), 20 April 2002.

[10]*Ibid.*, 6 April 2002.

INTRODUCTION

Without the container the global village would still be a concept, not a reality...[1]

Globalisation is the hallmark of our times. It is well-nigh impossible to escape the material and cultural webs spun by oil and energy companies, automobile firms, media corporations, tobacco and junk food conglomerates, the internet and many other transnational agents. But, although globalisation has become a household word, there is little recognition that our world could not function without the complex system of maritime transport sustaining intercontinental and regional trade.

Container shipping stands at the quality end of that infrastructure. At the turn of the millennium its 13.5 million boxes carried over ninety percent of the non-bulk trade of the world. The total value of all container cargoes exceeded seventy percent of all world trade.[2] After annual growth figures that more often than not ran into double figures, the turnover of all ports in the world has surpassed 200,000,000 containers per year. Although it cannot possibly match oil and bulk shipping in volume and tonne-miles, container shipping is the pre-eminent sector of the world's deep-sea merchant fleet. And through its spectacular growth and span, its still rising productivity and declining freight rates, and continuous improvements to the efficiency and quality of its maritime and door-to-door services, it has had a powerful stimulating effect on world trade – an aspect that, as the industry itself, is often overlooked.

The only "global" business history to give container shipping its full due was Fiona Gilmore's *Brand Warriors*, in which C.C. Tung, chairman, president and CEO of Orient Overseas Container Lines (OOCL) of Hong Kong took his place alongside fourteen leaders of other global companies.[3] Apart from giving revealing insights into the philosophy of his management of OOCL and the corporate strategy of the company, Tung also asserted that

---

[1]C.C. Tung, CEO of Orient Overseas Container Line, quoted in Fiona Gilmore (ed.), *Brand Warriors. Corporate Leaders Share Their Winning Strategies* (London, 1997), 80.

[2]Based on the figures in Niko Wijnolst and Tor Wergeland, *Shipping* (Delft, 1996), 19.

[3]Gilmore (ed.), *Brand Warriors*, 79-92.

1

global container transportation provid[es] the vital link to world trade...Without the container the global village would still be a concept, not a reality, because manufacturing would still be a local process. Car companies, for instance, would still have to insist that their components suppliers were located within 150 miles of their factory, as they once did.[4]

The reasons for this neglect are complex, but several features stand out. Shipping and ports, as indeed all seaborne activity, are rarely included in broader economic, trade or business studies.[5] All too often matters maritime are still – wrongly – regarded as non-mainstream subjects best left to professionals, afficionados and ship lovers. Oil tankers received more public attention, partly because of the flamboyant character of a few prominent shipowners in the trade, such as Niarchos and Onassis, partly because of their unprecedented dimensions,[6] and partly also because of their frequent involvement in flags-of-convenience controversies. Overall investment in the container industry is comparatively modest compared to that in manufacturing, energy and mining (total investments in containerisation between 1970 and the mid-1990s have been estimated at some US \$65 billion).[7] In view of its essentially international structure and service character, the industry does not lend itself easily to analysis.

Perhaps because of these reasons containerisation escaped the attention of British journalist Anthony Sampson, who devoted a series of books to global

---

[4]*Ibid.*, 79-80; see also H.A. Thanopoulou, "From Internationalisation to Globalisation: Trends in Modern Shipping," *Journal of Maritime Research* [electronic] (February 2000), 2.

[5]See, e.g., Mira Wilkins (ed.), *The Growth of Multinationals* (Aldershot, 1991); Jeremy Howells and Michelle Wood, *The Globalisation of Production and Technology* (London, 1993); Hans-Peter Martin and Harald Schumann, *The Global Trap: Globalisation and the Assault on Prosperity and Democracy* (London, 1996); and Peter J. Rimmer (ed.), *Pacific Rim Development: Integration and Globalisation in the Asia-Pacific Economy* (Sydney, 1997). For exceptions, see Gordon Boyce, *Information, Mediation and Institutional Development. The Rise of Large-Scale Enterprise in British Shipping, 1870-1919* (Manchester, 1995); and Gilmore (ed.), *Brand Warriors*.

[6]As evidenced, for example, by Noël Mostert's best-seller *Supership* (London, 1974).

[7]*Containerisation International* (April 1996), 9, based on a report from the International Council of Containership Operators. The market value of each of the seven largest stocks trading on Wall Street on 29 December 1995 was higher than that amount, Exxon topping the list with US \$145 billion; Otto Johnson (ed.), *1997 Information Please Almanac* (Boston, 1997), 62.

business sectors such as oil, the arms trade and civil aviation.[8] It might also be suggested that container terminals and ships are out of sight and out of mind, but that is certainly not always the case. At many ports huge container cranes are visible from afar, and the box itself has penetrated all six continents and is, in its global mobility, a routine sighting on road and rail. Yet historians have shunned the simple sea container, utilitarian and ubiquitous, and the highly sophisticated system of maritime and multi-modal transport which it has created.

The purpose of this book then is to present an up-to-date history of containerisation from its beginnings in the 1950s to the present, the first since Hans Jürgen Witthöft in 1978 published his remarkable *Container. Transport-revolution unseres Jahrhunderts.* Even more than Witthöft's work, the scope of this volume is fully global. Any such history must, in the first instance, focus on the container shipping industry, its expansion on all trading routes, and the technological and organisational revolutions that transformed liner shipping from a stagnating industry at the very limits of its technological capacity into a transport system of almost unlimited dynamism. The most prominent innovations of containerisation included radically new designs for vessels and cargo-handling facilities, global door-to-door traffic, early use of computers and the internet, and structural change in the industry through the formation of consortia, alliances and international mega-mergers. This growth was accompanied by significant diversification and projection of power ashore into container terminals, shipping agencies and inland transport. Finally, through the creation of global networks, enlargement of scale and worldwide investments by both shipping and port management companies, the container industry, from being a helpmate to globalisation, became one of its major exponents.

To achieve its purpose the book begins with a conceptual introduction to containerisation, after which four chapters discuss the growth and development of the container industry in an amalgam of chronological and thematic approaches. There is no alternative to that structure, as the introduction of successive innovations and their diffusion through the industry were very much the results of the conjunction of external historical circumstances and internal, industry-based, constraints and imperatives. Thus, each of the decades, in succession, can be characterised by a major advance: oceanic beginnings (late 1950s and 1960s); conquest of the world (1970s); the second revolution (1980s); and globalisation (1990s). But each of these themes subsume a host of inter-related subsidiary issues, such as the pioneering work, strong leadership, and ultimate demise of US shipping companies; the rise of the economies of East Asia

---

[8]Anthony Sampson, *The Seven Sisters. The Great Oil Companies and the World They Made* (London, 1975); *The Arms Bazaar, The Companies, The Dealers, The Bribes. From Vickers to Lockheed* (London, 1977); and *Empires of the Sky. The Politics, Contests and Cartels of World Airlines* (London, 1984), all of which were reprinted many times in soft-cover editions.

– a term used in this book to indicate the entire region stretching northeast from Indonesia and Singapore to Japan, Korea and Siberia – in synergy with the growth of their container fleets; the consortium system and its later, partial, replacement by global alliances and mega-mergers; and the increased attention paid to branding as a marketing strategy.

No history of containerisation would be complete, or even adequate, without reference to the enormous changes it wrought in ports and the port systems of the world. Container terminals, to a large extent, were created at virgin sites, either within established ports or at entirely new locations. As conventional liner facilities could hardly ever be reconstructed for container use, they were mostly left behind in derelict inner-city locations that worldwide became favourites of project developers and waterfront renewalists. The most significant change in the global port system, with its many and variant regional systems, was the significant but as yet incomplete transformation from conventional liner networks to hub-and-spoke models with a worldwide sprinkling of superports and pure entrepots. The supremacy of Singapore and Hong Kong, both the result of, and stimulus to, the economic growth of the larger region of East Asia, stand as monuments to the massive centripetal power of such hubs. And it is not coincidental that the Port of Singapore Authority and Hong Kong's major operator, Hutchison International Port Holdings, became two of the world's most active investors in, and managers of, overseas container terminals.

In a world of globalisation, constant restructuring and productivity increases through technological and organisational change, it is only fitting also to discuss the human and social consequences of containerisation. Aboard and ashore it decimated the numbers of seamen and dock workers whose trade unions – where they existed or were allowed to exist – naturally campaigned to minimise the losses suffered by their members. Seafarers faced not just severe reductions in crew size but also the registration of their vessels under flags of convenience, which mostly resulted in the total annihilation of their jobs. In principle, however, the employment of cheap, mostly Asian, crews is hardly different from the relocation of manufacturing from high-cost to low-cost economies. In container terminals, with the exception of the Arabian oil states, only national labour was used, but job losses were hardly less prominent. Nevertheless, it will be seen that even in the confrontationalist environment of the waterfront – in which a new brand of private or corporatised operating companies had replaced more placid traditional port authorities – understanding could still be achieved between employers and employees. Their agreements traded off down-sizing against permanency and significantly higher wages for those longshoremen who retained their jobs. Even the International Transport Workers' Federation acknowledged recently, albeit reluctantly, that it must overhaul its long-standing policies against flags of convenience and dockside downsizing.

Figure 1: The container links land and sea transport in an almost seamless and profoundly international continuum: an articulated lorry carries a container of Scandutch (the Swedish-Danish-Dutch consortium in the Europe-East Asia trade) high in the mountains of Switzerland past the Matterhorn.

Source: Eric Jennings, *Cargoes. A Centenary Story of the Far Eastern Freight Conference* (Singapore, 1980).

A final chapter draws together some important elements of the wider impact of containerisation in general and the box itself in particular. It begins with the cultural impact of the container, branded with the owner's name, through its ubiquity on roads and railways, often far removed from ships and ports. The sea, as never before, has invaded the land, and major company names and logos have become part of people's outlook throughout the world. Containers impinged also in other ways on cultural awareness, for example, as they became vehicles for the international drug trade or, more recently, the smuggling of refugees and illegal immigrants. But there are also alternative uses for the box, resulting from its sturdiness, mobility and adaptability, for example, for housing, canteens, prisons and many other ingenious purposes. Containerisation, finally, has become involved in what many now regard as the main problem besetting the future of our planet, the pollution and degradation of our environment. The construction of new, and the expansion of existing, container terminals at ecologically-fragile sites, and the dredging of ever-deeper access routes and wharfside berths in order to attract the largest container ships create serious environmental (and, occasionally, also heritage) problems at many locations.

And, perhaps rather ironically, not just the larger dimensions of container vessels but also their scrapping have become highly controversial because of the widespread use of asbestos in their construction and the presence of toxic anti-fouling paints on their hulls.

In a book of this format I could not possibly aim at presenting a comprehensive discussion of containerisation. The short-sea and north-south trades have not been neglected, but the emphasis is on the main east-west trades. The same applies to shipping companies and ports. Although it is vitally important to combine a structural approach to the industry with one that is heavily informed by the behaviour of individual firms and the thinking of their leaders, there always remains a fine balance to be drawn. Inevitably, selections must be made in choosing examples. There are also aspects that I have only mentioned in passing or touched upon lightly despite their obvious intrinsic interest. Thus, there are few references to the container shipbuilding industry in general and individual shipyards in particular, or the box-leasing business, which itself through takeovers and mergers has become something of a reflection of the industry at large.

Perhaps most important, I must stress that this is not a quantitative economic analysis of containerisation. I have specifically left aside issues such as market contestability, formation of freight rates and sustained cash-flow and profitability calculations. The former, a subject of lively debate in the second half of the 1980s,[9] was overtaken by developments and the realisation that it had no practical explanatory power. For a comprehensive accounting analysis of the industry, the collection of adequate sources is a major stumbling block, if only because many container operators form part of large maritime or general corporations. In any case, judging from the statements of some of the major participants in the industry, many of its leaders themselves had no precise insight into the financial position of their firms and made decisions based on gut feelings.[10] The formation of freight rates, finally, is a hoary problem, as old as the shipping industry itself, to which neither theory nor pragmatic analysis have been able to provide definitive answers. The container business, moreover, is far more complicated than the relatively transparent markets for bulk and oil carriers, with their relatively simple supply-demand models. An investigation

---

[9]See, e.g., J.E. Davies, "Competition, Contestability and the Liner Shipping Industry," *Journal of Transport Economics and Policy*, XX (September 1986), 299-312; J.A. Zerby, "Clarifying Some Issues Relating to Contestability in Liner Shipping (and Perhaps also Eliminating Some Doubts)," *Maritime Policy and Management*, XV, No. 1 (1988), 5-14; and J.E. Davies, "Impediments to Contestability in Liner Markets," *Logistics and Transportation Review*, XXV (1989), 325-342.

[10]See, e.g., APL's John M. Snow and OOCL's C.H. Tung, as quoted in *Containerisation International* (August 1996), 50; and (December 1997), 73.

carried out in 1995 to establish the cost of shipping electronic equipment from Singapore to Frankfurt, for example, found that ocean freight charged (and accepted) ranged from US $1700 to US $2400, and total point-to-point costs, including European port charges and inland haulage, from US $2883 to US $4253 per forty-foot container.[11]

As the first up-to-date history of containerisation, this book aims, in the first instance, at making a contribution to the history of modern shipping and business enterprise. But it should also be seen as a strong reminder that any study of the global economy should do more than pay lip service to the importance of its transport infrastructure. Shipping has always been an integral part of the world economic system and the rise, from the late 1960s, of mass long-distance civil aviation has made no fundamental change to that situation. Indeed, through its extraordinary growth and delivery of high-quality, low-cost services containerisation has probably stimulated global commerce more than any previous maritime technology and logistics system was able to achieve. Moreover, the container industry itself, through its round-the-world services and the worldwide expansion and intensification of its entrepreneurial influence, became a prime example of globalisation. The dynamics and results of the globalisation process stand as central themes in this book – as do its benefits and costs in human and social terms.

---

[11]*Containerisation International* (July 1995), 57.

Chapter 1
A Concept and Its Realisation

> The aim of the container operation is to replace this [conventional cargo handling] system with a through transport service which handles cargo in uniform, relatively large, but manageable units which, by application of mechanisation, can be moved from door-to-door with the minimum of hardship.[1]

Containerisation revolutionised liner shipping in all its physical, functional, organisational and human aspects. It industrialised the process of cargo handling and propelled the liner business into the modern worlds of computer and information technology. It was based on the application of two simple and related principles: the homogenisation of cargo into standardised units of a handy shape and volume in order to increase port productivity and reduce ship's time in port; and the use of such standardised units to create an effective multi-modal sea-and-land system with door-to-door transport from producer to consumer.

In the conventional maritime technologies that served the modern world economy until the 1960s, the piece goods carried by liner shipping were packed in bags, crates, boxes, packages, etc., of all kinds, sizes and shapes. For each successive stage of their voyage these had to be handled, sorted and stowed individually. This applied particularly to the land/sea interface, as the loading and discharging of the multitude of different cargo items between ship and wharf remained a slow and labourious process, even if since World War II some productivity gains had been made through the use of forklift trucks and pallets. Cargo-liners, on average, often had to spend a week or more in each port on their round-trip voyages, during which time not only they but also their cargoes were immobilised.[2] By 1960 often not even fifty percent of ship time was spent

---

[1]Sir Andrew Crichton, chairman of Overseas Containers Ltd., 1967, quoted in *Containerisation International* (December 1997), 72.

[2]A lively image of the "olden days" is offered in Richard Woodman, *Voyage East, A Cargo Ship in the 1960s* (London, 1988), as quoted in Sam Ignarski (ed.), *The Box. An Anthology Celebrating 25 Years of Containerisation and the TT Club* (London, 1996), 1-3; in a number of other reminiscences and company histories, such as Hans Georg Prager, *DDG Hansa. Vom Liniendienst zur Spezialschiffahrt* (Hereford, 1976); and in port handbooks, such as L. Wendemuth and W. Böttcher, *The Port of Hamburg* (Hamburg, 1927), 83-105. See also M.T. Tull, "Blood on the Cargo: Cargo-Handling and Working Conditions on the Waterfront at Fremantle, 1900-1930," *Labour History*, No. 52 (May

at sea, and current technology had reached the limits of its capabilities to achieve improvements in efficiency and productivity. By contrast, in the relatively young bulk sectors of the maritime freight market, ever larger oil tankers and dry-bulk carriers, operating in synergy with dedicated modern cargo loading and discharging facilities ashore, indicated the way ahead towards greater productivity through specialisation and enlargement of scale. In other words, while maritime bulk transport had been industrialised, the liner sector had progressed little further than its early twentieth-century semi-artisanal stage.

Conventional cargo-handling technology contained a second major inefficiency in that it kept the maritime and terrestrial legs of the total voyage of trade goods between producer and consumer almost totally isolated from each other. Ships loaded from and discharged into quayside warehouses and go-downs rather than directly into trains, trucks or vans. Inland and short-sea shipping could come alongside for loading or unloading, but that meant only delaying and relocating, not solving, the problem of the lack of articulation between water and land transport.

A few liner companies had diversified vertically into owning or controlling river, coastal or short-sea feeder shipping in order to increase their market share in contested hinterlands, but generally the successive modes of transport remained entrepreneurially and functionally autonomous, conditioned by their own technologies and market structures. Consequently, there was little or no change in the pace of cargo handling of overseas ships in port. The same can be observed with regards to the "real" forms of inland transport. Although many ports were served by railways, and increasingly also by the expanding road networks spawned by the 1950s explosion in the numbers of automobiles, trucks and vans, the advances made on land had no significant impact on ship's cargo-handling practices nor was there any degree of synergic coordination between the maritime and land sectors. Perhaps the most revolutionary aspect of containerisation was that it broke through the fetters of shipping's isolation in the transport chain and created physical and organisational multi-modal cooperation and, later, integration where none had existed before.

Containerisation, in the first instance, dramatically reduced the number of individual units to be lifted per ship, while the standard size and shape of the containers greatly simplified and accelerated stowage aboard. Ship's port time was slashed as the same volume of cargo was handled in a fraction of the time otherwise required. But of at least equal importance was the fact that the very same container could, without any sorting or repackaging of its cargo, be carried by rail, road or water (or any combination of the three) from the producer to the ship, and from the ship to the consumer. Even if true intermodalism, in the sense

1987), 15-29; and Tull, "American Technology and the Mechanisation of Australian Ports 1942 to 1958," *Journal of Transport History*, VI (1985), 79-90.

of the direct physical (seamless) transfer of containers between ship and land transport, took some time to develop and will probably remain largely limited to certain routes and commodities, the container successfully established door-to-door transport between producer and customer. The shipowner did not any more carry a mixed and complex number of piece goods but a number of cargo units of a standard shape and volume, each of which he rented out for the carriage of any kind of export cargo. Although he of course never stopped operating regular services, the container shipowner to some extent was influenced by the homogeneity of his cargo to adopt the philosophy of bulk shipping. As there was in principle no limitation on the movement of individual containers, they could be shipped through global networks of trunk-and-feeder services, not unlike messages shunted through the worldwide web.

The crux of the matter lies in the paradox that most of the container ship's cargo is no longer carried from port to port; instead, its boxes have an unlimited geographical mobility and move as their contents dictate, from any place on earth to any other. As global liner services operator Zim Israel Navigation Company declares in its motto, it is prepared to carry "All Cargo, To All Places, At All Times,"[3] a definition of function and purpose that is directly reminiscent of the "any cargo, anywhere, any time" creed of classical tramp shipping.

Still, the true meaning of Zim's motto goes further and far transcends the scope of that classical dictum as it relates not only to the maritime world of ports but also to the entire land mass of the economic world as the container reaches out into the furthest corners of the ports' hinterlands. By its capacity to be loaded and unloaded anywhere in the world, the container integrates land and sea as no previous technology has ever been able to do. Containerisation, in short, both required and created new transport philosophies. In combination with the organisational changes that containerisation brought to liner shipping, a new industrial culture emerged. Because of the international cooperation that it required, and following the experience of civil aviation, it also made English the working language of the container-shipping world.[4]

The vital advantage of the container was that during its entire voyage its contents could remain undisturbed, as it was the container itself that was moved through the multi-modal terrestrial and maritime transport chain. Loading (or "stuffing," as the jargon became) the container could be carried out at the producer's location, unpacking ("de-stuffing") at the final destination or consumer. The advantages of containerisation applied to all types of cargoes, but perhaps most to chilled and frozen meat carried in specially-equipped insulated

---

[3]Zim homepage, 1999 (http://www.zim.co.il/frmain.htm).

[4]See, for example, H.J. Korver, *Koninklijke Boot. Beeld van een amsterdamse scheepvaartonderneming 1856-1981* (Amsterdam, 1981), 196.

containers. Instead of the chaotic and labour-intensive motley of individual piece goods, a new and significantly larger standard unit of cargo was created, designed for both lowering the number of movements necessary to shift a certain volume of trade and achieving optimal loading capacity and speed in handling and stowage. The corollary of this transformation was a dramatic fall in the demand for dock labour; as will be discussed later, many shipowners also specifically saw containerisation as a method to break the power of maritime unions which, they felt, were responsible for the continued wage claims and strike action that held back the profitability of their companies.

Containerisation blew away the cobwebs that threatened to paralyse the liner trade. Its protagonists conceptualised and created the technology (and, in its wake, also the commercial infrastructure) to revolutionise quayside cargo handling, slash transshipment time and labour costs in port, and establish efficient door-to-door transport. In addition, the use of containers gave considerable benefits in reducing damage, loss and pilfering. US pioneer Sea-Land in its publicity claimed that the resulting savings in insurance premiums alone amounted to the freight it charged and, putting its money where its mouth (and the thirst of its American customers) was, targeted Scotland's whisky exports with its very first overseas service.[5]

But in order to apply the fundamental principles of containerisation and to achieve the resulting productivity increases, two elements were required: first, the adoption of a standard container of optimal size in which all break-bulk cargoes, irrespective of the shape and size of the individual goods, could be homogenised; and second, the construction of dedicated transport and transfer facilities designed to handle these standard-size containers both during transport and in the transfer from one mode of transport to the next. Moreover, as containerisation made no sense, if its geographical span remained limited to a few routes and ports, adoption of the system in principle meant that an entirely new infrastructure had to be constructed globally. This, in turn required huge investments and, in its wake, left traditional vessels to be cascaded down to secondary shipping and trading levels; ultimately, most of the traditional technology, like an obsolete ideology, ended on the scrap heap of history.

With regards to the shape of the new container, the last post sounded for casks, crates, bags, vats and the like, as a rectangular box provided maximum internal space, maximum volume given the maximum width dictated by the physical and legal limits of road and rail traffic, and minimum waste of space in loading containers aboard ship or parking them ashore, both horizontally and vertically. Special twist-locking devices were attached to the corners so they could be firmly slotted on to trailers, railway cars, ship's decks and, most

---

[5]Herman D. Tabak, *Cargo Containers. Their Stowage, Handling and Movement* (Cambridge, MD, 1970), 2-6; and Sea-Land, *Sea Notes*, Silver Anniversary Issue (1981), 2.

important, on top of each other. In addition to the totally enclosed steel box, with doors at either end, specialised containers of many different designs were built to meet the requirements of individual commodities. It was not in the least the humble container's great versatility that drove the rapid expansion of the industry as a whole. High-value liquid cargoes can be carried as effectively in boxed tanks as in open top-row containers and corn in containers with special loading and discharging sleeves. Containers for chilled or frozen cargoes initially were equipped with clip-on refrigeration units. Later, built-in refrigeration units were developed which in special reefer sections aboard could be hooked up to a shipboard plant.

During the very early stages, when containerisation was still restricted to isolated national niches of the general freight market, it was theoretically and practically possible for significant differences in box size to exist. The pioneering companies in American and Australian domestic waters indeed chose a variety of dimensions that apparently suited the conditions of their trading areas best. But as soon as container shipping broke out of its national confines to link continents and to establish global networks, it became vitally necessary to impose uniformity throughout the industry.

Testifying to the urgency of the issue, the standard container was defined in a fraction of the time needed in the railway era for the creation of national and international standard railway gauges. Even so, it was, somewhat ironically, conditions ashore that determined the maximum width, height and length of the box, as there were clear limits to the dimensions of truck and railway loads. In 1961 the American Standards Association adopted an eight by eight-foot width by height as the standard cross section, with ten-, twenty-, thirty- and forty-feet being offered as alternative lengths for the new box. Of these, the handy twenty-foot (eight by eight by twenty feet) and forty-foot (eight by eight by forty feet) containers soon became (and still are) predominant in both American and global business. Within a few years they were also covered by international standards agreements and became known by their acronyms, TEU (i.e., Twenty-feet Equivalent Unit)[6] and FEU (Forty-feet Equivalent Unit). Other-sized boxes did not entirely disappear,[7] and a number of shipowners stuck

---

[6]The term was actually developed by the journalist Richard Gibney: see Ignarski (ed.), *The Box*, 21. The standard box of forty-feet length became known as the FEU.

[7]As late as 1969, 50.9 percent of all containers built in the USA were thirty-five feet long, against 26.4 percent of forty feet, 9.5 percent of twenty feet, 6.8 percent of twenty-seven feet, and 6.7 percent of all other lengths and/or varying cross-sections; *ibid.*, 45.

to trailer loads, opting for Roll-on Roll-off (RoRo) systems with trailer loads (often in combination with the carriage of containers on deck).[8]

Another alternative technology was based on barge-carrying vessels (LASH: Lighter Aboard SHip) to be operated between ports located at the mouths of significant river systems. But RoRo and mixed vessels never captured more than a minor share of the market outside the short-sea ferry business, and generally were operated in niche areas. Their heyday was in the mid-1970s, when the construction boom in the Middle East caused massive congestion in ports like Jiddah, Dammam and Kuwait, and RoRo carriers enjoyed great advantages because their cargoes could simply be driven ashore; to a lesser extent, the same applied to Lagos in Nigeria. But since then RoRo has been restricted to routes with insufficient depth of trade to support pure containerisation, insufficient container handling capacity, or ports requiring additional cargo-handling flexibility.[9]

On the North Atlantic, Atlantic Container Line (ACL) remained the only major company to maintain its hybrid, container-RoRo technology, while mostly Scandinavian-led companies like Wilhelmsen and Barber Blue Sea have found their own ways in round-the-world services of a distinct niche character.[10] The major barge-carrying route between the Mississippi, New Orleans and upstream ports up to Catoosa (Tulsa, Oklahoma), and in the Rhine delta, collapsed shortly after the tragic sinking of the Hapag-Lloyd carrier *München* in 1978, leaving only the pioneering *Acadia Forest* and one sister ship in the transatlantic paper trade;[11] American experiments with LASH-carriers on the Pacific, notably by Pacific Far East and Farrell Lines, were abandoned around the same time and the vessels converted to ordinary container ships.

-----

[8]With regard to RoRo systems, overseas shipping developments should, of course, also be regarded as an extension of the rapidly growing car- and truck-carrying ferries across the Channel, North Sea and short-sea crossings in Europe and elsewhere.

[9]*Fairplay*, 5 March 1998, 47.

[10]The push for the adoption of RoRo capacity by ACL came from its Swedish partners, Wallenius, which had been deeply involved in car exporting (Volvo and Saab), and throughout there has been a strong correlation between RoRo enthusiasm and Scandinavian entrepreneurs; see, for example, Wilhelmsen's website (http://www.wlines.com/wl.html). Significantly, in 1999 Wilhelmsen, which also controlled the operation of a sizeable fleet of car carriers, merged with Wallenius.

[11]The operations of the *Acadia Forest* and its barges are succinctly explained in Hermann Schreiber, *Verkehr* (Darmstadt, 1972), 116; and G. Van den Burg, *Containerisation and Other Unit Transport* (London, 1975), 240-244.

From the late 1960s, the TEU became the universal yardstick of the brave new world of containerisation. The traditional measurement of a cargo liner's capacity in net register tonnage became obsolete, as containers were carried on deck as much as in the holds. Instead, capacity was now determined by the total number of standard containers a ship could carry. But, emphasising the conceptual convergence of liner and bulk shipping, the deadweight tonnage (dwt), i.e., the cargo-carrying capacity in weight, was also often given. Yet while individual containers might hold up to twenty tonnes of cargo, the TEU/dwt ratio of container ships usually did not reach more than fifteen or sixteen, and even less in the case of fast carriers. Still, the TEU became much more than a yardstick for ship capacity because it was also adopted to indicate the size of fleets operated or trade carried by companies or consortia, the volume of trade carried on particular routes or in commercial regions, the annual throughput achieved by ports and, more controversially, the turnover rate per hour of ports or individual terminals.

The creation of the TEU as the unit of measurement was a tremendous advantage to the industry in all its sections since statistics could be collected easily and manipulated into ranking tables, time series and other comparative indicators of the absolute size, market share and/or performance of companies, countries, ports, stevedores, waterside labour and much else in order to monitor the performance of the industry and make projections for the future.

The ramifications of the adoption of the standard container were enormous and went far beyond the calculations of the early pioneers. But the system could never have taken off without specialised facilities, both physical and commercial, at all stages of the transport chain. The most important of these innovations literally changed the sea- and landscape of the world as newly-designed container vessels with their heavy, angular lines and high, straight sides and dedicated terminals with huge portainer cranes dramatically transformed maritime horizons. In their wake, there were many other dramatic changes, for example in railway cargo terminals, insurance cover and information technology. But what should be emphasised is that, despite the historical roots of containerisation in the land-based US trucking industry, the revolution was soon driven by its maritime component and, in particular, by the changes in and requirements of the new container ships. Once the plunge had been taken and, in 1966, the point of no return passed, maritime technology was the most dynamic part of the global transport system and dictated the pace and extent of change to all its other parts.

Central to this massive process of transformation stood the fundamental design and structural changes that had to be made to both ships and ports. The conventional pre-container cargo-liners of the early 1960s differed, in principle, only slightly from those of half a century ago. They had increased in size and capacity, were powered by stronger and more economic engines for higher service speeds and sported more modern profiles and deck gear. But their design was still characterised by a multi-deck structure that provided both longitudinal strength and the necessary vertical subdivision for the cargo holds. These holds, almost without exception located before and aft the main deck house, were separated from each other by vertical walls which, structurally, gave stiffness to the ship. The access to the holds was through relatively narrow hatches, separated from each other by masts and other cargo-handling gear. Internally, the holds featured pillars for ceiling support. No other configuration was possible for traditional break-bulk cargo, yet for containers it was totally unsuitable. The only way to carry containers on conventional ships was as deck cargo, but that was patently unsatisfactory. Nothing less than a fleet of specially-designed and constructed vessels was required to make containerisation work. As we shall see later, this had a revolutionary impact on the shipping industry, but what matters here is the sea change in the ships themselves.

Figure 2: This bird's eye view of the loading of a container ship shows the cellular structure of its cargo hold. Very obvious is the total absence of waterside workers on board.

Source: Nederlandsche Scheepvaart Unie, *Annual Report* (1975).

To maximise efficiency the crucial requirement for the dedicated container ship was that its boxes could be stacked on board with least trouble and delay, which in practice meant in parallel rows divided by thin cell walls (hence the oft-used term "cellular vessel") and directly on top of each other. In the first instance, this meant the abandonment of all internal decks since they impeded the free vertical movement of containers and the maximum use of the ship's internal depth. To exploit the full width of the ship, hatch openings had to be made as wide as possible to enable the outer containers to be lifted on and off vertically. To shipbuilders this posed unprecedented problems for the structural strength of their designs. A particular problem was that they also had to ensure the rigidity of the rails in which the containers moved against vertical tensions. Solutions were found by doubling and/or reinforcing the ship's sides in combination with a significant heightening and by abandoning the traditional shelter deck. To protect its forward deck cargo, the ship's bows were redesigned. But the high deck cargo, in combination with the variable distribution of weight throughout the entire cargo of containers, also caused new problems with the stability of the ship.

To maximise ease of access to the containers, as well as cargo capacity, in most early designs all cellular holds were placed before the deck house which, as on tankers and bulk carriers, was fitted at the stern, above the engine room. But in contrast to tankers, the bridge was located in a more elevated position in order to exceed the level of a complete deck cargo of, say, three or four containers high, that is, up to ten metres. But when, following orders placed in 1969 and onwards, ship sizes escalated from 900 to about 3000 TEU, it proved advisable to shift the deck house forward again on larger vessels. The "third-generation" vessels of the Europe-East Asia TRIO-group, for example, carried eight rows of containers behind the bridge, as against twenty in front. By this time the dimensions of the largest container vessels far exceeded those of the conventional liners they replaced: P&O's 1972-1973 2960-TEU *Osaka Bay* (47,777 dwt), for example, measured 950 feet (289.6 metres) by 106' 1" (32.3 metres) with a depth of 80' 9" (24.6 metres, against the 563 feet x 79' 9" x 45' 10" (171.6 x 24.3 x 14.0 metres) of the same company's *Super Strath* (12,638 dwt) series.[12]

The same quest for economies of scale and greater productivity that lay behind containerisation and that rapidly pushed up the size of the container ships also became a powerful factor in increasing their service speed.[13] In the first instance this resulted in sharper bow forms, which necessitated new hull shapes

---

[12]Stephen Rabson and Kevin O'Donoghue, *P&O. A Fleet History* (Kendal, 1988), 260 and 403.

[13]An interesting article is "The Quest for Speed," *100A1* (Lloyd's Register) (December 1973), 4-11.

because the business part of container vessels had to be as rectangular as the box itself. But such gains were only marginal compared with those resulting from the increased power of engines. P&O's 1969 1530-TEU *Moreton Bay* for the Australian trade was equipped with two Stal-Laval steam turbines generating 32,000 shaft horsepower (shp) which gave the ship a service speed of 21.5 knots, but this performance was greatly surpassed by the *Osaka Bay*. Propelled by four Stal-Lavals totalling 81,132 shp, this ship attained a speed of twenty-six knots. Hapag-Lloyd, the German partners of P&O in the TRIO consortium, and its Dutch rivals, Nedlloyd, moved up to twenty-eight knots with their four quasi-sister ships that entered service in 1972-1973.[14]

The ultimate in the race for productivity-through-speed was achieved on the North Atlantic by the pioneering Sea-Land, which in 1969 ordered an entirely new fleet of eight 1086-TEU carriers at German and Dutch yards to be powered by gas turbines putting out 120,000 shp for a service speed of no less than thirty-three knots. The only ships ever to approach the 36-plus knot record of the Cold War-inspired passenger liner *United States*, these carriers almost immediately ran afoul commercially of a serious tonnage glut on the North Atlantic and the dramatic fuel price hikes caused by the first oil crisis. From the mid-1970s most companies slowed down their ships by four to seven knots and another five years began replacing their steam turbines with more economic diesels. Mitsui OSK, for example, in 1980 took the plunge, replacing the 80,000-shp turbine of its twenty-seven knot, 1836-TEU *Rhine Maru* with a 55,520-shp diesel – at a cost of nearly 3.6 billion yen.[15] Because of the complex requirements of US shipping subsidies, the transition to diesel-propulsion caused considerable additional problems to American companies.[16]

From the above it is evident that containerisation also caused a revolution in shipbuilding and marine engineering, as functional designs and demands for elevated speed levels had to be translated into physical reality. Initially, only a small number of yards were able to master the new art; German builders, such as Bremer Vulkan, Howaldtswerke Deutsche Werft (Hamburg and

---

[14]H.J. Witthöft, *Container. Transportrevolution unseres Jahrhunderts* (2nd ed., Hereford, 1978), 115.

[15][Mariko Tatsuki and Tsuyoshi Yamamoto], *The First Century of Mitsui O.S.K. Lines, Ltd.* (Osaka, 1985), 192. This conversion saved seventy-five tons of fuel a day. Other measures to reduce running costs included the adoption of duct propellers, improvement of automatic steering equipment, sandblasting and statistical process control (SPC) painting of ships' bottoms.

[16]John Niven, *The American President Lines and Its Forebears 1848-1984* (Newark, DE, 1986), 273-275. See also "US-built Slow-speed Diesel Completed," *Fairplay*, 11 September 1980, 23.

Kiel) and Blohm and Voss, were especially prominent, filling orders for many foreign companies.

By the late 1960s, as demand surged, expertise spread rapidly throughout the industry, although the building of container ships never became as diffused globally as container shipping itself. Indeed, after a short period in which all major shipbuilding countries gained a share of the market[17] – akin to the manner in which during the boom years of the early 1970s almost *everyone* built tankers and bulk-carriers – Japanese and Korean shipyards gained pre-eminence, with companies like Ishikawajima-Harima, Mitsubishi, Kawasaki, Daewoo and Hyundai taking the lion's share. As a result, especially after the deep crisis that gripped the tanker and bulk markets from 1973-1974 caused the collapse of orders, there was ample world shipbuilding capacity to meet the demand for new vessels.

The crucial advantage of the container ship resided in its ability to load and discharge unitised cargo at a far greater pace than traditional ships and ports had ever been able to do. By the early 1960s American container operators achieved loading speeds of 750 freight-tons per hour when conventional methods at Southampton yielded no more than twenty-eight to thirty.[18] A Belgian analysis showed that 100 men working in a conventional terminal could handle 1200 tonnes of freight in seven to eight hours, while twenty men in a container terminal achieved a turnover of almost 5000 tonnes.[19] It was estimated in 1970 at Hamburg that 2700 tonnes could be loaded in five hours with two container cranes, whereas the same amount in traditional packaging would have required six shifts working three days around the clock.[20] Although because of its easterly location Hamburg was always keen to drive up its productivity to maintain its competitiveness relative to rivals in the North Sea and Channel area, many similar results can be found elsewhere. In labour-intensive ports in the less-developed world, the contrasts were even more marked; in Venezuela, for example, eight men would have been able to replace a traditional gang of 112.[21]

---

[17]P&O's *Remuera Bay*, for example, was built by Swan Hunter at Newcastle (Rabson and O'Donoghue, *P&O*, 410), and CMB's *Mercator* was completed at France's oldest "modern" shipyard, La Seyne near Toulon (G. Devos and G. Elewaut, *CMB 100. Een eeuw maritime ondernemerschap* [Tielt, 1995], 228).

[18]Van den Burg, *Containerisation*, 264.

[19]Devos and Elewaut, *CMB 100*, 206.

[20]Witthöft, *Container*, 68.

[21]Susanne and Klaus Wiborg, *The World is Our Oyster. 150 Years of Hapag-Lloyd 1847-1997* (Hamburg, 1997), 354.

For the shipowner such productivity increases meant that the duration of expensive time in port was slashed accordingly; ships could be kept moving for a much larger proportion of the year; and capital used more productively. Because of its much greater productivity, each container ship replaced a number of conventional vessels. A calculation made in 1968, for example, demonstrated that the current fleet of approximately 130 conventional carriers on the then-leading route in the world, between Western Europe and the US East Coast, could be replaced by thirty-six container ships, at a ratio of about 3.6 to one.[22] In a similar analysis the previous year of the Australian trade, in which larger, second-generation, container ships were to be deployed, the ratio was estimated to be between five and six to one.[23] Generally, the five-to-one conversion rate became the standard assumption throughout the industry. From these figures it is easy to see why containerisation led to slashing employment at sea and ashore.

Only a fraction of the productivity gains could be realised, however, if container ships remained dependent on the conventional liner facilities of wharves or finger piers with roofed sheds and little or no open space.[24] From the beginning it was obvious that ports also had to undergo revolutionary transformations to enable the system to function. As will be seen, this posed serious spatial, financial and environmental challenges to many existing ports, but it also gave unprecedented opportunities to newcomers.

The essential requirements for a container terminal were four-fold: deep-water access and a long stretch of deep-water quayage; a large area of well-founded flat open space; specialised container cranes to lift boxes on and off ships and other equipment to move containers on the terminal; and good access to inland transportation networks. In principle, a terminal is little more than a giant parking lot designed to receive and exchange containers between sea and land, but from the beginning it was clear that ample space was needed to facilitate all the necessary box movements. Outbound cargo for a particular line or destination, for example, would accumulate over the period between sailings and had to be parked off-side not only until the ship for which the containers were destined had arrived but also until its inward containers had been discharged and removed to another off-side location. But boxes also had to be shifted for many other reasons, such as to prepare them for loading in a particular order to maintain the stability of the ship; to have those destined for the next port of call placed on top; or to manage the pool of empty containers that could be exported by any number of alternative services.

---

[22]Van den Burg, *Containerisation*, 265.

[23]James Taylor, *Ellermans. A Wealth of Shipping* (London, 1976), 162.

[24]Niven, *American President Lines*, 211-212.

Terminals were thus characterised by vast stretches of concrete with solid foundations to carry the weight of four- or five-high stacks of fully-loaded containers. If specialised boxes, such as freezer units, were involved, the necessary power points had to be provided. The problem of managing a container park and, especially, of keeping track of the location of individual containers was just one of the many elements of containerisation for which computers and, in more recent years, satellites have proved indispensable.

No terminal could operate without the appropriate equipment to load/unload ships and to shift containers across the terminal. With regards to the latter, many companies, especially those with origins in road transport like Sea-Land, initially left the containers on trailers moved by tractors. This procedure, of course, was also followed by RoRo operators and suggested a large degree of horizontal mobility. But experience showed that it led to an inefficient use of space because containers could not be stacked, and because mobility could better be assured by specialised container-handling equipment. Two major types of equipment soon came to dominate and, with only small alterations and innovations, still do. The first was the forklift-truck, redesigned and given sufficient power, weight and stability to lift a full forty-foot container (holding up to about thirty tonnes) stacked up to five or six high onto and down from a stack. The second was a totally new design, the transtainer or straddler crane, which stood on high legs in between which containers could be lifted, moved and deposited again. Both types of vehicles, of course, could also be used to load or unload trucks and trains. Where acreage was at a premium, as in many ports in East Asia, other solutions had to be found. By 1974, for example, an eleven-story container warehouse with lifts was constructed in Hong Kong.[25]

Although containerisation in its purest form can entail the loading of containers at the place of production, there were (and still are) many manufacturers and shippers whose output is too small to justify their own loading bays. They had to make use of facilities offered by alternative transport operators, including freight forwarders, trucking or railway companies, many of which began to establish their own inland terminals. Container loading/unloading centres could in principle be located anywhere inland where sufficient demand existed or commercial advantage could be gained. In England, for example, where containerisation was used as the vehicle for a massive attack against entrenched maritime unions, the shipping companies intentionally located their depots outside port boundaries in order to break the power of the Dockers' Union. In many cases, however, shipping companies and stevedores used the container terminals themselves, where sheds allowed less-than-container loads to be combined and imported containers to be destuffed.

---

[25]Witthöft, *Container*, 61.

Most characteristic of the new, and often downstream, terminals were the huge cranes that lifted containers between ship and wharf. Instead of the large number of waterbird-like gray structures with hooks and slings that characterised conventional liner shipping, an entire new breed of square-built container cranes of much greater height, dimensions and mobility was introduced.[26] The length of the crane could reach up to forty metres, spanning the full width of ship and quay, as well as several rows of containers ashore, to minimise movements within the terminal. With its capacity to move sideways, as well as forwards and backwards, one such crane could cover a large number of containers both ashore and aboard; with a brace of two or three it thus became possible to turn around a 2000-TEU carrier in the same number of days. To avoid obstructing ships during their arrival or departure, the waterside part of the crane could be lifted, thus defiantly enhancing its silhouette on the horizon. In principle, container cranes could move containers between all types of carrier platforms, such as trucks, barges and trains, as well as ships and terminal floors. From the beginning, such direct transfers occurred, but it was not until the mid-1980s that their potential regarding rail traffic was fully recognised; especially in the USA, ships and trains became dovetailed into a system that became known as intermodalism. The visible centrality of the gantry cranes was due not only to their huge dimensions but also increasingly to the abandonment of the drab gray-and-black conventional harbour cranes, which were replaced by brightly-coloured successors, including the sexy "Ferrari" red of Fujairah.

Especially when seaports in a region competed for trade (as on the US East and West Coasts, in Japan, or in the Havre-Hamburg range of North Sea ports), the quality of inland transport could be as important as the quality and/or price of the port facilities themselves. Short-sea and river traffic of course always had access to ports, but each needed to make significant adaptations to make it compatible with ocean-going container shipping in vessel design, terminals and the like. Special quays were often designated for such water transport, thus necessitating further expansion of terminal space. Least affected by containerisation was rail transport. Little was needed to adapt open freight cars, and by the early 1960s the world's railway network probably had gained its largest extension, although not all parts were suited for the carriage of containers. Most major ports already had railway spurs running onto liner wharves, but as terminals generally occupied new sites, extensions had to be built.

---

[26]For a historical sketch of conventional crane technology, see Hans Neumann, "100 Jahre Kaikräne im Hamburger Hafen," in Schiffahrts-Verlag "Hansa," *100 Jahre Schiffahrt, Schiffbau, Häfen* (Hamburg, 1964), 162-169. It must be pointed out, however, that the portal cranes used for the discharging of bulk ore and coal cargoes had already assumed larger proportions and in their design may be regarded as prototypes of the container cranes.

The main innovation, however, was in road transport, ultimately the only mode truly capable of door-to-door delivery. It was no coincidence that the beginning of containerisation coincided with the major spurt in the worldwide construction of freeways, *Autobahnen*, *Autostradas* or whatever the new multi-lane, intersection-free motorways were called. Sea-Land, after all, built its maritime assault on the back of the Highway Act of 1947 and, even more so, on President Eisenhower's Interstate Highway Act of 1956, which created a network of more than 79,500 miles throughout the continental United States. The early 1960s, similarly, marked the point from which the still relatively rudimentary motorway system of Europe exploded into the concrete and bitumen network that now covers much of the continent. Expansion, it should be stressed, was not uniform throughout western Europe; Britain, in particular, for a long time lagged behind enthusiasts like Italy, the Netherlands and Germany. Rail and road soon competed fiercely with each other and, with the spectacular growth of container transport from the late 1970s, that meant the involvement of other than purely commercial considerations.

In addition to its physical and highly visible hardware infrastructure, containerisation required dramatic changes in other aspects of the handling of cargo. Above all, it was totally dependent on electronic data processing for virtually every aspect of its operations; one might well say, paradoxically, that computers formed the software of the container system. The managment of the container park on a terminal has already been mentioned, but that task was simple compared to the global tracking systems that had to be created to help locate each individual box, loaded or empty, along the many sea routes operated by its owner (or lessor) and sent into the hinterlands of its ports. Moreover, there was not always the opportunity for the box to take exactly the same route home, if home it went, and each container, after all, represented not only a capital value of some £3000 (US $7500) in the initial years (by 2000 its cost had declined to under US $2000 from Chinese builders)[27] but also the capacity to carry revenue-earning cargo in the future. Even a company with a modest "fleet" of a few thousand containers would have had as many headaches without the computer. The optimal loading of ships, with boxes destined for a multiplicity of ports and destinations, was an equally useful field for computer application, but as each container could in principle have a different weight and centre of gravity, the ship's stability was of as much importance as was commercial efficiency.

Computers soon were indispensable in producing and handling the complex paperwork necessary to document the movements of each container, in which the shipborne leg often was but part of a complex chain of transport movements. Multi-layered forms replaced the conventional bill of lading, and

---

[27]Ignarski (ed.), *The Box*, 52; and *Containerisation International* (January 1999), 54-55.

through computerisation the shipping company could not only streamline its booking system but also monitor its transactions and performance. More recently, the internet has become the cutting edge of communications technology for freight bookings. Leading container operators were in the forefront of e-commerce. Two other aspects of global trade, however, were subject to much greater change than the "mere" adoption of new technology. National customs services and insurance companies had to adapt their practices to the full implications of the concept of door-to-door carriage of a sealed container.[28] It would, after all, defeat the purpose of the system if a box on arrival in port had to be opened and inspected for the presence of dutiable goods when its destination was in another country. The issue of transit trade had, of course, existed previously, but the container in this respect was literally far less transparent than conventional packaging had been. The legal problems of containerisation appeared so complex that some doubted whether the revolution could actually survive.[29]

An even more complex problem existed with regard to insurance because if a container contained damaged goods at its ultimate destination it was virtually impossible to establish on what leg of its multi-modal voyage the damage had been sustained. The container might have been under the legal liability of a number of quite diverse carriers in several different national jurisdictions. Yet here also the imperative to make containerisation succeed was so strong that comprehensive door-to-door insurance was soon introduced. In enabling these changes to be introduced rapidly, it was of great significance that containerisation sharply reduced the incidence of both damage and petty theft. Although entire containers were lost at sea or hijacked – in a number of ports protection money had to be paid[30] – such losses remained tolerable.[31] Research conducted in 1970 by the American Institute of Merchant Shipping showed that damage occurred to no more than one in 11,430 containers, while the British container consortium ACT found that damage on £125 million worth of goods it had carried was only five percent of that which would have occurred on a

---

[28]Van den Burg, *Containerization*, 217-230.

[29]James R. Woods, "The Container Revolution," *Journal of World Trade Law*, VI (1972), 661-692.

[30]*Dagblad voor de Scheepvaart*, 29 October 1970.

[31]A report of the Insurance Council of Australia, however, referred to the "appalling spate of containers overboard" during eighteen months in 1976-1977 (*Australian*, 27 October 1977). In the worst case, a South Pacific gale swept twenty-seven containers from Farrell Line's *Austral Endurance* and severely damaged another twelve. For later accidents, see chapter 7.

conventional shipment.[32] OCL's chairman, Sir Andrew Crighton, stated in 1970 that containerisation had reduced insurance claims for damage and pilfering from 1s. 8d. to 2d. a ton, a fall of ninety percent.[33] Farrell Lines claimed that containers could deliver ceiling tiles intact while previously hardly a consignment was undamaged.[34] It was, however, not until the late 1970s that the fundamental legal dispute as to whether the container was to be regarded as a single package or merely a "mode of conveyance" containing a multitude of individually-packed goods inside was solved. Because of the maximum liability per package of the shipowner under the Hague Visby rules, it was crucial that the latter interpretation was adopted. Insurance companies also had to come to terms with the immense concentration of value that containerisation represented, as the larger vessels, themselves built for US $80 to $100 million, could carry cargoes worth several times those amounts. The sinking of a single vessel could represent a financial catastrophe. Fortunately, in contrast to the oil and dry-bulk sectors, few major accidents have occurred with container vessels. The major losses were the sinking of the Hapag-Lloyd barge-carrier *München* in December 1978;[35] the destruction during the Falklands/Malvinas War (1982) of Cunard's *Atlantic Conveyor*; and the breaking in two of the *MSC Carla* in 1999.

Containerisation provides an almost perfect model of what may be termed complex innovation. Its first stage was extremely simple in theory and execution. But once the first steps had been taken and the true revolutionary power of the system could be imagined, it swept before it every aspect of liner shipping in a process of rapid transformation at sea, ashore on the wharf and in the office, and deep inland. Because of the profound nature of the resulting changes, the very process of change created its own momentum, as new physical and electronic facilities had to be fed with ever greater volumes of boxes. At the same time, it was not only container operators who were committed to the brave new world of containerisation: around the world demand from shippers, large and small, for the superior service also sky-rocketed.

---

[32]Witthöft, *Containerisation*, 25.

[33]*Australian*, 5 November 1970.

[34]*Intermodal World* (April 1975), 7.

[35]Wiborg and Wiborg, *150 Years of Hapag-Lloyd*, 374.

Chapter 2
The First Revolution

> Containerization made...a stormy, hectic era for shipping, embracing as it did changes comparable in scale to the great transition, seventy-five years earlier, from sailing ships to steamers.[1]

Conceptualising the solution to an economic problem is one thing; to bring it to practical application is another; and to make the new system work profitably is quite another matter again. The past is strewn with ideas and inventions that remained just that. But the progress of those that ultimately were successful often was slow and erratic, partly because the knowledge of materials and their properties was imperfect and needed to be developed simultaneously, partly also because the grim reality of the market and the financial bottom line.

The steamship, for example, did not replace the sailing ship and conquer the oceans either immediately or in a smooth and gradual process like the one so gracefully represented in the "ideal-types" offered by Griliches in his pioneering study on the diffusion of hybrid maize or by Harley to illustrate the transition from sail to steam.[2] The development and commercial diffusion of the steamship was characterised by alternating stages of spectacular innovation and careful piece-meal consolidation over a period of about a century. Moreover, the pace and extent of its diffusion varied markedly between the four main sectors of the shipping market: rivers, short-sea, deep-sea liner trade and global tramping. No single pattern can ever adequately describe the steamer's progress during the nineteenth century, if only because there was not a single "ideal-type" steamship in a single global freight market. Yet historians all agree that the adoption of the steamship brought a total revolution in international shipping, especially in the creation of the global liner industry.

---

[1][Mariko Tatsuki and Tsuyoshi Yamamoto], *The First Century of Mitsui O.S.K. Lines, Ltd.* (Osaka, 1985), 205.

[2]Zvi Griliches, "Hybrid Corn: An Exploration in the Economics of Technical Change," *Econometrica*, XXV (1957); and Charles K. Harley, "The Shift from Sailing Ships to Steamships, 1850-1890: A Study in Technological Change and its Diffusion," in D. McCloskey (ed.), *Essays on a Mature Economy: Britain after 1840* (London, 1971), 215-231.

27

Not surprisingly, in its historical significance and revolutionary impact containerisation is often compared by both historians and shipping professionals to the introduction of steam navigation. As Mitsui-OSK's president Kiichiro Aiura put it succinctly in 1985, "Containerization made...a stormy, hectic era for shipping, embracing as it did changes comparable in scale to the great transition, seventy-five years earlier, from sailing ships to steamers."[3]

But the diffusion of containerisation differed fundamentally from that of steam shipping or of similar seminal revolutions in modern transport – such as the elevator, railways, the motor car and commercial aviation – in that because of its very nature it both required and created almost instantaneous change on a truly global scale. Container shipping was like a shockwave to the liner industry. Many shipowners had no inkling of how fast the process of change would be and found themselves caught in the dizzying waves of containerisation, unconscious of the forces they had unleashed and only imperfectly understanding the full consequences of their own actions. Containerisation had a logic and momentum of its own that simply swept all before it and forced dramatic changes in everything it touched. Moreover, it came at a time when many other developments – technological, economic and political – reverberated through the shipping industry, such as economic nationalism in the non-industrialised world; the spectacular economic growth of Japan; the entry of the Soviet Union into merchant shipping; the temporary closure of the Suez Canal with its accompanying boom for tankers and bulk carriers; the globalisation of flags of convenience and crewing; and computerisation.

This chapter will analyse the first two stages of the process of containerisation: its early development in the domestic trades of the United States and Australia – two high-cost economies that were notoriously non-competitive in the international maritime arena – and its establishment as the predominant mode, and saviour, of liner shipping worldwide by its diffusion on the North Atlantic, in the Australian trade, and the transpacific route between Japan and the United States. It was during this period to about 1970 that the fundamentals of the new system were determined, on the basis of which containerisation during the 1970s could spread over all major trade routes of the world.

The common entrepreneurial thread linking these stages was the quest for productivity increases through technological change, enlargement of scale and increasing service speeds. The historical moment of these developments is given by the fact that containerisation required unprecedented huge investments in new ships, containers and port facilities both within an extremely brief time span and worldwide. Adding to the burden of these investments was the fact that containerisation instantaneously condemned entire fleets of conventional vessels to obsolescence, even if they sometimes could be "cascaded down" within the

---

[3][Tatsuki and Yamamoto], *First Century*, 205.

company or by sale to lower-quality services or secondary routes, and thus for some time to retain a value higher than scrap.

Some figures may indicate the sheer magnitude of the investments that containerisation required. The cost of OCL's six container ships (27,000 gross registered tons [grt], 1572 TEU) of 1967-1969 alone was US $100 million. Its containers, calculating that each ship needed one set aboard and two ashore for feeding and distribution, cost about US $3000 each, another US $85 million. The total cost of the twenty-one ships, ranging from 1840 to 2950-TEU each, ordered by the TRIO group for the Europe-East Asian trade, amounted to over US $1 billion and their boxes were another US $550 million.[4] Per deadweight ton, the three container ships of the Nederlandse Scheepvaart Unie required about 2.3 times as much capital as the company's conventional freighters (US $435 versus US $188).[5] The Compagnie Maritime Belge (CMB) estimated in 1970 that a fleet of six 1130-TEU ships would require some US $40 million worth of containers.[6] On top of these figures came the expenses for terminal facilities, cranes, stackers, trucks and, in some cases, short-sea feeder lines. As North German Lloyd director Sager observed in 1970, shipping managers suddenly realised that they incurred about half their expenses ashore.[7]

One observer estimated that between 1966 and 1970 some US $2.4 billion was invested in the maritime side of the container business. Yet, as Hugo van Driel has argued,[8] for some companies the overall capital invested did not significantly change; after all, conventional vessels did not come cheap either and more of them were needed. Crucially, however, the heavy demand for new investments came within short periods of time and in, for many companies, large individual parcels of unprecedented size.[9]

---

[4]Calculated from A.D. Couper, *The Geography of Sea Transport* (London, 1972), 152.

[5]Calculated from H. van Driel, *Samenwerking in haven en vervoer in het containertijdperk* (Delft, 1990), 114

[6]G. Devos and G. Elewaut, *CMB 100. Een eeuw maritime ondernemerschap* (Tielt, 1995), 100 and 208.

[7]H.J. Witthöft, *Container. Transportrevolution unseres Jahrhunderts* (2nd ed., Hereford, 1978), 18.

[8]Van Driel, *Samenwerking*, 114-115.

[9]It should be stressed that almost from the very beginning container-leasing companies sprung up, mostly in the USA, to help diminish investment requirements for shipping companies (Witthöft, *Container*, 105-106). By 1976 they owned about fifty-eight

The latter circumstance helped push many companies into joint ventures. But even then their equity resources were often insufficient, especially when they operated on a number of trade routes and were faced with the necessity of ordering a number of vessels. In addition, many established liner companies were under increasing pressure from their shareholders and/or bankers to raise their profitability through investments in the booming bulk and tanker sectors or to diversify into other promising areas. The Oyevaar and Rochdale reports, in the Netherlands (1968) and Britain (1970), had castigated liner companies for their low returns on capital, financial conservatism and lack of interest outside their own sector.[10]

The consequences of the trend towards diversification will be discussed in the next chapter, but what is of importance here is that established liner shipping directors by and large accepted the need to seek more external capital. For many this meant a philosophical sea change, especially in Britain where the ghost of the Royal Mail affair of the early 1930s still pervaded shipping circles. In the Netherlands, for example, during the reconstruction period of 1947-1954 only two percent of new investments were financed externally. By the mid-1970s, that figure had risen to about twenty-five percent, and in the case of the Belgian CMB to 38.5 percent.[11] P&O in 1965 had no external capital but in 1969 loans and debentures stood at seventeen percent, in 1972 at thirty-four percent, and in 1976 at thirty-eight percent.[12] The company's total capital during those years increased from £212 million to £710 million, a rise of 235 percent.

The prehistory of the container was long and varied. From as early as the 1840s railway companies in Europe and the USA used some kind of container, and in 1933 an international standard was adopted by the International

---

percent of the world's container stock, against the forty-two percent owned by shipping and transport companies; this ratio has roughly been maintained until the present day; see, e.g., *Containerisation International* (April 1988), 27-28 and 30, and (April 1996), 51; *Containerisation International Yearbook* (1998), 13 and 17; and Sam Ignarski (ed.), *The Box. An Anthology Celebrating 25 Years of Containerisation and the TT Club* (London, 1996), chapter 8.

[10]J.J. Oyevaar, *De nederlandse koopvaardij...Rapport uitgebracht aan het bestuur van de Koninklijke Nederlandsche Reedersvereeniging* (The Hague, 1968); Great Britain, Parliament, House of Commons, *Report of the Committee of Inquiry into Shipping* (Cmnd. 4337, London, 1970).

[11]Frank Broeze, "Rederij," *Maritieme Geschiedenis der Nederlanden*, IV (1978), 215.

[12]*P&O Annual Reports* (1965); and (1976), 31, "Ten Year Record."

Union of Railways.[13] Some of these containers were also carried on short-sea routes, and it has been claimed that the first ship to carry containers exclusively was *Clipper*, which in 1956 plied between England and Northern Ireland. Trains, of course, also had been carried on ferries, including Seatrain's international service (1928) between the fast-growing city of Miami and Cuba. At the same time, trucking companies adopted "piggy-back" methods to carry trailers on flat railway cars. But it was not until the mid-1950s that conditions in the American coastal trade led to the decisive experiments with containerisation.

To understand why it was in the USA, and soon afterwards in Australia, that containerisation was first introduced it is necessary to examine the conditions of the merchant marines of those two countries, neither of which belonged to the group of mainly European nations (such as Britain, France, Germany, the Netherlands, Greece, the Scandinavian countries and Japan) which constituted the dominant forces in international shipping. Fundamentally, both the USA and Australia (and one could also add Canada) were internationally non-competitive because of their high labour costs, but while Australian shipowners were at least free to import their vessels from overseas, American shipowners were bound by one of the very first acts of Congress, which from 1789 required American-flagged vessels to be built in the USA as well. Attempts to run a state-owned Australian shipping line in the 1920s had ended with its sale to a British rival, but American deep-sea liner shipping was maintained artificially on a number of strategically-important routes by a system of Constructional Differential and Operational Differential subsidies that in the Merchant Act of 1936 succeeded earlier ineffective schemes.[14]

Superficially, there is some irony in the fact that containerisation originated in two countries with such inefficient national fleets that cabotage legislation (put into effect in the Jones Act of 1920 and the Australian Navigation Act of 1921, respectively) was necessary to protect their domestic waters from foreign invasion. But it was that very lack of competitiveness in conventional maritime technology that provided the challenge and, because of their coastal reservation clauses, the opportunity to the capital-intensive new technology.

By the mid-1950s, liner shipping in American domestic waters (which also included trade with Puerto Rico, Hawaii and Alaska), as in Australia, was under increasing pressure from sharply-rising costs, industrial unrest and competition from rail and road traffic. At the same time, trucking companies began to send trailers by rail and even by ship in order to save on their wage

---

[13]Ignarski (ed.), *The Box*, 8-9; Jean Randier, *Histoire de la marine marchande française des premiers vapeurs à nos jours* (Paris, 1980), 347; and Witthöft, *Container*, 10.

[14]Benjamin W. Labaree, *et al.*, *America and the Sea: A Maritime History* (Mystic, CT, 1998), 536, 541 and 591-596.

bills. In hindsight, it was only a small step from across the threshold of containerisation to leave out the trailer from the seaborne part of the voyage by carrying only its container, lifting it on at the port of departure and off again on arrival. In its generous celebrations of the American pioneer of containerisation, Malcom McLean, the shipping community in 1997 made it very clear that although the separation of box and trailer may have been a mere step for him, it represented a giant leap for maritime mankind.

Undoubtedly, the time was ripe for the idea and, had McLean not made the move, someone else in the US coastal trade or perhaps in the "semi-protected" routes to Latin America might have done so. But in the tradition of Promethean entrepreneurs McLean not only changed the complexion of US coastal shipping but also soon afterwards invaded the North Atlantic and thus began the worldwide container revolution.[15] Moreover, his commitment, and that of several other American companies, made the USA for a considerable time the premier shipping nation in the new elite sector of maritime transport. McLean also propelled his own company Sea-Land, albeit later under the management of others and as a division of larger diversified corporations, to a position of global leadership that it surrendered only in 1999, when its international operations were taken over by its partner, the Danish giant Maersk.

Significantly, McLean's role began as a trucking operator.[16] In true Horatio Alger-style he bought a truck in 1934 and never looked back. By the early 1950s his McLean Trucking Company, headquartered in the heart of tobacco country in Winston-Salem, NC, was the largest operator in the South, with 2000 employees and thirty-seven truck terminals. It was from that position of strength that McLean Trucking in 1954 advertised a new door-to-door "sea-land" service in which land and sea transport were coordinated. Soon McLean understood that the strategic centre of gravity in his new service had shifted from land to sea, as the shipping leg became the functional and entrepreneurial centre in his new multi-modal transport concept. In 1955, he and his brother James and sister Clara through McLean Industries bought the Pan-Atlantic Steamship Corporation, and on 26 April 1956 they opened the first trailer-and-container carrying service between Port Elizabeth (Newark, New Jersey), and Houston (Texas). As a significant pointer to the future of established ports, no suitable site was available in New York, while Port Elizabeth connected immediately with the freeway network of the Northeast and Midwest; Manhattan would play no role in containerisation (although much later the port authorities of New York and New Jersey would be merged into one business unit).

---

[15]Ignarski (ed.), *The Box*, 13-20.

[16]The following account is largely based on Sea-Land, *Sea Notes*, Silver Anniversary Issue (1981).

The ship McLean used, sporting the advertiser's dream name *Ideal-X*, was a conventional World War II tanker fitted with a platform above deck capable of holding fifty-eight trailers. McLean almost immediately realised that even better results could be achieved if he dispensed with trailers on board, as they were only standing idle, and had the ship's holds remodelled for the carriage of containers. Six conventional C-2 freighters were converted into mixed carriers with a capacity of 226 containers (size: eight by eight by thirty-five feet) each. From 1957 the number of ports served rapidly increased, as did the volume of traffic. Miami and Tampa were included, and the weekly "West Side Service" between his main terminal at Port Elizabeth and San Juan, Puerto Rico, opened. In 1962, Port Elizabeth was linked by intercoastal service with Oakland, and two years later a west coast service began between Seattle and Anchorage.

From the beginning McLean had adopted a policy of owning or at least controlling his own terminals. Two examples show the impact of his decisions. Since insufficient space was available in San Francisco, he opted for Oakland, which now set out on its path to maritime ascendancy at the Golden Gate. At the other end of the continent, in 1966 he leased for twenty-five years the container terminal that the Boston Port Authority had made available to ensure that no other company could attack his base at Port Elizabeth.[17] Symbolising both the purpose and success of his enterprise, McLean in 1960 changed the name of his company to Sea-Land Service, Inc. When he sold it in 1969 to the tobacco giant, R.J. Reynolds Industries, the company operated thirty-five ships and 30,000 containers; its revenues stood at more than US $250 million.

Sea-Land's initiative was soon followed by another from one of the west coast's established shipping companies, the Matson Line, a firm of long standing in the trade between California and Hawaii. Its monopoly did not protect it from the general pressures in its industry, and in 1956 it was the first US company to establish an "integrated research department" to investigate Hawaii's transport requirements and to suggest solutions to the problem of rapidly-escalating port and cargo-handling costs.[18] This initiative resulted a year later in a report which recommended the adoption of containerisation for general cargo in a two-phase programme. In August 1958 the first boxes were carried as deck cargo on conventional vessels, and two years later Matson introduced converted all-container tonnage, starting with *Hawaiian Citizen*.

Matson's transition demonstrated that the containerisation concept could also be developed from the shipping industry's perspective. It may, indeed, be suggested that Matson thought through the consequences of containerisation further than Sea-Land since, in contrast to McLean's company, from the

---

[17]Van Driel, *Samenwerking*, 183-184.

[18]William L. Worden, *Cargoes: Matson's First Century in the Pacific* (Honolulu, 1981), 143.

beginning it dispensed with ship-based gear for handling containers. Instead, it relied on specially-designed gantry cranes ashore, thus initiating the transformation of general ports into dedicated container terminals.

In 1960, Grace Lines opened the first foreign-going container service when it sent its *Santa Eliana* to Venezuela, but in a move that foreshadowed the massive industrial unrest that was to accompany containerisation throughout the world, the opposition of La Guaira's dockworkers aborted the project. For the time being, most observers and shipping executives believed that containerisation was only possible in the domestic trade. As the rapid expansion of the Sea-Land and Matson networks demonstrated, the companies could never satisfy the demand for their new high-class services. Significantly, what had begun as a supply-driven revolution to increase productivity and cut costs was now also spurred by demand as customers became aware of the advantages the new technology had to offer.

This argument was confirmed when the American example was followed in Australia, another high-cost, protectionist country without any significant participation in international shipping. Due to its geographic, economic and demographic configuration, Australia had always relied heavily on coastal shipping. Since World War II, however, significant shifts had taken place in the maritime sector of its national transport infrastructure. While the bulk sector grew with the development of mineral and energy industries, passenger and cargo-liner services contracted rapidly in the face of many of the same factors as those in the USA.

In 1960 the first containers had been carried experimentally on conventional vessels. But in 1963 Associated Steamships (AS), the product of a merger between two ailing companies, decided that survival rested upon systematic containerisation. While the American companies still relied on converted tonnage, it took the bold step to order the first specially-designed and newly-built cellular container ship, *Kooringa*, which in 1964 was berthed in the Melbourne-Fremantle and later the Melbourne-Brisbane trades. As it brought terminals on stream in its various ports of call, AS added two sister ships, *Kanimbla* and *Manoora*, to establish a fortnightly service. Although it handled more than sixty percent of the admittedly low volume of Fremantle's container traffic, the company was brought down by two specifically Australian factors: the exceptionally high inflation levels from 1972 and the low freight rates charged by the heavily-subsidised, government-owned transcontinental railway. In 1975 its container service was liquidated, having lost most of its Aus $17 million capital; to see this failure in perspective, it should be observed that the Commonwealth Railways in 1974 operated with a loss of no less than Aus $200 million.[19] But by then, in stark contrast to its coastal demise, containerisation

---

[19]John Bach, *A Maritime History of Australia* (West Melbourne, 1976), 380-381.

reigned triumphant in Australia's overseas trade, as it did on all major trade routes of the world. To understand how that had come about, we need to return to Malcom McLean and Sea-Land.

With his successful expansion from Port Elizabeth and on the west coast, McLean felt confident that containerisation could also be applied to foreign trade; "it was the next logical step," as he explained succinctly.[20] Between 1966 and 1969 Sea-Land successively opened services to northern Europe, Southeast Asia, Japan, Hong Kong, Taiwan and Singapore. Working outside the realm of coastal reservation and entirely without operating subsidies, the company challenged the established conventional liner companies with its superior productivity and one formidable additional advantage: long-term contracts with the US military. It is a moot point whether McLean would ultimately also have made the jump into the deep without this guaranteed income, but it can safely be claimed that the Cold War, with America's massive commitment to the European front and the Vietnam War, significantly hastened the pace of global containerisation. While its main business on the North Atlantic was to supply the US Army in Germany, across the Pacific military and other government cargo was carried to Okinawa, the Philippines and, above all, Vietnam. In the latter theatre, Sea-Land convincingly proved the superior productivity of container shipping, if that was still necessary. Its seven ships carried about ten percent of all US cargo, while the remaining ninety percent required about 250 chartered conventional ships.

The full importance of Sea-Land's Vietnam contract and the flexibility that it possessed by not being subsidised can be best understood from the perspective of one of its rivals, American President Lines. Tracing its roots back to 1848, APL was the prestige US liner company operating a heavily-subsidised round-the-world service. Based on San Francisco, it avidly followed Sea-Land's successful strategies but as yet felt unable to decide how to respond. As APL Vice-President John Espey later recalled:[21]

> We were just helpless. I mean all of our ships were subsidized... To go out and buy ships out of the lay-up fleet and convert them would take too long. It would have been extremely expensive...So Sea-Land secured a tremendous container contract with MSC [Military Sealift Command]. basically, from Oakland to Cam Ranh Bay. They put a crane and equipment out there. Well, they operated outbound, fully loaded, under their contract, and came homebound empty. Containers empty. They did that for a year. Then they signed

---

[20]Ignarski (ed.), *The Box*, 19.

[21]Interview, quoted in John Niven, *The American President Lines and Its Forebears 1848-1984* (Newark, DE, 1986), 225.

a new contract with the government and made the logical decision that instead of coming back with the containers empty, they would start serving Japan. So they went into Kobe and into Yokohama.

While Sea-Land was thus laying the basis for a long-term position in the transpacific trades, McLean's historic moment came in April 1966 when he dispatched *Fairland* from New York across the North Atlantic, opening the first truly commercial intercontinental container service. He had prepared his ground thoroughly, establishing an extensive network of agents throughout Europe and contracts with 365 trucking companies to carry his containers and generate cargoes for the homeward run. The service was built around three ports on the North Sea: Bremerhaven, the supply base for the US military in Germany; Rotterdam, the region's largest and most central port; and Grangemouth, on the Firth of Forth west of Edinburgh, the gateway to Scotland's whiskey distilleries.[22]

McLean originally intended to follow his American model and obtain a terminal in Rotterdam for his company's exclusive use, but the Rotterdam Port Authority (owned by the city of Rotterdam) refused to make the required large tract of quayside and land available because it feared locking up too much of its scarce assets by ceding control to a single customer. As existing liner facilities were unsatisfactory, a new company had to be created which caused almost open warfare between Rotterdam's prominent stevedoring firms.[23] Significantly, the manager of the new terminal was Frans Swarttouw, the young and ambitious leader of the stevedoring firm Quick Dispatch which previously had operated only in the bulk sector.

Europe Container Terminus (ECT), named to emphasise Rotterdam's claim as the continent premier port in containerisation, was the result of a consortium formed in 1965 by QD, liner shipping stevedores Thomsen and the national railway company Nederlandse Spoorwegen (NS). It signified that ashore as much as at sea Europe's immediate future in containerisation had to be secured by joint ventures which often incorporated novel elements. Thomsen, by contrast to its Rotterdam colleagues, had developed an early interest in containerisation that was fanned by regular contacts with Sea-Land and pressure from one of the Netherlands' leading trucking companies. The participation of NS was welcomed

---

[22]The choice of Grangemouth was surprising because it housed a large BP oil terminal with associated petrochemical industries and was located at a considerable distance from the open sea. But Scotland's whiskey exporters greatly valued the reduced incidence of damage and pilfering that Sea-Land suddenly offered them.

[23]For an incisive analysis of the Rotterdam stevedoring scene and the early history of Europe Containers Terminus see Van Driel, *Samenwerking*, 183-223.

to ensure that the new terminal would have adequate connections with the national network. The formation of ECT to handle Sea-Land's business, however, was not welcomed by the greater part of the Rotterdam shipping fraternity. At the reception to celebrate the opening of the new terminal, McLean and Swarttouw were booed by many of their guests, and the latter broke down and cried.[24] But jeers could neither delay *Fairland* nor stop the inevitable. Sea-Land's service was an unqualified success, and the container revolution had been unleashed.

It soon was evident that the gates had been opened both in the United States and abroad. Although many of the subsidised foreign-going shipping companies in the USA had been highly sceptical about McLean's project, several eagerly jumped onto the bandwagon while others remained cautious. Within a few years Sea-Land was joined on the North Atlantic by American Export Isbrandtsen, Moore McCormack and the prestigious United States Lines; later, newcomer Seatrain also entered the fray.

At the same time, shipping (as well as stevedoring) companies across the Atlantic had been anxiously watching McLean and developments in the American and Australian trades, while Roll-on Roll-off and, to a lesser extent, container shipping was gaining ground in European ferry and short-sea services. It was not difficult to perceive the huge gains in productivity that containerisation could bring, but what about the financial returns under international competitive conditions? It was evident that huge investments were required, and European and other shipowners found themselves caught on the horns of an extremely sharp dilemma, characteristic for situations arising from a quantum leap in technology.[25] On the one hand, it was possible that containerisation was the wave of the future, even if the proportion of liner cargo that could be containerised was by no means fathomable. Failure to make the transition would mean certain extinction or relegation to low-quality or secondary services. If, however, one invested and container technology turned out to have been a bubble, money, but not one's existence, might be lost.

The dilemmas facing the leaders of Europe's traditional liner shipping companies were all the more acute for three structural reasons: first, that unprecedentedly high investments were necessary for container ships and their boxes, as entire fleets had to be replaced and little value remained for the discarded tonnage; second, that containerisation was not restricted to the maritime sector but required specialised new port and other transport facilities, insurance and customs arrangements, and a much closer cooperation with port

---

[24]Ignarski (ed.), *The Box*, 19. Swarttouw, of course, had the last laugh when his opponents soon joined ECT and he remained its Managing Director.

[25]Interview with the late Mr. Hans Reuchlin, President of the Holland America Line, 5 January 1978.

authorities and the non-maritime transport industries; and, third, that the productivity of the new container ships was so vastly superior – the rule-of-thumb figure usually given was that one container ship could replace five conventional vessels – that the major question became how in any given service the frequency of sailings could be maintained with only a fraction of the number of ships presently deployed. Since McLean started from scratch he was not troubled by such considerations, but for the established liner companies on the North Atlantic and elsewhere it seemed impossible to slash the number of departures to which exporters and importers had become accustomed.

Ultimately it was the very success of the container, demanded by more and more customers for their shipments, which cut the Gordian knot. And once a few sheep had passed the gate, virtually all others followed. By 1968, 200,000 containers were carried eastwards and westwards across the North Atlantic.[26] But the fundamental economic reasons for the adoption of the container in Europe (as also in Japan) were of a much deeper and longer-term nature. Throughout the 1950s, liner freight rates had climbed steadily, while those in the bulk trades had declined. In a marked reversal of the interwar trend, bulk carriers and specialised vessels, such as reefers, took cargoes away from the liner sector in a process that Van Driel evocatively has described as the "massification" of general trade.[27] At the same time, costs in the liner industry had risen faster than could be recouped through rising revenues, and the years from 1956 to the early 1960s were characterised by great pressures on profit margins.

Although there had been a minor recovery since 1963, the future for conventional liner shipping looked increasingly bleak, in part as well because its passenger and high-value, small-volume sectors were being invaded by civil aviation. Where geography was favourable, such as around the European continent, heavy lorries and semi-trailers also proved ever-more powerful challengers on their expanding network of freeways. With containerisation all these problems could be addressed and international road transport turned into an ally. Strong evidence of the advantages of such an alliance was already emerging from the European short-sea ferry sector. From the early 1960s, traditional vessels were being replaced by Roll-on Roll-off tonnage, specifically designed with ramps to accommodate not only tourists with their passenger vehicles but also the fast-growing number of trucks. By 1965, early short-sea pioneers, such as Bell Lines, were converting to container traffic. As a result, once containers were introduced on main lines, regional feeder services already existed in some regions.

---

[26]Witthöft, *Container*, 32.

[27]Van Driel, *Samenwerking*, 178.

About sixteen months after the arrival of *Fairland* in European waters, the first effective response was made to Sea-Land when the Atlantic Container Line's (ACL) *Atlantic Span* entered service.[28] In view of the magnitude of the problems and uncertainties the European shipowners faced, that time lag was remarkably short. The first steps in the formulation of that response had, in fact, been taken about two years previously. In 1965, the Holland-America Line, which would be most directly affected by Sea-Land's service to Rotterdam, reached agreements with three Swedish companies (Wallenius, Transatlantic and the Swedish America Line) to establish a joint venture, which was formalised in 1966 under the ACL name. Wallenius was the real mover as, following from its interest in car-carriers, it had already ordered two Ro-Ro combi container ships. Hamburg-America Line (HAL) took over one of these, and each of the other partners also contributed a sister ship to the consortium.

Even before ACL was formed legally, the main French operator on the North Atlantic, Compagnie Générale Transatlantique (CGT), joined and soon the British Cunard Line completed its membership. The Swedish companies, mindful also of the nature of Scandinavian exports, did not believe conditions were suitable for the use of fully cellular vessels, and the new consortium in succession ordered two series of hybrid ships that were part Roll-On Roll-Off, part container carrier, with flexible deck configuration to maintain maximum flexibility. Significantly, the cooperation was cast in such a form that ACL became the operating and marketing company. The participating companies chartered their vessels to ACL, thus abandoning their individual identities on the North Atlantic. But their joint venture did not apply to any other trade route, where they remained totally free to act as they wished. Cunard, in fact, from 1965 had been a member of another consortium in the Australian trade. For the time being this strategy of forming separate consortia for individual trade routes would be adopted by many liner companies wishing to containerise. Most simply did not have large enough market share to be able to continue standing alone. And, born from necessity, consortia became one of the most dynamic forces in the rapid diffusion of container shipping in the late 1960s and early 1970s.

Two additional aspects of the formation of ACL and the nature of the North Atlantic market for liner services must be highlighted. First, US anti-trust legislation prohibited the formation of similar consortia by American companies or the participation of US companies in foreign consortia. It is a moot point whether companies like Moore McCormack and US Lines would have been interested in joining forces, although the former did work closely with HAL in shore-based container activities.[29] Sea-Land certainly was too independent-

---

[28]Van den Burg, *Containerisation*, 123.

[29]Van Driel, *Samenwerking*, 117; H.A. Dalkmann and A.J. Schoonderbeek, *125 Years of Holland America Line* (Edinburgh, 1998), 46.

minded for such a step, and after its takeover in 1969 by the Reynolds tobacco group it was assured of ample funds for both defensive purposes and further expansion into mainline and feeder services. But most other American companies existed far more precariously, and many would not live to see the end of the 1970s. Second, and most important, the economic and marketing imperatives of containerisation, which forced established liner companies to cooperate, did not halt at national boundaries.

The long-standing regime of shipping conferences on the North Atlantic and many other routes had, of course, brought shipping leaders together to manipulate markets and to create a certain culture of working towards common objectives, but container consortia demanded unprecedented degrees of commitment, confidence and cooperation. Although individual companies, as shareholders in ACL, retained their national identities, a certain degree of trans-nationalism crept into their beings. On top of all the other changes of outlook that containerisation demanded, it was a truly new professional culture in the liner business when traditional rivals like HAL and Cunard could work together.

Yet at least for the time being, there were limits to the size and membership of the new consortium. The two German companies, Hamburg-America Line (Hapag, after its German name) and North German Lloyd (of Bremen), despite serious misgivings, found their destiny first in a joint container line venture and then, in 1970, finally laying to rest an often bitter rivalry that spanned more than a century, in a complete fusion. As Lloyd director Karl Heinz Sager acknowledged in 1970, big companies like his, despite the uncertain financial future, had no option but to containerise wherever that seemed possible.[30] And, after "careful consideration," Hapag-Lloyd chose "the risky course of going alone,"[31] believing the new company would be able to capture sufficient market share.

As a result of these moves the Compagnie Maritime Belge (CMB) of Antwerp fell between the stools.[32] Its application to join ACL was refused and negotiations with Hapag-Lloyd and US Lines remained fruitless. Estimates of the high investments needed for a fleet that could provide the same frequency of service, however, demonstrated that CMB could not act alone. A joint venture was created in June 1968 with two total newcomers, Bristol City Lines and the Montréal freight forwarder and coastal shipowner, Clarke Traffic Services, under the name Dart Container Line. Dart's headquarters were located in Bermuda. It marketed its new container services (which included the first between northern

[30]Witthöft, *Container*, 17-18.

[31]Hapag-Lloyd director Karl-Heinz Sager, quoted in *Fairplay*, 24 September 1981, 24.

[32]Devos and Elewaut, *CMB 100*, 208-211.

Europe and Canada)[33] itself and operated by chartering new container ships, ordered and owned by each of the partners. For a short time in 1970 *Dart Europe* and its sister ships (1556 TEU, 28,500 dwt – a remarkably high deadweight/TEU ratio) were the largest container ships in the world.

In the five years after Sea-Land's *Fairland* initiated the container revolution, the North Atlantic had been the stage for a frenzy of entrepreneurial activity, technological and organisational change, and exponential growth of container capacity. Several years later Sager recalled the absolute turmoil of the time:[34]

> The time lag between placing orders and delivery of the new containerships, a period of some 18 months, was extremely turbulent. We assumed rightly that the transition from a traditional vessel to a fully cellular containership could not be made from one day to the next. So conventional freighters were packed to their mastheads with containers. The costs were horrendous...After the introduction of a fleet of containerships, each at least double the capacity of its predecessor, substantial over-tonnaging prevailed...The resulting rate war entailed tremendous losses for shipowners, but brought on the other hand the breakthrough of the "box" with shippers.

Two international consortia had been formed (three if one includes the trade with the Great Lakes),[35] and a number of European companies had lost their identity on what still was the most important trade route of the global economy. The carefully-crafted conference agreements on the North Atlantic had exploded under the combined impact of technological and organisational change, on the one hand, and a tonnage glut on the other. Under these conditions a new agreement between all container operators became both desirable and necessary; as usual, varying calculations fired enthusiasm. Weak lines were glad to find protection, while strong ones regarded the agreement as a good opportunity to consolidate and strengthen their positions for the next struggle for market share, which they knew would come as surely as day follows night. The pool agreement (see table 1) that was concluded in June 1971 "to stabilise the rate structure and

---

[33]The service ran to Halifax, NS, from where rail connections were maintained with Montréal, Toronto and Hamilton.

[34]Quoted in *Fairplay*, 24 September 1981, 24.

[35]Its members included CGT, Oranje Lijn (Netherlands), Fjell Line (Norway) and Cunard; Randier, *Histoire*, 322.

curtail over-tonnage" demonstrated the current balance of strength in the trade.[36] Together, the American lines accounted for no less than fifty-five percent, eloquent evidence of the tremendous advantages Sea-Land's pioneering role and entrepreneurial drive, the early development of container infrastructure ashore, and the capital-intensive nature of containerisation had given them.

Table 1
North Atlantic Pool Agreement, June 1971

Consortium/Company	Market Share (%)
Atlantic Container Line (S, NL, F, GB)	20.250
United States Lines (USA)	18.000
Sea-Land (USA)	17.000
Hapag-Lloyd (D)	14.175
Sea-Train (USA)	11.250
Dart Container Line (B, GB, CND)	10.575
American Export Isbrandtsen Lines (USA)	8.750
	100.000

Source: See text.

But containerisation did not remain limited to the North Atlantic or the initiative of American businessmen. Virtually at the same time as the first steps toward consortium formation were taken for the North Atlantic, British companies in the long-distance trade to Australia had begun conducting their own research on the topic. Under pressure from sharply-rising costs and numerous labour disputes in both Australia and Britain, they soon came to the conclusion that only far-reaching cooperation between previously independent partners in the form of a consortium could overcome the fundamental problems of conventional liner shipping sketched above. They were concerned in particular about the huge investments required and the need to maintain the same frequency of sailings with container ships. As P&O's leader, Sir Donald Anderson, expressed it, "A solution is likely to be achieved only by very close co-operation within a group small enough to act effectively but strong enough to command the necessary contacts and resources."[37] The membership of the first two consortia in the Australian trade, which actually predated the formal creation of ACL, fully confirms the revolutionary impact of containerisation.

---

[36]Van den Burg, *Containerisation*, 131.

[37]Quoted in Stephen Rabson and Kevin O'Donoghue, *P&O. A Fleet History* (Kendal, 1988), 219.

The first breakthrough was achieved in September 1965 when Overseas Containers Limited (OCL) was founded by four British shipping companies with the specific mission to initiate containerisation in the trade between Britain and Australia. The four constituted a truly remarkable combination of forces, as they were Britain's first, second, third and fifth largest liner companies, with fleets (in 1960) of 2,007,000, 1,291,000, 971,000, and 769,000 million grt, respectively.[38] Each of the four, moreover, possessed a long tradition and well established identity in the Australian trade: the Peninsular and Oriental Steam Navigation Company (P&O), Furness Withy and Co., Ocean Steamship Company (also known as Blue Funnel), and British and Commonwealth Shipping (B&C).

P&O, which had sailed to Australia since 1852, was Britain's largest and most traditional imperial mail company. Since the beginning of the century it had built an unassailable position as leader of the trade. Its field of operations far transcended Australia, covering much of the trade East of Suez and across the Pacific; with its numerous subsidiaries it was the Port of London's largest customer. Ocean Steamship of Liverpool from the 1860s had been the pioneer of unsubsidised steam shipping in the trade with China and Southeast Asia. It had entered the Australian trade in the 1890s, but despite close collaboration with P&O in later periods, over the years the companies had maintained a lively rivalry. Furness Withy and B&C were successors to a number of other lines in the Australian trade (notably the Clan and Scottish Shire Lines, and Shaw Savill and Albion) that dated back to the 1880s and 1890s; but, as their partners, they also had interests elsewhere. The financial participation of OCL's members, and hence their internal balance of power, was determined roughly according to market share, with Ocean Steamship gaining the lion's share of forty-nine percent; P&O (whose strength lay foremost in the doomed passenger trade), thirty percent; Furness Withy, 13.4 percent;, and B&C, 7.6 percent. OCL was not just a unique combination but also a uniquely powerful bundling of forces.

As Anderson's words suggested, OCL's partners did not want their group to be too large, and they specifically refused entry to several other leading companies such as Ellerman, Blue Star and Cunard. A number of these in the Australian – still a traditional British stronghold – and Asian trades had been following events closely. Ellerman (Britain's sixth largest company with 631,000 grt), for example, learned that "four titled shipping men, each chairman of a major shipping line, had been meeting regularly....[and had] under consideration...the consolidation of the four large companies."[39]

---

[38]S.G. Sturmey, *British Shipping and World Competition* (London, 1962), 360.

[39]James Taylor, *Ellermans. A Wealth of Shipping* (London, 1976), 161.

Although they misunderstood the nature of the new consortium, Ellerman's leaders immediately applied to join OCL, once its formation and purpose had been publicly announced. When they were rebuffed, they immediately invited a number of colleagues for emergency talks. They found a receptive audience, as the Cunard-owned Port Line and Blue Star had been similarly snubbed. Cunard's managing director, Philip Bates, was convinced that OCL was determined to gain control over the entire British liner industry and let all others fade into obscurity.[40] With that spectre hovering above them and Cunard, in particular, also in an acute crisis as the result of rapidly-declining passenger traffic on the North Atlantic,[41] the group soon reached agreement. Before the year was out, Associated Container Transportation (ACT) was formed as the second British consortium, with Ellerman, Blue Star, Ben Line, Harrison and Port Line as partners. As Ben Line and Harrison were not involved in the Australian trade (they traded mainly with East and South Asia, respectively), the three remaining partners formed ACT (Australia) (ACTA) as the immediate counterweight to OCL.

Blue Star was a relative newcomer to the Australian trade, having entered in the 1930s with a fleet of modern refrigerated freighters; it had testified to its origins in the cold storage business by staying out of the Australian conference until 1958. Port Line was, as Furness Withy, successor to a number of pre-World War I companies but since 1916 had been owned by Cunard, Britain's fourth largest liner group (947,000 grt). Cunard, whose main interests were in the Atlantic trade, for some time occupied a rather ambivalent position *vis-à-vis* containerisation. Although, primarily for purposes of self-preservation, it pushed ahead with ACTA and the planning for a container service to Australia, it was less certain about the future of containerisation on the Atlantic. In a 1966 report all the arguments for and against were enumerated and the question put, whether it was possible to devise a hybrid scheme that would enable the company to enjoy all advantages without suffering any of the disadvantages of the new technology; this fit neatly the philosophy of ACL, which it joined late that year.[42]

The magnitude of the technological, organisational and logistic problems ahead of OCL and ACTA can be measured from the fact that they did not order their container ships until early 1967 and did not open their services until two

---

[40]Howard Johnson, *The Cunard Story* (London, 1987), 179.

[41]As early as 1958 the number of passengers carried by air equalled that of shipboard passengers, and the balance was shifting rapidly in the direction of the airline companies (Dalkmann and Schoonderbeek, *125 Years*, 44).

[42]Johnson, *Cunard Story*, 179.

years later. Ellerman's former director, James Taylor, gave an eloquent impression of the tasks involved:[43]

> A totally new type of ship was required, several times larger than those with which most of the partners had been accustomed to dealing in the past. They were to cost as much as three or four traditional cargo ships, but each was expected to replace five or six of the traditional type in providing an improved service to the shippers. Not only were they to be larger and faster: they would turn round at the end of the voyage in a matter of a few days, the improved dispatch being made possible by the container nature of their cargo and the equipment on the quayside or terminal for handling containers. This multi-million-pound commitment did not end with the ship and its containers, as depots and terminals were required and needed to be constructed or leased.

During the process of implementing the containerisation decision, moreover, the rate of change in liner shipping accelerated so much that virtually every month brought structural and material developments. ACT and OCL soon realised that cooperation between the two consortia was needed to develop terminals and to schedule sailings. Old and more recent enmities were cast aside with the joint construction of the London container terminal at Tilbury and the establishment of shared facilities in Australia.[44]

In 1967 the Australian government decided that the Commonwealth-owned Australian National Line, which until then had only operated in domestic waters, should make use of the window of opportunity that capital-intensive containerisation offered to enter the foreign trade, especially on the old imperial line with Britain. This decision will be discussed in more detail later, but here it will suffice to note that the ANL's resources were to be spread over all Australia's major trade routes; in consequence, the line would be utterly incapable of offering a service of any acceptable frequency on any route if it stood alone. Negotiations with ACTA led to its inclusion in this consortium, which now gained a new complexion, indicative of new patterns in both joint venturing and liner shipping in general. Within the context of the former it meant the inclusion in container consortia of members located at both ends of the trade route, which gave the consortium additional strength and legitimacy. And, in more general terms, it meant the entry into container shipping, beyond the USA,

---

[43]Taylor, *Ellermans*, 162.

[44]John Hovey, *A Tale of Two Ports* (London, 1990), part 1, gives a highly interesting inside account of the preparations at Tilbury for the new service.

of countries that until then had been consumers rather than providers of shipping services.

In 1968, ACTA's British principals decided also to enter the trade between Australia and New Zealand and the US East Coast where, on top of all the usual problems, competition from American newcomer Farrell Lines was beginning to bite.[45] ANL and OCL also became involved, but with minority shares only. The new service, opened in 1970 under the name Page Line, used a further three ACT ships and one each from ANL and OCL; it joined Farrell Lines and the dominant cross-trader Columbus Line, a subsidiary of the West German company, Hamburg-Süd.[46] OCL at that stage had already decided to enter the Europe-East Asia trade, and it was apparent that the cooperative consortium structure provided a most effective method to expand into other trading regions. How far cooperation could extend was demonstrated later in 1969 when the combined ACT and OCL formed a mega-agreement with the recently formed Seabridge consortium of continental European companies in the Australian trade, Nedlloyd (Netherlands), Hapag-Lloyd (Germany), Messageries Maritimes (France) and Lloyd Triestino (Italy).

The formation of Seabridge eloquently confirmed, if that was still necessary, that the economic logic of containerisation broke down not only traditional company rivalries but also national boundaries. With a total of fourteen container ships of the second generation (approximately 1300-TEU each), the Australia Europe Container Service (AECS) was the most formidable concentration of power yet. It offered a minimum of one sailing every ten days, and its marketing arms covered the entire European continent, Britain and Ireland. In 1977, AECS was transformed into ANZECS when it incorporated New Zealand, both as a market and as a participant, through the newly-founded New Zealand Shipping Corporation, whose contribution consisted of a single vessel, *New Zealand Pacific*.

While European liner companies formulated their answers to the American challenge, the Pacific was rapidly turning into a technological and

---

[45]This company from the 1920s had run services to South, East and later also West Africa, but in 1965 had opened an entirely new line from the US East and Gulf coasts to New Zealand and Australia. Initially, Farrell carried only a few containers, but gradually the traffic thickened and in 1972-1973 the company introduced fully cellular vessels. As an indication of their superior productivity, these four new 1050-TEU carriers could carry twice as much freight as Farrell's six older ships and annually make twenty-two round voyages against only thirteen previously. For a brief historical portrait of the company see the special report in *Intermodal World* (April 1975).

[46]Hamburg-Süd carried about sixty percent of the trade; in 1971 it introduced three full-container ships with 1187-TEU capacity, of which 758 could be refrigerated (Witthöft, *Container*, 39-40).

entrepreneurial maelstrom. When Sea-Land entered the transpacific trade, it threw down the gauntlet to US operators, like Matson and American President Lines, and long-standing Japanese companies, like Nippon Yusen Kaisha (NYK) and Osaka Shosen Kaisha (OSK), after its merger with Mitsui known as Mitsui-OSK. The contrast between the responses from Matson and APL, and between NYK and Mitsui-OSK, reflected in their respective arenas the worldwide differences of view on containerisation.

While Matson's President, Stanley Powell, was a container enthusiast with grandiose visions of integrated ship-train-ship traffic between Japan and Europe,[47] APL's leadership was divided and indecisive.[48] In October 1965 Powell made a trip to Japan to sound out Japanese shipping leaders on the establishment of transpacific container services. Mitsui OSK's attitude was "initially negative" because the company – quite exceptionally in the liner industry – was making good profits, saw no good reason to abandon the *status quo*, and felt that a shipping company could "not control all the elements" of the new infrastructure that containerisation required, such as large terminals and matching land transport arrangements.[49] NYK, by contrast, reacted enthusiastically and agreed to the establishment of a joint service. But while Matson ordered its first fully cellular ships, Japan's Ministry of Transport intervened, believing that containerisation was too serious to leave to the whims of individual shipping companies, especially now that NYK had tied itself to a foreign company. Characteristically, a national study group was established on which the ministry and the major liner companies were represented.

In the USA, as a result of its shipping regulations, containerisation was achieved through bilateral negotiations between the Maritime Administration and the shipowners, and European governments encouraged voluntary cooperation between interested companies. In contrast, Japan adopted the path of bureaucratic intervention. Such a strategy fit perfectly into the ethos and policies of guided economic development that Japan had adopted from the early 1950s, and it was no coincidence that a body already existed that was perfectly suited to deal with the issue, the Japanese Council for the Rationalization of the Shipping and Shipbuilding Industries (CRSSI). Established in 1952, by the 1960s it was concerned with restructuring the Japanese merchant fleet in the wake of the depression early in that decade.

---

[47]Worden, *Cargoes*, 150.

[48]Niven, *APL*, 211-228. It should be taken into account that APL was one of three steamship companies owned by a holding company; its main owner, George Killion, had interests in several other sectors, including oil and the film studio Metro-Goldwyn-Mayer.

[49][Tatsuki and Yamamoto], *First Century*, 168-169.

The container study group passed on its brief to CRSSI, which in September 1966 released a report with a number of specific recommendations for the containerisation of the transpacific trade. Among the most important were the adoption of the TEU and FEU as standard containers; the proposal that containerisation take place within the framework of existing conferences (I shall later return to this theme); the integrated use of terminals and containers; and, as most companies were still recovering from the recent depression, the strong recommendation that they adopt policies of voluntary cooperation rather than excessive competition. The first route to be containerised would be Japan-California.

Since the necessary investments were estimated to amount to some twenty billion yen, the Ministry of Transport in December intervened to accelerate the process of establishing joint ventures. It combined the lines into two groups: NYK, still with its joint venture with Matson, was assigned the Showa Line, while Mitsui-OSK, Yamashita-Shinnihon Kisen (YS Line), Kawasaki Kisen (K-Line) and Japan Line formed the second group. Integration of the companies was achieved at sea through mutual space charter agreements, ashore by the creation of jointly-owned terminal companies.[50] The first ship to leave Kobe for the four-line consortium in October 1968 was Mitsui-OSK's appropriately named *America Maru* (705 TEU), but this had been preceded by several months by NYK's *Hakone Maru* (851 TEU), the first container ship built outside the USA. NYK had achieved in six months what had been believed would take three years. Moreover, by Japan's rapid action, the Pacific had overtaken the Atlantic in challenging American dominance.

Ironically, the flood of vessels that now entered the Pacific caused the demise of Matson Line as an international operator. Burdened with heavy debts due to its containerisation programme and led by men whose main interest still lay in Hawaii, the company in 1970 abandoned its East Asian service and Powell's premature dreams of intermodalism. Its ships were sold to Sea-Land and Pacific Far East Lines. In future it would focus again on the California-Hawaii trade.[51] Honolulu's ambitions to become the oceanic hub of the entire Pacific area collapsed with Matson's shipping dreams. Without Matson's active intervention, and with the establishment of direct lines between the USA and East Asia by Japanese and other American rivals, Honolulu was simply dropped from the schedule of transoceanic services.[52]

---

[50]*Ibid.*, 170-173.

[51]Worden, *Cargoes*, 152-153.

[52]Edward D. Beechert, *Honolulu. Crossroads of the Pacific* (Columbia, SC, 1991), 170-179.

The two major American lines on the Pacific were APL and Pacific Far East Lines (PEFL), both members of the Natomas group (a third company, American Mail Lines, operated in the coastal trade). Natomas' leadership was undecided about containerisation because of its uncertain future and the huge investments required. Their hesitation was increased by the fact that many East Asian ports were chronically congested, which suggested that a barge system like LASH might be more suitable. W.R. Grace/Prudential Line, which operated in the Caribbean and Latin American trades, had already opted for the LASH system, partly because it operated out of New Orleans, partly because it could outflank congested ports and hostile waterside workers in this manner.

Under the terms of US shipping legislation, new technology had to be adopted by two operators and, accordingly, the Maritime Administration invited APL as the next company on its list to join Grace in the development of the barge carriers; should APL refuse, PFEL would be next. Put on the spot in this manner, Natomas' management became involved in what can only be described as a bitter civil war.

Sea-Land and Matson had made the container a household word in California, but LASH was deemed to be more suitable for conditions in East and Southeast Asia, where competition with Japanese and European lines was fiercest, and also the Mediterranean.[53] As presidents came and went, a temporary solution was found when PFEL was sold to the transport conglomerate Consolidated Freightways, which concurred in adopting LASH, while APL continued to operate with a fleet of break-bulk vessels with container capacity. In 1967-1968 five new "Sea-masters" (14,000 grt) were introduced, while the boardroom battle for the construction of fully-cellular ships continued. It was not until 1973-1974 that APL took delivery of the first two of these ("Pacesetters" of 1508 TEU), at the same time as all its existing conventional vessels were lengthened and reconstructed as container ships. The question, of course, was whether this massive transformation was too little, too late, as Sea-Land and its Japanese colleagues had forged ahead.

The fifth major trade route to be containerised from the late 1960s was that between Japan and Australia.[54] Its evolution demonstrated just how complex consortia and other cooperative structures had become. The first step was taken when NYK, Mitsui-OSK and YS Line began operating a three-ship service, with one ship owned by each of the former two and the third by all three lines jointly. A second three-vessel consortium soon joined them, the Eastern Searoad Service

---

[53]Niven, *APL*, 224-225. APL had considerable additional problems as it also had to face the demise of its round-the-world passenger ships.

[54]Keith Trace, "Shipping Links between Australia and Japan: An Analysis of Current Problems and an Agenda for Further Research" (Unpublished paper, Melbourne, 1977), 4-6.

of the Australian National Line, K-Line, and Flinders Shipping (a privately-owned Australian company), with one ship each. From 1971, the first group cooperated with the Australia-Japan Container Line, which was owned half by Australia West Pacific Line, a Swedish cross-trader, and half by Overseas Containers Pacific Line, itself a joint venture of John Swire and Son (Hong Kong) and OCL, Britain's very first consortium. It is noteworthy that, apart from the complex arrangements that more-or-less reflected the pre-containerisation balance of power in the trade, OCL here acted as an independent entity, an issue to which I shall return later in the context of the Britain-East Asian trade.

By 1970, the outlines of a global container network had become clearly visible. Although the system had suffered plenty of problems and many shipping people and observers still were not convinced that containerisation could deliver what enthusiasts promised, it was firmly established on five of the six trade routes (USA (and Canada)-Britain/Europe; USA-Japan; Britain/Europe-Australia; Australia (and New Zealand)-USA; and Japan-Australia) between the four most developed regions of the capitalist world economy.

The one link still missing was the longest and most challenging route of all, between Britain/Europe and Japan, but several consortia had been formed and orders placed for their ships (the maiden voyage began on 31 December 1971, with the departure from Tokyo of NYK's 1950-TEU *Kamakura Maru*).[55] In the meantime the number of containers handled worldwide was increasing exponentially, as were the number and capacity of vessels in service and on order. By adopting the consortium strategy, British, European and Japanese companies had successfully taken up the challenge thrown down by Sea-Land and its American rivals. In all major ports of the world container terminals, often on green sites, were ready for operation, under construction, or on the drawing board. Massive investments, increasingly drawn from external sources, were committed to container shipping and its associated activities ashore. The next chapter will discuss its triumphal march through the 1970s, when many of the constraints that had been thought to limit the potential of containerisation were removed. But while the system expanded faster and further than expected, the shipping industry itself was buffeted by many forces, external and incidental as well as internal and systemic. By the end of the decade its structure and appearance was dramatically transformed.

---

[55]Witthöft, *Container*, 2.

Chapter 3
The 1970s: Conquering the World

> The towering containership, with its slab-sided building blocks
> of cargo and dramatically flared bow, is ubiquitous and
> commonplace today.[1]

By the late 1970s, containerisation had become a worldwide system. From its foundations in the trades between the industrialised and wealthy poles of the global economy, the revolution had spread like a nuclear chain reaction across the world, sweeping all before it. The degree to which liner cargoes could be containerised had surpassed all expectations, as that European veteran of containerisation, Karl-Heinz Sager, recalled in 1981:[2]

> I still remember how piles of cargo manifests for certain trades
> were analysed at our [i.e., North German Lloyd] offices, in
> order to establish which goods could reasonably be packed in
> containers. At the time we arrived at a proportion of only
> about 25-30 per cent for the North Atlantic, though today [i.e.,
> 1981] 80-90 per cent of all cargo there is carried in containers.
> For the US/Far East trade our calculations were only slightly
> more encouraging.

A survey instigated by the Far Eastern Freight Conference in 1978 found an even more complete transformation in its field: of all Europe/East Asian cargoes, eighty-three percent was already containerised; of the trade between East Asia and Europe, ninety-two percent was; while ninety-nine percent of the trade from Europe to Japan was carried in boxes.[3] But it was not just the rapid growth and intensification of containerisation on the main routes that amazed experts and propelled the industry forward. It was also the extent to which

---

[1]*The Australian*, 29 March 1979, 15.

[2]Quoted in Sam Ignarski (ed.), *The Box. An Anthology Celebrating 25 Years of Containerisation and the TT Club* (London, 1996), 68; Sager supplied the full text of his speech to *Fairplay*, 24 September 1981, 24. See also Hermann Schreiber, *Verkehr. Schienenbahnen, Schiffahrt, Luftverkehr* (Darmstadt, 1972), 114.

[3]Eric Jennings, *Cargoes. A Centenary Story of the Far Eastern Freight Conference* (Singapore, 1980), 59.

containerisation (including, to a much lesser extent, RoRo) invaded the trade with the less- developed areas of the global economy – what, adopting the economic-ideological imagery of the Club of Rome, became known as the North-South trades. While many insiders had believed that the industry would take a breather after the containerisation of the Europe-Singapore-East Asia route, the second stage followed almost without interruption (see table 2).[4]

Table 2
Introduction of Container Shipping on Major North-South Routes

1972: Europe-East Asia
1973: USA-Latin America
1974: USA-Middle East and India
1976: Europe-Caribbean
1977: Europe-South Africa
1977: Europe-Middle East
1978: Japan-Middle East
1978: Europe-India/Pakistan
1978: Europe-West Africa
1979: Europe-China
1980: Europe-Latin America

Source: See text.

The capacity of the world container fleet between 1973 and 1983 grew from 278,000 to almost 2,000,000 TEUs, an increase of approx. 620 percent. (Its effective productivity rise was somewhat lower, as the excessive and costly service speeds of the early- and mid-1970s were reduced to more modest levels.) With the exception of 1974-1976 annual growth rates of twenty percent and more were common. A comparison of the growth rate of container shipping with that of the other main sectors of the shipping industry puts its exceptional dynamism in even greater relief. Between 1970 and 1984 total international seaborne trade increased over twenty-seven percent from 2605 million to 3320 million tons. Oil shipments actually fell over that period by more than two percent, while dry bulk increased by sixty-three percent. World container cargoes, however, rose over six times from forty-eight million to over 305 million tons, an average annual growth rate of over thirty percent, compared to just 1.5 percent per annum for all seaborne trade.[5] In terms of the accumulated turnover of all container ports,

---

[4]H.L. Beth, A. Hader and R. Keppel, *25 Years of World Shipping* (London, 1984), 76.

[5]Ernst Gabriel Frankel, *The World Shipping Industry* (London, 1987), 103-105.

global container traffic by 1983 amounted to forty-six million TEUs, more than three times the figure for 1973.[6]

Within the overall pattern of growth, however, significant regional differences can be observed, reflecting developments in the container shipping industry as well as the impact of structural changes and fluctuations in the world economy. Perhaps the most important aspect of the latter was the spectacular rise of oil prices from less than US $2 per barrel in 1970 to over US $40 by the early 1980s. The two oil crises, in 1973 and 1979, dealt sharp blows to economic activity and world trade. The first stopped the boom of the early 1970s dead in its tracks and led to a modest attempt at energy conservation. But the higher oil price proved a strong stimulus to growth, as it was translated into a consumer and building boom in the Middle East and petrodollars lubricated global economic activity. The second crisis, however, had no such redeeming features and plunged the industrial world into a recession which only deepened further when the oil price itself collapsed.

Rising energy prices slowed down the growth of the USA and Europe but affected Japan much less and did little to slow the rapid rises in the newly-industrialising countries of East and Southeast Asia, such as South Korea, Taiwan, Hong Kong and Singapore. Moreover, as labour costs in Western countries continued to rise, manufacturing production was increasingly moved offshore to low-cost countries. East and Southeast Asia were the main beneficiaries of this strategic and irreversible relocation of manufacturing production.

The unprecedented strong economic performance of Japan and the "small dragons" of its region, especially in the production of automobiles, electrical goods, toys, hardware, plastics and other consumption goods, precipitated a dramatic shift in the balance of economic power from the North Atlantic to the North Pacific, where the total value of trade approached that of the traditional major axis of global commerce. Further, as imports in East Asia from the USA and Europe were significantly smaller in volume than exports to those areas, on both the USA-East Asia and Europe-East Asia container routes it increased the systematic imbalance regarding TEU requirements, creating serious problems in the repositioning of empty boxes. This was one of the problems that inspired the planning and opening of global services, which will be analysed in the next chapter.

This epochal shift from the Atlantic to the Pacific was most immediately visible in the stagnation of New York as the largest port of the world and the relative rise of US West Coast ports. Between 1974 and 1983, New York/New Jersey (including Port Elizabeth) increased its turnover by only twenty-five percent, from 1,657,500 to 2,065,000 TEUs, only a little over one-half of the combined figures for Seattle, Oakland, Long Beach and Los Angeles, which

---

[6]*Containerisation International Yearbook* (1985).

together grew from 1,678,300 to 3,286,200 TEUs, a rise of ninety-six percent.[7] Total American figures were clearly influenced by the Pacific dawn, growing from 5,382,500 to 9,477,700 TEUs (up seventy-six percent). But the overall figures for Japan during the same time moved from 1,906,800 to 4,105,500 TEUs (up 115 percent), while Taiwan rocketed from ninth to fourth position in the list of nations with a growth from 388,900 to 2,429,300 TEUs (up 525 percent), and Southeast Asia's entrepot, Singapore, enjoyed an even faster rate of growth (up 731 percent), jumping from 153,400 to 1,274,300 TEUs. Hong Kong had been an early starter in containerisation (726,200 TEU in 1974), but made solid gains as well, to 1,837,000 TEUs, up 153 percent. About two-thirds of the cargo from East Asia loaded for the USA now originated from Taiwan, South Korea, Singapore and Malaysia.[8] The People's Republic of China was hardly a major player in 1983, although the signs that this giant was emerging from its international isolation were unmistakable. The other region that suddenly became a major economic player, of course, was the Middle East and, in particular, the Gulf. None of its littoral countries appeared among the top thirty container users in the world in 1974, but nine years later Saudi Arabia (twelfth), the United Arab Emirates (twentieth) and Kuwait (twenty-eighth) together accounted for almost two million TEUs.

The explosive expansion of container shipping through the 1970s and early '80s was characterised by a pattern consisting of three mutually reinforcing elements: intensification, i.e., increasing the level of the containerisation of trade on established routes, intercontinental and/or short-sea; diffusion, the opening of new main lines; and penetration, the establishment of new regional feeder and distribution networks. From the perspective of the individual company, there was a certain element of chronological sequence in this pattern, but once a company was established on a number of routes, its development assumed an almost organic quality, as increases on any one line provided the stimulus for others in adjacent areas. The opening and intensification of the main east-west lines between the industrialised and consumer-rich poles of the world economy, particularly as the TEU capacity of vessels on those services was large, increasingly demanded the acquisition of greater numbers of boxes which could only occur through building up regional feeder services ashore and on short-sea routes. Thus, the container invaded existing hinterlands and created new ones; at the same time, avenues were found to use the box in the North-South trades. Although initially many believed that containerisation was only possible in regions that possessed extensive and sophisticated transport infrastructures, container companies quickly transformed existing facilities and built new ones

---

[7]*Containerisation International Yearbook* (1977 and 1985).

[8][Mariko Tatsuki and Tsuyoshi Yamamoto], *The First Century of Mitsui O.S.K. Lines, Ltd.* (Osaka, 1985), 196.

in many parts of the Less-Developed World to accommodate the maritime revolution. A prime example of this rapid transformation was the container terminal at Colombo which, benefiting from the 1967 closure of the Suez Canal, regained its former importance as a regional hub for liner shipping (the "Clapham Junction of the East"),[9] but others could be found all across the globe, including Africa.[10]

The key to the containerisation of the North-South trades, according to many analysts, was the flexible application of the consortium model. The first generation of consortia in most cases had not only achieved all that their principals anticipated – in terms of joint research, planning, marketing, freight acquisition, and spreading the burdens of investment afloat and ashore – but also had proven successful in managing joint ventures and overcoming the fierce sense of independence of the individual partners. OCL, ACT, ACL, Seabridge and the two Japanese groups in the transpacific trades stood as beacons in the industry. From the viewpoint of the individual company, Cunard was satisfied with its participation in both ACT and ACL; as its Chairman, Sir Basil Smallpeice, put it, "I was now more than glad that P&O and Ocean Steamship, who had thought we were fit only for breaking up, had spurned my original merger offer."[11] And while the first consortia generally had been formed by established liner companies (the only exception being the Australian National Line), they showed themselves willing to accept newcomers to the business, so that the system maintained a remarkable flexibility and dynamism.

Just how successful the consortium formula was could be seen when the world's longest and third-most important trade route, between Europe and East Asia, was containerised. After all the dust had settled, in the late 1970s four large international consortia existed, none more powerful than the TRIO-group that had initiated the process. It combined the interests of five companies in a joint venture that involved investments of DM 2.7 billion and the building of

---

[9]K. Dharmasena, *The Port of Colombo 1860-1939* (Colombo, 1980); and Dharmasena, *The Port of Colombo. Vol. II, 1940-1995* (Tokyo, 1998), esp. chapter 5.

[10]See, e.g., B.S. Hoyle, "Maritime Perspectives on Ports and Port Systems: The Case of East Africa," in Frank Broeze (ed.), *Brides of the Sea. Port Cities of Asia from the 16th-20th Centuries* (Honolulu, 1989), 188-206; and the advances in inland transportation made in central Africa, as reported in the *Annual Reports* of the Compagnie Maritime Belge.

[11]Howard Johnson, *The Cunard Story* (London, 1987), 180.

seventeen third-generation ships to maintain two weekly services,[12] a feat that no individual company could have achieved on its own. As table 3 shows, membership in the group encompassed three countries; roughly reflecting respective market shares, the three British and German partners brought in twelve ships of about 3000 TEUs and the two Japanese lines five of a smaller capacity:

Table 3
Membership of the TRIO Group, 1972

Company	Country	Participation
Overseas Containers Ltd. (OCL)	Britain	5 vessels, 3000 TEU
Hapag-Lloyd	Germany	4 vessels, 3000 TEU
Ben Line	Britain	3 vessels, 2800 TEU
Nippon Yusen Kaisha	Japan	3 vessels, 1950 TEU
Mitsui-OSK Lines	Japan	2 vessels, 2000 TEU

Source: See text.

Each of the European ships measured little short of 60,000 grt, four times larger than the conventional ships used in the trade. With their service speed of twenty-six knots, they reduced transit time between Europe and East Asia, through Suez or Panama, to twenty-one to twenty-three days, and the total length of the round-trip voyage to sixty-three days compared to the previous fastest voyage of 110 days. One container vessel replaced six or seven conventional ones.[13] The productivity gain could also be measured in the ratio of sea time to time in port, which increased from sixty/forty to eighty/twenty.[14] A highly significant feature – until then only visible as a minor feature in the ACTA consortium – that provided strength to TRIO was that its membership was solidly established at both ends of the trade route, with major partners in Europe and Japan. OCL, of course, also was special because strictly-speaking it was not a company but a consortium. Originally formed for the Australian trade, all its partners were multi-trade operators whose experience had taught them that it was most efficacious to keep their joint venture together. Later, OCL would enter several other trades beyond East Asia, including the Middle East and South

---

[12]J. Witthöft, *Container. Transportrevolution unseres Jahrhunderts* (2nd ed., Hereford, 1978), 41; and Susanne and Klaus Wiborg, *The World is Our Oyster. 150 Years of Hapag-Lloyd 1847-1997* (Hamburg, 1997), 363-364.

[13]G.J. de Boer and A.J. J. Mulder, *Nedlloyd. 25 Jaar Maritiem* (Alkmaar, 1995), 13.

[14]Witthöft, *Container*, 41.

Africa. The fifth partner, the Edinburgh-based Ben Line, by contrast was not a "general" company with an elaborate network of long-distance liner services and large interests in other sectors of the shipping industry but rather the quintessential one-route company with its headquarters in a maritime backwater; its London agents, Killick Martin and Co, largely represented its interests.[15]

Figure 3: K-Line's *Verrazano Bridge* was a typical example of the Japanese carriers of the third generation. This photo, taken during its trial voyage, shows how much the deck structure of container vessels differed from that of traditional freight liners.

Source: R. Kolbeck, *Zukunft der Schiffahrt.das neue Gesicht d. christl. Seefahrt* (Berlin, 1974).

---

[15]David R. MacGregor, *The China Bird. The History of Captain Killick, and the Firm he Founded: Killick Martin & Company* (2nd ed., London, 1986), 178-181.

The formation of TRIO in its complex double-ended form was based on the perceived necessity to integrate totally the acquisition powers of all companies which, individually, were dominant in their own national markets. The resulting marketing strategy dictated that all companies acquired cargo for each ship through slot-leasing agreements based on each company's historical performance, similar to pool-based conference agreements. Periodic meetings of all partners, in which the number of slots per company could be re-allocated according to recent performance, ensured that real shifts in company strength could be reflected in the number of box each participant was entitled to carry. The agreement also contained clauses to regulate the expansion of the group's fleet, which occurred in 1976-1977 when NYK and Mitsui-OSK -- whose carriers had been the smallest of the group -- brought in TRIO's eighteenth and nineteenth vessels, respectively. The immediate success of TRIO was based not just on meticulous planning and cooperation but also, as the group itself acknowledged, on massive demand resulting from the economic boom of 1972 to 1974. The East Asian trade did not in fact not stop growing until the early 1980s, and TRIO was fully able to satisfy its partners. But the consortium also held together during the difficult 1980s and only outlived its usefulness in the early 1990s. Its participating companies performed very strongly, with Hapag-Lloyd in the mid-1970s yielding dividends of twelve percent and OCL contributing "an extremely satisfactory" £29 million to P&O in 1976 and 1977.[16]

Hard on the heels of TRIO, three Scandinavian cross-traders, which lacked the advantage of large national markets, pooled their interests in a second consortium. In 1971 Sweden's Broström group (which in 1974 was to take over the Holland-America Line's interest in ACL), Norway's Wilhelm Wilhelmsen and Denmark's East Asiatic Company (EAC), in a proportion of one to one to two, formed Scanservice, whose four 2400-TEU ships were to maintain a fortnightly service from Göteborg. By now the East Asian trade, still operating within the broad confines of the Far East Freight Conference, was in turmoil as other conference members started to jockey for positions; for the first time in many years, aggressive outsiders were lured into the trade by the splendid profits resulting from the boom conditions. The first to act was the Dutch company Nedlloyd. Unable to join TRIO, it negotiated its way into Scanservice which in 1972 became ScanDutch. Nedlloyd put in two ships, with a full-blown third-generation capacity of 2952 TEUs, which allowed the frequency of service to be increased to three times per month.[17] One of the most outstanding features of

---

[16]Wiborg and Wiborg, *150 Years of Hapag-Lloyd*, 372; and P&O, *Annual Report 1977*, 36.

[17]ScanDutch for some time maintained a conventional service besides its high-quality container service. Hapag-Lloyd for this purpose used the autonomous Rickmers Line, thus benefitting from the high reputation and brand recognition of this well-

ScanDutch was the extraordinary speed of its fleet, designed for service speeds of thirty knots; indeed, Broström's *Nihon* achieved thirty-two knots on its maiden voyage. More fundamentally, ScanDutch differed from the other groups in that its partners did not market their ships individually but, like OCL, operated as a single entity.

In contrast to TRIO, which maintained the same membership throughout its lifetime, ScanDutch welcomed expansion as a means of increasing market share through privileged access to additional national markets. Thus, France's Messageries Maritimes (from December 1973, CGM), which had been in the East Asian trade since the 1860s, joined in July 1973. Its *Korrigan*, virtually a sister-ship to Ben Line's 2804-TEU carriers, allowed ScanDutch's frequency to be increased to four sailings per month and accelerated its penetration of the French market. In another significant step, in 1977 the Malaysian International Shipping Corporation (MISC) was added, bringing in another two ships and the nationalist ambitions of Muhammad Mahathir and his *bumiputra* government.

A third consortium took shape in 1975 as the ACE Group. Again, partners from both sides pooled their resources. On the East Asian side they were the Japanese K-Line and newcomers Orient Overseas Containers Line (OOCL) of Hong Kong and Neptune Orient Lines (NOL) of Singapore, the latter two representing national home markets. No less significant, however, was that this meant the entry of the K-Line as the third Japanese company into the trade with Europe. The European side was represented by the Franco-Belgian Service, itself a joint venture between France's minor East Asian representative, the Compagnie Maritime des Chargeurs Réunis, and Belgian newcomers, CMB and Ahlers Line.[18] From the beginning ACE offered a weekly service, beginning with the departure from Hamburg of OOCL's 2068-TEU *Seven Seas Bridge*. Around 1980 ACE expanded further, reflecting the rapidly-accelerating growth of Korean exports, by embracing two new Korean lines, Korea Shipping Corporation and Cho-Yang, as members.

The fourth consortium was slightly different in purposes because its western domain was the Mediterranean rather than northwest Europe; in consequence, there was a partially overlapping membership with each of the other three consortia. Med Club included Chargeurs Réunis (France), Lloyd Triestino (Italy), Japan's "traditional twins" NYK and Mitsui-OSK, and the intriguingly but appropriately named Orient Mediterranean Express, a joint venture between OOCL, NOL and Korean newcomers Cho Yang.

As the practices of ScanDutch and ACE demonstrated, the Europe-East Asia trade grew so rapidly that ample opportunities existed for newcomers.

---

established company. It was only sold in early 2000.

[18]Ahlers Line soon afterwards was absorbed by CMB.

Those who were willing or able to find shelter within the consortia were only a few of a large number of challengers of all kinds and nationalities. Some represented the aspirations of even more national markets served en route (Taiwan, Thailand), while others were cross-traders or competitors from established shipping nations.

Apart from those challenges already mentioned, two stood out by the early 1980s. The most prominent was Evergreen, a company which had emerged in the late 1960s in Taiwan and, led by former seaman Chang Yung-fa, rose on the back of the extraordinary export performance of that island economy, in the process making big waves itself with its green boxes and ships. Not far behind came Maersk from Denmark, a well-established shipowner but until now only a modest participant in the liner business.[19] For both companies the East Asia-Europe trade provided a short and sharp learning curve that, within a decade, they were able to master with great advantage throughout the entire world.

In addition to these profoundly capitalist newcomers, the expanding merchant fleet of the Soviet Union also made its appearance. At the time its significance was vastly overrated because many Westerners nervously saw it as the commercial arm of the Soviet "grab for sea power" that found its major expression in the rapid expansion of the Soviet Navy and possession of the world's largest fishing fleet. Although the most dynamic of the Soviet companies, the Far Eastern Shipping Company (FESCO), was based on Vladivostok, it was not that company that entered the East Asia-Europe trade, but the Leningrad-based Balt-Orient Line. With its modestly sized RoRo-carriers it never picked up more than a few of the crumbs that were left on the rich East Asian table. Another, more traditional, Russian bogey man, the Trans-Siberian Railway, was often regarded as a more dangerous challenger.[20] Marketing itself as JESCO (Japan-Europe Shipping Company), it reached its zenith in the early 1980s, but then sank back into insignifice.

A review of the market situation in 1982 offers an insightful snapshot of the relative position of the various players in the Europe-East Asian trade. Again, the leading role of TRIO and the rise of the East Asian players are apparent (see table 4).[21]

---

[19]Ove Hornby, *"With Constant Care..." A.P. Møller: Shipowner 1876-1965* ([Copenhagen], 1988), 106-118.

[20]See, e.g., *Fairplay*, 19 July 1979, 15.

[21]De Boer and Mulder, *Nedlloyd*, 56.

Table 4
Market Shares in the Europe-East Asian Trade, 1982

Consortium/group	Nationality of Partners	Share
TRIO	Britain, Germany, Japan	39%
ScanDutch	Sweden, Norway, Denmark, Netherlands, France, Malaysia	17%
ACE	France, Belgium, Hong Kong, Singapore, Japan, Korea	17%
Total Consortia		**73%**
Single companies		
Maersk and others	Denmark, East Germany, Poland, West Germany, Thailand	9%
Evergreen	Taiwan	9%
Balt-Orient Line	Soviet Union	3%
Trans-Siberian Railway	Soviet Union	6%
Total Independents		**27%**

Source: See text.

The group "Maersk and others," which included a small number of remaining conventional operators (such as the Hapag-Lloyd subsidiary Rickmers and Unithai) along with the consortia (TRIO, ScanDutch and ACE) comprised the membership of the Far Eastern Freight Conference which, with its eight-two-percent market share, could still boast to be highly successful. The consortia had been able to withstand most pressures and were now ready to fight Evergreen and the Russians, which it generally if erroneously believed sailed "irrespective of costs" in order to capture market share and disrupt the overseas trade of the capitalist world. The great absent power, for the time being, was China. Having just gone through the traumatic events of the Cultural Revolution, and with many of its more liberal politicians and business-minded officials only now re-emerging from rural exile, it was still largely withdrawn from the sea. Within a few years, however, this would be decisively reversed as China threw out a maritime challenge and almost imperceptibly began its campaign to reclaim Hong Kong.

The financial and entrepreneurial success of TRIO, ScanDutch and ACE, even more than previous developments in the Atlantic, Australian and Pacific trades, were proof of the unprecedented structural changes containerisation caused in liner shipping. Necessity was the mother of cooperation, a realisation that resulted in a measure of entrepreneurial unity and decisiveness which in most cases transcended the traditional rivalries, prejudices and suspicions that even the strict régime of the Far Eastern Freight Conference, under the quasi-neo-imperial chairmanship of P&O, had not been able to bury. Consortia now became the vehicle to achieve the breakthrough in the North-South trades.

The invasion of the Less-Developed Countries began with the Caribbean and the east coast of Central America. Although regarded as a most difficult region because of its maritime configuration, the multitude of its small individual economies and ports of call, and the rudimentary state of its transport infrastructure, it nevertheless had the advantage of being compact and relatively immune from incursions by outsiders. In 1973 three of the established companies – Hapag-Lloyd, Harrison Line (Britain) and KNSM (Netherlands) – formed the Caribbean Overseas Lines (CAROL – euphonious acronyms now also penetrated the shipping market), which France's Compagnie Générale Transatlantique joined a year later. Each company brought in two identical 1160-TEU vessels, including 220 TEUs that had a cooling capacity for the carriage of fruit.[22]

The pace of development now increased rapidly. One year after the Caribbean, it was South Africa's turn. The fact that the Republic of South Africa (RSA) was a political outcast because of its repugnant system of apartheid deterred only few large corporations, and no shipping firms, from dealing with its regime. The Southern Africa-Europe-Container-Service (SAECS) that put its first vessels in service in 1977 was largely based on a combination of the successful formulas that underpinned the Australian, East Asian and Caribbean containerisation models. It consisted of two branches, covering northern Europe and the Mediterranean, respectively, and included not only European companies but also the newly- established, government-owned shipping corporation of RSA, Safmarine. In its final composition, SAECS involved seven companies that brought in twelve identical 2450-TEU container ships, with considerable freezer capacity and service speeds of twenty-three knots. Up to one hundred conventional freighters were replaced as round trips shrunk from 104 to forty-nine days.

In the national composition of SAECS, South African economic nationalism – which had manifested itself as early as 1905 when it precipitated one of the biggest inquiries into, and the first legislation against, the conference system – found powerful expression, as Safmarine was allotted no less than five of the twelve carriers. The Italian company, Lloyd Triestino, was allowed two ships, with one each going to OCL, Ellerman's Harrison Container Line (Britain), Nedlloyd, Compagnie Maritime Belge, and Deutsche Afrika Lines (German Africa Lines of Hamburg). This configuratrion was quite flexible, incorporating important shifts in relative power; this was further highlighted as the containership originally allotted to a joint venture of French companies CGM

---

[22]Witthöft, *Container*, 46.

and Chargeurs Réunis was transformed into two Ro-Ro carriers to serve minor ports in RSA, Namibia, and Mozambique.[23]

It would be impossible to record all the details of the numerous consortia that were formed during the late 1970s and early 1980s. Suffice it to say that their number rose to well over fifty and that they covered the Middle East, Latin America, Indonesia, West Africa and many other routes throughout the world. In most cases fully-cellular vessels were used, but port congestion in several areas, such as Nigeria, favoured RoRo with its instant unloading capacity. For some time after 1974, RoRo was the preferred form of containerisation in the Middle East, as Saudi Arabia and some of the Gulf emirates went through construction booms, including a number of gigantic turnkey projects, which totally outpaced port infrastructure.

Table 5
Consortia and Participation of the Australian National Line, 1980

Route	Vessels	Consortium	Partners
Europe/UK	2x container	ACTA	ACT consortium
Japan	2x RoRo	ESS	K-Line, NYK, MOL, YS
Eastern USA	1x container	PACE	ACT consortium
Western USA	1x RoRo*	PAD	Broström, EAC
Hong Kong, Taiwan	2x RoRo	AnLine	Asia Australia Express, OOCL
ASEAN	1x RoRo	ANRO	NOL, OCL, Swire, Nedlloyd

Note: * Twenty-five percent participation only

Source: See text.

But the specific choice of cargo system made no difference as far as consortium formation was concerned. A number of companies became almost religious believers in the system, especially those that represented smaller nations, both newcomers and established powers. The Australian National Line, for example, as a matter of policy elected not to invest its relatively modest means, as RSA did, in only one or a small number of routes; instead, until it reached the end of its means – opponents would argue, until it paid out enough rope to hang itself – it became a partner in seven consortia on seven different routes, using both fully-cellular vessels and RoRo carriers. The latter, it must be stressed, often involved cooperation with Scandinavian companies which, from the very beginning in the 1960s (e.g., ACL) had shown a marked preference for this technology. Table 5 shows just how complex the entrepreneurial environment of a single firm could become.

---

[23]*Ibid.*, 47.

But many majors in Europe and elsewhere also systematically used the consortium system, as not just the three great consortia in the East Asian trade but also the geographical diffusion of OCL, Hapag-Lloyd, CMB and CGM. Nedlloyd in particular became known as a great believer in consortia. In 1981 it served a complex worldwide network of no fewer than thirty-six services, of which nineteen were containerised/RoRo and operated through consortia.[24] Altogether, Nedlloyd had entered joint ventures with over thirty companies, a remarkable form of global policy and tactical flexibility. Among its partners were OCL, Hapag-Lloyd, CMB, CGM, Lloyd Triestino, Japan's NYK and Mitsui-OSK, Singapore's NOL, Malaysia's MISC, the Australian National Line, Transportación Marítima Mexicana (TMM), and Compañia Sud Americana de Vapores (CSAV) of Chile.

It would be entirely wrong, however, to assume that the consortium was the only method of access or expansion in the industry. In the first place, no American company was allowed by law to establish or join any joint venture, and it is inconceivable that someone like McLean would ever have contemplated such a restriction on his freedom to move. All American companies, like Sea-Land, APL, US Lines, Prudential Grace Lines, Seatrain or Lykes Lines, operated independently. This did not mean that some, as the European and Japanese research of the 1960s had suggested, did not suffer from the problem of maintaining services of adequate speed and frequency with a small number of highly productive vessels. Although most were heavily subsidised (but, in principle, only up to the point of reaching cost parity with non-American operators), it was no wonder that several collapsed in the late 1970s and early 1980s, when market conditions deteriorated.

From both a theoretical and practical viewpoint, most US lines would have fared better if they had been able to join one or more consortia. Nevertheless, for the time being not only were experienced operators like Sea-Land, APL and US Lines doing well, but so too were newcomers Seatrain and Farrell Lines, which branched out from the African trade into the North Atlantic and Australasia. Significantly, its competitors on the Pacific route included the ACTA and PAD consortia, formed by established lines and the Australian National Line, and another independent newcomer, the Columbus Line, a subsidiary of Hamburg-Süd, the German company that for a century had focussed on South America and also used containerisation to expand its network. The other major German company, Hapag-Lloyd, also operated independently on several routes. Although it joined a good number of consortia, its merger had

---

[24]Nedlloyd, *Annual Report 1982*.

been achieved to enable it to maintain its independence on the North Atlantic, and in 1977 it single-handedly opened its new transpacific service.[25]

The consortium, in short, had been a powerful but not indispensable instrument during the first highly uncertain phase of containerisation. Once the success of the system was apparent, newcomers commanding an adequate acquisition base and marketing performance and possessing the ability to maintain a frequency that was acceptable to the trade could enter the container business. Attention has already been drawn to the East Asia-Europe trade, which included several "lone wolves," notably Maersk, Evergreen and Balt-Orient. The same observation applied even more to the North Pacific. By 1980, the world's fastest growing container region was being served by a host of companies which, in addition to the members of the Japanese and international East Asian consortia and the American pioneers Sea-Land, US Lines, APL and Seatrain, included a number of highly energetic independents like Taiwan's Evergeen, Korean Shipping Corporation and cross-traders Maersk, Zim, Hapag-Lloyd and the Vladivostok-based FESCO.

Table 6
World's Fifteen Largest Container Companies, 1981

Rank	Company	Country	Ships	Capacity in TEU	% world
1	Sea-Land	USA	30	41713	5.3
2	Hapag-Lloyd	Germany	27	40491	5.2
3	Maersk	Denmark	25	36552	4.7
4	OCL	Great Britain	18	35180	4.5
5	NYK	Japan	26	29047	3.7
6	OOCL	Hong Kong	21	27742	3.5
7	CGM	France	18	22713	2.9
8	Evergreen	Taiwan	15	20768	2.7
9	APL	USA	14	19689	2.5
10	US Lines	USA	19	19346	2.5
11	Mitsui-OSK	Japan	13	18614	2.4
12	NOL	Singapore	9	16539	2.1
13	Nedlloyd	Netherlands	11	15927	2
14	ZIM	Israel	12	14982	1.9
15	Kawasaki K-Line	Japan	13	14641	1.9
Total					95.5

Source: See text.

The 1970s were marked by a revolution in the structure of the container shipping industry as established companies were joined and challenged by

---

[25]Witthöft, *Container*, 48-49.

newcomers from virtually the entire world. An analysis of table 6, which lists the world's fifteen largest container-shipping companies in 1981, shows the dramatic changes the decade had wrought in the industry:[26] Four of these companies – Maersk, OOCL, Evergreen and NOL – were newcomers which had no presence of any significance in liner shipping in 1970, while Sea-Land, APL and US Lines represented the tremendous boost containerisation had given to the ailing US fleet. Pioneer Sea-Land was still defending its first rank, albeit by a small margin. Europe and East Asia were represented by five and six companies, respectively, a clear reflection of the general economic rise of the latter area. It was a highly significant indication of its greater vitality, however, that three of the six East Asian companies were newcomers (OOCL, Evergreen and NOL), while in Europe there was only one, Maersk.

Maersk was the shipping arm of the A.P. Møller group, which had rapidly eclipsed the East Asiatic Company (EAC) as Denmark's leading liner company. OOCL had emerged as an aggressive player from the worldwide shipping empire of Hong Kong magnate C.Y. Tung, father of the future leader of Hong Kong under Chinese rule. Its takeover in 1980 of the container interests of the British company, Furness Withy and Co., had been a landmark of epochal proportions since it marked the beginning of the penetration of Europe and the North Atlantic by Asian shipping interests. Through its subsidiary Manchester Lines, OOCL became the first Asian line to operate a service across the North Atlantic, and at the same time it acquired control over Britain's major container port, Felixstowe. Evergreen and NOL had emerged as the leading shipping companies of Taiwan and Singapore, respectively. The three new East Asian companies represented not just the rapid economic growth of their region's economies and export sectors but also the increasing participation of "non-traditional maritime nations" in liner shipping that became of increasing political interest. By contrast to NOL and OOCL, however, Maersk and Evergreen operated predominantly outside the conferences, using quality service and lower cost structures through economies of scale to good advantage.

Another highly significant feature of table 6 is that all European companies, with the exception of newcomer Maersk, were traditional in origin but not identity. Without exception, they were the result of mergers that were unprecedented in the history of their national maritime industries. The most novel operator was OCL, the consortium that since 1965 had combined the container investments of four traditional British companies, first in the Australian and then in the East Asian, South African and Middle Eastern trades. It was, however, not quite the same company any more. When Furness Withy was taken over in 1980 by OOCL, the remaining three partners denied membership to the Hong Kong company and used the opportunity to renegotiate their internal

---

[26]*The-Australian*, 29 July 1982.

balance of power. The loser was Ocean Steamship, whose share dropped from forty-nine to 40.5 percent, while P&O moved up from thirty to 36.7 percent and British and Commonwealth made the largest gain, trebling its share from 7.6 to 22.8 percent. After the shipping crisis of 1982-1983, P&O would move to buy out both its partners and make OCL a fully-owned subsidiary, but for the time being OCL constituted Britain's answer to the need for enlargement of scale in the 1970s.

With the exception of Maersk, all the other European companies in the list were the result of mergers designed to achieve the concentration of power that OCL represented. Chronologically, the first of these mergers had been between the Hamburg-America Line and the North German Lloyd to form Hapag-Lloyd. The amalgamation of the two lines in 1970 put an end to well over a century of intensive rivalry between not just Germany's leading liner shipping companies but also the Hanseatic sister cities, Hamburg and Bremen. From 1965, the two companies had cooperated closely in the development of their container ventures, but by 1968 they felt that only a full merger could bring that concentration of power in the freight and financial marketplaces that the high levels of investment and cargo acquisition required. In addition, the merger enabled the new Hapag-Lloyd to retain its independence on the North Atlantic.[27]

During the 1970s, Hapag-Lloyd actively pushed the containerisation of many significant trading routes. It showed its flexibility by joining several consortia, including one with the Holland-America Line in the Combi Line that operated two LASH vessels in the Europe-US Gulf trade. New confidence and aggressiveness were visible in establishing the last link of its global chain of services in 1977 with the inauguration of a service between East Asia and the US West Coast.[28]

Besides Hapag-Lloyd, only two other significant cargo companies, albeit of entirely different background and structure, remained in Germany: the Hamburg-Südamerikanische Schifffahrtsgesellschaft (usually known as Hamburg-Süd) and the Bremen-based DDG Hansa. The Hansa was a pure shipping company operating an extensive network of relatively low-volume freight services focussing on the Middle East. By the late 1970s, it was in severe trouble,[29] and when merger talks with Hapag-Lloyd failed, the company filed for bankruptcy in August 1970. Its Middle East and Indian Ocean interests were

---

[27]Wiborg and Wiborg, *150 Years of Hapag-Lloyd*, 356-357.

[28]*The-Australian*, 8 September 1977.

[29]Ironically, but not uncommonly, only very shortly after the company had produced a celebratory company history: Hans Georg Prager, *DDG HANSA* (Hereford, 1976).

taken over by Hapag-Lloyd.[30] Hamburg-Süd since the 1870s had operated in the South American trade and, as its opening the new Columbus Line in the cross-trades between the USA and Australia demonstrated, it was fiercely committed to remaining independent. Despite its relatively small size the company was able to sustain this policy because it was a subsidiary of the large (and private) Oetker Group of companies, best known to the public for its vast range of baking powders.

A concentration process that began with many more players but resulted in an almost complete national hegemony occurred in the Netherlands.[31] As a small nation, in the maritime and economic shadow of both Britain and Germany, its liner operators, though autonomous, had already been articulated by networks of joint ventures before World War I. From the late 1950s, under the pressures of low profitability and the need to rationalise, the process of concentration had begun, including in 1963 the amalgamation of the cargo services of the traditional "mail" companies,[32] the Stoomvaart Maatschappij Nederland (headquartered in Amsterdam) and the Royal Rotterdam Lloyd, into Nedlloyd Lines. Three years later the KPM, which until its expulsion from Indonesia had operated intra-colonial and regional lines in and around the former Dutch East Indies, and the JCPL (Java China Japan Line) merged into the KJCPL. Under its English trademark, Royal Interocean Lines, based in Hong Kong, it had become a major regional player. In 1969, the holding company of the Nederland, KRL and KJCPL, Nederlandse Scheepvaart Unie (NSU), at its formation in 1908 only intended as a defence mechanism against foreign takeovers, was activated into an operational company. It immediately absorbed the African, Asian and Australian lines of the Vereenigde Nederlandse Scheepvaart Maatschappij (VNS), a joint venture of eight Dutch liner companies dating from 1920.

Within a few years a loose federation of often jealously independent firms was turned into a powerful concern possessing 185 vessels of 1.5 million grt; a few years later it established its internationally recognisable identity as *the* Dutch company by adopting the name Nedlloyd. In this way Dutch liner interests

---

[30]*Fairplay*, 4 September 1980, 7; *Economist*, 23 August 1980.

[31]This process has been analysed in H. van Driel, *Samenwerking in haven en vervoer in het containertijdperk* (Delft, 1990), chapter 5; and van Driel, *Een verenigde nederlandse scheepvaart. De fusie tussen Nedlloyd en KNSM in 1980-1981* (Delft, 1988).

[32]"Mail" lines because both companies had started life on the imperial mail run between the Netherlands and the Dutch East Indies. During the 1950s they had been excluded from Indonesia but were granted compensation by their conference partners in the Europe/East Asia trade. They also served the Gulf. They were the main shareholders in the KPM, Koninklijke Paketvaartmaatschappij (Royal Mail Shipping Company) of 1888.

East of Suez found the strength necessary to become successfully involved in the container revolution in the Australian, East Asian and other trades in their region. While Dutch North Atlantic interests had been lost by the sale of the Holland-America Line's container interests to the Swedish Broström concern, Nedlloyd's smaller counterpart in the Caribbean and South American trades was formed in 1970 through the absorption by the KNSM of the KHL.[33] In 1981, an enlarged KNSM was taken over by Nedlloyd, which in the meantime had played a leading role in the containerisation of its own main lines. In short, containerisation had propelled Nedlloyd in the space of a few years to an overwhelming position in the Netherlands, only excluding the North Atlantic. As the next chapter will show, thanks to Malcom McLean that final step was soon taken.

The creation of CGM (Compagnie Générale Maritime) in December 1973 was France's strategic answer to the containerisation revolution.[34] But its formation represented neither a bundling of already-related interests, as in the Netherlands, nor a merger of two largely similar global operators, like Hapag-Lloyd. Instead, in merging the Compagnie Générale Transatlantique and the Messageries Maritimes it amalgamated two companies with liner networks in separate hemispheres. The two, however, possessed similar historical traditions, as both were more than a century-old and were heavily subsidised imperial "mail" companies which in the late 1940s had been nationalised. Both had also clocked up considerable losses, and Messageries Maritimes was in the process of closing many of its conventional services. Besides CGM, which like Nedlloyd was an enthusiastic consortium partner, a number of smaller private companies remained, like the Société Navale Chargeurs Vieljeux-Delmas (itself the result of a 1971 merger). But these firms operated mostly on other routes, so that CGM could lay claim to being France's premier company; it also was the only of the majors to serve both the USA and East Asia.

The logic behind these mergers, and similar ones in smaller shipping nations like Belgium and Australia, was not just the need to achieve economies of scale, rationalisation of services and the creation of the most effective and aggressive management team but also to achieve an uncontested identity as a

---

[33]KNSM: Koninklijke Nederlandse Stoomboot Maatschappij (Royal Netherlands Steamship Company), founded at Amsterdam in 1856 for the European coastal trade but since 1912 also involved in the West Indies, Caribbean and Central America; KHL: Koninklijke Hollandsche Lloyd, founded at Amsterdam in 1908 for the trade with the east coast of South America. Supported by government subsidies and the Amsterdam commercial and banking world, it became a strong competitor of Hamburg-Süd and other German lines.

[34]Jean Randier, *Histoire de la marine marchande française des premiers vapeurs à nos jours* (Paris, 1980), 186 and 328.

"national carrier." A particularly interesting example of all the above motives in the context of Arab nationalism and Gulf cooperation was the United Arab Shipping Company (UASC), which in 1976 emerged from the recently-founded Kuwait Shipping Company. Its shareholders were the governments of Kuwait, where its headquarters was located, Iraq, Bahrain, Qatar, United Arab Emirates, and a few years later Jordan.[35]

By only listing the top fifteen players, table 6 concealed the fact that from the 1960s, coincidental with the technological-commercial container revolution, an ideological-political revolution had also taken place in the liner shipping world. This had made it more international in structure and gave the concept "national carrier" special significance and legitimacy.[36] Political decolonisation after World War II brought in its wake a strong economic nationalism aiming at liberating national economies from dominant foreign economic interests; fostering comprehensive economic development; and establishing within a "New International Economic Order" a more equitable balance between North and South. Major milestones were the foundation of the Organisation of Petroleum Exporting Countries (OPEC) in 1960 and the first conference of the United Nations Conference on Trade and Development (UNCTAD) in Manila in 1962. In liner shipping, in particular, which many newly independent countries regarded as the vital link between their national economy and the world market, the control exercised by foreign shipping companies – often belonging to the former colonial master – appeared vexatious and opposed to the national interest. India and Israel were early examples of new states entering deep-sea shipping, but from the late 1950s the pace quickened. Ghana's Black Star Line, named by that country's leader Kwame Nkrumah after the shipping company of America's black nationalist Marcus Garvey in the 1920s,[37] was soon followed by many others.

Participation of Less-Developed Countries in liner shipping became an important item on the UNCTAD agenda. At its fourth conference in 1974, a Code of Practice for Shipping Conferences was adopted which included the "forty-forty-twenty" formula which, it was anticipated, would give developing countries the legal entry into liner shipping that they found it so difficult to

---

[35]Fatimah H.Y. Al-Abdul-Razzak, *Marine Resources of Kuwait* (London, 1984), 152; and USAC, *USAC. Liner Break-bulk and Container Services around the World* ([Kuwait, 1983]).

[36]The following discussion is entirely focussed on the liner sector. It does not take into account developments in the dry- and wet-bulk sectors. Thus, for the time being, the rise of flags-of-convenience, above all Liberia and Panama, is of no consequence.

[37]E. David Cronon, *Black Moses: The Story of Marcus Garvey* (Madison, WI, 1969).

achieve commercially. Bilateral trade was to be divided according to the nationality of participating companies, with shipping belonging to both terminal states receiving forty percent each and cross-traders twenty percent. Great excitement was created at the time, but the resolution only came in force in 1983. By that time, events had overtaken both the sentiments and the assumptions behind the UNCTAD document.

The container world was extremely dynamic, with internationalisation and soon also globalisation as driving forces. But already in 1974 the idea that liner shipping could be reduced from its immense complexity to a series of bilateral relations and subjected to legal prescripts and mathematical manipulation rather than the chilly winds of international competition was quixotic. Yet, it would be foolish to underestimate the immense power of economic nationalism in both developing and developed states, as the continued state subsidisation of the US merchant fleet, the informal flag preference of most East Asian countries, widespread overt and covert government subsidies, and the rise of state-owned companies, even outside the communist blocs of the Soviet Union and China, demonstrated only too eloquently. More important, in contrast to the Black Star Line, which despite assistance from Zim Israel never flourished, many newcomers entered container shipping, especially from Asian, but later also Latin American, countries (which, in fact, had long traditions of shipping nationalism).[38] The 1970s, for example, were marked by the emergence of companies like Orient Overseas Containers Line, Evergreen and Yang Ming from Taiwan, Neptune Orient Line (Singapore), the Australian National Line, Malaysian International Shipping Corporation, the National Shipping Corporation of Sa'udi Arabia, the United Arab Shipping Corporation, the Korean Shipping Corporation, Transportación Marítima Mexicana and Compañia Sud Americana de Vapores of Chile.

The shipping world, in the final analysis, is one of cold figures, and the survival of any company, either large or small, is not guaranteed. But there was a strong element of national legitimacy in the origins and growth of these new national companies, as the "traditional maritime nations" had to acknowledge that fundamental changes had occurred in global political economy and that the far-reaching internationalisation of the liner trade also reflected the rising share of such commerce produced by the "new" maritime nations.[39]

---

[38]S.G. Sturmey, *British Shipping and World Competition* (London, 1962), chapter 5.

[39]Interestingly, several of the new companies laid claim to national maritime traditions stretching back to the era of the first European traders and before. It is inviting, but misleading, to compare the concept of the "national shipping company" with the seemingly similar phenomenon of the "national airline." Although both were fueled by the same forces of economic nationalism and the desire to obtain optimal links with global

In explaining the growth of container shipping and the great structural changes caused by it, several additional external and internal factors need to be considered: shipping conferences, finance and, finally, the simple box itself. Ever since the 1870s, the liner shipping industry had revolved around the conference system, i.e., the cartel agreements on individual trade routes which governed competitive conditions and attempted to establish the hegemony if not monopoly of the participating companies. Restrictive practices, coupled with high entry costs for newcomers, had made the conferences powerful instruments against outsiders. Many conferences operated on the basis of market-sharing and/or pooling arrangements and the existence of a mutually-accepted key to establish the relative share of each participant greatly facilitated consortium formation, as was shown by the genesis of OCL, ACT and ACL.

In addition, in the early years many shipping leaders and others believed that the shipping conferences would continue to oppose participation by outsiders and, in fact, would be strengthened by the high capital-intensiveness of containerisation. But what they too easily forgot was that new companies had always been admitted, though not necessarily without a bitter fight, especially when a newcomer flew the flag of a nation served by the conference but not yet represented in its membership; a certain element of "national legitimacy" had always been present. This ideological attitude remained unchanged and applied equally to consortium formation and admittance of new independent container companies to conference agreements. But the developments of the 1970s also showed that, as so often is the case when a revolutionary new technology is introduced into an industry, existing defence mechanisms and attitudes lost much of their strength as the sheer volume of new opportunities enabled many newcomers to overcome entry problems. Several of these newcomers, moreover, demonstrated no desire at all to join conference agreements and, indeed, made it clear that they were in principle unwilling to contemplate membership. In addition to companies from the various communist bloc nations, Maersk, Evergreen and Zim were satisfied to remain outside conferences – stressing their independence from what they claimed were antiquated and unresponsive bureaucracies – and relying on competitive rate structures and a quickly acquired reputation for service and punctuality.[40] Since American companies also largely operated outside conferences, as they by law were prohibited from joining conferences with restrictive practices, the conference system by the early 1980s was under considerable pressure.

---

transport networks, the shipping industry was characterised by its free access to all ports, while civil aviation was subject to an exclusivist régime of landing rights strictly ruled by bilateral intergovernmental agreements and negotiations.

[40]See, e.g., *The Australian*, 27 May 1982.

Apart from service and marketing, the key to expansion always remained finance, especially as containerisation was highly capital intensive. Indeed, as chapter 2 showed, the vast expense of a container fleet with its triple set of boxes and additional facilities had been one of the major reasons for the formation of the British, European and Japanese consortia of the early years. But it must be stressed that the companies involved had been traditional liner companies whose leaders were thoroughly imbued with the liner trade's long-standing aversion against using loans or other external sources of finance; if necessary, expansion was financed from reserves or the raising of new share capital. The Royal Mail failure cast a very long shadow indeed.[41]

Ironically, the initial impetus for liberalising finance policies came virtually simultaneously with the first challenges of containerisation and constituted the reverse side of the coin of shrinking profits in the liner business. At the same time, as containerisation appeared to be an avenue to the reversal of profit trends, liner companies became aware of the huge profits that could be made in the bulk sectors of shipping. Especially after the closure of the Suez Canal in the Six Days' War of 1967 and again in 1973, freight rates for bulk carriers and especially oil tankers – whose dimensions were rapidly inflated from super-tanker to VLCC and ULCC with a tonnage ultimately surpassing 500,000 dwt[42] – reached unprecedented levels. "Oldtimers" like Niarchos and Onassis, and many newcomers with them, made fortunes.[43] While most Japanese and East Asian shipowners had already begun to diversify, European liner owners were pushed hard – in Britain by the Rochdale Inquiry[44] – to invest in the booming bulk sectors. Clearly, reserves and ordinary financing techniques were insufficient for the purpose, all the more so as containerisation itself also demanded huge funds.

The consequence of these pressures was the widespread adoption of a number of external financing methods. Some of these, like mortgages and debenture bonds, were traditional instruments in the industry, but many other

---

[41]Sturmey, *British Shipping*, 394-403.

[42]VLCC stood for Very Large Crude Carrier, ULCC for Ultra Large Crude Carrier.

[43]Frank Brady, *Onassis* (Melbourne, 1978), 198-199: and N. Fraser, *et al.*, *Aristotle Onassis* (London, 1980), 314-316 and 458.

[44]Great Britain, Parliament, House of Commons, *Report of the Committee of Inquiry into Shipping* (Cmnd. 4337, London, 1970). For the Netherlands, see J.J. Oyevaar, *De nederlandse koopvaardij...Rapport uitgebracht aan het bestuur van de Koninklijke Nederlandsche Reedersvereeniging* (The Hague, 1968), a report commissioned by the Dutch Shipowners' Association.

forms had emerged in the oil and bulk sectors, such as loans against charter contracts or loans made directly to companies or even individual owners. At the inflated prices they could command in the first half of the 1970s, shipyards were willing to offer considerable credit facilities. Newcomers in particular were able to build up close relations with general banks and other financial institutions which suddenly took a great interest in the shipping sector, of which they understood next to nothing.

In New York, London, Singapore and elsewhere banks established shipping departments, and once petrodollars started rolling from 1974 and trade with the Middle East and exports from East Asia rose rapidly, most liner companies adopted new financing practices and in the process sharply increased their gearing ratios. The availability of large funds for the shipping industry was particularly beneficial for many newcomers which were able to expand their operations at an extraordinary pace. Many of them, like Evergreen and Maersk, were private companies, and it is regrettably only possible to observe the spectacular results and not the methods of their financing policies. But the extraordinary advertisement placed by Morgan Guarantee Trust Company of New York in *Fairplay*, proudly announcing its role in a US $800,000,000 project financing arranged for Maersk, lifted a tip of the veil and suggested that shipping had become a field of investment like any other.[45]

Ironically, just when many of the tankers and bulk carriers ordered by liner companies were ready for service, their freight market had collapsed. The re-opening of the Suez Canal, conservation measures in energy-consuming countries (car-free Sundays did not achieve all that much in themselves but were evidence of a new mentality), and over-building had created an acute tonnage glut that was not overcome until the 1980s. Although, as will be seen in the next chapter, this crisis would be extremely harmful to many members of the liner industry, it also had a positive effect. As shipbuilding capacity throughout the world had mushroomed in response to the demand for VLCCs and ULCCs, their demise left shipyards desperately chasing orders just when the containerisation boom was still gaining ground. Contract prices dropped and those with faith were able to expand at much lower prices. The results could be seen in the continued penetration of the Less-Developed Countries through new consortia and services, the intensification on main container lines, and the rapid growth of several new companies, as evidenced in table 6.

The final and certainly not least important factor in the explosive growth of container shipping in the 1970s was the impact of the box itself. More than was ever possible in the days of conventional shipping, when cargo vessels were often specially designed to carry the commodities that characterised specific routes and the shipowner's expertise in a particular trading region had been built

---

[45]*Fairplay*, 2 December 1982, 6.

up over many decades, the box and its carrier were dynamic elements. They could, after all, be used for any cargo and any route. Less knowledge was required about specific trading conditions, commodities and loading requirements, which greatly facilitated entry into the business by newcomers and expansion into new areas by established shipowners. As ever-larger container carriers were introduced on main routes, previous classes could be cascaded down into secondary trades, new trunk lines, routes with lower-density volumes or feeder services.

Figure 4: Scandutch's *Francesca*, a regular trader on the Singapore-Bangkok run. During the 1970s the major operators began supporting their main-line services by establishing their own dedicated feeder networks.

Source: Eric Jennings, *Cargoes. A Centenary Story of the Far Eastern Freight Conference* (Singapore, 1980).

Figure 5: UASC container vessel *Jebel Ali*, 1160 TEU, Arabian Gulf-USA service. Named after Dubai's largest port, this carrier represented the cooperation of the Arab Gulf states in the process of localisation in the container shipping business. It shows a typical design of the late 1970s.

Source: UASC website (http://www.uasc-sag.com).

Equally as important as the physical flexibility of containerisation were its psychological and entrepreneurial consequences, which induced shipowners to think far more readily than before about entering new trades. Container shipping required and created a different mind, and the characteristic of that mind was its ability to think horizontally as well as vertically; in other words, expansion was not seen only in greater market share but also in entering new trade routes. Companies like Zim, Evergreen and Maersk demonstrated all the flexibility and geographic mobility that the box incorporated, but they were not alone; many of the traditional companies were transformed in spirit and outlook. The Compagnie Maritime Belge, awkwardly squeezed between ACL, OCL, Hapag-Lloyd and CGM, used containerisation to enter a number of new trade routes and established a European feeder service that ranged from Portugal to Scandinavia. In addition, it involved itself in trucking, a container terminal in its home port of Antwerp and the development of inland freight stations in Zaire. Although such vertical diversification in other transport sectors had not been uncommon in conventional liner shipping, the box and its integrated movement through successive modes of transport began creating the idea that the container shipping company should draw the consequences from its centrality in the transport chain. The next stage of containerisation would be dominated by taking the box idea to its logical consequence through global services, true intermodalism, and the concept of logistics management.

Chapter 4
The 1980s: Crisis and the Second Revolution

> Gone was the glamorous growth that had characterised the
> industry for much of the 1970s; probably never to return again
> to an industry that had finally come of age.[1]

Containerisation had made extraordinary progress during the 1970s. In contrast, market conditions throughout most of the 1980s were anything but favourable; in consequence, "fierce competition between carriers was sustained."[2] The decade began with a rapidly-escalating crisis which reached its deepest point by 1983 as the impact of a structural tonnage glut was exacerbated by a severe global trade recession.[3] Container shipping, with only a few exceptions, was beginning to look as unhealthy as the long-suffering bulk sector. A brief recovery was followed by a second recession in 1985-1986 when trade with the Middle East, which had already slowed down since the Iranian revolution and the outbreak of the Gulf War in 1980 collapsed due to a huge fall in the price of crude oil from c. US $40 to US $10 and even lower per barrel. As well, the sharp devaluation of the US dollar, in which most freight was paid, after the Plaza agreement of 1985 and the stock market crash of October 1987 had a negative effect. NOL later declared that the years 1984-1989 were "probably the toughest" for the company,[4] and that sentiment was echoed by many of its colleagues.

Although some powerful newcomers emerged during the decade, the 1980s were also marked by the demise, takeover or withdrawal of a number of traditional companies. Rationalisation and cooperation of various kinds between companies helped to reduce both cost levels and the surplus of tonnage, and across the board rates showed modest improvements. Nevertheless, by 1990 the industry remained in turmoil, and its instability was accentuated by a number of

---

[1]*Containerisation International Yearbook* (1981), 7.

[2]*Ibid.* (1990), 5.

[3]*Ibid.* A leading analyst, Fearnley and Eger of Oslo, could find no area of world shipping that was profitable.

[4]Quoted in *Lloyd's List*, NOL 30th Anniversary supplement (December 1998), 55.

contradictory trends and fuelled rather than calmed by the apparent return to profitability.

Figure 6: CMB's *Maeterlinck* (2257 TEU), a medium-size vessel of the mid-1980s on the Europe-East Asia.

Source: CMB, *Annual Report* (1986).

Yet despite the gloom which dominated so much of the decade, container shipping continued to grow at a remarkable rate and exhibited evidence of such significant structural changes that there may well be said to have been a second revolution. Between 1980 and 1990, the total capacity of the world's container fleet increased from 1,200,000 to 3,200,000 TEUs, a growth rate of 167 percent or about thirteen percent per annum, compared with the roughly twenty-percent expansion of the previous decade. Total global port turnover rose at almost the same remarkable pace: by 150 percent, from 33,700,000 to 84,200,000 TEUs. New trunk routes and feeder services were opened annually as both the scope and rate of containerisation continued to climb. Trade with East Asia, driven by Japan and the "little tigers;" the ever-more important intra-Asian traffic; and the remarkable growth of China's economy and export industries demonstrated remarkable growth rates.

This was the decade in which Hong Kong and Singapore took over from Rotterdam and New York as the two leading container ports in the world. At the same time, the structure of the container shipping industry – despite the entry of several prominent newcomers, such as the China Overseas Shipping Corporation (COSCO) and the Korean trio, Hanjin, Cho Yang and Hyundai – became more concentrated as the top twenty companies steadily increased their share of global capacity.[5] The average size of the leading companies was also rising fast – Evergreen topped the list in 1990 with 117,418 TEU, almost three times Sea-Land's fleet of 1981, and had another eleven 4000-TEU carriers on order – in their furious drive to reduce costs through economies of scale. Significantly, several strategic alternatives existed to achieve corporate growth through merger, buy-out of consortium partners or individual expansion, but at the same time cooperation between the majors also entered a new phase.

Economies were achieved in many more ways than merely increasing the size of the enterprise. Crew numbers were cut sharply; the capacity of the largest container ships rose from the 3000 TEUs of TRIO's third-generation vessels to over 4000 TEUs, which included a number of post-Panamax carriers too wide to transit the Panama Canal. At the same time the 1000-TEU-range ship, once the flag carrier on the North Atlantic, was becoming a handy-sized vehicle for the feeder trades.[6] Malaysian International Shipping Corporation (MISC), for example, in 1990 introduced the first of four 1234-TEU ships on its Taiwan-Hong Kong-Singapore-Port Kelang run.[7] Equally important was the adoption of fuel-saving engines and lower service speeds, as well as the continuous re-designing of network lay-outs; the most spectacular examples of the latter strategy were the round-the-world services initiated in the second half of 1984 which would in the early 1990s be matched by post-Panamax pendulum services. In addition, the overall strategic position of container shipping companies within the total transport infrastructure at sea and ashore was decisively expanded through far-reaching intermodal integration with railroads and the introduction of through-traffic responsibility on the part of the shipping companies. Major companies saw themselves increasingly as comprehensive transport providers or, as NYK described it, "logistics megacarriers."[8]

Only from late 1986 were there signs that changes had been put in place to tackle the serious problems of a tonnage surplus and the erosion of freight

---

[5]*Containerisation International Yearbook* (1990), 6.

[6]*Ibid.*(1991), 5.

[7]*Fairplay*, 25 October 1990.

[8]*NYK Annual Report*, quoted in *Containerisation International Yearbook* (1991), 6.

rates. While new orders finally dropped in volume, for the first time older vessels were actually replaced rather than cascaded down to secondary routes or other operators. At roughly the same time, three other structural, though paradoxically also incidental, factors helped towards recovery. First, in 1984 the long-expected US Shipping Act was passed. Its major purpose was to rectify the failures of the hugely defective 1970 subsidy system by giving the US merchant fleet a more flexible regime, enabling it to become an effective instrument in world shipping and assisting in the global deployment of US intervention forces. American companies were liberated from the straightjacket of the 1936 system of "strategic routes" with regard to the payment of subsidies and also gained the freedom to adopt many of the methods of their European and Asian competitors, such as slot-leasing and autonomous consortium management. To world container shipping, its crucial clauses were those that greatly reduced the anti-trust restrictions on agreements between shipping companies in the US trades.

A second, often overlooked, important positive factor was a change in Germany's tax laws, which drastically reduced the incentive for the building of the so-called "dentists dodges." These were container vessels ordered and operated on the free market by speculative German owners/managers who mainly raised their investment capital through spectacular tax avoidance schemes for high-earning professionals like dentists. By 1986, this German tramp fleet had mushroomed to about ten percent of total world capacity.[9]

The third factor may best be described as a double negative. Although the 1974 UNCTAD Conference Code of Practice, which prescribed the forty-forty-twenty formula for flag sharing between exporters, importers and cross-traders, gained sufficient ratifications by 1983 to come into force, the fear that shipowners outside the Less-Developed Countries had of its impact never materialised. It was soon evident that it was almost totally irrelevant in the cutthroat capitalist world of containerisation with its international consortia, slot-leasing agreements and complex network layouts.

It should be stressed that the competitive behaviour of the Soviet and other communist lines, apart from their staying aloof from consortia and conferences, was no different than that of the West and East Asia. Although communist ideologues and supporters of UNCTAD regretted the brushing aside of the "New International Maritime Order,"[10] they lacked the means to challenge

---

[9]*Containerisation International Yearbook* (1987), 5. The main motive for these tax laws had been the desire to provide employment to Germany's ailing shipbuilding industry, which had seen its leading position in the container sector during the late 1960s and early 1970s dwindle as first Japan, and then Korea, gained dominance.

[10]See, for example, Wolfgang Lutze, "Containerkonsortien der führenden Linienreedereien aus westeuropäischen Ländern und Regulierung des wissenschaftlich-technischen Fortschritts im Linienkodex," *Gesellschaftswissenschaftliche Reihe*, XXXIII

the *status quo*. Moreover, even in relatively simple shuttle trades it was extremely difficult to use mathematical formulas to impose market shares on vessels under specific national flags; the only area where the UNCTAD guideline approximated reality was in West Africa. A 1988 review showed that container technology had well and truly buried maritime revisionism.

By the late 1980s, the effects of restructuring, intermodalism and concentration gradually became visible as the overall market trend of the early 1980s was reversed. Traffic again considerably outpaced capacity (1986-1990: thirty-eight as against twenty-four percent). The appetites of the major players were whetted after several years of uncertainty and, as they began moving forward, the industry again became the scene of a global power struggle. Enlargement of scale through expansion, mergers and further forms of cooperation, and the establishment of brand identity throughout networks, became the major strategies. On the eve of the new decade, these developments were still in full flux. Though it was evident that a second revolution had occurred, its outcomes were as yet far from clear.

General Developments

The crisis that struck container shipping from the late 1970s, the ramifications of which were to dominate the industry during the next decade, could, as all fluctuations in the shipping market, have been foreseen. But, as is so often the case in the maritime economy, the dynamics of the young industry and the ambitions and optimism of a host of operators conspired to lull many into a false sense of security.

When in 1981 Karl-Heinz Sager referred to the surprise of all experts, including himself, at the fast rate of containerisation on the main east-west lines and the speed of its diffusion into the Less-Developed World,[11] he was still speaking optimistically, even though his own company, Hapag-Lloyd, had been sailing in the red for two years.[12] As early as June 1979 Sir Ronald Swayne, Chairman of OCL, had acknowledged that "liner profits are very unsatisfactory and for strong currency and relatively higher cost owners they are negligible."[13]

(1984), 60-62.

[11]*Fairplay*, 24 September 1981.

[12]Susanne and Klaus Wiborg, *The World is Our Oyster. 150 Years of Hapag-Lloyd 1847-1997* (Hamburg, 1997), 385.

[13]Speech, "Shipping in the Year 2000," circulated as a memorandum within Overseas Containers Australia Pty. Ltd., 16 July 1979, courtesy of Mr. R.W. Eaton, Executive Director, OCA P/L.

The decline of the fortunes of Mitsui-OSK eloquently illustrates how rapidly the container market had shifted after the collapse of the bulk sector. In 1976, all sectors recorded profits, but in 1977 only the liner sector did, and the next year even it plunged into the red.[14] From 1978, most liner operators began fleet reductions and staff sackings.[15] Ironically, many of the traditional companies, having been stung by the criticism of conservatism levied against them during the 1960s and early 1970s, had invested, in some cases quite heavily, in the bulk sector – but often too late, so that vessels ordered at top prices entered service only after the market had collapsed. Many were immediately mothballed.

By 1982 Sager's Hapag-Lloyd was forced by its major shareholders (three financial institutions) to adopt a thorough restructuring of its operations and to conduct a fire sale of its assets to raise some DM 300 million (US $160 million) to restore an even financial keel.[16] The pride of the company (and its home port of Hamburg) was deeply hurt when the Supervisory Board meeting deciding on the rationalisation measures was held in the offices of the company's largest shareholder, the insurance company Allianz, in Munich. To add insult to injury, its headquarters on the Ballindamm was sold and leased back to raise cash. Several of the company's leaders, including Sager himself, were forced to resign. Although Hapag-Lloyd suffered severely as a result of its ill-timed diversification into bulk shipping and land transport (its ULCC *Bonn*, for example, built at a cost of DM 190 million, yielded a modest DM twenty-five million), its difficulties were symptomatic of the severe crisis that container shipping in general and many individual companies in particular experienced between 1980 and 1986. But for those who survived, as Hapag-Lloyd chairman Hans Jacob Kruse noted, it had been "a salutary lesson to be confronted with the prospect of extinction as a reality."[17]

One newcomer that almost collapsed was OOCL, swamped in red ink as a result of the huge loans contracted by its bulk-shipping arm, Worldwide Shipping. Only a few years after he had taken over the traditional British firm Furness Withy and Co., C.Y. Tung, once regarded as one of the most visionary

---

[14][Mariko Tatsuki and Tsuyoshi Yamamoto], *The First Century of Mitsui O.S.K. Lines, Ltd.* (Osaka, 1985), 190.

[15]*Fairplay*, 15 February 1979, already referred to extensive fleet reduction plans by the major West European liner companies.

[16]Wiborg and Wiborg, *150 Years Hapag-Lloyd*, 384-390.

[17]Quoted in *Containerisation International* (December 1997), 73.

shipowners of his age, had to be rescued by a huge cash injection from Beijing[18] – a telling case of how China began to operate behind the scenes to prepare for its takeover of Hong Kong. China gradually became involved in many more Hong Kong companies – including shipping and banking – and it was no coincidence that when COSCO left its splendid isolation in the late 1990s it was OOCL with which it associated. Even more telling, the first appointed leader of government of Hong Kong after its return to China was C.H. Tung, son and successor to the great C.Y. himself. It is interesting to speculate just how much information China was able to gain about the West through OOCL, as it provided both a window onto the shipping scene and secure passage for material collected in the USA.

Virtually all companies had their own peculiarities, such as Seatrain's disastrous "social" investment in a Brooklyn shipyard; Farrell's equally ruinous takeovers of American Export/Isbrandtsen Lines and Pacific Far East Line; or ANL's near-suicidal ordering of four bulk carriers for the iron-ore trade with Japan. But the independent Zim Lines also plunged into losses of almost US $100 million for 1983 and 1984 before returning a profit of US $1 million in 1985 – but at the same time, restructuring had forced its debt up to US $500 million.[19] The plight of these companies was only too common throughout the industry, although a small number, including OCL and Nedlloyd, whose exposure in the east-west main lines was relatively small compared to that in the less affected north-south routes, came through relatively unscathed.

The fundamental reason for the crisis was that after a decade of "sensational" growth averaging some 18.5 percent annually,[20] the industry faced a severe surplus of tonnage as volumes on the North Pacific and North Atlantic, which together accounted for more than half of all container movements in the world,[21] fell by six to seven percent. While bulk freight rates, after a brief muted revival in 1978-1979, went back into the doldrums and by 1983-1984 reached new lows, the container sector was also hit hard. Between 1977 and 1980 total new capacity of 646,000 TEUs was added to a world fleet which, until then, had counted only 530,829 TEUs.[22] To some extent, this rapid growth was stimulated

---

[18]*Lloyd's Maritime Asia* (April 1994), 48, interview with C.H. Tung; and *Fairplay*, 20 August 1998, 4, commenting on OOCL's official website history.

[19]Anon., *All Ways Zim. 50 Anniversary Album 1945-*1995 [Tel Aviv, 1995], 133-135.

[20]*Fairplay*, 24 June 1982.

[21]*Containerisation International Yearbook* (1981), 10.

[22]*Ibid.*, 10.

by subsidies given in many nations to shipbuilding, because that industry was seen in developing countries as a spearhead in economic modernisation strategies or, by the traditional maritime powers, as a political instrument to maintain employment and prestige. But demand factors were of much greater significance when many shipowners put larger ships into existing trades, ordered tonnage for new services and replaced their semi-container freighters. As a result, the downturn in freight volume was met by an increase in capacity that was believed to be as high as twenty percent, and about twice that rate on the North Atlantic.[23]

The first reaction of all the big companies to the tonnage glut on the main routes was to reduce costs and capacity. In the first instance, this meant cutting crew sizes to the absolute minimum (some critics, indeed, would argue that they went below that minimum); renegotiating loans contracted at the high interest rates of the late 1970s; and giving consideration to transferring vessels to cheap registers to obtain tax advantages and the opportunity of employing inexpensive foreign crews (mostly Asians from the Philippines, India, China and Korea). To leave a national flag, however, was by no means as easy to achieve or as immediately advantageous in liner shipping as it was in the bulk sector, where flags of convenience had been prevalent since the 1950s. Both dry-bulk carriers and oil tankers operated on open markets where shippers chartered whatever vessel was available at a specific time on the best terms, irrespective of nationality. Liner shipping, by the nature of its business, operated and competed under entirely different conditions, where national identity was extremely important, partly to achieve preponderance in the home market and partly also to give legitimacy to shipping companies on routes touching their home countries.

Although Europeans often condemned their Asian rivals for such informal cargo preference, they had long been keenly aware of the promotional potential of pride in their national identity. OCL, Nedlloyd, CGM and Hapag-Lloyd continued to hold to attitudes first cultivated by their predecessor companies at a time when no significant overseas shipping was owned in Asia or Latin America. But now Evergreen and Yang Ming enjoyed the status of "official carrier" for Taiwan, as did OOCL for Hong Kong, COSCO for China and the Korean and Soviet companies for their respective states. All, moreover, had access to cheap national labour; only Taiwan, because of its non-recognised status, used the Liberian flag for its foreign-built vessels. For Taiwanese-built vessels, however, its government insisted that they use the national flag. As yet,

---

[23]G. Devos and G. Elewaut, *CMB 100. Een eeuw maritieme ondernemerschap* (Tielt, 1995), 244.

no major companies from Japan,[24] Europe or the USA had switched as to a flag of convenience, but their problematic costs, combined with the lingering desires of many governments to retain a strong shipping industry, soon led to the adoption – in those countries, like the USA, that did not already have subsidy legislation – of a kaleidoscope of supportive tax schemes. By the late 1980s these included the rather farcical scheme of establishing "second registers," under which shipowners could continue to fly the national flag but operate under flag-of-convenience conditions. Few companies followed the example of NOL, whose directors accepted a cut in their salaries.

A second general response was to reduce vessel speed and thus both costs and capacity as sailings per year dropped. On the North Atlantic and in the Europe-East Asian trade, container ships during the 1970s thundered along at thirty knots and more – a fetish for speed that culminated in the extraordinary gas-turbine carriers of Sea-Land and US Lines. With fuel prices rising rapidly in the second half of the 1970s, it is difficult to see how such practices could have been maintained, but a sudden awareness of the tonnage surplus caused vessels to be slowed down to the low twenty-knot range. At the same time, new vessels were powered by diesels, albeit of ever-larger output, that achieved considerable savings over steam turbines. Moreover, in a process reminiscent of the 1870s, when conventional ocean steamers were re-equipped with compound engines, all big-turbine vessels were gradually brought in and re-engined with diesels. From an engineering viewpoint, but no less that of the accountants in head office, the TRIO and Scandutch consortia provided the most rewarding jobs.

Curiously, American companies had considerable trouble staying abreast of developments elsewhere: until 1978 not a single large ship's diesel had been built there, and the 1970 subsidy system required the cooperation of two companies in order to develop a new technology. As so often, Sea-Land was the US pioneer. As it did not receive subsidies, between 1978 and 1980 it had its entire new series of twelve diesel-engined ships for the Pacific trade built in Japan. Yielding service speeds of twenty-two knots, their Sulzers were thirty-percent more efficient than previous steam turbines, thus enabling the entire round-trip voyage to be made without refuelling.[25] America's next landmark was the completion in the USA itself in September 1980 of the first modern, large,

---

[24]Shin Goto, "Globalization and International Competitiveness: The Experience of the Japanese Shipping Industry," in David J. Starkey and Gelina Harlaftis (eds.), *Global Markets: The Internationalization of the Sea Transport Industries since 1850* (St. John's, 1998), 355-384, deals mainly with bulk carriers, although crew-reduction schemes applied to all vessels.

[25]Sea-Land, *Sea Notes*, Silver Anniversary Issue (1981), 7.

low-speed diesel engine.[26] Producing 43,200 horsepower, it was the first of a series of three to power the largest container ships yet built in the USA, 2494-TEU units for APL's East Asian service.

Figure 7: APL's *President Truman* (1988, 4340 TEU) leaving Oakland through the Golden Gate for East Asia.

Source: Courtesy American President Lines.

Individual Trade Routes

On the North Atlantic, which, because of the large-scale participation of US companies had never been able to achieve any comprehensive conference agreement, a "murderous rate war" raged from 1978-1979.[27] A shakeout began with the withdrawal of Farrell Lines (whose stoppage left Amsterdam without an American connection)[28] and the sale of Seatrain to Trans Freight Lines, owned by the Australian freebooter, Thomas Nationwide Transport (TNT). Swedish operator Broström underwent restructuring and put its Dutch subsidiary Incotrans

---

[26]*Fairplay*, 11 September 1980; and John Niven, *The American President Lines and Its Forebears 1848-1984* (Newark, DE, 1986), 274-275.

[27]Wiborg and Wiborg, *150 Years of Hapag-Lloyd*, 384.

[28]*Dagblad voor de Scheepvaart*, 17 October 1980.

(the former Holland-America Line and a partner in ACL) up for sale.[29] Rumours suggested that Nedlloyd might be interested in buying Incotrans, but the appalling state of the transatlantic market – "battlefield" and "bloodbath" were common descriptive terms – was an effective deterrent to any adventurism on its part. Nedlloyd's entry into the North Atlantic had to wait another six years.

Under great pressure by early 1983, the five "establishment lines" (Sea-Land, US Lines, Hapag-Lloyd, ACL and Dart) appeared to close ranks against outsiders TFL and Cast, but their conference agreements had no more substance than wallpaper, barely disguising the "total disarray" in the trade, where the tariffs quoted were still those of 1978.[30] Cast was a Canadian newcomer with a twist, operating an innovative type of hybrid vessel, the "conbulker," that carried containers westward and bulk cargoes eastward across the Atlantic, thus taking advantage of the reverse imbalances in both sectors. Later in the year, the first modest rate increases since the late 1970s were announced, and TFL and Cast even joined the existing conferences.[31] But with the introduction of round-the-world services imminent, any semblance of order was bound to be short-lived.

On the transpacific routes, full-scale rate war broke out in 1980, when Sea-Land withdrew from the existing agreements, and soon rates were about seventy percent of what they had been in 1976.[32] Pressure had been mounting as a result of both a tonnage surplus in general and the entry of new and aggressive companies from East Asia's "little tigers" (Taiwan, South Korea, Hong Kong, Singapore and Malaysia), such as Evergreen, Korea Shipping Corporation (KSC), OOCL, NOL and MISC.

Greatly assisted by the rapid growth of their own economies – exports from these countries by now amounted to twice those from Japan[33] – these newcomers were powerful contestants. In an unprecedented move, the five American companies on the Pacific route, including APL and Sea-Land, in 1981 applied for permission from the Federal Maritime Commission to enter into a

---

[29]*Fairplay*, 4 December 1980.

[30]*Ibid.*, 10 February 1983, 12-13; and *Dagblad voor de Scheepvaart*, 18 February 1983.

[31]*Fairplay*, 15 September 1983, 6; and 27 October 1983, 6.

[32]Niven, *American President Lines*, 271.

[33][Tatsuki and Yamamoto], *First Century*, 196.

mutual slot-leasing agreement such as the two operated by their Japanese rivals.[34] Hard times brought traditional individualists and opponents together in a proposal that was clearly designed not just to test how far the existing anti-trust legislation might be bent but also to support the campaign to overthrow that legislation altogether.

APL and Sea-Land had been outspoken critics of the legislation, and it was no coincidence that their action came shortly after the strongly Pacific-minded Senator Daniel K. Inouye of Hawaii introduced his Ocean Shipping Act. This act, of course, aimed at achieving exactly the outcome that America's leading companies desired. Although the time was not yet ripe for any departures from US policy, two years later APL and Sea-Land, in a landmark decision, gained permission from the Federal Maritime Commission for the first deep-sea joint venture, a common feeder service linking Manila and Subic Bay with Kaohsiung.[35] As APL plunged into the red in early 1983, from its US \$44.6 million profit for 1982, it was evident to all inside and outside the industry that US companies should not be denied access to the tactical tools used by so many of their foreign rivals. Within a year the new US Shipping Act was passed.

Cooperation was also the response from several newcomers from the "little tigers." OOCL, KSC and NOL in March 1982 obtained permission from the Korean government to form the Three Parties Consortium Agreement. While KSC pulled out two years later, when it wanted to increase its share of the trade,[36] the alliance between OOCL and NOL strengthened over time. KSC's resumption of its independence was entirely rational, considering the rapid growth of the Korean economy and the small share of its exports carried by national shipping, but Singapore and Korea were also geographically too far apart for a satisfactory integration of services. Under increasing pressure, the "big six" Japanese companies initially clubbed together even more tightly in their two groupings, relying above all on their domination at home to survive the crisis. Criticism of the resulting restrictive and exploitative practices culminated in 1984 in a speech by the Chairman of the Japan Shippers Council, entitled "The Seven Wonders of the Japanese Shipping Industry." He castigated Japan's container operators for refusing to operate terminals on weekends, disadvantag-

---

[34]*Fairplay*, 21 May 1981. The other three companies were Lykes Bros., US Lines and Waterman Steamship. In view of the "heroic" nature of Niven's history of APL, this episode is not mentioned in the book.

[35]*Fairplay*, 10 November 1983, 8.

[36]*Ibid.*, 19 March 1981, 8; and 14 June 1983, 9.

ing national exporters by cutting rates for foreign competitors, and protecting the weaker members of the group.[37]

By 1984, however, the first signs of a fundamental reorganisation and internationalisation of Japanese container shipping were becoming visible. While the *"pater familias,"* NYK, was unwilling to act, it was Japan's more impatient and innovative numbers two and three which took the initiative. Mitsui-OSK started the ball rolling in March 1983 when it asked permission from the Ministry of Transport to withdraw from the six-line agreement to the US West Coast. From the early 1980s, moreover, Mitsui-OSK and K-Line had established direct services from mainland East Asia and Taiwan, in which they entered into immediate competition with the new lines from those countries, including Evergreen and the NOL-OOCL consortium. The centrifugal forces thus set in train gained further impetus from the Ministry of Transport's decision to allow a reorganisation of Japan's US West Coast trade into three groups of two; the deregulation of transpacific trade in the wake of the US Shipping Act; and the shock rise in the value of the yen after the 1985 Plaza Accord (from 260 yen/US$ in March 1985 to 175 yen/US$ one year later).[38] The break-up of the "great six" and the creation of international consortia soon dramatically changed the structure of the Japanese industry.[39]

The two East Asia-USA cross-traders, Mitsui-OSK and K-Line, teamed up on the run to California, but failed to agree on all other routes. To strengthen its position in the East Asia-USA trade, Mitsui-OSK in March 1985 entered into a consortium with the Danish cross-trader East Asiatic Co.[40] A few months later, K-Line provided a partial response by leaving the five-line agreement on the Japan-US East Coast run and joining the NOL-OOCL consortium, recreating the grouping that already existed in the East Asia-Europe trade within the ACE-group. This left the weak YS-Japan Line group (which in 1988 merged into Nippon Liner Services) and the unbalanced pairing of Showa and NYK. Showa, the smallest of the six lines and already absent from the five-line agreement on the Japan-New York run, in 1988 withdrew entirely from liner shipping.

Many other main-line and feeder routes were affected by the slump, partly because box ships could easily be moved onto new routes and partly also because new tonnage continued to come on stream. The most complex of all main-line trades, Europe-East Asia, provides a telling example. Load factors and freight rates had steadily declined since 1979, and the Far Eastern Freight

---

[37]*Lloyd's Maritime Asia* (June 1986), 12.

[38]*Ibid.* (May 1986), 18.

[39]A good overview of developments is given in *ibid.* (May 1985), 30-31.

[40][Tatsuki and Yamamoto], *First Century*, 196.

Conference (FEFC) came under increasing pressure – ironically, as so often happens, exactly at the moment it produced a handsome celebratory history.[41] Exceptionally, the customary loner Maersk had for some time aligned itself with the conference, but it announced it would pull out in June 1982.[42] Nonetheless, other outsiders, including Zim, Evergreen and Balt-Orient, continued to erode the hold of the FEFC over the trade. Understandably for a company that prided itself on the quality of its service,[43] Maersk threatened to throw the trade wide open. The three northern consortia, FEFC's main constituents and the main targets of Maersk, responded by making space available to the Danish company through their Inter-Group Agreement (IGA).[44] At the same time, FEFC entered into what is best described as an "uneasy truce" with Evergreen; on the Japanese part, this consisted of little more than a series of verbal assurances.[45]

The price for these concessions soon had to be paid: in early 1983 the TRIO group reduced its capacity by having each partner successively lay up a ship and cut one round-trip voyage from its schedule.[46] This, however, did not restore order to the trade; on the contrary, from 1982 four significant new players emerged: Yang Ming, a second Taiwanese company that was focussed on containers from the beginning, Cho Yang from Korea, Blasco (Black Sea Shipping Company), the Odessa-based Soviet entity that was the descendant of the Russian Volunteer Fleet of 1877, and, most importantly, COSCO. With the defeat of the last Maoist faction at the 12th Communist Party Congress of 1981, the last barriers isolating China's economy were removed, and COSCO began its meteoric rise as the official and independent carrier of the new "workshop of the world." By the early 1990s, it became one of the top five container companies. Moreover, within several consortia members were itching to renegotiate deals and increase market share. Pressures were rapidly building toward a showdown, and it came as no surprise that in July 1984 the FEFC and Evergreen, locked in

---

[41]Eric Jennings, *Cargoes. A Centenary Story of the Far Eastern Freight Conference* (Singapore, 1980); the year of publication suggests that the preoccupation of the conference's principals with other priorities caused a delay in production.

[42]*Australian*, 27 May 1982.

[43]*Ibid.*, 30 September 1982.

[44]"Europe/Far East Conference is Ready for the Storm," *Containerisation International* (May 1985), 38-47; and "Europe/Far East Lines Play for High Stakes," *ibid.* (December 1986), 35-39.

[45]*Fairplay*, 12 July 1984, 7.

[46]*Hamburger Abendblatt*, 15 February 1983.

mutual recriminations, terminated the 1982 agreement. But by then the liner scene had adopted an entirely different complexion, as Evergreen launched the first round-the-world services, incorporating the three main east-west lines – North Atlantic, Europe-East Asia, and East Asia-North America – in a single operation.[47]

Figure 8: An M-class Panamax carrier (4344 TEU, 1988/1990) of Maersk.

Source: Courtesy Maersk Sealand.

Rumours about plans for round-the-world services had been rife since the late 1970s. Although they promised to provide huge economies of scale, almost all shipowners had looked upon such projects as recipes for disaster, both for the companies themselves and for the industry as a whole, as huge volumes of TEU would be added to the already excessive stock. As Karl-Heinz Sager (Hapag-Lloyd) succinctly stated, under those circumstances there was "no

---

[47]As opposed to the operations of companies like the former Hamburg-America Line, which for some time had operated large numbers of individual services in all major trading areas, but without any coordination within the network. Over time there had also been companies whose vessels actually sailed around the world (e.g., before World War II the Federal Steam Navigation Company with cargo to Australia and meat from the Argentine, or during the 1970s and early 1980s Atlanttrafik Express Service, Barber Blue Sea and Hoegh Lines), but these firms had always remained small players on the periphery of the liner industry. APL had actually terminated its round-the-world service in 1977 (Niven, *American President Lines*, 273).

stability in sight."[48] But this did not deter two of the world's most creative and aggressive operators, Evergreen's Chang Yung-fa and US Lines' president Malcom McLean, from implementing the idea. Evaluating their initiative as the most significant event of 1984, *Containerisation International* rightly declared 1984 the "year of the entrepreneur."[49]

As had been expected, both projects involved huge newbuilding programmes, altogether of more than 110,000 TEUs, or over five percent of total world numbers, indicating the confidence of both men that they could make money where others struggled to make ends meet. Evergreen's outlay amounted to US $1 billion,[50] while US Lines' twelve ships alone cost US $570 million in a total investment of over US $1 billion.[51] Before going into the details of their vastly different strategies, it must be stressed that both, despite the perilous state of the industry, appeared to time their moves perfectly. Since shipbuilders had been thrown into disarray by the shipping crisis, they could order their vessels at rock-bottom prices and benefit from significant mass discounts. In addition, their fleets could incorporate the latest developments in fuel-efficient engine design and automated technology. Crew sizes were reduced to sixteen or seventeen for Evergreen and twenty-one for the US Line ships. It was estimated that per TEU-mile, Evergreen's costs were as little as 3.5 to four US cents and those of US Lines about four to 4.5 cents, while competitors were still calculating on a basis of 6.5 to 9.5 cents.[52] Equally important were the advantages to be gained from a round-the-world service, as it was believed that an occupation rate per (albeit longer) completed voyage of three containers per slot could be achieved against only two for conventional end-to-end operations. And, on the other side of the ledger, the US dollar, in which most freight was paid, enjoyed a considerable rise as a result of the strengthening of the American economy in 1984.

In short, if Evergreen and US Lines were able to fill their ships, they would leave their rivals in a heap. The volume they had on offer was gigantic. Evergreen's plan was by far the most ambitious, based around weekly services both eastbound and westbound with a fleet of twenty-four G-class 2728-TEU carriers, only slightly smaller than the largest TRIO ships in the Europe-East

---

[48]Quoted in *Fairplay*, 24 June 1982, 7.

[49]*Containerisation International Yearbook* (1985), 5.

[50]*Lloyd's List*, 15 January 1985, special report, "Round the World Services," 5.

[51]*Fairplay*, 15 August 1985, 6; *South* (July 1986), 102; and *Containerisation International* (January 1987), 37.

[52]*Containerisation International Yearbook* (1985), 6.

Asia trade but an advance of some thirty percent on the maximum capacity of individual ships on the North Atlantic and North Pacific. Reflecting its almost immediate success, Evergreen's last eight vessels were delivered with a capacity of over 3000 TEUs.

In contrast, McLean's gamble was based on a totally different calculation: a single-direction eastward circumnavigation, including both the US East and West coasts, to be performed by twelve "econoships" with the unprecedented capacity of 2129 FEU (4258 TEU) each. McLean had conceived of his "global bus service" during the high fuel prices of the late 1970s when he had purchased US Lines specifically for that purpose. Banking on fuel prices rising again and mindful of his disaster with Sea-Land's thirty-three-knot, gas-turbine express trains of the early 1970s, he give his fleet a speed of only eighteen knots, against the by now customary twenty-two to twenty-four knots. Evergreen's first sailing took place in July 1984, the very time it cancelled its agreement with FEFC, and new vessels followed in quick succession. US Lines, all of whose ships, in the largest ever order, were built in Korea by Daewoo, followed in December.

With their round-the-world services Evergreen entered the North Atlantic, and US Lines the Europe-East Asia trade, for the first time. There and on all other main lines they boosted both capacity and oversupply volumes to new heights, while combing all regions for boxes to feed into their ports of call. No company, large or small, could ignore their impact. Evergreen established several new feeder services in the intra-Asian trades, particularly through its subsidiary, Uniglory, while McLean purchased Moore McCormack Lines and most of Delta Steamship to gain footholds in the South American and African trades.[53]

The first response of the FEFC has already been indicated. On the North Pacific the majors reshuffled their consortia or, alternatively, re-established their identities to withstand the onslaught the easily-recognisable green ships and boxes of Evergreen. APL and Sea-Land pressed ahead with their intermodal strategies. ACL opened a new service with the southern region of the USA, based on Wilmington.[54] On the North Atlantic other companies adopted creative maritime strategies that helped to transform the face of that ocean. P&O, under the aggressive leadership of Jeffrey Sterling, showed its hand for the first time in 1985 by taking a strategic ten-percent stake in its OCL-partner (and traditional rival) Ocean Transport and Trading and by having OCL buy half of the deeply-troubled Trans Freight Lines from its Australian owners.[55] With the latter move

---

[53]*Containerisation International* (January 1987), 37.

[54]*Fairplay*, 9 August 1984, 9.

[55]*Ibid.*, 16 January 1986, 7.

P&O, for the first time in history, entered the North Atlantic. Within a few months it was followed by Nedlloyd, which had attempted to bolster its position by a short-lived coalition with Barber Blue Seas on the US-Middle East run.[56] But with the collapse of the Middle East market – which also affected US Lines more heavily than Evergreen – its vessels, for the first time in the history of this "imperial" company, were shifted to the Atlantic.

Similar in background and outlook, Nedlloyd and OCL soon found each other in a slot-leasing agreement with TFL.[57] The pace of developments now increased. In May 1986, P&O bought out its partners in OCL, cleverly re-naming it P&OCL, and in July 1987 took over the remaining fifty percent of TFL.[58] At the same time ACL "jumboised" part of its fleet and entered into a slot-leasing agreement with the previously fiercely-independent Hapag-Lloyd[59] – which soon afterwards rationalised its network in a deal with Hamburg-Süd and shifted its priorities to the Europe-East Asia run.[60] Almost unbelievably, neither main-line tonnage gluts nor the considerable strategic activity of all major players were able to deter yet more newcomers, who thus added to the almost explosive mix.

In 1986, Hyundai began a five 2970-TEU vessel East Asia-USA service,[61] while the French Compagnie Maritime d'Affrètement (CMA) of Marseilles in the same year entered the Europe-East Asia trade as a cut-price outsider with a fleet of six 1600-TEU carriers.[62] Perhaps most extraordinarily, Karl-Heinz Sager, the German veteran who had been shown the door at Hapag-Lloyd, during the summer of 1986 set up plans for his own round-the-world service, to be started in the spring of 1987 as the Senator Line. He planned to use a fleet of about twenty vessels, of a modest 700 to 1500 TEU, to be chartered from German tramp owners, for a service targeting niche cargoes left out by the

---

[56]*Ibid.*, 10 July 1986, 3-4.

[57]*Ibid.*, 3 July 1986, 6.

[58]Stephen Rabson and Kevin O'Donoghue, *P&O. A Fleet History* (Kendal, 1988), 474.

[59]*Fairplay*, 12 June 1986, 5.

[60]*Ibid.*, 4 December 1986, 8; and Wiborg and Wiborg, *150 Years of Hapag-Lloyd*, 399.

[61]*Fairplay*, 25 September 1986, 9.

[62]*Ibid.*, 23 October 1986, 9.

majors.[63] His venture would never make a profit, but he cleverly based it on Bremen, calculating – correctly – that the state-city's government would repeatedly step in to his rescue.

By the time Sager entered the fray, the contrasting commercial fates of the two round-the-world services had become evident. Evergreen went from strength to strength, boosting its loadings in 1984 by eighty percent and in 1985 by another fifty percent.[64] It delivered quality door-to-door service on all routes, had no difficulty attracting sufficient cargo in the USA despite charging the same rates as the North Atlantic agreements, focussed on the dominant twenty-foot container, and in July 1986 established its own double-stack train between Los Angeles and Chicago. From the very beginning it made a profit, despite low revenue levels per container on almost all legs of the route.

In contrast, US Lines lagged behind from the beginning. Its ships were too slow, losing especially valuable time in transit between California and New York. The company suffered from the desperately low rates on the Pacific, which it undercut by fifteen percent to attract business. It made no impact on the Europe-East Asia trade, as it carried only forty-foot slots while the trade was mainly structured around the twenty-foot box. To service its debt (US $180 million per year) it was forced to charge high rates which it could never recoup under current conditions.[65] By July 1986, McLean had to reschedule his debt repayments, and four months later he filed for his companies to be placed under Chapter 11 protection.[66] Laying up the econoships and continuing trading on US Lines' transpacific and South American routes could not prevent liquidation. The econoships were auctioned in December 1986. Understandably, no shipowners were ready to purchase the flawed vessels, and its was US Lines' banks who ended up with the dozen – paying a mere US $4 million per ship as against their building cost of US $46.5 million each.[67] In the meantime, Evergreen and others benefited from McLean's demise.

The liquidation of US Lines, however, was not the end of the matter; developments had just been so rapid that no one in the industry had been able to formulate a response. That the econoships could yet have a future emerged in

---

[63]*Ibid.*, 25 September, 8; and 30 October 1986, 9.

[64]*Ibid.*, 26 June 1986, 21-22.

[65]Claude Abraham, "Lignes tour du monde: viable ou non, pas de miracle," *Transports* (January 1987), 35-37. A timely overview of the Pacific trade is in *Fairplay Pacific*, 11 December 1986, xxv-xxvi.

[66]*Containerisation International* (January 1987), 37-41.

[67]*Economist*, 9 January 1988, 71.

1988 when Sea-Land bought them (at a bargain price of US $162 million). After a refit to give them a smaller 3400-TEU capacity and slightly higher service speeds, they became the material with which Sea-Land, P&OCL and Nedlloyd (in proportions of fifty-five/twenty-five/twenty) began a new joint North Atlantic service.[68] As the ships had been built with US government subsidies, they could not be sold overseas, so Sea-Land owned them while P&OCL and Nedlloyd had access to their slots through a leasing agreement – a clear example of how flagging legislation could be circumvented by technology.

Although a certain amount of rationalisation was achieved in this manner, with P&OCL and Nedlloyd redeploying their own tonnage in other trades, the Atlantic remained grossly overtonnaged. A reorganisation of the main conferences in 1989 could provide neither relief nor additional defence against outsiders like Evergreen. But it created the opportunity for the formulation, one year later, of a Tonnage Stabilisation Agreement on a similar basis to the agreement in 1989 that had been introduced on the North Pacific. Significantly, besides the conference stalwarts ACL, Hapag-Lloyd, CGM, Nedlloyd, P&OCL, Sea-Land and OOCL, it also included outsiders Evergreen, Polish Ocean Lines and Mediterranean Shipping Co., a Geneva-based aggressive newcomer offering cut-rate services with second-hand tonnage.

Significantly, by now any agreement would have to comply with both US and European Community rules.[69] The overall outlook, however, was still bleak, with load factors at best at seventy-five percent, overcapacity still at around thirty percent, and most rates fifteen to twenty-five percent below 1988 levels. Although the idea of a tonnage stabilisation scheme, as was adopted in the Pacific in 1988, began circulating,[70] industry opinion was expressed succinctly by Sea-Land executive, Wilford Middleton who stated that "We will have to weather the next three/four years with sluggish rates."[71]

On the transpacific routes, the response to the round-the-world services was a return to cooperation. This was shown in the evolving arrangements between the main Japanese container companies as well as in broader agreements.[72] Early in 1985 the TransPacific Westbound Rate Agreement (TWRA), the first tangible result of the new US Shipping Act, was concluded between no less than nineteen companies, which thus established a limited form

---

[68]*Fairplay*, 11 February 1988; and 5 May 1988, 14-16.

[69]*Ibid.*, 22 February 1990, 5; and 22 March 1990, 5.

[70]*Lloyd's Maritime Asia* (January 1990), 9.

[71]Quoted in *Containerisation International* (August 1990), 43.

[72]For an overview of all Japanese transpacific services see *ibid.* (June 1989), 50.

of conference covering almost the entire liner trade between the west coasts of North America and East Asia. With an occupancy rate chronically between twenty-five and forty percent less than that in the eastward trade (depending on the relative value of the US dollar), it was vital to provide at least a minimum floor for backhaul container rates. Significantly, as on other routes at the time, there was a gradual move away from the extremely complex rate structures of the liner industry, which dated from the 1870s and perhaps even earlier, when different rates were fixed for almost every individual commodity. This practice had then been accepted as fair and realistic. Moreover, it was flexible enough to stimulate certain export trades and thus strengthen the common interest between owner and shipper. But now it ran counter to the interest and strategic logic of the container shipowner, for whom a box was a box was a box.[73]

With the fall in the value of the US dollar after the early 1985 Plaza Agreement among the G-7 nations, TWRA was transformed by its manager, Ron Gotschall, into an effective and increasingly valuable instrument.[74] Nevertheless, agreement on the main haul direction of the trade, in which competition had become ruinous, was even more important. It was achieved in late 1985 with the establishment of ANERA, the Asia North America Eastbound Rate Agreement. Although never as comprehensive or powerful as TWRA, ANERA did become a permanent feature of the trade and by the late 1980s assisted in reversing the downward trend of freight rates.

An important instrument towards that end was the conclusion in November 1988 of the Transpacific Stabilisation Agreement, the first of its kind in the world. Its thirteen participating lines, the most notable absentee being NYK, agreed to cut their collective capacity by ten percent during the first year and to aim at a total reduction of thirteen percent. As a diplomatic feat and a first step in addressing the huge problems of the trade – total overcapacity eastwards was still a huge forty percent – this was a promising, if modest, beginning.[75] In 1990, the TSA became the vehicle through which the members hesitantly attempted to enforce a rate hike; not surprisingly, calculating realists, like APL's Bruce Seaton, remained sceptical.[76]

In the Europe-East Asia trade rapprochement of any kind was as far away as ever, even if some diplomatic contact occasionally took place between FEFC representatives and the major outside lines, such as Evergreen, Yang

---

[73]*Fairplay*, 21 March 1985, 8.

[74]*Lloyd's Maritime Asia* (September 1990), 7-9.

[75]*Ibid.* (May 1991), 11-12.

[76]*Fairplay*, 25 January 1990, 7; and *Lloyd's Maritime Asia* (May 1991), 8-9.

Ming, COSCO, Hanjin and Cho Yang.[77] The ACE consortium had split in two when the French-Belgian part was sold to Maersk, and its Korean members strained like dogs on a leash. As the 1989 orders from Hapag-Lloyd (five 4400-TEU carriers for its TRIO service) and Nedlloyd (five hatchless 3568-TEU vessels) demonstrated,[78] plenty of dynamism existed within the other consortia that formed the backbone of FEFC. With the TRIO agreement scheduled to run out in 1991, utter uncertainty was the rule of the day.

In short, although there were some hesitant signs of improvement, on most routes the problem of overcapacity had not been solved and whatever cooperation existed between companies and consortia fell far short of what was required to bring stability to the trade. What had been demonstrated, however, was a determination by all major players to defend status and market share through enlargement of scale, rationalisation of services, slot-leasing agreements and expansion into new trading areas; in following such strategies, traditional firms and newcomers struggled side by side. A number of new coalitions were formed which pointed the way toward the early 1990s when many of the existing consortia were dissolved and large-scale re-alignment of alliances took place. At the same time, there were some notable examples – such as Evergreen, Maersk, APL, COSCO and OOCL – of companies which preferred isolation.

During the 1990s, the clash between these apparently diametrically-opposite strategies – consortium or independence – would become one of the main issues in the industry. But virtually all agreed on one point: they saw their future in establishing, maintaining and advertising a strong individual identity and brand recognition.[79] To understand the developments of the next era adequately, two other fundamental changes in the structure of container shipping need to be considered: the external diversification of shipping companies into intermodalism and further concentration of power within the industry through mergers, takeovers and other methods.

Intermodalism

The crisis on the North Pacific not only led to retrenchments and new forms of cooperation but also to the development of true intermodalism in the United States through the integration of container shipping and rail services. Although in principle this was a "natural" progression in transport organisation and infrastructure, it must be stressed that it was the peculiar geographic and

---

[77]*Fairplay*, 1 February 1990, 5.

[78]Wiborg and Wiborg, *150 Years of Hapag-Lloyd*, 399; and G.J. de Boer and A.J.J. Mulder, *Nedlloyd. 25 jaar maritiem* (Alkmaar, 1995), 78 and 169-170.

[79]*Fairplay*, 9 February 1989, 8.

economic situation of the USA and its location in relation to Japan and East Asia that provided both context and stimulus.

Figure 9: The intermodal box: an APL stack-train passing the traditional "gateway to the West," St. Louis, Missouri.

Source: Courtesy American President Lines.

Traditionally, the US West and East coasts had been served separately, and each had possessed its own hinterland, with that of New York and other east coast ports stretching well westwards of Chicago and Kansas City. Initially, this pattern had remained after the trade was containerised. But when, stimulated by piggy-backing and containerisation, the American railroad system was modernised, restructured and deregulated, it became capable not just of competing with road transport but also of hauling freight economically over much longer distances. In consequence, deliveries from East Asia by ship and rail through west coast ports began penetrating more deeply into the continent than previously. Thus, it could reach the vast consumer markets of the eastern USA, effectively taking traffic away from the all-sea services through east coast ports as a result of competitive advantages in delivery time and overall transfer costs. One of the main issues that had kept K-Line and Mitsui-OSK apart was the difference in their approaches to the US market. K-Line regarded the entire USA as a single market to be approached through a comprehensive strategy, while

Mitsui-OSK viewed the lower-volume New York run as a totally separate route from the high-volume shuttle trade with the West Coast.[80]

Apart from offering access to a rapidly-growing regional market, dominated by the explosive economy of California,[81] the US west coast ports offered three rail corridors to mid-America and the eastern and southeastern states. The northern route ran from Seattle, Tacoma and Portland and had Burlington Northern as its main railroad company. The central passage started at Union Pacific's terminus in Oakland. In the southern corridor, leading eastward from the adjacent ports of Los Angeles and Long Beach, Southern Pacific was the main operator. Sea-Land was the first to realise that shipping companies should not be satisfied with merely delivering boxes to railroads but had to integrate the successive transport stages into a single, intermodal operation.

In 1980 it commenced through transport to inland destinations under a system called Interior Point Intermodal (IPI). But it was APL's leaders, especially Bruce Seaton,[82] who more perfectly understood both the principles and the requirements of successful intermodalism. Their solution was to take control of train movements out of the hands of the individual railroad companies. In 1981, APL concluded agreements with three US railroad companies whereby it made its containers and trailers available to them for domestic use, thus ensuring a much higher utilisation rate on the backhaul to west coast ports.[83] In addition, APL gained the benefits of railroad deregulation in the USA, as large rail users were now permitted to contract for freight services with mutually-agreed rates instead of having to accept public tariffs. Equally importantly, Sea-Land and APL realised that existing railroad technology was inadequate. Freight cars that had been built for piggybacking operations rather than the carriage of containers were to be replaced with material dedicated for the transport of containers. Making use of light-weight metal and adopting a revolutionary design, Southern Pacific developed a double-stack train capable of carrying up to 150 FEU, or 300 TEU, at a time, thus dramatically increasing railroad productivity.

---

[80]*Lloyd's Maritime Asia* (May 1985), 30.

[81]Between 1970 and 1985 California's international trade had trebled (*Fairplay Pacific*, 11 December 1986, xxv). See also Grahame Thompson (ed.), *Markets. The United States in the Twentieth Century* (Milton Keynes, 1994), chapter 9.

[82]For an illuminating "profile" of Seaton, see *Lloyd's Maritime Asia* (May 1991), 7-9.

[83]Niven, *American President Lines*, 267-271; and *Fairplay*, 16 April 1981, 11; and 11 July 1985, 33-44.

Sea-Land actually was the first to use the new system between Los Angeles and the US Gulf, but APL caught up fast and took the lead by realising the necessity of the shipping company taking control over the movements of the trains from the railroad companies. APL time-chartered trains and ran them on schedules it determined and, where necessary, serviced by ramps it owned. In this way it was possible to have dedicated double-stack APL Linertrains standing ready to receive their boxes from the moment a ship tied up to the terminal. This, in turn, made it all the more important for container shipping companies to control their own port terminals, a subject discussed elsewhere.

With these innovations APL achieved the seamless transfer from ship to train, true intermodalism. There were some teething problems, mostly due to congestion in existing facilities, but both the system itself and the new technology worked. Despite their light construction and much heavier usage, the freight cars performed more than adequately. The economic outcomes surpassed all expectation: APL, which had never made a profit of more than US $12 million, in the early 1980s averaged US $45 million per year, a result that contrasted brilliantly with the global trend. Although this result was also influenced by APL's early decision to focus its East Asian operations on Kaohsiung, Taiwan's booming gateway, it was a resounding confirmation of the soundness of both its strategy and intermodalism in general.

In its strategy to control train space and movements, APL went far. It established a subsidiary to control its rail and trucking operations, bought three domestic freight-broking firms to gain access to their markets, and by 1985 invested some US $17 million in double-stack rail equipment. It built up an extremely complex railroad network that covered the entire country and was managed by the most up-to-date computer technology – an aspect of APL's operations that has remained until the present day. By July 1985, APL had firmly established its leadership. It ran eight dedicated double-stack trains in four corridors: Los Angeles-Chicago, Los Angeles-New York, Seattle-New York, and Los Angeles-Atlanta.

The next largest intermodal company was Sea-Land, with services to Chicago and New York from Tacoma, and to Chicago and the US Gulf from Los Angeles. The latter could carry up to 300 FEU.[84] It had, in fact, taken other companies and ports only a little time to realise that intermodalism was the way of the future in North America. Burlington Northern introduced common-user trains from Seattle, the Norfolk and Southern from Norfolk, and Conrail between New York and Chicago.[85] US Lines followed suit with a dedicated Union Pacific

---

[84]*Fairplay*, 11 April 1985, 12-14.

[85]*Ibid.*, 11 July 1985, 39.

train from Oakland. What a decade earlier would have been unthinkable, foreign shipowners also started contracting with US railroad companies.

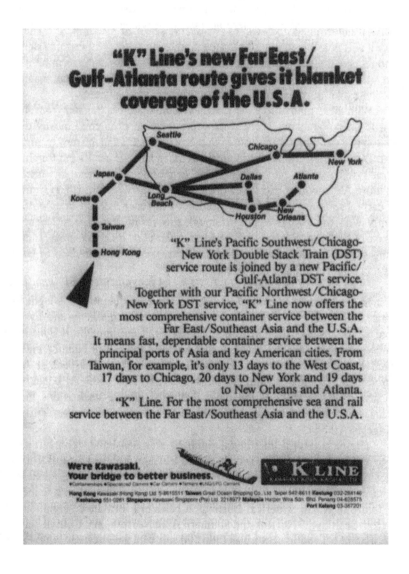

Figure 10:   The Intermodal Revolution: K-Line's East Asia-USA stack-train network.

Source: *Lloyd's Maritime Asia*, Intermodal Asia, part 1, K-Line advertisement (1987).

The first, in 1985, were Maersk; NYK, which was finally awakening from its slumber; and K-Line. Five years later they had been joined by other majors such as Evergreen, Hanjin (which had absorbed KSC), Hyundai, Mitsui-OSK, Nippon Liner Services (formerly YS-Japan Line), and OOCL. American ports gained international rivals when Vancouver and Montréal were developed by Canadian National and Canadian Pacific Rail to serve as intermodal gateways into Canada and adjacent regions of the USA; both gained double-stack services with Chicago, which more than ever was the centre of the US rail infrastructure. The rapid expansion of the industry, which included a fierce rate war lasting several years and the belated but then all-the-more aggressive entry of the Santa Fe Railway, did much to transfer a significant market share of the US domestic container traffic from the trucking industry to rail.[86]

Speculation was rife, but mostly of an academic nature, as to whether any railroad company – as had been the case in the pre-1914 days – would be interested in reversing the tables and, rather than being forced to accommodate itself to the demands of its shipowning customers, invest in shipping. Nothing of the kind eventuated, with one notable exception: the acquisition of Sea-Land by the Richmond-based railroad conglomerate, CSX. Its motives were simple and a significant recognition of the importance of containerisation in the increasingly globalised economy. As the domestic market was static, the company had to expand overseas by entering into shipping: "If we were going to continue to participate with an aggressive and growth-oriented base in the transportation market, then we have to be in a position to be able to compete globally and not be reduced essentially to the role of landlord in the USA providing delivery services."[87]

Nowhere else in the world by 1990 did a landbridge rail infrastructure exist that could in any way be compared to that of the USA. In Europe there was very little movement towards a unified railway infrastructure, although Nedlloyd, CMB and Maersk began building up inland networks, partly because of the competitive advantages to be gained from door-to-door service contracts and partly with an eye on the creation of the single European market in 1992. The Trans-Siberian Railway, which in the early 1980s had frightened so many capitalist shipowners on the East Asia-Europe run, never gained any momentum. Nevertheless, intermodalism became a global reality in the realm of operator-customer relations and freight rates through the increasing practice of quoting through-rates for container movements.

There was in principle nothing new in the concept of through-rates, which overseas shipping companies had introduced well before World War I for

---

[86]*Lloyd's Maritime Asia* (January 1987), 19-25; and (September 1990), 11-13.

[87]CSX Corporation spokesman, Tom Hoppin, quoted in *ibid.* (January 1987), 25.

cargo shifted through successive legs of maritime transport or, as in the case of Germany, for successive domestic train and overseas shipping movements. Container companies from the beginning had quoted freight rates that involved feeder as well as main-line movements, but with intermodalism it became possible to quote through-rates from origin to destination. In the first instance, it was freight-forwarders who had taken up the practice, but now the shipping industry itself began to take responsibility for inland conveyance. Two companies stood out as pioneers in their aim to provide total transport services: APL and Nedlloyd. The latter gave a telling description of the changes in its self-image during the 1980s:[88]

> Nedlloyd developed [after its takeover of KNSM in 1981] from a shipping company into a company where the accent is placed more and more on logistics services: the total control of physical cargo flows on behalf of shippers and recipients anywhere in the world.

CSX's Tom Hoppins' vision for his company after the takeover of Sea-Land expressed the same point in different terms, when he promoted it as a one-stop transport shop:[89]

> Whatever the customer needs, be it truck, train, barge, container or whatever, we can provide on the basis of one call to us...The customer does not have to worry about dealing with a variety of suppliers of services. His life becomes much simpler and his costs should come down.

Control over intermodal transfers could be decisively extended if the shipowner also controlled the onward mode of transport. The first two areas for such expansion were trucking and feeder shipping. Many owners in the late 1960s had bought trucking companies (Sea-Land's reverse example again providing the model), but in the course of time they moved out of the business, satisfied to rely on long-term contracts with independents. Short-sea shipping was a more natural extension of their core business, and beyond concluding slot leasing arrangements on dedicated carriers, some began operating their own feeder lines, either as joint ventures or on their own accounts.

---

[88]Nedlloyd, *Annual Report 1988*, 7.

[89]*Lloyd's Maritime Asia* (January 1987), 25.

As early as 1970, CMB started the Ibesca Line as a European feeder for Dart,[90] and from then the practice spread gradually through the industry. Evergreen (with its regional subsidiary Uniglory), Maersk and Sea-Land became leaders in this field, and during the 1980s major-owned regional networks expanded at a pace with general traffic. As main lines grew, global services multiplied and post-Panamax vessels were introduced, the "feeder" concept was gradually stretched to include long-distance north-south trades, such as Singapore-South Asia and the Gulf or from California southward along the west coast of Central and South America. This certainly did not mean that the independent short-sea company disappeared, as the examples of Bell Line, probably the oldest short-sea operator in northern Europe,[91] and Regional Container Lines, the major Singapore-based operator, demonstrated.

A major impetus to these developments was the globalisation of the world economy, in which individual exporters in East Asia, the USA and Europe generated many thousands of TEUs per year, and multi-national corporations decentralised production over many countries and/or distributed their products to stores around the globe. Automobile manufacturers like General Motors, Ford or Volkswagen, electrical and electronic goods suppliers like Philips or Sony, or international supermarkets like IKEA became increasingly interested in long-term contracts and other value-adding services, such as comprehensive transport packages and electronic data information. Swedish carmaker Volvo as early as 1983 had explained the advantages of "materials management" and the total control over material movements.[92] In order to maintain minimum stocks and hence to minimise inventory financing, insurance and the like, external transport flows became governed by the "just-in-time" principle – which, of course, could only be maintained by guaranteed services of the highest quality. As the shipping company became the one-stop transport provider, the relationship between shipper and shipowner could become close based on joint planning. On the one hand, this required both capacity and flexibility; on the other, it encouraged the development of a single identity and a single marketing organisation – at the same time that increasing cooperation and slot-leasing between companies was necessary to provide that capacity and flexibility.

Ironically, both APL and Nedlloyd initially found the challenge of controlling their immensely complex multi-modal networks beyond the capacity of their management, agency networks and computer technology. Both companies had disappointing results in 1989 and 1990, and a hostile minority group of shareholders forced Nedlloyd to divest itself of many non-core

---

[90]Devos and Elewaut, *CMB 100*, 210.

[91]Bell Lines, however, was liquidated in the late 1990s.

[92]*Containerisation International Yearbook* (1988), 6.

activities. APL went through several financially difficult years from 1988, when its five new 4300-TEU post-Panamax carriers came into service. But by 1992 these problems were overcome as APL consolidated its railroad and transpacific business and looked back on eight years of over fifteen-percent growth in the intra-Asian business.[93] As NYK's self-description as a "logistics mega-carrier" demonstrates,[94] the future of big container companies lay as much ashore as on the water. NOL symbolised its transformation by a change in its corporate logo; the Neptunic trident was replaced by three blue waves pierced by six upward and downward shafts representing the movement of goods by land, sea and air.[95] The full implications of that invasion of the land by maritime entrepreneurs, however, would not be felt until the early 1990s.

The Structure of the Industry: Concentration

The relentless search for economies of scale and, increasingly towards the end of the decade, company identity, resulted in an increased rate of concentration in the container shipping industry. While the top twenty companies steadily increased their market shares,[96] the size of the largest companies rose dramatically. In some cases, like that of Evergreen, such growth was purely internal to the corporation, while in others it was achieved through mergers, takeovers and other external moves.

At the top a number of companies emerged that were active on at least two of the three main east-west lines. Most of these, for historical and/or strategic reasons, were also represented in a number of regional and north-south trades. Other companies were increasingly characterised as niche players. It must not be forgotten, of course, that many companies had interests in other shipping sectors – as NYK and Mitsui-OSK did in bulk shipping and tankers, or P&O in cruise liners and ferries – or in other only remotely-related fields, as exemplified by Hapag-Lloyd's extensive investments in tourism. APL, through its intermodal subsidiary, was a major owner in the railroad sector. Many companies also were subsidiaries of much larger conglomerates. The container shipping interests of

---

[93]*Lloyd's Shipping Economist* (July 1992), 27-31, esp. 28; and *Containerisation International* (July 1992), 29-36.

[94]NYK, *Annual Report*, quoted in *Containerisation International Yearbook* (1991), 6.

[95]*Fairplay*, 9 November 1989, 7.

[96]*Containerisation International Yearbook* (1990), 6.

EAC formed but a small part of the overall EAC group that in 1982 counted 137 companies.[97]

In other cases shipping companies were taken over by large corporations outside the shipping or even transport sectors. This trend had begun as early as 1969 when the Reynolds group bought Sea-Land and was confirmed two years later with the takeover of Cunard by the real estate and hotel giant Trafalgar House. CMB and Hapag-Lloyd for a long time were wholly or predominantly owned by banks and/or other financial institutions. Other companies, like CMG, Lloyd Triestino and NOL, were state-owned and/or heavily subsidised. There is little doubt that being part of a larger conglomerate, whether in private enterprise or belonging to the public sector, helped companies survive financial pressures. But what is of importance here is that the structure of the container shipping industry itself became more concentrated during the late 1980s through the resumption of a pattern of mergers and takeovers, as well as voluntary exits from the industry, such as that of the Showa Line. These took two major forms: the combination of existing companies or the buying out of consortium partners. In both cases the result was an enlarged control over cargo space, vessels and sailing rights.

One of the most interesting examples of the complexity of corporate identity, strategy and ownership is provided by P&O, whose fortunes were mixed but which managed to come out on top as one of the leaders in the 1990s. From the 1970s it controlled an international construction company, Bovis; had an uncertain presence in the cruise business; and had an exposure to the large bulk sector as well as heavy investments in European ferries. Its container section, moreover, was not autonomous but was integrated into OCL, in which it had used the opportunity of OOCL's purchase of Furness Withy (1980) to increase its share to forty-nine percent.

The various parts of the P&O empire, moreover, formed anything but a synergic network. A few years into the 1980s the company, as so many others, was in serious trouble, and in 1983 Trafalgar House, the owners of Cunard, were interested in buying P&O – a curious reversal of an offer made by Trafalgar House itself several years earlier to sell its Cunard interests to P&O.[98] But as Trafalgar House became disenchanted with its container shipping activities, a white knight appeared in the shape of Jeffrey (later Lord) Sterling, the leader of a City financial group, who later in 1983 took control of P&O. In hindsight it is clear that from the outset Sterling had a strategic vision aimed at making P&O *the* British company. For traditional English shipowners this was an entirely new and baffling ambition – as their German rivals had cause to remember, the

---

[97]*Lloyd's Shipping Economist* (February 1987), 27.

[98]Rabson and O'Donoghue, *P&O*, 473-474.

traditional strength of British shipping had resided in the multitude of its liner companies, even when incorporated into larger groups, which were dedicated experts in their own particular fields. But Sterling understood much better than anyone in Britain at the time that such specialisation had been made obsolete by the box. Under his leadership P&O was to became what the Hamburg-America Line had been in 1914, a truly global company whose field was the world.

Sterling wasted no time once he had given P&O a health-providing cash injection. Decentralising the company, he instilled identity and strategic purpose into its container division. In the kind of financial manoeuvre that had been only too rare in shipping, in 1985 he bought a strategic ten-percent share in his major partner – and traditional rival – OCL (Ocean Transport and Trading).[99] Threatening enough in itself, especially as OT&T clearly was crippled by the shipping crisis, Sterling next showed the magnitude of his ambitions. In early 1986 OCL took a fifty-percent share in Trans Freight Line, the transatlantic subsidiary of the Australian TNT group. Despite TNT's warm relations with the forces that controlled the New York/New Jersey docklands,[100] TFL had always lost money on a grand scale. For the first time in its history, P&O had a presence in the North Atlantic. Further moves now followed rapidly, as developments elsewhere showed that, following the introduction of the round-the-world services during a period of a severe tonnage glut, these were going to be the decisive years. Perhaps this should have caused no surprise as shipowners, at least those who afford to do so, often behave anti-cyclically by going for expansion exactly when times are hard and newbuildings or companies in trouble are cheap.

In April 1986, almost at the worst point of the depression, P&O gained full control of OCL, paying £270 million for the fifty-three percent held by OT&T and British and Commonwealth. In January 1987 the company was cleverly renamed P&OCL, reincorporated as a division within P&O and strengthened a few months later by the purchase of the remaining fifty percent of TFL. In a significant re-alignment, which uncannily presaged later developments, P&O associated itself with Nedlloyd when both companies shifted ships and interests from the ailing Middle East trade to the North Atlantic. Their commitment to the North Atlantic and their association deepened further when they concluded a "Vessel Sharing Agreement" with Sea-Land, which had bought

---

[99]*Fairplay*, 11 April 1985, 8. P&O, at the same time, sold its LNG- and LPG-tankers, a clear indication of its new strategic priorities.

[100]Gossips always maintained that TNT knew a lot more about other controversial businessmen (See Morris West's novels *Cassidy* and *The Ringmaster*), but a critical business history of this fascinating and multi-faceted company (which also owned half of the now-defunct Ansett Airlines of Australia) remains to be written.

US Lines' twelve econoships. By late 1988, a broader agreement was reached which also included OOCL and Maersk.

Nothing less than a totally new order ruled on the North Atlantic. But P&O did not neglect its traditional fields, as became clear in 1991 when it also purchased the remaining container operations of Cunard (which a few years earlier had gained control over ACT) and Blue Star. In one blow it about doubled its market share in the Australasian trades. With ACT also came its 1989 "neo-colonialist" purchase, at a fraction of the real price, of the Shipping Corporation of New Zealand.[101] (New Zealand embraced Thatcherite privatisation and deregulation policies with a commitment and devastating completeness matched in no other country.) To be complete, P&O also aimed at gobbling up the Australian National Line, but strong resistance by the Maritime Union of Australia and ANL management prevented a sale at that time.

The fate of ACL demonstrated that reduction of ownership could also come through a process of attrition. It has already been recounted that a first reduction of partners occurred in 1974 with Broström's takeover of the liner operations of the Holland-America Line, which became a subsidiary under the name of Incotrans; for political and commercial reasons it continued to fly the Dutch flag. Dedicated as it was to the North Atlantic, ACL suffered badly from the rate wars of the early 1980s. Cunard in addition had been hit by the sinking of one of its ships in the 1982 Falklands/Malvinas War. Broström, with its heavy investments in shipbuilding and other industries making it "the pride of Gothenburg," was dragged down by its debts and liquidated. Its liner interests, including its participation in ScanDutch and the shares of the Swedish American Co. and Incotrans in ACL, were taken over by its more cautious and entirely shipping-focussed neighbour, Transatlantic.[102] In the context of the weakening of Sweden's economy, security for that company was achieved as Transatlantic in 1988 became a majority subsidiary of the trucking and forwarding conglomerate, Bilspedition – a telling reverse of the predominant diversification of shipping companies into land-based transportation.

In 1989 Transatlantic in two steps made ACL a fully-owned subsidiary. First, Wallenius, the initiator of this very first international consortium, and CGM sold out – the former to concentrate on its car-carrying business, the latter to establish its own North Atlantic service and identity ("French Line").[103] A few

---

[101]*Fairplay*, 30 March 1989, 5.

[102]Martin Fritz and Kent Olsson, "Twentieth-Century Shipping Strategies: Broström and Transatlantic, Gothenburg's Leading Shipping Companies," in Simon P. Ville and David M. Williams (eds.), *Management, Finance and Industrial Relations in Maritime Industries* (St. John's, 1994), 107; and *Fairplay*, 21 June 1984, 17-21.

[103]*Fairplay*, 12 October 1989, 5 and 10.

months later the last remaining partner, Cunard, parted with its twenty-two percent minority share which had now lost all strategic meaning and attraction, especially as ACL in 1989 had lost US $40 million.[104] This, however, did not mean that Transatlantic absorbed ACL or planned to operate its services independently. On the contrary, the ACL brand name was retained and extended to the other USA-based trades that Transatlantic now controlled and could restructure into a coordinated network, including the Gulf Container Line and Incotrans' Pacific Express Service between Europe and the US West Coast.[105] The very purpose, moreover, of gaining a strong individual identity and position was to become a more effective player in slot-leasing and other agreements to be concluded with the majors, such as APL, Hapag-Lloyd, P&O and Sea-Land.

Very much the same strategy inspired CGM. Despite a regular diet of subsidies its survival during the crisis of the early and mid-1980s had been a real issue. The election of the Chirac government in March 1986 brought not only another massive injection of funds (Fr780 million, or about US $120 million) but also a fresh approach that was intended to help it to recuperate from its heavy losses and to renew its fleet.[106] Because of the sheer size of the CGM's restructuring task within the global network of its services, the French shipping secretary did not allow CGM to take over France's second-largest private liner operator, Chargeurs Réunis, although most observers believed this would have made strategic sense. Instead, CR's loading rights in the Europe-East Asia trade were sold to Maersk with the rest of the French-Belgian group within the ACE consortium,[107] while its African operations and ships were snapped up by France's largest private shipowner, Delmas-Vieljeux.

From the very moment of Chirac's election Delmas-Vieljeux had become France's most aggressive shipping group. Taking over a string of minor companies as well as CR, it also acquired the US-based Australia-New Zealand Direct Line and, together with CGM, the Pacific Australia Direct Line (PAD), thus establishing a firm presence in the US-South Pacific trades.[108] For CGM the purchase of PAD meant a welcome reinforcement of its Europe-Australia and New Zealand and Pacific Islands-Europe services in a strategy aimed at reinforcing its traditional strengths. CGM's director, Claude Abraham,

---

[104]*Ibid.*, 9 August 1990, 11.

[105]*Ibid.*, 4 January 1990, 16.

[106]*Ibid.*, 2 October 1986, 5; 9 October 1986, 6; and 24 September 1987, 15-20.

[107]Devos and Elewaut, *CMB 100*, 250.

[108]*Fairplay*, 31 March 1988, 10; and 31 August 1989, 16-19.

specifically rejected a round-the world main-line approach for his company.[109] More important, these moves pointed the way to the massive consolidation of France's liner services in the 1990s.

Conclusion

The American transport expert Carl S. Sloane suggested in 1989 that the lesson of the 1980s was that in the intermodal transport world "instability [was] the norm."[110] This judgement could equally well be applied to the entire container shipping industry. Francis Phillips, editor of *Containerisation International*, in 1990 observed that "the scene all around was one of massive uncertainty and major change."[111] *Fairplay*'s John Guy spoke about "The second revolution – a struggle for identity."[112]

Economic conditions had buffeted all but the strongest. Despite massive rationalisation through new joint ventures, extensive slot-leasing arrangements and innovative tonnage stabilisation agreements, the surplus of tonnage remained. While several established owners left the trade or were taken over, there seemed to be no barriers to aggressive newcomers. Consortia were increasingly subject to internal tensions, and several had been consolidated into one hand or disbanded. The will to establish individual identities had to be matched with the continued need for cooperation. The ultimate rationale was the ever-more frenetic search for cost reductions and economies of scale – paradoxically expressed in the building of ever-larger fleets and individual container ships, which only helped to make the tonnage glut into an almost permanent feature of the industry. As if these problems were not enough, the identity of the leading operator was dramatically changing from a maritime entrepreneur into a total transport service provider. These were exciting times with much at stake – reminiscent of the pre-1914 liner-shipping world with its social-Darwinist struggles. As the shifting alliances and takeovers of the 1990s would show, there was very little certainty in this corporate jungle.

---

[109]Abraham, "Lignes tour du monde," 37.

[110]Quoted in *Containerisation International Yearbook* (1990), 5.

[111]*Containerisation International Yearbook*, 1991, 5.

[112]*Fairplay*, 9 February 1989, 8.

Chapter 5
The 1990s: Globalisation

Getting that "third ocean" is a goal every liner operator is pursuing right now, representing the great leap towards a global service.[1]

The most important success factor for the future is the need for total customer awareness by container operators.[2]

Despite their huge size, most container shipping giants have little control over their destiny.[3]

Since 1990, the container shipping industry has above all been characterised by globalisation and the relentless drive of operators to lower costs through enlargement of scale in an industry environment of a chronic tonnage surplus and falling freight rates. Almost all leading companies followed Evergreen's example and expanded their operations, either individually or as members of consortia and, from the mid-1990s, global alliances. Their specific objective was to include the three main east-west trade routes in their service networks. The resulting globalisation was partly driven by supply-side factors, such as the enlargement of scale of individual companies, ensuring that sufficient external funds remained available for investment,[4] and adopting changes in transport, computer and telecommunications technology. But shifting market conditions also created strong demand impulses, as the shipping companies increasingly had to deal with the needs of large trans-national manufacturers such as General Motors, Ford and Volkswagen in cars, Sony and Sanyo in electronics, Du Pont, ICI and Union

---

[1]*Fairplay*, 29 August 1996.

[2]*Containerisation International* (December 1997), 55, quoting Mr. Tony Farr, managing director of Safmarine, September 1992.

[3]*Fairplay*, 26 August 1999, 3.

[4]In addition to the new sources of external capital mentioned in chapter 3, this now also included Islamic funding, which was particularly suitable for the shipping industry (see David Hudson's articles in *Fairplay*, 26 September 1996, 23; 13 March 1997, 40; and 15 May 1997, 32-33).

Carbide in chemicals, and Heineken and Guinness in beer.[5] As these corporations shipped high volumes of trade on many routes, they preferred to deal with single operators rather than a large number of separate companies or consortia; only global companies could satisfy this demand.

But globalisation soon became more than the industry's economic context and a marketing strategy for individual companies. Operating global services, expanding company capacity and increasing market share almost became aims in themselves, a demonstration of "going with the times" and vital elements in the creation of new corporate identities. Because of their growing land-based interests and door-to-door commitments, moreover, container shipowners became increasingly aware that they stood at the heart of the transport infrastructure of the entire world economy and constituted an ever more powerful agent for change.[6] In C.C. Tung's words, "container transportation...provid[es] the vital link to world trade."[7] But their dynamic influence was not only created by the synergies resulting their entrepreneurial diversification but also, and perhaps even more, by the continuous decline in freight rates. As the *Journal of Commerce* in 1997 suggested, "the real driving force behind globalization is...the declining costs of international transport."[8] Whether this observation provided any consolation to shipping shareholders who suffered with "stoicism and patience"[9] in the hope that the trade cycle might one year turn their way was not recorded.

The problem of the tonnage glut, which had been endemic in the industry since the late 1970s, was never solved on the mainstream lines and rarely elsewhere. Occasionally there were glimpses of hope and rates rose, but these faded away as quickly as they had arisen under the crushing weight of ever-more orders for ever-larger ships. APL's post-Panamax carriers of 4300 TEU of the late 1980s were outpaced as Evergreen exceeded the 5000-TEU barrier, and

---

[5]Interesting and highly enlightening articles under the generic heading "Shippers" are in *Containerisation International* (July 1997), 57-59; (November 1997), 75-77; (March 1999), 59-63; (May 1999), 67-69; and (August 1999), 33-35. See also Fiona Gilmore (ed.), *Brand Warriors. Corporate Leaders Share Their Winning Strategies* (London, 1997), 88, where it is pointed out that 1.5 percent of OOCL's customers account for over thirty percent of the company's business.

[6]Brian Slack, Claude Comtois and Gunnar Sletmo, "Shipping Lines as Agents of Change," *Maritime Policy and Management*, XXIII (1996), 289-300.

[7]Quoted in Gilmore (ed.), *Brand Warriors*, 79.

[8]*Journal of Commerce*, 15 April 1997.

[9]*Containerisation International* (September 1996), 3.

soon afterwards Maersk, P&O Nedlloyd and Maersk again lifted the maximum capacity of their newbuilds over the 6500-TEU and even the 8000-TEU levels.[10]

As still bigger vessels were taking shape on the drawing boards,[11] a snapshot in mid-July 1998 revealed that no less than 106 ships of 4500-plus TEU had already been delivered or were on order from twelve companies.[12] Overall capacity rose by eleven percent in 1997 and another thirteen percent the next year. Such high growth rates could not be sustained, but 1999 and 2000 still registered increases of over nine percent.[13] Post-Panamax carriers, physically unable to perform round-the-world services, linked East Asia, Europe and North America through three-ocean pendulum voyages between the US West and East coasts via Asia and Europe or, alternatively, were employed on two-ocean or single east-west lines: most commonly East Asia-Europe or East Asia-North America. The productivity of these ships was further enhanced by rising service speeds, which again reached twenty-four or twenty-five knots. They had now become the dominant ship type, with almost sixty of them on order for 2001, over sixty percent of all slots to be delivered, and another forty-four ordered for 2002.[14] But construction activity also remained feverish in smaller classes of ships. In part this could be blamed on the stimulating effect of Germany's shipping tax laws, as was conceded even by Karl-Heinz Sager, head of the DSR-Senator Line, which chartered so many of their products,[15] and partly also on the fact that the major companies were increasingly penetrating feeder systems.

The tonnage glut remained despite the fact that the total capacity of the world's container fleet increased fractionally less than the turnover of all container ports. Total TEU slots operated increased by about nine percent per

---

[10]Jan Hoffmann, "Concentration in Liner Shipping: Its Causes and Impacts for Ports and Shipping Services in Developing Regions" (report prepared for the Economic Commission for Latin America and the Caribbean, [1998] (http://www.eclac.cl/research/dcitf/lcg2027), section IA, "Vessel Sizes." See also Mitsui-OSK, "The Present Situation of Liner Shipping 1997/98" (http:// www.mol.co.jp/JE3/e3/nenpo/frame.html), ch. 3, esp. section 2 (1), "The Shocking Debut of *Sovereign Maersk.*"

[11]*GL-Magazin* [magazine of the Germanischer Lloyd Group], No. 1 (August 1998), 4-6.

[12]*Fairplay*, 23 July 1998, 47. See also *Containerisation International* (September 1994), 47-51.

[13]*Fairplay*, 3 August 2000, 26.

[14]*Ibid.*

[15]*Ibid.*, 8 July 1999, 17.

annum between 1990 and 1997, from 3.2 million to 5.3 million TEUs.[16] The latter rose at a compound rate of some thirteen percent per year, from 84.2 million TEUs in 1990 to 170.3 million TEUs in 1997. This growth reflected the continued expansion of the already-containerised trade in manufactured commodities on the three east-west main lines, where the degree of containerisation had already exceeded ninety percent by the turn of the decade, and continued intensification on north-south and minor routes. The weakness of the US economy in the early 1990s and patchiness in the performance of Europe was more than matched by the strong growth of East and Southeast Asian exporters. The economic unification of the European Community (later European Union, EU) and the North American Free Trade Agreement (NAFTA) between the USA, Canada and Mexico provided moderate stimuli and expanded the scope of the North American market. On a smaller scale, the same applied to the South American trading bloc Mercosur, which united Brazil, Argentina, Uruguay and Paraguay, with Chile and Bolivia contemplating applying for membership. Figure 11 shows the geographic distribution of global container traffic in 1993, clearly confirming the prominence of the three main economic regions.[17]

Figure 11
Container Traffic, 1993 (in million TEU and percent of global total)

Transatlantic

> > eastbound > >: 1.3 - 4.5%
< < westbound < <: 1.9 - 6.6%

Transpacific	**Europe/East Asia**
> > eastbound > >: 4.6 - 15.9%	> > eastbound > >: 1.9 - 6.6%
< < westbound < <: 3.5 - 12.1%	< < westbound < <: 2.1 - 7.3%

Short sea:	Europe	5.2 - 17.9%
	Asia	3.5 - 12.1%
	USA/Caribbean	1.1 - 3.8%
	India/Middle East	3.0 - 10.4%

Other seaborne trades: 0.8 - 2.8%

Total Seaborne Container Traffic: **28.9 million TEU**
Total turnover of all ports: **108.6 million TEU**

---

[16]*Containerisation International Yearbook* (1991 and 1998).

[17]Niko Wijnolst and Tor Wergeland, *Shipping* (Delft, 1996), 38; see also Elizabeth Canna, "The Second Reshuffling," *American Shipper* (August 1993), 40B-40E.

Neither the Second Gulf War nor the Yugoslav and Bosnian crises seriously disrupted the pace of growth until the sudden Asian currency crisis of 1997. The next year was marked by significant shifts in the trade between the three poles of the global economy. Asian exports to Europe and America went up by ten and thirteen percent, respectively, while Asian imports from the same areas decreased by seven and fourteen percent; trade between America and Europe, however, showed healthy growth in both directions, eight percent eastwards and no less than sixteen percent westwards.[18] As fears of an Asian financial meltdown receded, the region was stabilised and exports, cheaper than ever as the result of widespread devaluations, rose to unprecedented levels, thus helping to turn the tide. Boom conditions in the American economy further boosted the growth of container shipping in its import trades. In August 2000, total capacity offered in the eastbound Pacific trade exceeded the "landmark" ten million TEUs, the equivalent of forty post-Panamax carriers every week, much earlier than the respected research group of NYK had forecast.[19] Interestingly, the market share of the four alliances, Evergreen and Maersk dropped from eighty-seven to eighty-three percent, as newcomers like China Shipping, CMA-CGM and MSC increased their capacity by an incredible forty percent in six months.

Shipowners, however, now had to contend with a second evil beyond the never-ending slide in freight rates, as the imbalance in trade volumes on the Pacific became extreme. Against the 5.8 million TEUs shipped eastwards to the USA in 1997, only 3.6 million TEUs went in the opposite direction. The costs and logistics of the repositioning of empty boxes became of ever-greater concern, even if, partly in response to back-haul problems, the container increasingly made inroads into what had traditionally been specialised trades, such as the reefer business in fruit[20] and even some "semi-bulk or neo-bulk" trades that Pearson as late as 1988 had identified as "non-containerisable"[21] because freight rates in that sector could be set by the marginal costs of the intermodal system rather than the full costs of bulk handling.[22]

---

[18]Hapag-Lloyd, *Annual Report 1998*, 29.

[19]*Shipping Times Online*, 24 July 2000, "Eastbound Trans-Pacific Route Hits 10m TEU Mark" (http://www.nyk.com/nyk21/scale/container/index.htm).

[20]See, e.g., *Containerisation International* (January 1999), 69-71 and 73-75.

[21]Roy Pearson, *Container Ships and Shipping* (London, 1988), 18.

[22]*Fairplay*, 10 June 1999, 20-21.

        Despite its expansion into adjacent trades, the container shipping
industry continued to be plagued by chronic overcapacity. Even during the early
1990s, when the fleet rarely increased by more than five percent per year, it had
been unable to make a substantial inroad into this problem. In August 1993,
NYK Senior Managing Director Hiroshi Takahashi estimated that space
utilisation rates in the east-west trades ranged from eighty-five to sixty percent.[23]
From 1994 onwards, growth rates of ten percent have again become the norm
rather than the exception, decidedly outpacing the average seven-percent growth
rate of global trade.[24] With shipbuilders offering highly competitive prices for
newbuildings (with prices falling from US $15,000 per TEU slot in 1995 to
under US $10,000 by late 1999)[25] and Germany's fiscal legislation again
favouring that nation's dentists and other "extreme tax write-off artists,"[26] a
strong supply-push added to the expansionary policies of the major operators.
        This stimulus was enhanced by the greater operational and financial
flexibility operators enjoyed as more vessels became available for short- or
medium-term charter from large independent lessors, such as German Conti-
Reederei, Niederelbe and Nordcapital, or the fast-rising Greek shipowner,
Costamare. While the German companies, fed by the specific regime of tax
concessions, from the beginning used newbuildings, others began mainly with
second-hand tonnage. Most recently, however, in a significant development
Costamare ordered its own post-Panamax tonnage and was, with good grounds,
declared a "heavyweight" of the industry.[27]
        In its wake other Greek owners entered the business which they had
shunned for such a long time, concentrating instead on bulk carriers and oil
tankers, leading one observer to comment that finally the Greeks, too, had been
bitten by the "box bug."[28] Overall, the rationalisation of services carried out by

---

[23]*American Shipper*, August 1993, 40C.

[24]*Shipping Times Online*, 9 March 1999, "Preparing for Era of Giants" (from
ABS Surveyor).

[25]*Fairplay*, 23/30 December 1999, 47.

[26]*Fairplay*, 11 March 1999, 3; the quotation is from Germany's short-lived SPD
finance minister, Oskar Lafontaine.

[27]*Containerisation International* (August 1998), 3.

[28]*Journal of Commerce*, quoted in InforMARE, Press Review, 4 June 1998. For
an excellent review of the Greek merchant marine since 1945, see Gelina Harlaftis, *A
History of Greek-Owned Shipping. The Making of an International Tramp Fleet, 1830 to
the Present Day* (London, 1996), chapter 9.

the main operators, i.e., the productivity gains achieved by structural changes within the industry and its operations, the introduction of larger and faster vessels and the increased use of chartered tonnage, more than compensated for the two-percent gap in overall growth rates. And despite continued expansion in global container throughput, the heavy ordering, especially of post-Panamax tonnage, is threatening to undermine all the benefits gained from industry consolidation, with severe overcapacity once again looming large.[29]

Enlargement of Scale and Concentration of Power

Under these circumstances increases in market share, revenue and profitability could only be ensured by further increases of scale and rationalisation.[30] As Evergreen's chairman, Chang Yung-fa, put it simply, "Unit costs can be decreased by carrying even more cargo,"[31] which principle, as long as capacity continued to expand faster than trade volumes, could only help to widen the gap between demand and supply. The year 1996 was "one of the toughest...on record."[32] A vicious circle was created, which resulted in sixteen leading companies in 1997 all increasing their liftings, but generally suffering "declines in profits, due to sharp plunges in freight rates."[33] The next year was worse, "an *annus horribilis* for most."[34] Even Maersk reported "a difficult year" for its container operations.[35] As the London-based industry experts Drewry Shipping Consultants concluded in October 1999, "Container shipping companies are no

---

[29]*Shipping Times Online*, 23 March 2000, "World Box Volume to Rise 10%: P&O Nedlloyd;" and 24 July 2000, "Overcapacity May Become an Issue Given Recent Large Ship Orders."

[30]For good theoretical discussions of this point, see Hoffmann, "Concentration in Liner Shipping," section IID; and *Containerisation International* (January 1999), 51-53.

[31]InforMare, Press Release, 5 October 1998 (quoting *Shipping Times*).

[32]*Containerisation International* (September 1997), 45.

[33]Mitsui-OSK, "The Present Situation of Liner Shipping 1997/98," chapter 5. The companies involved were Mitsui-OSK, NYK, K-Line, Sea-Land, Maersk, P&O Nedlloyd, Hapag-Lloyd, OOCL, Evergreen, Yang Ming, Hanjin, Hyundai, Cho Yang, NOL and MISC.

[34]"An *Annus Horribilis* for Most," *Shipping Times*, 5 January 1999.

[35]*Containerisation International* (May 1999), 24.

nearer solving the riddle of how to turn growth into profit."[36] Pointedly asking, "High Risk, High Stakes, Where's the Payback?," Drewry estimated that operators in 1998 carried 14.7 percent more cargo in an additional 7,200,000 TEUs but "somehow contrived" to earn 1.2 percent less revenue.

Although this debacle was partly due to the Asian crisis, Drewry saw no reason for any significant improvement in the market. Its pessimistic views echoed the thrust of many previous studies into east-west freight rates and the profitability of major container operators. An American report of 1992 showed that the US ocean liner industry's pre-tax return on assets for 1991 was well below two percent, and had been only 1.47 percent for the 1985-1989 period.[37] A few years later *Containerisation International* carried out an international review that found that the ratio of net profit to total revenue for the years 1990 to 1993 had been no more than zero percent, one percent, one-half percent and one percent, respectively. For 1996, the data were only marginally better. Of twenty-three companies, only three had a net profit margin of ten percent or more, six made less than one percent, and the average was a paltry 3.6 percent.[38] Interestingly, three of the four best performing companies (returns between nine and eleven percent) were niche operators: CP Ships, ACL and UASC; the other was Evergreen. Maersk was close to the average, at 4.3 percent. Most traditional lines fared badly, as table 7 shows.

Table 7
Profit Margins of Traditional Liner Companies, 1996

Company	Profit Margin (in %)
P&O	2.8
APL	2.5
Sea-Land	2.1
K-Line	1.3
NYK	1.3
Hapag-Lloyd	1.2
NOL	1
Nedlloyd	0.8
MOL	0.8
CGM/CMA	0.7
CMB	(-0.4)

Source: See text.

---

[36]*Shipping Times Online*, 26 October 1999, "Low Freight Rates Here to Stay."

[37]*Containerisation International Yearbook* (1992), 5.

[38]*Containerisation International* (September 1997), 45.

Probably the consistently worst results were booked by the three large Japanese companies; until 1998 K-Line, NYK and Mitsui-OSK had made losses on their container operations in each of the previous eighteen years.[39] But it is evident that many more operators had to find cost reductions and chase enlargements of scale.

The chronically low profitability of large segments of the container industry raises the vital questions as to how and why many of these companies stayed in the business. At present no systematic information is available that would allow any authoritative answers, but some suggestions may be made. In many cases, container lines were operated by multi-sector shipping companies, or even larger conglomerates, and evidently supported by transfers of funds from other sectors. In the case of the three Japanese majors, for example, it was largely profits from their car-carriers that enabled them to tolerate and offset their container losses. *Mutatis mutandis*, very much the same observation can be made with regard to most large European shipping companies, with the additional comment that several benefited greatly from their being part of multi-divisional corporations.

This applied particularly to P&O, with its 1970s takeover of Bovis Construction and 1980s rescue by the financial conglomerate of Lord Sterling, but also to Hapag-Lloyd's recent revitalisation after its takeover by tourism and manufacturing giant Preussag. Hyundai Merchant Marine is an integrated sector of the huge Hyundai Corporation, MISC of the Malaysian oil conglomerate Petronas. Maersk is a multi-divisional enterprise with multi-sector shipping interests, its own shipyard, aviation and oil interests, and excellent connections with successive Danish governments. CP combines shipping, railroad and other industries, and one could go on. In a different and perhaps extreme scenario, DSR Senator was bailed out year after year by the state government of Bremen, which evidently saw large social returns arising from the survival of its locally-based line. But the USA, despite an increasing number of policy changes and qualifications, never abandoned its shipping subsidy regime. Many European states have changed tax laws to reduce cost levels for companies using their flags. And the UASC has behind it the commitment of its various Arabian Gulf state owners to maintain its position "despite ups and downs" in the market.[40] Evidently, both governments and the shipping companies themselves fully realise the wider economic and social importance of continuing to provide high-quality container services.

---

[39] *Shipping Times Online*, 19 May and 2 June 1999 (quoting *Bloomberg*).

[40] Http://www.uasc-sag.com/High_res/english/_Noindex/Default.htm, UASC, "Establishment and Objectives: Corporate Profile."

Enlargement of scale may also be the result of psychological factors. It is hard to escape the conclusion that the personal outlooks and ambitions of the operators in the corporate jungle of the deregulated 1990s – as in so many other branches of the global economy – played a role in lubricating the fast-turning carousel that container shipping had become. As one commentator mused,[41]

> The question has to be asked whether the international container shipping market and its seemingly unassuagable demand for economies of scale is driving the development of faster tonnage with higher capacities, or if shipping lines have begun to fall victim to a syndrome in which the mere announcement of a new range of larger, faster vessels is enough to precipitate a rush of orders.

The desire to operate on all three oceans and the fight for market share had become intertwined with the egos of company leaders and a competitive *zeitgeist* that resembled that of the social-Darwinist 1890s.[42] In consequence, stability eluded the grasp of the industry as a whole and became all the more difficult to achieve. As "mega" became a word of common usage and, as in the oil, banking and automobile industries, mergers and takeovers became a standard strategic tool, a certain element of growth for growth's sake began to pervade the industry in this stage of rationalisation. Characteristically, Hiroshi Takahashi, whose NYK was one of the first to use the concept "mega," was unable to state why his company and its rivals were engaged in their almost suicidal cycle of rate cutting in order to maintain or expand market share.[43] A related issue was that many leaders in the industry were not perfectly aware of the details of the cost structures of their firms and/or in the final analysis made decisions based on gut feelings. As John W. Snow, chairman of the US intermodal giant claimed, "I don't think this industry knows its costs well. People do a lot of back of the envelope stuff."[44] C.H. Tung, albeit before the almost fatal crash of OOCL, admitted that he took all the available advice on supply and demand and favoured

---

[41]*Fairplay*, 19 October 1995, Newbuildings, 2.

[42]See Frank Broeze, "Shipping Policy and Social-Darwinism: Albert Ballin and the Weltpolitik of the Hamburg-America Line 1886-1914," *Mariner's Mirror*, LXXIX (1993), 419-436.

[43]*American Shipper* (August 1993), 4E.

[44]Quoted in *Containerisation International* (August 1996), 50.

sound planning, but that at the end of the day, it was his feelings that counted. "A decision has to feel right. If it doesn't then you probably shouldn't make it."[45]

Structural change within the industry to some extent mirrored the drive for ever-larger ships and globalisation. The concentration of power, through the growth of the individual company, mergers and takeovers, and/or the creation of global consortia (for which soon the new term "alliance" was adopted), became an ever-more salient feature. The share of the top twenty companies in the total fleet rose from thirty-nine percent in 1990 to forty-six percent in 1994 and fifty percent in 1999.[46] The top five in 1997 accounted for thirty percent.[47] The fleet of the largest company, Maersk, increased proportionally much faster than the total fleet, from 117,418 TEUs in 1990 to 378,205 TEUs (a gain of 223 percent) in early 1999;[48] its acquisition of the international liner business of Safmarine Container Lines and Sea-Land in 1998-1999 further boosted its capacity to well over 600,000 TEUs.[49] Another indication of its awesome thirst for boxes is that its fleet in 1993 made sixty calls per month at Hong Kong.[50]

Maersk's takeover strategy, which was not limited to these two examples, was symptomatic of structural change throughout the industry. The most salient aspect of this form of concentration was not so much the number of takeovers but the fact that they increasingly involved the merger or absorption of foreign companies. The ties between the emergent trans-national shipping corporations and their home ports and states loosened, especially as their corporate strategy was increasingly dictated by commercial calculation rather than historical loyalty, and their vessels were flagged out to whatever country appeared to provide the best advantages. Within an industry, in which round-the-world voyages and global networks with extensive overseas investments became the norm, the national identity of individual companies was gradually eroded.

A clear distinction could now be made between the leading group of companies, numbering between eighteen and twenty-two, and the others, among which some might be identified as niche specialists of one kind or another. Over

---

[45]Quoted in *ibid.* (December 1997), 73.

[46]*Containerisation International Yearbook* (1995), 5.

[47]"Backbone of Global Shipping," *Shipping Times*, 2 September 1998.

[48]"Asian Share of Global Container Fleet Slips," *ibid.*, 3 March 1999.

[49]"A.P. Møller to Buy Sea-Land for US $800m," *ibid.*, 26 July 1999.

[50]*Lloyd's Maritime Asia* (September 1993), 7. By 1997 Evergreen and its regional subsidiary Uniglory made eighty-five calls a month at Singapore (*Fairplay*, 9 January 1997, 48).

time, the gap between the two categories grew wider, making the transition into the elite ever more difficult. It was then also suggested that within the elite a widening divide existed between the top six and the companies of the next tier, putting pressure on the latter to seek survival in amalgamation and close cooperation.[51] In addition, after a period of rapidly-changing relationships, by 1998 six alliances emerged, which integrated the operations of the majors on the east-west routes and occasionally extended into other areas as well. The largest of these, the Grand Alliance, brought together the fleets of P&O Nedlloyd, NYK, Hapag-Lloyd, OOCL and MISC, with a total capacity of some 650.000 TEUs; the New World Alliance followed at a distance, with NOL/APL, MOL, and HMM totalling some 440,000 TEUs. To put these figures in the broadest perspective, the capacity of Maersk after its July 1999 purchase of Sea-Land exceeded 650,000 TEUs. Of considerable assistance was the further deregulation of US legislation in the 1998 Ocean Shipping Reform Act, which from 1 May 1999 freed ocean carriers from the requirement to file both general tariffs and individual contracts with the Federal Maritime Commission.[52]

Marketing and External Relations

Tellingly, in all major consortia and alliances each partner retained its own identity and marketing; ScanDutch, which expired in 1991, had remained the only major consortium to take over these tasks from its individual members. Slot-leasing agreements were the central feature of alliances, and cooperation often extended to the joint running of land-based facilities and electronic services as well. Under pressure to fill their main-line slots many companies, which had not done so before, invaded the regional and north-south trades, adopted a strong commitment to service contracts with large individual shippers, and began to take agency work into the firm. These practices contrasted strongly with the current economic fashion of out-sourcing, but only in this way could the smooth flow of boxes from one line to another be assured. The same applied to control over terminals in ports and, almost exclusively in the United States and its neighbours, intermodal links with railroads. All US and East Asian majors by mid-1999 had acquired control over dedicated terminal facilities on the US West Coast.

In order to achieve just-in-time delivery and no-inventory objectives, operators began offering many new value-adding services. These included the

---

[51]"Smaller Carriers Turn to Consolidation to Survive," *Shipping Times*, 16 November 1998.

[52]For a discussion of its impact, see *Containerisation International* (May 1999), 59-61.

provision of door-to-door logistics, Electronic Data Interchange,[53] tracking of individual containers,[54] planning of total material movements, competitive pricing, and the use of the internet for public relations, information and soon also the booking of containers. As the chief information officer of OOCL, Ken Chih, declared, "It is not an option not to connect to the Internet."[55] The container shipping company became an organism that was capable of remarkable innovation and flexibility in meeting the demands of the market and its major customers.

NYK, in its 1996 "21st Century Plan" focussing on the transportation requirement of the world economy during the next century, summarised its long-term vision in simple but comprehensive terms that could apply to many if not most of its rivals: "to reinforce its global position as a logistics megacarrier, using its well-established strength as a base. On the sea, on land and in the air, NYK aims to continue making use of its complete transportation network, offering its customers safe, punctual door-to-door service."[56] APL put its self-image in even more succinct but only slightly different terms:[57] "APL provides worldwide container transportation and logistics services with state-of-the-art information technology." APL was one of the pioneers in using the internet, partly for institutional advertising and general information, but also to provide additional services, information and advice for its customers; its latest innovation is an interactive schedule.[58] The greatest advantages are being seen in the

---

[53]*Ibid.* (June 1999), 72-75.

[54]See, for example, the internet-based container exchange scheme of the San Francisco firm International Asset Systems, established in October 1999 with the cooperation of the cross-alliance syndicate of main-line and feeder operators China Navigation Co., Hapag-Lloyd, OOCL, PT Lines, P&O Nedlloyd, Samudera Shipping and Wan Hai Lines, designed to help owners reduce the cost of repositioning empty boxes (*Fairplay Daily News*, 25 October 1999).

[55]*Ibid.*, 24 March 1999; see also his CEO, C.C. Tung, in Gilmore (ed.), *Brand Warriors*, 82-83.

[56]Http://www.nyk.com/corpinfo/Euhist.htm [1997]. K-Line two years' later launched its equivalent, "The Spirit for the 21st Century Plan" (*Containerisation International* [May 1998], 19.

[57]Http://www.prnewswire.com/cgi-bin/microstories.pl?ACCT =107003&TICK=APL&STORY=/www/story/04-06-1999. See also *Containerisation International* (April 1999), 45.

[58]Http://www.apl.com/content/about/sched.html.

maritime version of e-commerce: the paperless booking of slots and the capability to track individual containers during their entire voyage.[59]

The ideological corollary of their new policies was that the companies regarded themselves as embodying both global power and concern for every one of their customers. As Evergreen's advertisements proclaimed: "Global Reach. Local Responsiveness;" P&O Nedlloyd put it: "Hardware configures the network, but we still think shipping is a matter of people, relationships and service. As a global company, we give you local treatment."[60] OOCL was even more simple and direct in its slogan: "We take it personally."[61] The company's mission statement reflected all modern business-speak as it aimed to be "the best and most successful global container transportation company for our customers, employees, shareholders and partners, providing the vital link to world trade."[62] Rotterdam container terminal ECT went one step further, into space, with its promotional video featuring Dutch astronaut Wubbo Ockels and the message that containers brought humanity together.[63] NYK echoed OOCL's mission and strategy in its detailed "New Millennium Declaration," vowing to secure reasonable profits and increasing corporate value to shareholders, customers, employees and the international community.[64] In view of all such statements, one almost wonders why shippers across the globe increasingly band together to counter the power of the container giants and their alliances. In this context the following Freudian slip cannot be regarded as a surprise: while OOCL's online mission statement was designated by the sub-heading "philosophy," that of NYK unashamedly carried the sub-heading "profit."

An important extension of the projection of a clearly marked independent corporate identity was "branding," i.e., the building up of a globally recognisable brand name, like Coca Cola, Heineken or Sanyo. From the very

---

[59]See, for example, "Who is Pushing IT?," *Containerisation International* (July 1999), 35-37; and "Services Set to Go On-line," *Shipping Times*, 10 November 1999. The APL website (http://www.apl.com) also included a section on the US Ocean Shipping Reform Act, as did that of Maersk (http://www.maerskline.com).

[60]Evergreen advertisement on the back cover of *Containerisation International* (July 1999); and P&O Nedlloyd, "Company profile" (http://www.pokl.com/welcome/profile.htm [1997]).

[61]Gilmore (ed.), *Brand Warriors*, 84.

[62]Http://www.oocl.com/philosophy/philosophy.htm.

[63]Personal communication, Dr. Hugo van Driel.

[64]Http://www.nyk.com/nyk21/profit/index.htm.

beginnings in the 1950s and 1960s individual companies and consortia, as well as container lessors, applied their names and sometimes also logos to their containers.[65] Some operators, still in the grip of a conventional past in which institutional marketing had not yet been invented, were modest in the size and/or artistic flair of their markings, while others realised the advertising and marketing potential of their boxes that carried their name through the world. Mitsui-OSK's boxes popularised its alligator mascot. ScanDutch's orange propeller matched the impact of SeaLand's black-and-red logo. OOCL's first design sported a small plum blossom as logo; later the flower, in seductive pink, gained pride of place in the second O of OOCL on the walls of ships and containers alike. As C.C. Tung explained,[66]

> the plum blossom has "soft" values. We deliberately put [it] on a massive ship of 50,000 tonnes of steel. [Also], it says something about our character, our resilience. In the late 1980s we could have easily packed it in, and the brand would no longer exist. But in China the plum is a flower that blooms in the harshest conditions."

Figure 12:   The most recent version of the OOCL logo with its flower emblem.

Source: Private Collection.

Designs changed rapidly, partly according to fashion, partly to keep track with corporate developments, such as the sequence that transformed OCL into P&OCL, P&O, and, most recently, P&O Nedlloyd. Maersk's seven-pointed

---

[65]The following selection is based on H.J. Witthöft, *Container. Transportrevolution unseres Jahrhunderts* (2nd ed., Hereford, 1978); Roy Pearson, *Container Ships and Shipping* (London, 1988); and *Fairplay Container Operators, 1996* (London, 1996).

[66]Gilmore (ed.), *Brand Warriors*, 86.

white star on an ultramarine field has appeared in a great variety of positions with or without the company's name and must be ranked second only in brand recognition to the entirely green boxes of Evergreen, almost superfluously painted with the company's name. (It was a few of these boxes that were splashed across the world's newspapers and TV news programmes in 1999 as the collision between the *Ever Decent* and *Norwegian Star* dumped them unceremoniously on the foredeck of the latter vessel.)

The nomenclature of the ships also became subordinated to the necessity of brand recognition. Many shipping companies had established policies on this point dating from the era of conventional shipping, but containerisation intensified the development and made the purpose marketing rather than maintaining cultural traditions. OCL stood out with its adoption of *Bay* names, while Hapag-Lloyd used the suffix *Express*, and the K-Line *Bridge*. Other companies used their own name or an obvious derivate (*Ever, Ming, Nedlloyd*, etc.) The most extreme system, fortunately not imitated, was that of the early ACT consortium that simply called its ships *ACT 1, ACT 2*, and so on to *ACT 7*. From the late 1980s branding became a high priority of marketing managers. OOCL switched from *Oriental* to plain *OOCL*. P&O dropped the *Bays* after its takeover of OCL, adopting the *P&O* prefix instead. Consequent to the end, P&O Nedlloyd, after its merger, introduced the double prefix. The full extent of this phenomenon (see table 10) may be judged from the fact that of the twenty largest operators in January 1999 no fewer than sixteen used the company name as prefix. Hapag-Lloyd and K-Line never abandoned their traditional suffixes, *Express* and *Bridge*, and only culturally-minded COSCO and UASC named their ships individually, mostly after historical persons or geographic landmarks.[67] Interestingly, Costamare adopted the nomenclature of the individual charterers of its vessels, retaining not just Pireaus as their home port but also the Greek alphabet to paint their names.

Three other dimensions were added during the 1990s to the global standing of the container shipping industry. First, the combined force of mega-carriers and alliances provoked parallel moves on the part of individual shippers and national shippers' councils. Regulatory bodies such as the Federal Maritime Commission in the USA and the European Commission's competition watchdog, Directorate General 4, were continuously pressed by shippers' organisations that argued that it was "totally unacceptable to industry that the present antiquated system which permits and supports price fixing is allowed to remain in place."[68]

---

[67]See, for example, the regular column "Behind the Ship's Name" in the house journal of the UASC, *Al-Mirsat Al-Arabiyah (Arab Anchor)*. In recent joint ventures with Evergreen, however, COSCO has begun to use the company prefix.

[68]Garry Mansell, chairman of the European Shippers Council, quoted in *Fairplay Daily News*, 23 September 1999.

National shippers' organisations began meeting in regional forums. Harried by these prosecutors, the International Council of Containership Operators (the "Box Club"), which until then had been almost entirely invisible, found it necessary to counterattack with a brief study entitled "Container Shipping – Backbone of World Trade."[69]

It made no impact on the critics. In 1997 the European Shippers' Council warned that regulatory authorities needed to be watchful to ensure that the big alliances did not develop into monopolistic transport providers and that consolidation should not be allowed to result in only few players being left.[70] The EC's Directorate-General 4 in September 1998 fined the fifteen members of the Trans Atlantic Conference Agreement a total of US $313 million for anti-competitive behaviour.[71] In the wake of the adoption of deregulation in the US Ocean Shipping Reform Act, a global conference of shippers organisations was held in 1999 at Vancouver.

In order to present for the first time united views and voices an Asian alliance of shippers' councils was formed, consisting of representatives from Japan, Korea, Hong Kong, ASEAN, Australia, New Zealand, Sri Lanka and India.[72] Asian interests had already been present in the Shippers Tripartite Group that met annually from 1994. In all these global forums the customers' counterpoint to P&O Nedlloyd's marketing slogan was made: yes, we want individual and confidential service contracts, but do not forget that we do not stand alone. Interestingly, it was the same P&O Nedlloyd that warned that deregulation had led too much to one-to-one contracting.[73] Coordinating the efforts of the various shippers' organisations, the OECD has taken up the task of formulating plans for the regulatory reform of liner shipping. The European Shippers' Council did not mince words in expressing its opinion that action was long overdue: "the present system of regulation of the liner shipping industry is unacceptable to its customers and...reform is necessary."[74] Whether this firm stand will bear any fruit remains another question.

---

[69]*Containerisation International* (April 1996), 9.

[70]"Shippers Warn of Too Many Liner Alliances," *Shipping Times*, 5 December 1997.

[71]*Fairplay*, 24 September 1998, 7; and *Containerisation International* (October 1998), 3 and 7.

[72]*Shipping Times*, 15 July 1999.

[73]*Fairplay Daily News*, 9 November 1999.

[74]*Fairplay*, 28 September 2000, 22-23.

Second, the consortium and alliance forms of cooperation between individual companies – especially in its slot-sharing, joint marketing of ships and services, and electronic data sharing, and more recently also internet booking systems – which after twenty-five years had been developed into a highly sophisticated system, became the model for the civil aviation industry. Initially, this mainly concerned bilateral agreements dealing with simple shuttle services, but in due course these led to much closer integration of operations and seat-booking systems. With the indispensable assistance of mega-computers, alliances were created which brought together a number of airline companies from across the globe. At the moment of writing the Star and One World Alliances have emerged as the two industry leaders, each representing massive concentrations of power that, in their sphere, aim at providing the same advantages as the container alliances at sea.[75] The third area in which containerisation, albeit to some extent together with the other sectors of the shipping industry, pioneered and carried through dramatic change was in decimating its workforces in port and at sea. This downsizing, which during the 1990s increasingly involved the flagging-out of container carriers, is discussed in chapter 7, but here it may be emphasised that especially the sharp reductions in the number of waterside workers resulting from the establishment and growth of container terminals became examples for entrepreneurs in non-transport industries. Especially, though by no means exclusively, in countries like Japan and South Korea, where employment cultures had developed that appeared to cushion workforces against the impact of economic downturns, the experiences of the docks provided lessons in efficacy and, occasionally, ruthlessness.

From Consortia to Alliances

While the North Atlantic and Pacific trades in 1990 were still wallowing without any specific direction, the first signals of change appeared on the East Asia to Europe route, which in the late 1980s had undergone an extraordinary increase in capacity. From August 1988 to late 1989, slot capacity had increased by an amazing twenty-four percent for conference members and thirty-one percent for outsiders. At the same time, the first stage of the disintegration of the consortium system began. Between 1987 and 1990 the ACE Group lost half of its members, as first the Franco-Belge Services (a combination of Chargeurs Réunis and CMB) withdrew, selling its sailing rights to Maersk. Soon afterwards the two Korean

---

[75]The Star Alliance (established in 1997) currently comprises Lufthansa, Singapore Airline, United Airlines, Scandinavian Air System, Varig (Brazil), Thai Airways and Air Canada; One World, which followed a year later, includes American Airlines, British Airways, Qantas, Canadian Airlines, Cathay Pacific, Finnair and Iberia. Several smaller alliances have also been created, such as that between Air France and Delta Airlines.

companies Hanjin (which had absorbed KSC) and Cho Yang left out of dissatisfaction with their share of Korean exports. Yet the three remaining lines (K-Line, OOCL and NOL) had increased their capacity by over fifty percent, thus putting immense pressure on conference members and outsiders alike.[76] But the crucial factor was that the twenty-year terms of the TRIO and Scandutch consortia would expire in 1991 and 1992, respectively, and that chances of their extension or even renegotiation appeared increasingly remote. Within both, relations had increasingly turned sour as the agreements made in the early 1970s outlived their usefulness and stronger companies felt restrained by the weaker ones in pursuing their interests. Especially within TRIO, which operated a complex pooling system of revenues and costs, the competitive pressures of the late 1980s and the ambitions of the individual partners had created sharp divisions. As Hapag-Lloyd judged the situation, "Looking inwards and concentrating on maintaining its members' market shares rather than on consolidation, let alone expanding, its initially dominant market share, the consortium positively invited flexible outsiders to offer competition."[77]

Soon to be released from their mutual obligations, the members had to decide how best to combine the two great imperatives: enhancing both individual identity and market share. All companies realised that to the latter end cooperation with others was almost indispensable since otherwise their services would lack in frequency, regularity and range of ports. Shippers had become accustomed to the vast choice offered by the consortia, and they would not be satisfied with any arrangements of lesser quality. Only the largest companies or those which for one or more reasons – for example, quality of service, cost and/or nationality – were assured of a market share might contemplate operating in splendid isolation. Thus, while it was evident that the consortium system as such would not be given up, great uncertainty existed about what new combinations would emerge and on the basis of what calculations about cost reductions, compatibility, etc., carriers would decide to team up. In addition to factors specific to the East Asia-Europe trade and the position of its main conference, FEFC, the companies of course also considered their interests in other trading areas. Although the era of the route-specific consortia was by no means finished, far-seeing shipping leaders and commentators could already envisage the creation of more global relationships.

The realignment of the liner-shipping world was assisted by two important developments. First, since the passage of the 1984 US Shipping Act,

---

[76]*Lloyd's Maritime Asia* (November 1989), 9.

[77]Susanne and Klaus Wiborg, *The World is Our Oyster. 150 Years of Hapag-Lloyd 1847-1997* (Hamburg, 1997), 404-405.

American companies had become "Europeanised,"[78] i.e., they had adopted a willingness to consider participating in joint ventures. Second, by contrast to their US rivals, the three major Japanese liner companies (NYK, MOL and K-Line) no longer tolerated being restrained by all-Japan agreements such as those that existed on the Japan-US West and East Coast services and were desirous of entering into alternative international arrangements.[79] In addition, they were buoyed by the prospects of an upturn which, indeed, eventuated in 1991.[80] Probably the biggest surprise to come out of the melting pot was the teaming up of P&O, which left TRIO to do so, with the fiercely independent Maersk. This alliance came after P&O had rejected a similar agreement with Ben Line, which would have united the British sector of TRIO but left P&O short of its desired aim to offer two sailings each week from both ends of the long line. In conjunction with Maersk, however, the required capacity was achieved. An alliance of a similar kind, but with less capacity, was concluded shortly afterwards by Sea-Land, which only a few years previously had entered the trade, thus adding the third ocean to its network, and Korean newcomer HMM, the shipping arm of the giant Hyundai conglomerate.[81]

TRIO lost another member as a direct result of the break-up of Scandutch, in which the relationship between Nedlloyd and its Scandinavian partners had gradually deteriorated.[82] Realignment became guaranteed when the Danish member, East Asiatic Co., in June 1990 took over the interests of its Scandinavian partners, Transatlantic and Wilh. Wilhelmsen, and became the single largest operator.[83] Too small yet to manage on its own, EAC soon afterwards allied itself with Ben Line, whose welcome in TRIO had evidently come to an end, in a sixty-six/thirty-four-percent joint venture, EacBen. In July 1992, however, Ben withdrew from the trade, explaining that it was simply too small a player to continue. EAC used the opportunity to obtain further rationalisation, but to no avail. Simply too small for the trade and with little or no prospects to return to prosperity, a year later it was sold by its parent company

---

[78]*Containerisation International Yearbook* (1991), 5.

[79]"Pacific Revival: Japanese Carriers Seek Separate Routes," *Containerisation International* (June 1989), 47-51.

[80]*Fairplay*, 28 May 1992, 10.

[81]*Ibid.*

[82]*Lloyd's Maritime Asia* (November 1989), 11.

[83]*Fairplay*, 21 June 1990, 35.

to Maersk – which thus became the uncontested "national" carrier of Denmark.[84] As a result of these reshuffles, four long-established companies had disappeared from the trade, which was left with two unstable rump consortia, TRIO Mark 2 (Hapag-Lloyd, NYK and MOL) and ScanDutch Mark 2 (Nedlloyd, CGM and MISC). Their respective sources of weakness, however, were of a quite different nature. While TRIO 2 still had considerable capacity available, the renewed rivalry between NYK and Mitsui-OSK was bound to destroy the consortium from within. Scandutch 2, by contrast, was weak in all its links: Nedlloyd's financial losses resulting from its premature embracing of the total logistics doctrine; CGM's single-ship contribution, rudderless direction and continuous financial haemorrhaging; and MISC's modest capacity. CGM actually withdrew from the East Asian trade in 1994, two years after it left the North Atlantic, selling its rights on a fifty-fifty basis to Nedlloyd and MISC and leaving those two companies in a very awkward position.

Significant developments also took place outside the conference consortia, including the aforementioned Sea-Land/HMM consortium. In June 1990, the partnership between the two Korean companies, Hanjin and Cho Yang, which had been forced on them by the Korean Maritime and Ports Authority, broke up. Hanjin was very much the larger of the two and was loathe to be restrained. It was ambitious to strike out its own path by establishing a post-Panamax pendulum service linking Europe-East Asia-US West Coast, rather similar to what Taiwan's second line, Yang Ming, was inaugurating.[85] Cho Yang, too small to stand on its own, in turn joined the new all-German consortium DSR-Senator in its round-the-world service. With that support at its back, it also possessed a platform for expansion which in turn became of vital importance for the health of the new alliance, Tricontinental Services (TriCon), and the ambition of its founder, Karl-Heinz Sager, to create a weekly service in both directions.[86] The Senator Line, established with the support of a group of German investors which included the long-suffering city of Bremen, had run up heavy losses in its first years, while the DSR (Deutsche Seereederei Rostock) was the former state-owned shipping company of East Germany; it which was going through several painful years of privatisation.[87] Ironically, but not unexpectedly, only several years later Hanjin and TriCon found each other again in a much

---

[84]In fact, the position of Maersk within Denmark is much more than that, but the subject falls outside the scope of this work.

[85]*Lloyd's Maritime Asia* (July 1990), 17.

[86]*Containerisation International* (December 1991), 39-43.

[87]On DSR-Senator, see http://www.svz.de/cgi-bin/aglimpse/ 33?query=DSR-Senator.

happier embrace, which in the late 1990s was to make them one of the big six in the business.

The purpose, it may be repeated, of all consortia was to offer greater frequency of services and choice of ports than could be achieved by most individual companies, Evergreen and Maersk excepted. The weekly sailing was gradually replaced with a bi-weekly service as the new standard of the trade. Fast direct links between as many ports as possible and fixed-day sailings became other benchmarks of service quality. But, in a vicious circle akin and very closely related to that of the tonnage surplus, the quest for ever-higher frequencies and ever-denser networks was never satisfied. As Maersk's Hong Kong manager explained the *raison-d'être* of his company's sixth transpacific string, which included a direct Hong Kong-Long Beach leg, timing had come down to an extremely fine art:[88]

> Our service offers a late weekend cut-off in Hong Kong.
> Normal time for this is Saturday 2300 hours, but we do have
> a late cut-off which is Sunday 1200 hours. Shippers in Hong
> Kong value this because it allows up to one extra day for
> production and still connects to an end week sailing.

It was market forces like these that provided the dynamics for further rationalis-ation and intensification of networks and the service capacity of individual firms.

By the beginning of 1990, the disastrous trading conditions on the North Pacific demonstrated that, although TWRA and ANERA had not been entirely inefficacious in restraining expansion, there was a clear limit to what such agreements could achieve for individual companies. The only solution became the formation of slot-sharing consortia. The first to join were NYK, Nippon Liner System (the result of the merger between Yamashita Shinnihon and Japan Line) and NOL, which thus gained vastly improved access to each other's regions and the US West Coast with its intermodal network into the central and eastern sections. Interestingly, NOL did not see the transpacific route as the most profitable way to New York, and in 1991 the company opened a direct route from Singapore, the Asia East Coast Express, but not as was customary via Panama but rather through the Suez Canal.[89] Maersk demonstrated that its isolation was not a matter of principle but of strategy, as it concluded a slot-sharing agreement with "Europeanised" Sea-Land. Developments in Japan then followed quickly. NYK swallowed its minor partner, Nippon Liner System, and five days later MOL and K-Line, which had both broken loose from the all-Japan

---

[88]Quoted in *Lloyd's Maritime Asia* (June 1993), 10.

[89]"NOL 30 Years," 56; and *Containerisation International* (June 1998), 62-63.

mould in the late 1980s, teamed up. In view of earlier statements to the contrary and great contrasts in operations and philosophy, their reunion came as a considerable surprise. Still, it underlined the need to combine forces to compete with NYK-NOL and to maintain market share.[90]

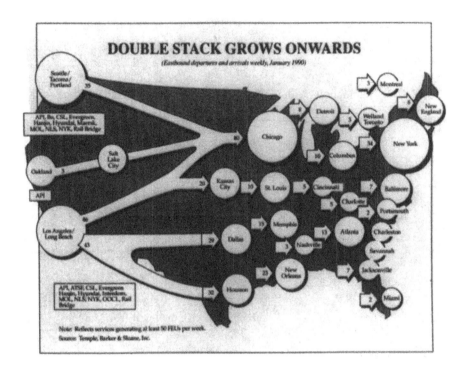

Figure 13:   Intermodalism quickly broke through: weekly stack-train services, 1990.

Source: *Lloyd's Maritime Asia* (September 1990).

---

[90]*Lloyd's Maritime Asia* (June 1991), 29.

While many doubted whether the K-Line/MOL combination could long survive, a new consortium was planned that would within a few years create the greatest shake-up yet seen in the container industry. The key to these new developments was the rejuvenation of Hapag-Lloyd as a container shipping company through the vast profits generated in its tourism and aviation sectors. Having gained new shareholders who saw the company as a way to cash in on the insatiable "wanderlust" of the German people, Hapag-Lloyd between 1989 and 1992 was able to invest, "without tears," some DM two billion (US $1.2 billion) in new aircraft, computer systems and, most important, eight 4400-TEU Panamax container ships.[91] In the first instance these were intended to give the company strength in the Europe-East Asia trade, but their restrained beam gave Hapag-Lloyd the flexibility to employ them anywhere, including on round-the-world voyages. As MOL and NYK had become implacable opponents, Hapag-Lloyd could now make use of the opportunity offered by the imminent demise of TRIO 2. Negotiations with NYK quickly led to an understanding, and a full agreement was signed in September 1992 with NYK and its Pacific partner, NOL.[92]

The NYK/NOL/Hapag-Lloyd agreement marked a milestone in the development of container shipping in the 1990s. While the previous consortia had been restricted to a single route, the new alliance was global. In its span and ambitions it transcended all that had existed before. It included all three continents, as it covered both the Asia-US West Coast and Europe-US East Coast routes. Through slot-chartering, Hapag-Lloyd returned to the Pacific and also gained access to the intermodal systems of NYK and NOL in America, while it offered the same service to its Asian partners on the Atlantic. In 1994, Hapag-Lloyd and NYK joined NOL's highly successful service from East Asia to New York, which *en route* also captured a significant share of South Asian exports. The direct Europe-East Asia route remained out of reach until the expiry of the ACE consortium to which NOL belonged; it was included from January 1996. As if this was not enough, in late 1995 the consortium was joined by P&O, which earlier had pulled out of its arrangements with Maersk. To emphasise the importance of their agreement, the new four-company coalition was called the "Grand Alliance." With a capacity of some 360,000 TEUs, and linking the premier container lines from Japan, Singapore, Germany and Britain, it represented an unprecedented concentration of power, with two equally strong leg positions in East Asia and Europe. The time of global strategies had well and truly arrived.

---

[91]Wiborg and Wiborg, *150 Years Hapag-Lloyd*, 396-399. The company was also able to buy back its head office on the Ballindamm.

[92]*Ibid.*, 405-406.

If 1984 had been the "year of the entrepreneur," 1994 was the year of the alliance. The formation and implementation of the NYK/NOL/Hapag-Lloyd mega-consortium had acted as a catalyst in shipping diplomacy and led to the creation of new combinations of global coverage and much greater capacity and geographic span than any previous consortia. Maersk, alone again after P&O's departure, rapidly developed links with Sea-Land, and by May 1995 the two companies operated their "Worldwide Alliance" on the Atlantic and Pacific and shared services around Latin America, the Middle East and Europe. In May 1996, they closed the gap in their global web with their own joint Europe-East Asia service, thus giving Sea-Land its third ocean.[93]

In 1994, in direct opposition to these two groups, another five companies joined together in what was called the "Global Alliance:" APL, OOCL, MOL, and Nedlloyd, with MISC cooperating on the Asia-Europe route.[94] The Global Alliance not only introduced intermodal pioneer APL to the Europe-East Asia and transatlantic trades but also testified to the total disintegration of the previous consortium system, with Nedlloyd and MISC representing the last surviving partners of Scandutch and MOL and OOCL the latest defectors from TRIO and ACE, respectively.

Finally, the fourth alliance resulted from the *rapprochement* of Hanjin and Cho Yang in its TriCon consortium with DSR-Senator. For the time being no new identity was created, but by 1998, after Hanjin had taken over seventy percent of DSR-Senator's shares and the United Arab Shipping Corporation had joined as a further member, the new group became known as the United Alliance.[95]

Alliances were a qualitative as well as a quantitative step forward to greater consolidation. They represented much more than just the enlargement of scale achieved in consortia, as cooperation between partners was not restricted to a single service but applied to the Europe-East Asia and transpacific trades; from early 2000 they also began to include the North Atlantic. They set out to reduce costs and rationalise maritime and shore resources to an unprecedented degree. Their formation was also inspired by the necessity of offering their global customers (like Sony, Volkswagen, Union Carbide or Heineken) assurances of efficiency and quality of service on global networks with greater choice of sailings, destinations, direct connections, forward intermodal connections and many other value-adding services. Only a greater bundling of forces could achieve such comprehensive logistics packets while maintaining the

---

[93]*Fairplay*, 25 May 1995, 6.

[94]Originally, CGM also was included, but the troubled French line withdrew before the alliance started operations.

[95]On UASC see http://38.15.18.26/news.html [written early in 1998].

individual identity of alliance partners which continued to market themselves separately but had access to all vessels of their chosen alliance. The Grand Alliance, for example, offered four different services from Europe to Singapore and East Asia, including three sailings from Rotterdam, Hamburg and Southampton, two from Le Havre and one each from Antwerp and Bremerhaven.[96] On the Pacific the big alliances could operate up to six loops, including a greater variety of ports and opening the prospects of daily services for some major ports. Maersk went one better, as table 8 shows.

Table 8
Main Line Services of Maersk Line, June 1997

Route	Frequency	Partner(s)
Asia-Europe	4 per week	Sea-Land
Asia-USA	7 per week	Sea-Land
Europe-USA	4 per week	Sea-Land, P&ONL, OOCL
Asia-Middle East	1 per week	Sea-Land

Source: *Containerisation International* (July 1997), 46.

The sheer size of the competition broke COSCO's isolation when it teamed up with K-Line, which had been left alone after the great realignment. The compelling commercial logic of the alliance system applied to all but the biggest and most individualistic. Only Evergreen entered no main-line alliances, although it did join a number of minor consortia,[97] and those of the top twenty that had been left out of the global alliances scrambled to team up, often in different combinations on various oceans. In the Europe-East Asia trade, for example, K-Line joined Yang Ming, and Hyundai paired with the two Swiss lines, MSC and Norasia. In the process, another set of Asian carriers outside the big alliances – COSCO, Yang Ming and K-Line – went global and opened discount services on the North Atlantic, thus adding to that region's financial woes.[98] But as *Fairplay* put it in August 1996, "Getting that 'third ocean' is a goal every liner operator is pursuing right now, representing the great leap

---

[96]Michel Neumeister, "Extrême orient: l'axe majeur," *Journal de la marine marchande*, 11 October 1996.

[97]In this context, it is relevant to mention that strong differences of opinion existed between Evergreen's founder, Chang Yung-fa, and his eldest son and heir-apparent, Chang Kuo-hua, who subsequently resigned from the company (*ibid*. [October 1998], 11).

[98]*Fairplay*, 29 May 1997.

towards a global service."[99] K-Line (Europe)'s CEO, Mitsuo Mori, explained that it was the pressure from major trans-national shippers, who wanted "global packages," that made network globalisation attractive for his company.[100]

The emergence of the alliance system did not end specialised consortia. On the contrary, on secondary routes and within regional networks it remained the indispensable method to establish new services and create capacity, frequency and flexibility. In some cases, members of opposite alliances could find each other, while elsewhere otherwise fiercely-independent operators teamed up, and there was also the opportunity for small players to get the necessary leg-up. A good example of the continued usefulness of the consortium was that formed in early 1999 by Yang Ming, Zim and the Shipping Corporation of India for the direct India-to-Europe trade, which until then had languished as much as the SCI itself.[101] Zim, although never prepared to ally itself globally or even regionally to one partner, maintained and expanded its network mainly through the agency of consortia.[102] From a political viewpoint, the consortium formed by COSCO, Evergreen and Yang Ming for the trade between East Asia, South Africa and the East Coast of South America is particularly interesting, but not surprising after the opening of the direct trade between Taiwan and mainland China in 1998.[103]

Larger Ships, Mega-Mergers and Further Concentration of Power

Alliances, consortia and globalisation, however, did not achieve the final configuration and optimal level of magnitude in the trade because sudden quantum leaps were made in two other variables, ship capacity and the size of the individual firm. The size of the largest, post-Panamax container ships had been gradually creeping up toward 5000 TEU when in early 1996 Maersk revealed that the first of its new series of twelve vessels, *Regina Maersk*, had a 6000-TEU capacity. Six months later it became known that P&O had ordered a new series of ships exceeding 6600 TEU. The imminent arrival of such gigantic ships caused much excitement and speculation, and it was with a sigh of relief that the market in October 1996 received the unexpected announcement of a merger

---

[99]*Ibid.*, 29 August 1996, 11. Cf. *Lloyd's List* (April 1993), Containerisation Supplement, 5: "One of the 'buzz' words in the container shipping sector at present is 'globalisation.'"

[100]*Containerisation International* (October 1997), 40.

[101]*Fairplay*, 25 February 1999, 12.

[102]*Containerisation International* (June 1997), 56-57.

[103]*Ibid.* (June 1999), 10.

between the container divisions of P&O and Nedlloyd. The new British-Dutch company (*à la* Royal Dutch Shell or Unilever) possessed the largest individual container fleet in the world. This move was justified by the expectation of savings on the order of US $200 million per year and a guarantee of the survival of both companies. Nedlloyd's financial position was difficult after disappointing results for 1995 and, as Sterling explained later, the P&O Group could not continue to support its under-performing container division.[104] The merger, in short, gave hope to the "long suffering shareholders" of both companies that their fortunes might finally be reversed.[105] Within weeks P&O Nedlloyd negotiated a credit facility to the tune of US $1 billion.[106]

Figure 14:   The first of the "super" carriers, *Regina Maersk* (6000 TEU, 1996).

Source: Courtesy Maersk Sealand.

But while the P&O Nedlloyd merger was of considerable and immediate benefit to both partners in their competition with low-cost competitors and market leaders Maersk and Evergreen, it only moved instability onto a higher level because the two partners were members of opposite alliances; realignments would

---

[104]"Coping with Weaker Market," *Shipping Times*, 20 April 1998.

[105]*Containerisation International* (October 1996), 3.

[106]*Fairplay*, 5 December 1996, 7.

be inevitable. One insider's view, that "Chaos threatens liner trades,"[107] succinctly summed up the state of affairs. Before any alliance realignments were undertaken, the suggestion that the industry-wide process of rationalisation was entering a new phase driven by mergers was confirmed by a second bombshell.

In April 1997 Singapore-based (and Global Alliance member) NOL announced it was taking over Grand Alliance member American President Lines. Paying US $825 million, a forty-seven-percent premium over APL's current market price, NOL swallowed a company that owned about double its tonnage of container vessels. Equally important, it acquired a highly-regarded American company with a prestigious brand name, sophisticated electronic data systems, an extensive logistics network both in the USA and, in cooperation with TMM, on the west coast of Latin America.[108] Significantly, NOL dropped its own name from its container operations and replaced it with that of APL. NOL's strategy was splendid, but the premium paid (which forced it to increase its gearing ratio from two-to-one to 3.9-to-one) raised many questions. NOL chairman Herman Hochstadt claimed that he had acted to protect his relatively small company but also acknowledged that he had been inspired in his decision by the P&O-Nedlloyd merger.[109] A factor of considerable importance in his thinking was that Singapore's home market was too small a base for a mega-carrier and that only a larger identity could bring security.

With survival at stake, it soon transpired that Hochstadt had bitten off far more than he could chew. The promised economies of scale did not materialise; instead, losses and debts mounted. Assets had to be sold, including APL's much-vaunted intermodal operations in the USA. New equity capital had to be raised. NOL sailed on "a sea of red ink," losing US $258 million in 1998, and at the end of the year its total group borrowing stood at about US $5 billion, a gearing ratio of 14.6 to one.[110] Significantly, NOL's new CEO, Flemming Jacobs, was a man with thirty-nine years' experience at Maersk, including two years as regional manager in Singapore.

Driven by the two mergers, the great alliance realignment was finalised in early 1998 with the surprising switch of OOCL to the Grand Alliance and the formal and full-scale inclusion of Yang Ming and Hyundai, which had already

---

[107]*Ibid.*, 2 January 1997, 17.

[108]*Fairplay*, 24 April and 1 May 1997, 13. TMM reportedly was also interested in buying parts of the soon-to-be-privatized Mexican railways, thus enabling it to become the intermodal leader "south of the border;" *Ibid.*, 4 July 1996, 5.

[109]*Fairplay*, 24 April 1997, 18.

[110]*Ibid.*, 8 July 1999, 14-15. Container shipping accounted for about seventy percent of NOL's total shipping activity.

signed a far-reaching slot agreement with the Global Alliance for the transpacific and Asia-Europe routes.[111] How much the concentration of power was advanced by the new configuration, which also included the renaming of the largely transformed Global Alliance, became evident when the fog lifted (see table 9).

Table 9
Membership of the Two Major Container Shipping Alliances, 1999
(with company capacity, as per 1 January 1999)

Grand Alliance	P&O Nedlloyd	UK/NL	263,248 TEU
	NYK	Japan	164,331
	Hapag-Lloyd	Germany	100,216
	OOCL	Hong Kong	90,944
	Total capacity		618,739 TEU
New World Alliance	NOL/APL	Singapore	198,163
	MOL	Japan	129,210
	Hyundai	Korea	109,192
	Total capacity		436,475 TEU

Source: See text.

With an increase of 250,000 TEU over its capacity of 1995, the Grand Alliance in its most recent composition demonstrated just how desperate the quest for economies of scale had become. The capacity of Maersk and Sea-Land rose during the same period from about 350,000 to 587,500 TEUs, an equally formidable jump. Hanjin and DSR-Senator, which in 1998 carried through their own merger, advanced less forcefully, yet still grew from about 150,000 to 233,000 TEUs.

With the P&O Nedlloyd, NOL/APL and Hanjin/DSR-Senator mergers, a significant new phase of structural reorganisation of the container shipping industry began in which takeovers became a prominent method for consolidation and expansion. Consolidation through mergers and takeovers had been an integral part of the liner-shipping scene from its very beginnings, but from the mid-1990s they assumed unprecedented importance as they constituted a strategy for concentration of power, network intensification and growth which did not add to the industry's overcapacity. In this, container shipping merely followed the

---

[111]*Asian Shipping* (August 1997), 8.

example of many other sectors of the global economy, such as oil, banking, automobile manufacturing, media and accountancy. This, it must be stressed, did not mean that shipping executives put a halt to the growth of their own firms. On the contrary, as table 10 shows, all major companies, with the single exception of languishing Sea-Land, followed that path, as the top twenty companies increased their capacity by between fifteen and over 100 percent. It was, of course, the tearaway pace of Maersk and Evergreen that set the standards for the industry and, by doing so, forced others into their takeover strategies.

These tendencies were further strengthened by significant shifts in the cost structure of container shipping. With rising investments in ships, port and other land-based facilities, and computer systems, and relatively lower costs for fuel, personnel and port-handling charges, the proportion of fixed to variable costs was estimated to have moved from fifty-fifty to as high as ninety-ten.[112] Although mostly caused by the structural dynamics of the container shipping industry, as was also shown by Hanjin's takeover of DSR-Senator,[113] the current fashion for privatisation provided additional opportunities in several countries, notably France, Italy and Australia. It should be stressed, though, that privatisation does not inevitably lead to mergers or foreign takeovers, as is testified by the case of Yang Ming. Between 1994 and 1996 the Taiwan government reduced its stake from 100 percent to forty-eight percent with highly positive results for the company.[114]

Some of the earliest and most interesting examples of expansion-through-takeover strategies were adopted by niche players and north-south operators. Perhaps the most striking case was that of CP Ships, the London-based subsidiary of the Calgary-based Canadian Pacific conglomerate. During the 1980s, CP Ships was one of the real minnows on the North Atlantic trade. But capitalising on the intermodal strength of its railroad network and its Montréal container terminal, it moved heavily into shipping after 1990.[115] First it bought out its partners in Canada Maritime (successor to Dart, the original Montréal-

---

[112]Hoffmann, "Concentration in Liner Shipping," section IID. This should not be taken to mean that shipping companies are no longer vulnerable to sharp increases in bunkering charges.

[113]An interesting insight into the connections between DSR-Senator, Bremen and the German shipping tax laws is given in *Fairplay*, 8 July 1999, 17. One of the side-products of the company's crisis was the enforced departure of its initiator and container pioneer, Karl-Heinz Sager.

[114]*Containerisation International* (August 1996), 21.

[115]A brief overview of the growth of CP Ships is given on its website (http://www.cp.ca/cp/e/div) [1998].

Europe consortium) and took over Cast, the Canadian conbulker operator. This enabled it to achieve considerable economies of scale and in 1996 to become the largest single operator on the North Atlantic.[116] In 1997, CP Ships went international with the purchases of the US-based Lykes Lines and Contship, a lively newcomer with a global network and brightly painted vessels.[117] It then expanded its interests into South America and Australia, taking over the Norwegian Ivaran Line, which added services between the USA and the Caribbean and South America, and the Australia New Zealand Direct Line between the US West Coast and Australasia, which complemented Contship's services in this region. In July 1998 CP Ships concluded an agreement with Latin America's largest intermodal operator, TMM, in which TMM's container operations and those of Lykes and Ivaran were combined in a new company, Americana Ships.[118] CP Ships initially was careful not to approach the east-west main lines, but eventually it was drawn into the main pool and in July 2000 Americana entered the North Atlantic as partner of the Grand Alliance.[119]

On a smaller scale, but within a geographically rather similar context, the German line Hamburg-Süd acted like CP Ships. In the early 1990s it had mopped up a number of small West European lines in the South American trades, including Furness Withy, which it bought from OOCL.[120] Still too small to stand alone, Hamburg-Süd in 1996 became subject to a takeover bid from Hapag-Lloyd, but negotiations showed the incompatibility of the two companies and their leaders. Hamburg-Süd then decided that attack was the best means of defence. Making use of the financial resources of its mother concern, the Oetker Group, it went on a shopping spree, adding in quick succession to its existing

---

[116]*Fairplay*, 1 February 1996, 21.

[117]*Containerisation International* (September 1995), 54-58: and *Fairplay*, 21 August 1997; and 6 November 1997, 7; Contship operated services Europe-Australasia, Europe-Middle East-India; round-the-world, Mediterranean-Gulf of Mexico, and North Europe-East Coast Latin America. Contship was (and still is) the only company managed by a woman, Cecilia Battistello.

[118]"CP Ships, TMM Form US $1b Joint Venture," *Shipping Times*, 30 July 1998. TMM, a short time previously had gobbled up Colombia's Flota Mercante Grancolombiana (*Fairplay*, 12 December 1996, 13); for assessments of the CP Ships conglomerate, see *Containerisation International* (December 1997), 42-43; (September 1998), 47-49 and 55-57; and (April 1999), 65-69.

[119]*Shipping Times Online*, 21 April 2000, "Grand Alliance in Deal to Operate on Transatlantic Trade;" and *Fairplay*, 18 May 2000, 18.

[120]*Fairplay*, 1 November 1990, 6; the purchase included agencies on the west and east coasts of Latin America.

interests in the South American and US-Australian trades the Brazilian companies Aliança and Transroll, the South American lines of US operator Crowley, South Seas Steamship Lines and the San Francisco-based South Pacific Container Line.[121] Working in close cooperation with Chile's CSAV (Latin America's largest independent shipping company), Hamburg-Süd built up a strong network that offered "an unparalleled level of service between the Pacific Islands, the west coast of the United States and Australia and New Zealand"[122] – a perfect description of a niche operator. At least for the time being, the company appears to have found profitability and security.

Figure 15:   An OOCL stack-train traverses the USA.

Source: OOCL website (http://www.oocl.com).

---

[121]*Ibid.*, 7 May 1992, 13; 11 May 1995, 6; 27 August 1998, 49; 8 July 1999; and 29 September 1999. See also *Australasian Ships and Ports* (November 1999), 19.

[122]*Australasian Ships and Ports* (November 1999), 19.

The takeover activity in the north-south trades to some extent was a direct consequence of the concentration of power on the east-west main lines. As capacities of individual ships, companies and alliances grew, they invaded the regions they served by establishing their own feeder services. CMA-CGM, for example, in Europe operated a weekly service between its northwest European ports and St. Petersburg, Tallinn and Riga, and in Southeast Asia one between Singapore and Vietnamese ports.[123] Not satisfied with these short-sea "trawling" operations, the majors soon also entered the major north-south routes, such as those covering the South American East and West coasts, the Caribbean, and East and/or South Africa in order to fill their slots.[124]

The Australian trade, one of the highlights of the pioneering phase of containerisation, began to be turned into a regional operation feeding into hubs like Singapore with its few remaining direct links under the control of niche operators. MSC went one step further by opening an Auckland-Melbourne mini-relay service to feed into its Australia/New Zealand-Singapore line.[125] This north-south expansion of main-line operators was illustrated, above all, by Maersk's purchase in early 1999 of South Africa's Safmarine Container Line. This company had only shortly before taken over the East African-Indian Ocean network of CMB,[126] aiming to construct a solid niche network. But despite its size, some 56,000 TEU, it had no adequate defence once Maersk showed its interest and was prepared to pay US $240 million.[127] Only partially in the container sector, but displaying the same inexorable financial logic, was the Scandinavian merger, effective from 1 July 1999, of RoRo operators and specialist car carriers Wilhelmsen and Wallenius.

Privatisation in those countries that still possessed state-owned fleets created additional opportunities for national and international corporate power plays. It was immediately responsible for the more traditional takeover of long-suffering CGM by its young and ambitious private rival, CMA, for the paltry

---

[123]*Containerisation International* (August 1998), 46; and (January 1999), 9.

[124]Highly informative on this issue is Hoffmann, "Concentration in Liner Shipping," section F.

[125]*Fairplay Daily News*, 29 November 1999.

[126]For the rapid decline of CMB's liner interests see Devos and Elewaut, *CMB 100*, 271-276. After a reorganisation in the mid-1990s CMB had been renamed CMB Transport (CMBT).

[127]*Fairplay Daily News*, 11 February 1999.

price of about US $4 million.[128] CGM had lurched from crisis to crisis until the French government in 1996 finally cut the Gordian knot by deciding to privatise its merchant fleet. Combining the best of old and new proved an arduous task made all the more difficult by a bitter feud between CMA's leaders, the brothers Jacques and Johnny Saade. Yet, the evidence suggests that France, once again, had not just a major shipping operator but also one that was profitable.[129] That the engine of the new company turned in Marseilles was evident from the beginning and sealed by the closure a few years later of the CGM head office in Paris. Initially aiming especially at the Asian and Australian trades, it was the surprise buyer of the Australian National Line, which ended Canberra's seemingly interminable privatisation saga.[130] While P&O Nedlloyd, after its purchase of ANL's rights in the Europe-Australia trade,[131] had lost interest in the ailing Australian company, by picking up Blue Star Line and New Zealand's Tasman Express Line it effectively strengthened its position in Australia's refrigerated trades.[132]

The privatisation of the Italian state-owned holding company Finmare was responsible for enmeshing Evergreen in the takeover scene, as it bought the entire fleet and operations of Lloyd Triestino, the oldest steamship company in Europe and the world.[133] Evergreen had already collaborated closely for several years with the Italian company but, despite the great differences in corporate culture of the two companies, regarded complete control as absolutely indispensable. Only after the takeover, however, did Evergreen discover just how deep Lloyd Triestino's problems had been; as Chang Yung-fa later admitted, "it was a booby prize."[134] But Chang immediately set out to make his purchase a success by abandoning Lloyd Triestino's direct Europe-Australia service with P&O

---

[128]*Fairplay*, 31 October 1996, 9; and *Containerisation International* (September 1997), 65-69; and (August 1998), 45-47.

[129]*Fairplay*, 8 April 1999, 14.

[130]*Shipping Times Online*, 26 October 1999, quoting *Journal of Commerce*, 25 October 1999.

[131]*Containerisation International* (February 1996), 15.

[132]"P&O Nedlloyd buys UK's Blue Star Line for US $60 million," *Shipping Times*, 10 February 1998; and *Fairplay*, 4 March 1999, 20-21.

[133]*Fairplay*, 30 July 1998. Lloyd Triestino had been founded in 1836 as the Austrian Lloyd and became Italian after World War I.

[134]*Ibid.*, 28 October 1999, 4.

Nedlloyd in favour of the establishment of lines feeding west and east Australian cargoes for transshipment into Singapore.[135]

While this service restructuring was a prime example of the strengthening of east-west traffic resulting from the expanding power of a leading operator, Evergreen also was flexible enough to acknowledge that the brand name Lloyd Triestino was still a valuable asset. Rather than absorbing the Trieste company into its own corporate identity, it actually began moving some thirty to forty vessels from its own fleet to Lloyd Triestino. Evergreen also used its new Italian arm to establish a slot-charter agreement with Mediterranean SC on the Europe-South Africa run, thus terminating Lloyd Triestino's connection with Safmarine after its takeover by Maersk. It also fuelled speculation that Evergreen might contemplate a global slot arrangement with MSC, which would lift concentration in the industry by another notch. It should be noted, too, that at the same time that Evergreen announced the transfer of ships to Lloyd Triestino, it also revealed plans to order another twenty-five vessels measuring 90,000 TEUs.[136]

In July 1999 came the last and, until now, largest takeover when Maersk bought the international operations of Sea-Land from its parent, CSX, for what was generally regarded as a relatively low US $800 million.[137] But CSX kept a number of overseas terminals and its domestic shipping interests; these were subsequently renamed CSX Lines. Although not unexpected, as rumours had been circulating since the NOL/APL merger, the sheer size of the new company – with a capacity of close to 600,000 TEUs – set new standards for the industry.

In many ways a "natural development" of the close relationship that already existed between the two companies, it confirmed not just the scope of Maersk's ambitions but that it also still believed that considerable cost reductions could still be achieved through the integration and rationalisation of the new company. Moreover, one of Maersk's partners claimed that "Maersk-Sea-Land will offer a wide range of services unmatched in the industry, for the benefit of our customers worldwide."[138] The purchase of Sea-Land also confirmed the validity of an earlier statement made by Thomas Anderson, managing director of Maersk UK, in which he expressed his company's ambitions and driving force to be "ever larger ships and further company mergers or take-overs...in order to

---

[135]InforMare, Press Release, 31 December 1998, quoting *Shipping Times*.

[136]*Fairplay*, 4 November 1999, 16; for an extensive review see *ibid.*, 11 November 1999, 22-26.

[137]*Lloyd's List*, 23 July 1999, 1; *Shipping Times*, 26 July 1999; and *Fairplay Daily News*, 23 July 1999.

[138]Quoted in *Shipping Times*, 26 July 1999. In early 2000, to the horror of traditionalists, Maersk simplified the name of the new combination to Maersk Sealand.

service the increasing number of global customers."[139] Chris Bourne, Mitsui-OSK's European managing director, also foresaw the number of global carriers diminishing to ten to fifteen through rationalisation, emphasising the importance of the bottom line: "Volumes are going up; profitability is going down. It is essential to make money."[140] Bourne's boss, MOL President Masaharu Ikuta, soon clarified that MOL believed that, although he did not rule out mergers if a good opportunity offered itself, at the time he preferred alliances as instruments for cost cutting; after all, "size does not matter, what we seek is profit."[141]

Table 10
Top Twenty Container Operators, 1 January 1999

Rank (1995)	Name	Country	Capacity in TEU
1. (2)	Maersk*	Denmark	378,205
2. (3)	Evergreen*	Taiwan	297,030
3. (8,7)	P&O Nedlloyd*	UK/Netherlands	263,248
4. (9,15)	Hanjin*/DSR-Senator*	Korea/Germany	232,911
5. (4)	COSCO	China	227,137
6. (1)	Sea-Land*	USA	209,226
7. (11)	Mediterranean SC*	Switzerland	199,226
8. (18,10)	NOL*/APL*	Singapore	198,163
9. (5)	NYK*	Japan	164,311
10. (-)	CP Ships*/TMM	Canada/Mexico	139,085
11. (6)	MOL*	Japan	129,210
12. (20,-)	CMA/CGM*	France	115,843
13. (14)	Zim*	Israel	113,673
14. (19)	Hyundai*	Korea	109,192
15. (12)	K-Line	Japan	105,643
16. (16)	Yang Ming*	Taiwan	101,094
17. (13)	Hapag-Lloyd	Germany	100,216
18. (17)	OOCL*	Hong Kong	90,944
19. (21)	UASC	Arab Gulf states	68,553
20. (25)	Wan Hai*	Taiwan	56,194

Note: * denotes companies whose container vessels carry double names, beginning or ending with the company name (e. g., ss *Maersk, Ever xx, Hanjin yy, Ming zz*).

Source: *Fairplay Container Operators Yearbook 1996*, 2.

---

[139]*Fairplay*, 24 April 1997, 5. It is only fair to relate a rival's comment: "[but] even Maersk has to face up to its costs." (Angiolino Vignodelli, CEO of Lloyd Triestino, quoted in *ibid.*, 26 June 1997, 39).

[140]*Ibid.*, 25 March 1999, 64.

[141]*Containerisation International* (August 1999), 10.

The results of the concentration process are, above all, visible in the rankings and size of the top twenty container operators. While Maersk was the largest company in 1991 with a capacity of 117,418 TEU, eight years later no fewer than eleven companies surpassed that figure (see table 10).[142]

Even bearing in mind that Maersk's takeover of Safmarine and Sea-Land took place after the date of this table, the sheer power of the Danish company stands out, as does its meteoric rise. The effect of recent mergers is equally visible, including the emergence from nowhere of CP Ships, the only newcomer among the top eighteen, all of whose fleets dwarfed those of the 1980s. Despite Maersk's supremacy and P&O Nedlloyd's strong showing, the European Union accounted for only twenty-five percent of the world's TEU capacity, against thirty-four in 1985. Even sharper was the decline of the USA, from twenty-one to ten percent. This contrasted with the predominant position of East Asia, where eleven of the twenty companies were based, with an overall capacity share of fifty-eight percent, remarkably strong growth from the thirty-eight percent of 1985.[143] Another indication of the power of Asian carriers was that they carried about seventy percent of all Asia-Europe trade, over eighty percent of the containerised trade between Asia and the USA, and ninety percent of the Intra-Asian trade.[144] Within the East Asian sector, however, the relative position of all three Japanese lines had deteriorated sharply, as might be expected from their woeful financial results.

As the number of international mergers had demonstrated, however, nationality seemed to count for far less than previously. The increased use of flags of convenience, which in late 1994 had over thirty-five percent of total TEU capacity (see chapter 7) further emphasised the growing distance between operator and home country.[145] With their global networks and the increasing deregulation of maritime and inland transport, container operators could behave increasingly like trans-national corporations, whose loyalty was less to their home ports and nations than to their identity as global operators. K-Line America, for example, markets its image specifically as "not an American company, not a

---

[142]"Asian Share of Global Containership Fleet Slips," *Shipping Times*, 3 March 1999.

[143]Mercer Management Consulting and Partners, *Analysis of Supply and Demand of Shipping Services. First Interim Presentation* (London, 1996), 20.

[144]Hoffmann, "Concentration in Liner Shipping," Section I, B1.

[145]*Containerisation International* (February 1989), 23-27; and (March 1995), 53-55.

Japanese company, but an international company."[146] The same point was made in a different fashion when NOL removed limits on foreign shareholding and non-Singapore directors.[147]

Notably absent from the list of big companies were any of the former Soviet lines that in the late 1960s and 1970s had so alarmed shipowners and governments in the West. In the absence of a *rouble* tree to be shaken at will, Soviet – and other former East Bloc – lines had found it difficult to maintain their modest positions in the transition to fully-containerised traffic. The collapse of the USSR and the huge problems caused by privatisation decimated fleets (and made Russian seafarers into "crews of convenience"). The only company left with its strength more or less intact was Vladivostok-based FESCO, a fact which was due to its nature and operations more on an East Asian than a European model. In early 1999 the company became the subject of a fierce power struggle between the governor of the Primorsky region, Yevgeny Nazdratenko, and a group of foreign investors.[148] While the latter accused Nazdratenko of blackmail and illegal behaviour, the governor claimed he was attempting to protect Russia's interests by keeping FESCO, as Vladivostok's last surviving big company, under Russian control: "I can't watch indifferently how rapaciously and uncontrollably our fisheries companies, sea transport and mining industry are robbed."[149] For the time being FESCO, with an annual turnover of about US $300,000,000 and a fleet of some 22,000 TEU,[150] appears safe after Nazdratenko – a fierce Russian nationalist who increasingly orchestrated a Stalinesque personality cult – was able to maintain a majority on FESCO's board. The company did not lose its combativeness during troubled times, as the opening of the first direct service between Yantian, southern China and eastern Australia shows.[151]

---

[146]K-Line website (http://www.k-line.com/Company/news/notamer.htm), reprinted from *American Shipper* (November 1998).

[147]*Fairplay*, 18 November 1999, 13.

[148]This highly controversial affair is best followed through the columns of *Vladivostok News Online* (http://vlad.tribnet.com/1999).

[149]Quoted in *ibid.*, 18 June 1999.

[150]Fleet list in http://www.fesco.com.au (25 October 1999).

[151]Http://www.fesco.com/newsletter2.htm [1998].

The main "reality" of the global container shipping market in the "age of mega-competition"[152] remained a chronic tonnage surplus. Despite the rising volume of container traffic and the incidence of takeovers, huge newbuilding programmes maintained its structural overcapacity and depressed freight rates and company revenues.[153] When P&O Nedlloyd CEO, Tim Harris, in August 1999 revealed that average revenue per container for his company fell from over US $1500 in 1997 to US $1258 in the second quarter of 1999, it was clear that further economies of scale had to be made. Since the acquisition of other lines appeared to be the only strategy to increase capacity without adding to the global tonnage glut, observers speculated whether P&O Nedlloyd should make an offer for debt-ridden NOL, and/or first pick up Hapag-Lloyd, in order to match the huge power of Maersk/Safmarine/Sea-Land and the continued expansion of its own alliance partners. Economies of scale and network diversification must be pursued and, whether Harris wanted to or not, he was committed by circumstance. And so were the Japanese companies who must restructure in order to regain their influence. As *Fairplay* commented, "Despite their huge size, most container shipping giants have little control over their destiny."[154]

If the unspoken suggestion was "small can be beautiful again," this was strongly supported by Hapag-Lloyd's CEO, Bernd Wrede, who acknowledged that his company had been approached by several players.[155] But exactly because Hapag-Lloyd had been doing well in recent years, Wrede was adamant that "at the end of the day it has always been better to remain alone." Claiming that P&O Nedlloyd still was to make its first profit (in which he was patently wrong)[156] and that the NOL/APL merger had been little less than a financial *Titanic*, mergers *per se* were not his way. In February 2000, on the occasion of the naming ceremony of the first of a new seven-vessel series, Hapag-Lloyd's leaders returned to the theme that mega-mergers had "so far not been convincing,"[157] but they also suggested that their company might become predator rather than prey.

---

[152]Mitsui-OSK, "The Present Situation of Liner Shipping 1997/98" (http://www.mol.co.jp/JE3/e3/nenpo/frame.html).

[153]See the interview with MOL's president, Masaharu Ikuta, in *Fairplay*, 3 July 1997, 22-23, and C. Heideloff, B. Lemper and M. Zachcial, "Changing Times Ahead?" *Hansa*, CXXXV, No. 9 (September 1998), 12-14 and 17-19.

[154]*Fairplay*, 26 August 1999, 3.

[155]*Ibid.*, 23 September 1999, 3.

[156]See, e.g., *Fairplay Daily News*, 19 November 1998.

[157]*Shipping Times*, 21 February 2000.

In particular, Wrede acknowledged that "a stake in P&O Nedlloyd" might be "useful."[158] In a situation not dissimilar to that of Hapag-Lloyd, Japan's third and non-alliance company, K-Line, strongly restated its intention to avoid a takeover by ordering eight post-Panamax vessels.[159]

A day is a long time in container politics, as new developments soon showed. Both P&O Nedlloyd and NOL announced solid profit returns, thus removing lingering doubts about the financial wisdom of mega-mergers.[160] In April 2000 a landmark agreement was signed between the second and third largest combinations in the industry (New World and Maersk-Sealand) in preparation for the introduction of joint services on the North Atlantic.[161] With this pact, which in an ironic reversal of life-long hostility united the successor companies Sea-Land and APL, the alliance system now also entered the third east-west route.

The unprecedented concentration of power of the new super-alliance was countered only a few weeks later by the Grand Alliance, a clear sign that the vast scale of its operations had in no measure diminished its capacity to respond to market changes. In July it began its own Atlantic services. In a significant recognition of the need for even greater concentration of market power, this step was taken in association with CP's Americana Ships.[162] To the twelve loops the Grand Alliance operated on the two other main east-west routes it now added another five, "providing shippers with an extended range of direct port calls in Europe, the USA, Canada (Halifax), and Mexico." A series of "very detailed" schedules was announced for targeted express services between important port pairs and growth regions. And within the Grand Alliance P&O Nedlloyd soon began shifting the balance of power as in quick succession it mopped up two small companies, the US-based Farrell Lines and Harrison Lines, the last

---

[158]*Fairplay Daily News*, 24 February 2000.

[159]*Shipping Times Online*, 16 December 1999, "K Line Orders 8 post-Panamax Ships."

[160]*Fairplay*, 24 August 2000, 27; and 28 September 2000, 12.

[161]*Shipping Times Online*, 13 April 2000, "Shipping Alliances in Trans-Atlantic Pact;" and *Fairplay*, 24 August 2000, 5-6.

[162]Http://www.nyk.com/what/000420/000420.htm; http://www.ponl.com/news/news/n_04000c.htm, "Joint Press Release Issued by the Grand Alliance Members and Americana Ships;" and *Shipping Times Online*, 21 April 2000, "Grand Alliance in Deal to Operate on Transatlantic Trade."

surviving traditional British liner company.[163] At the same time, NYK increased its orders for post-Panamax tonnage. Hapag-Lloyd's future once again looked uncertain in an industry in which many observers expected further mergers and a reduction in the number of majors to perhaps twelve or fifteen.[164]

The comment about the "force of destiny" may also be made about the manner in which the character of shipping companies inexorably changed when their drive for enlargement of scale, rationalisation and quality control had consequences far beyond their seaborne operations. As they increasingly took charge of the entire door-to-door chain of transport and became total transport service providers, they discovered, somewhat to their consternation, that non-shipping expenses amounted to anywhere between forty and sixty percent of total costs and could occasionally run as high as seventy-five percent.[165] Control over inland-generated costs and their sources became crucially important.

One aspect of this vertical diversification was a significant increase in terminal investments and port operations to ensure the prompt handling of ships, the seamless transfer to intermodal railroad networks and other forms of inland transport, and the integration of feeder and mainline networks. In the USA intermodalism was confirmed as the indispensable foundation of door-to-door operations, as one major after another expanded inland – the sale of APL's railroad interests by NOL was an exception, caused by the financial stress of NOL's takeover. The growing pressure on services and costs also resulted in a first wave of mergers between Burlington Northern and Santa Fe (BNSF), Union Pacific and Southern Pacific, and Canadian National and Illinois Central, and the splitting up of Conrail by CSX and Norfolk Southern.[166] As at sea, here a mega-merger also followed, although at the moment of writing no definitive permission had as yet been given for the amalgamation of BNSF and Canadian National.

The vast increase in rail traffic showed the limits of the US system as a gridlock in October 1997 caused total paralysis and damage to shippers

---

[163]Http://www.ponl.com/news/news/h_06000a.htm, 6 June 2000; and P&O Nedlloyd, Press Release, 11 September 2000.

[164]For a dissenting view, see *Shipping Times Online*, 1 September 2000, "Limited Scope for Asian Mergers," in which it is plausibly argued that while the USA and Europe have already gone through their wave of consolidation, little chance exists of the same phenomenon striking Asian shipowners because there is little government willpower in either Japan or Korea to enforce mergers; Evergreen and Yang Ming are large enough to stand side-by-side in Taiwan; and COSCO, OOCL and NOL are healthy global players.

[165]Hoffmann, "Concentration in Liner Shipping," section III, E2; and Gilmore (ed.), *Brand Warriors*, 87.

[166]For a good overview, see *Containerisation International* (April 1999), 49-55.

estimated at some US $4 billion. It took almost a year before Union Pacific, the largest rail carrier, was released from federal oversight, and even then services in the west had not been returned to "uniformly improved levels."[167] During the 1990s, in both Canada and Mexico intermodalism, pushed by Canadian Pacific, APL and TMM made great progress, but outside North America national and/or private railway companies and operators did not provide anything comparable.[168] Both the Trans-Siberian and Australian transcontinental railways patently failed to lift their performance. And despite the formation of a single economic area, the European Union still has not progressed much further than the infant stages of an effective continental railway policy; the intermodal performance of its many rail operators has remained patchy.[169] National divisions and conservative attitudes remained strong. P&O Nedlloyd's director of continental operations, Greg Guthrie, who had experience running a shuttle service between Rotterdam and Milan, reserved his strongest criticism for the German *Bundesbahn*. This organisation, he claimed, was "bureaucratic, overmanned, riddled with practices which make no commercial sense and which seriously inhibit performance and are a burden on the state."[170] Guthrie's boss, Tim Harris, had been even more outspoken: "There is no continental railway worth speaking about."[171] It was left to individual shipping companies to explore opportunities as, for example, OOCL initiated from 1996 in cooperation with the Chinese national railways.[172]

The quest for quality control and closer relations with global customers also had profound consequences for the organisational structure of container operators who saw the need to take greater control of their entrepreneurial nodes. Reflecting the fundamental contradiction between concentration and cooperation inherent in the industry, this involved both centrifugal and centripetal tendencies. Decentralisation occurred as subsidiary offices were established overseas in

---

[167]*Fairplay*, 13 August 1998, 10; and *Containerisation International* (September 1998), 75-77.

[168]See, for example, *Fairplay*, 8 October 1998, 20.

[169]*Containerisation International* (November 1997), 83-85; and (February 1999), 35-39. The Trans-Siberian Railway in 1998 carried a paltry 40,000 TEU against 140,000 ten years previously (*Containerisation International* [December 1998], 31).

[170]*Fairplay*, 6 March 1997, 21.

[171]*Ibid.*, 12 December 1996, 9.

[172]Indicative of the increasingly important role of port authorities, the Port of Singapore Authority has become assisted with the opening of a container service from Dalian Container Terminal, in which it owns a share, to Harbin (*Ibid.*, 22 May 1997, 16).

regional hubs. Singapore, Hong Kong, New York and London, for example, became the seats of many such regional offices for global companies wanting to establish a presence in all three major trading areas. Greater power, by contrast, was achieved through replacing or taking over previously independent shipping agencies. Traditionally, most liner shipping companies used well-established independent commercial and/or agency firms to handle their overseas business, the major exceptions being "imperial" companies like P&O and CMB.

Figure 16:   A modern feeder, MISC's *Bunga Delima*, in the port of Fremantle.

Source: Chris Rowett and Selima Baxter, *Working Port* (Fremantle, 1997).

Initially, container operators followed the same practice, but from the late 1980s the larger companies and consortia increasingly desired undivided loyalties and turned over enough business to warrant keeping agency work in-house.[173] Again, the innovators often were Maersk and Evergreen, "whose concepts of global organisation and aggressive image-making have been years

---

[173]"Feeling the Squeeze," *Lloyd's Maritime Asia* (June 1989), 27-28; and *Fairplay*, 13 December 1990, 13.

ahead of other lines."[174] But all the majors followed the same policies and built up regional or even global networks of in-house agencies. A good example was provided by NYK, which in 1991 established a Logistics Management Division in London, charged with the development of land-based logistics services such as custom formalities, warehousing, distribution and interfacing with its European customers. Three years later NYK took control of its own liner agencies in Sweden, the Netherlands, the UK and Germany.[175] UASC established offices in London, New York, Singapore and Tokyo before building up regional agency networks in continental Europe and the USA. The latter, significantly, was constructed around railroad nodes and port cities: Lansing, Chicago, Cleveland, Baltimore, Norfolk, Atlanta and Houston. Long-standing connections were jettisoned as quality control, exclusive market information and personalised customer service were regarded as vital ingredients to successful management.[176] As advertising gurus strongly believed in the success of projecting company colours and logos, container operators during the 1990s "mopped up" independent agencies in the main ports of call, often taking their employees into their own service. Yet, as globalising operators continued to penetrate new markets, the role independent shipping agencies have not been eliminated, as is strongly demonstrated by the resilience of firms like the Inchcape and Kanoo Groups, although in this sector mergers and rationalisation have also become common.[177]

The State of the Conference System

One last theme remains to be addressed: the impact of concentration and alliance formation on the competitive structure of container shipping and, in particular, on the conference system.

In the late 1980s significant developments in the transpacific and transatlantic trades had occurred through the formation of tonnage stabilisation schemes and general, but not necessarily binding, rate agreements. Only in the Europe-East Asia trade was the Far Eastern Freight Conference holding out, but

---

[174]*Fairplay*, 15 August 1996, 33 and 41.

[175]"A Brief History of NYK (Europe)" [1997] (http://www.nyk.com/corpinfo/Euhist.htm). For the comparable, albeit slightly later, policy of MOL see *Containerisation International* (August 1997), 13; and (February 1999), 40-41.

[176]*Fairplay Container Operators 1996* (London, 1996), 154 and 259-260; and *Containerisation International* (October 1998), 13.

[177]See, e.g., *Lloyd's Maritime Asia* (January 1994), 13-14; *Fairplay*, 8 July 1999, 41-54; *Containerisation International* (February 1996), 53; *Fairplay Daily News*, 29 November 1999; and *Fairplay*, 6 July 2000, 15 and 28-37.

it gradually lost all its traditional functions as it became an integral part of complex global and pendulum services. With the much more far-reaching deregulation of the industry in the 1990s and the emphasis put on greater individual freedom of action, most of the regulatory functions of conferences simply faded away. By the mid-1990s many had simply lapsed or were replaced with a series of vague regional pacts. On some routes, such as the well-defined Europe-South Africa run, conferences survived longer in their original form. The more common kind of agreement has become similar to those that were concluded on the North Atlantic.

By 1990, existing conferences were collapsing under the weight of rapidly-rising overcapacity, aggressive competition from outsiders like Maersk, Evergreen and OOCL, and novel organisational forms on the model of transpacific agreements.[178] Two years later, the Trans-Atlantic Agreement was formed as an umbrella organisation to incorporate conference lines and outsiders like Maersk and OOCL; its first priority was to increase rates. Almost immediately the British Shippers' Council began proceedings against TAA and soon afterwards the European Commission began an investigation for "grave abuse" of EC law through its dominant position in the trade – a sure sign that the cooperation between the fifteen participating lines on tonnage rationalisation and the imposition of higher box rates was working.[179]

Although the EC's Directorate-General 4 for the time being preferred not to lay charges, which could have resulted in the lines being fined up to ten percent of their annual turnover, TAA was transformed into the Trans-Atlantic Conference Agreement in order to escape prosecution. TACA continued with the task of restoring order and profitability to the trade.[180] Interestingly, this was achieved under the chairmanship of the Norwegian Olav Rakkenes, leader of ACL, which in its identity as a specialised niche player with the longest experience in the trade, was perfectly suited for its diplomatic role.[181] As the European Commission later claimed, TACA was extremely successful, as it "reimposed the member discipline that conferences had lost, and in so doing turned a catastrophical loss-making trade into a profitable one. But it had to break

---

[178]"Atlantic Conferences Start Getting It Together," *Containerisation International* (August 1990), 41-45.

[179]*Fairplay*, 16 December 1993, 6.

[180]*Ibid.*, 21/28 December 1995, 4.

[181]ACL, moreover, was a totally independent firm again after its 1994 sale by Swedish transport conglomerate Bilspedition to Norwegian interests.

the rules to do so."[182] Specifically, the EC claimed, TACA's members "abused their joint dominant position by restricting the availability of individual service contracts and by actively discouraging independent market entry by potential competitors."[183] Although Rakkenes pointed out that his members had allowed several major Asian operators, such as MOL, Yang Ming, COSCO and K-Line, to enter the trade without interference and forcibly argued against accusations of illegal discrimination and other restrictive practices, the EC took an historic decision by fining TACA for its behaviour. The total penalty amounted to over US $310 million and was apportioned to its members according to their market share (see table 11).

Table 11
Members of TACA (1994) and Their 1998 EC Fines

Company	Fine	TACA Share
P&O Nedlloyd	47.2m US$	15.1%
Maersk	31.6	10.1
Sea-Land	31.6	10.1
OOCL	23.7	7.6
NYK	23.7	7.6
Hanjin	23.7	7.6
Hapag-Lloyd	23.7	7.6
Hyundai	21.3	6.8
MSC	15.8	5.0
DSR Senator	15.8	5.0
NOL	15.8	5.0
Cho Yang	15.8	5.0
TMM	7.9	2.5
ACL	7.9	2.5
Polish Ocean Lines	7.9	2.5

Source: Fairplay, 24 September 1998, 3.

This list also shows the global nature of TACA's membership, with seven European, six Asian and two North American companies. Taking into account that TACA accounted for more than sixty percent of transatlantic capacity, and that in addition to Evergreen another four Asian companies entered the North Atlantic, it is evident that the preeminence of East Asian shipping now also extended to what for it essentially was a cross-trade.

The deregulation resulting from the 1998 US Ocean Shipping Reform Act and the continued attention of the European Commission's anti-trust Directorate-General 4, as well as the arrival of powerful Asian cross-traders, led

---

[182]*Fairplay*, 24 September 1998, 3.

[183]*Ibid.*, 7.

in February 1999 to the formation of a broader-based North Atlantic Agreement (NAA). NAA brought together nineteen lines, accounting for some eighty-five percent of total slot capacity, including all previous members of TACA and now also COSCO, Yang Ming and K-Line; Evergreen and MOL specifically elected to remain outside.[184] Indicative of the turmoil in the trade, "despite, or because of" NAA holding eighty-five percent of the market, NAA was withdrawn and replaced with a TACA, Mark 2, with only eight members.[185] With the legalisation of confidential rates and service contracts there was no longer a need for a rate-setting cartel; instead NAA and TACA 2 announced that they would function like the Transpacific Stabilisation Agreement, a body mainly dedicated to discussions rather than negotiations and to voluntary tonnage rationalisation rather than the imposition of restrictive measures. The change in purpose of TACA on the North Atlantic was, very much for the same reasons, followed by the end on 30 April 1999 of the two similar rate agreements that existed since the 1980s on the North Pacific, eastbound ANERA and westbound TWRA. ANERA's membership had gradually decreased to nine lines, while TWRA was little more than a walking corpse after four of its remaining six lines resigned because the agreement restrained their flexibility in the area of individual contracting with customers.[186] Only the broader and less restrictive Transpacific Stabilisation Agreement still existed, more recently complemented by a Westbound Transpacific Stabilisation Agreement.

The survival of shipping conferences under changing technological and organisational circumstances has long been a subject of debate. On the eve of the new millennium, the formation and nature of TACA 2, ANERA and TWRA suggested that shipping conferences of the traditional kind, at least on the main lines of global shipping, might be institutions of the past. Globalisation of demand and supply for total logistics services, unprecedented increases in the scale of company and alliance operations, intermodalism, deregulation, and a maritime market place characterised by an excess of capacity have gravely undermined the old order. Yet, if "conferences are no more,...nobody has told the Far Eastern Freight Conference."[187] It was FEFC that after the Asian currency crisis was the shipowners' body to initiate rate increases, while the 1992

---

[184]"19 Shipping Lines Set to Form North Atlantic Pact," *Shipping Times*, 16 February 1999, and "Proposal to Set Up Larger Cartel to Replace TACA," *ibid.*, 18 February 1999.

[185]*Containerisation International* (July 1999), 39.

[186]"Two Cartels on Asia-US Trades to Stop Operations," *Shipping Times*, 22 March 1999.

[187]*Ibid.*, 8 March 1999.

Europe Asia Trades Agreement, struck between FEFC and leading Asian independents, was abandoned.[188] Even independently-minded COSCO is set to join FEFC.[189] When UASC joined the United Alliance in 1996-1997, it belonged to one "modern" rate agreement but also to eight conferences.[190] When finally in 1999 rates between Japan and the US West Coast were pumped up again, it was done through the agency of the Japan US Eastbound Freight Conference.[191] The same applied to the Anscon/Anzesc consortium in the trade between Australia and East Asia.[192] And, when it actually came to the point, both TSA and TACA 2 were used as instruments to raise freight rates.

Nevertheless, with the increased influence of main-line operators in feeder networks, secondary and north-south trades, there can be little doubt that the conference system will be pushed back. A prime example is the Europe-South Africa trade after the takeover of Safmarine Container Lines and Lloyd Triestino by Maersk and Evergreen. In South America and Australia concentration of power, restructuring and rationalisation point into the same direction. This does not mean that there will be no more conferences. But liner agreements will predominantly be of different kinds: either loosely-structured tonnage, rationalisation and service quality discussion forums or tightly-structured consortia and alliances of ever-greater capacity.[193] As it is unlikely that in the foreseeable future any effective international regulatory regime will be established, the nature and incidence of agreements will remain to be determined by market forces in the industry and the perceived self-interest of the companies. Rather than adopting a "live and let live" attitude,[194] container operators use every tactic to protect and promote their interests.

---

[188]*Shipping Times Online*, 1 September 1998, quoting *Journal of Commerce*; and *Containerisation International* (July 1999), 23.

[189]*Fairplay Daily News*, 6 July 1999.

[190]Http://38.15.18.26/services.html.

[191]"Box Operations Sail Back to Profit," *Shipping Times Online*, 2 June 1999, quoting *Bloomberg*.

[192]*Containerisation International* (July 1999), 15.

[193]See Hoffmann, "Concentration in Liner Shipping," Section III, C1-2.

[194]Hugo van Driel, "Collusion in Transport: Group Effects in a Historical Perspective," *Journal of Economic Behavior and Organization*, XLI (2000), 394.

Chapter 6
Ports, Port Systems and Liner Networks

> We do not feel that just because a ship is bigger it is necessarily better. Not all ports can accommodate larger vessels.[1]

The impact of containerisation on the world's ports and port systems was as revolutionary as its impact on shipping. Containerisation required shore facilities totally different in nature and appearance from those that had served for a century or more during the supremacy of the conventional passenger ship and cargo-liner. Intermodalism required further expansion and adaptation, not just in physical facilities but also in organisation and control. From the beginning container operators became directly involved in developing and managing terminals, a trend reinforced by the introduction of intermodalism. Although a number of ports remained public utilities that were not necessarily run on purely commercial criteria, others were exposed to the harsh world of the marketplace.

Port rivalry was nothing new, but ports now also had to be able to operate profitably – which, of course, did not mean that local or national authorities did not occasionally provide financial and other support. In their drive to cut costs, rationalise and become more efficient, many port authorities began to out-source functions and were corporatised and/or privatised. In its interaction with the big container companies and alliances, whose custom could make or break a harbour, the world's port industry became as globalised as its customers. During the 1990s, moreover, it became evident that running a port was a service function which could be exported through providing consultancy services to other port authorities, management contracts, joint ventures, and even direct investment abroad. A number of specialised port operators emerged which themselves built up networks of projects and investments around the world.

As individual ports were transformed, regional port systems followed suit. In the first stages of containerisation it appeared that conventional patterns might be duplicated, but the high capital intensity of the container industry at sea and ashore gave a fresh impetus to port rivalry, especially because terminals could, in principle, be built at almost any location. The rise of Felixstowe and Southampton in the early 1970s in England as container ports was a signal to all. Since shipping companies aimed at limiting the number of ports of call, a process of concentration took place, with stronger container ports obtaining

---

[1]Isao Shintani, president K-Line, quoted in *Containerisation International* (May 1996), 55.

regional hegemony and subordinating others. On the other hand – in a contradiction that was once again characteristic of the entire containerisation process – many second-rank ports and even some well-established or entirely new creations continued to fight for inclusion in main-line schedules and to forge direct links with overseas forelands. Many factors played a role in these rivalries, political as well as economic and commercial, and shipping operators, consortia and alliances did not hesitate to expand into gateways of new areas of production – most notably mainland China – to obtain maximum utilisation rates.

Figure 17:   Port of Singapore container terminal with a third-generation OCL carrier.

Source: Eric Jennings, *Cargoes. A Centenary Story of the Far Eastern Freight Conference* (Singapore, 1980).

Alliance formation, which enabled member companies to offer a number of main-line services, especially stimulated the inclusion of minor ports and hence port decentralisation. The introduction of round-the-world services and post-Panamax vessels, however, gave an additional impetus to port centralisation, as shipping companies tried to reduce sailing distances by replacing port strings and loops with single hubs in geographically-favourable locations. During the late 1980s and 1990s, the emergence of a number of new hubs, like Khor Fakkan, Dubai, Gioia Tauro and Algeciras, and the strong relay function of pre-eminent ports like Singapore, Hong Kong and Rotterdam underscored the extent to which the global system had changed.

In their global collectivity, ports create a complex web consisting of regional and supra-regional systems. Over time each of these port systems is inherently dynamic as ports respond to economic factors in their hinter- and forelands and vie with each for supremacy on national, regional and global levels. In some regions clear hierarchies exist, with one or two ports having gained the ascendancy; in others a cluster of ports with similar regional functions and power form the top echelon, with minor ports subordinated to one or more members of the cluster. While there are "objective" geographic reasons for the port system of East Asia to differ from that of the North American West Coast, each system is as inherently unstable as the container shipping industry itself since container port systems have become subjected to the same interplay of opposite forces. On the one hand, there are strong tendencies towards concentration, the strong growth of individual ports and hubs whose feeder services replace long-distance trunk lines. On the other, there are the impulses towards creating new ports and hubs, and including a greater variety and range of existing minor ports on main-line services and thus emancipating them from their subordinate status by providing them with direct access to their forelands.

This chapter will first trace the development of container ports and terminals and how they evolved over time. Second, it will discuss the dramatic changes in management and control over terminals. Particular attention will be given to the role of container shipping companies and the rise of global port corporations. Third, it will analyse how since 1965 the major regional port systems have been transformed in response to changes in world trade and the layout of shipping networks. The emergence of Dubai will be used to highlight the interaction of all the factors that drive port development in the container era.

Global Port Rankings

Ports and shipping are the two sides of the coin of world trade. Ships carrying trade need ports to load and discharge; ports need ships and trade to exist. The three elements have always lived in dynamic synergy. Throughout world history shipping technology and trade volume have determined the nature of port facilities.[2] As important as their location and transport infrastructure *vis-à-vis* their hinterland in terms of generating trade is the access and facilities ports offer to overseas shipping in terms of quayside space, water depth, cargo-handling equipment, experienced workforces and the means of onward transport. But, in turn, improving existing ports and/or building new facilities has stimulated and relocated both shipping activity and the flows of commerce. Responding to and, at the same time, stimulating world trade growth since the 1960s, container ports increased their business by leaps and bounds. Total world turnover rose from seventeen million TEU in 1975 to 55.8 million TEU in 1985 and 170.3 million TEU in 1997. Estimating average growth per year conservatively at seven percent, for 2000 a figure of well over 200 million TEU may be anticipated.

The changing distribution of container ports between 1975 and 1996 offers benchmarks of the global diffusion of containerisation, spatial shifts in

---

[2]J.H. Bird, *Seaports and Seaport Terminals* (London, 1971).

world production and consumption, and the influence of pre-eminent ports such as Hong Kong, Singapore and Rotterdam. Table 12, ranking the top twelve countries in containerisation, demonstrates the continued dominance of the USA as the world's leading consumer nation, as well as the clear shift of manufacturing production and shipping activity to East Asian countries.

Table 12
World Container Traffic, 1975-1996
(Per country, in millions TEU)

Rank	1975		1986		1996	
1	USA**	6.1	USA**	12.3	USA**	22.2
2	Japan	1.9	Japan	5.6	China***	18
3	Great Britain	1.5	Taiwan	4.1	Singapore*	12.9
4	Netherlands*	1.1	Netherlands*	3	Japan	12.4
5	Hong Kong*	0.8	Great Britain	3	Taiwan	8.1
6	Australia	0.7	Hong Kong*	2.8	Great Britain	5.1
7	W. Germany	0.7	W. Germany	2.3	Netherlands	5.1
8	Belgium	0.5	Singapore*	2.2	S.Korea*	4.7
9	Taiwan	0.5	Belgium	1.5	Germany	4.7
10	Canada	0.4	France	1.5	U/A/Emirates	3.8
11	France	0.4	Spain	1.5	Italy	3.8
12	Italy	0.3	S. Korea*	1.4	Spain	3.5
Total World		17		59.4		147.3

Notes: * country with only one or one dominant (greater than ninety percent of traffic) port; ** including Puerto Rico; *** including Hong Kong.

Source:All data taken from *Containerisation International Yearbook*, various years.

The share of the early leaders dropped significantly between the mid-1970s and the mid-1980s (from 83.5 to 64.4 percent) as con-tainerisation diffused rapidly into Asia and the north-south trades. From then onwards, however, little overall change took place (1996: 65.9 percent), but the relative decline of the USA (from thirty-six to fifteen percent), Japan and the northwest European nations is particularly noticeable. Despite Japan's decline, by the late 1990s East Asian ports overall accounted for about one-half of all containers moved in the world. Interestingly, too, Taiwan's greatest gain was made during the first period while, by contrast, the meteoric rise of Singapore and Hong Kong occurred during the latter years of the decade. The latter were, of course, assisted by the fact that they had a full monopoly within their political borders and that their ports stood at the heart of two powerful commercial and financial entrepots at the apex of fast-growing hinterlands. Hong Kong was, in addition, a major manufacturing location. To gain a more precise impression of historic growth patterns and their dynamics, the shifts in the relative positions of the leading ports rather than nations need to be examined (see table 13).

Table 13
Top Twenty Container Ports in the World, 1975-1999
(turnover in million TEU)

Rank	1975 Port	Turnover	1983 Port	Turnover	1991 Port	Turnover	1999 Port	Turnover
1	New York	1.6	Rotterdam	2.3	Singapore	6.4	Hong Kong	16.2
2	Rotterdam	1.1	New York	2.1	Hong Kong	6.2	Singapore	15.9
3	Kobe	0.9	Hong Kong	1.8	Kaohsiung	3.9	Kaohsiung	7
4	Hong Kong	0.8	Kobe	1.6	Rotterdam	3.8	Rotterdam	6.3
5	Oakland	0.5	Kaohsiung*	1.5	Kobe	2.6	Busan	6.3
6	Seattle	0.5	Singapore*	1.3	Busan	2.6	Long Beach	4.4
7	San Juan	0.5	Antwerp	1	Hamburg	2.2	Shanghai*	4.2
8	Baltimore	0.4	Seattle	1	Los Angeles	2	Los Angeles	3.8
9	Bremerhaven	0.4	Keelung*	0.9	Keelung	2	Hamburg	3.7
10	Long Beach	0.4	Hamburg	0.9	New York/NJ	1.9	Antwerp	3.6
11	Jacksonville	0.4	Yokohama	0.9	Yokohama	1.8	New York/NJ	2.9
12	Melbourne	0.4	San Juan	0.9	Tokyo	1.8	Dubai	2.8
13	Tokyo	0.4	Busan*	0.9	Long Beach	1.8	Tokyo	2.7
14	Hamburg	0.3	Bremerhaven	0.8	Antwerp	1.8	Felixstowe	2.6
15	Yokohama	0.3	Oakland	0.8	San Juan	1.6	Port Kelang*	2.6
16	Los Angeles	0.3	Long Beach	0.8	Felixstowe	1.4	Gioia Tauro*	2.3
17	Antwerp	0.3	Jiddah*	0.8	Bremerhaven	1.3	Bremerhaven	2.2
18	Norfolk	0.3	Los Angeles	0.7	Dubai*	1.3	Manila*	2.1
19	Sydney	0.3	Tokyo	0.7	Oakland	1.2	Yokohama	2.1
20	London	0.3	Felixstowe*	0.7	Bangkok*	1.7	San Juan	2.1

Note: * new entry

Sources: All pre-1999 figures taken from *Containerisation International Yearbook;* for 1999: http://195.38.155.61/cgi-bin/tabelle.pl (website of the Port of Hamburg).

A summary of these rankings, arranged according to economic region, is given in table 14.

Table 14
World's Top Twenty Ports, 1975-1999, According to Region

Region	1975	1983	1991	1999
United States	9	6	5	4
Europe	5	5	5	6
Asia	4	9	10	10
Australia	2	-	-	-

Source: See table 13.

The unprecedented economic growth of Asia and its participation in the high-quality container trade are particularly evident, as is the relative decline of the pioneering United States. In particular, the waning of New York/New Jersey between 1983 and 1991 even in absolute terms, is remarkable; only in the last few years has the negative trend been reversed. A product of the relative fall of the transatlantic trade, the intermodal revolution and strong competition from other east coast ports, New York was also hampered by its lack of post-Panamax water depths and a significant delay in developing its own intermodal railroad links into the interior. Leaving aside San Juan, the origin of the original "West Side run" and monopoly gateway to Puerto Rico, the only two US ports in the list were neighbours and strong rivals, Long Beach and Los Angeles. Often changing places, with Oakland and Seattle (1998 rankings: twenty-sixth and twenty-seventh, respectively), they testified to the American passion for Asian imports, the success of intermodalism, and the primacy of the Pacific in America's economic destiny.

Within Asia itself, apart from the remarkable ascendance of Dubai – the only port outside the three main centres of global industrial activity – the extraordinary upsurge of Singapore and Hong Kong to undisputed regional and global leadership is the most striking feature. Both ports grew at rates of two or three times that of world traffic and have maintained that pace until the late 1990s. While their lead over third-ranking Kaohsiung increased to more than that port's entire annual turnover, they changed ranks several times. Despite predictions to the contrary, Hong Kong's return to China – but with a special political and economic status, and under the leadership of C.H. Tung, OOCL's saviour – has not yet impacted on the fortunes of its port. It has successfully withstood the promotion of free-trade zones in its close vicinity, several of which (like Shenzhen and Yantian) obtained direct links with overseas markets, and the rapid emergence of Shanghai as a major maritime and financial centre and gateway to central China.[3] Singapore simply continued to power ahead as the busiest and best-equipped hub in the world.

The growing importance of Kaohsiung and Pusan is an eloquent reflection of the growth of the export trades of their *de facto* island economies of Taiwan and South Korea, with the former brushing aside its erstwhile challenger Keelung and the latter catering for over ninety percent of South Korea's exports. The general decline of Japan is evidenced as much as the yoyo-like rivalry of Tokyo and Yokohama, in which the relocation of one company or alliance can shift the tables. Overshadowing events in Tokyo Bay, however, is the slump of Japan's long-standing premier container port Kobe, which was not able to recover fully from the disastrous Great Hanshin earthquake of January 1995 and after a seventeenth-place ranking in 1998 did not figure in the 1999 top twenty.

The economic growth of Southeast Asia is reflected partly by the transit trade of Singapore (estimated to run at about seventy-eight percent)[4] and partly by the emergence of secondary container ports. These include Bangkok, Leam Chabang, Tanjung Priok and of course Port Kelang and Manila. Significantly, no port in South Asia ever came close to the top twenty.

The traditional jewels of the British Empire, Mumbai (Bombay) and Kalkota (Calcutta), were dragged down by the general malaise of the Indian economy, and it was, in fact, Colombo, Sri Lanka, which developed into a hub for South Asia. Overall container traffic, however, remained too modest to propel it to any higher ranking than twenty-sixth in 1996. Very much the same can be said in relation to South America, Africa and also Australia, where a modest-sized economy could not transform an early start into solid volumes of general trade. The Middle East offers a unique situation because of the remarkable growth of Dubai, which will be discussed later because it provides such a remarkable combination of hub function and port industrialisation. The short-lived appearance of Jiddah in the mid-1970s resulted from the Saudi building boom of those years; the "bride of the Red Sea" soon afterwards slipped down the rankings.

The European ports on the list are no longer identical to the members of the traditional "Havre to Hamburg range" of conventional cargo shipping; instead, they vividly demonstrate how containerisation has led to "green field" creations, mixed fortunes and significant shifts in rankings. First and foremost, London dropped away very quickly. Though at the pioneering edge of

---

[3]See, for example, *Fairplay*, 2 December 1999, 32.

[4]Jan Hoffmann, "Concentration in Liner Shipping: Its Causes and Impacts for Ports and Shipping Services in Developing Regions" (report prepared for the Economic Commission for Latin America and the Caribbean [1998], website www.eclac.cl/research/dcitf/lcg2027), section ID, table 1.

containerisation, it soon lost trade to Felixstowe and Southampton, especially the former which, unhampered by the existing British system of dockside industrial relations on its virgin site, soon forged ahead. From a modest ferry port it became, and remained throughout the period, by a long distance Britain's leading container port. The other leaders in the North Sea area, Rotterdam, Hamburg, Antwerp and Bremen/Bremerhaven, containerised successfully and maintained the lustful rivalry that had characterised their relationship since the late nineteenth century and earlier. Rotterdam's hegemony was never in doubt, but behind it Felixstowe and the others never ceased to jostle for position. Le Havre was never able to command a leading position, but recently adopted the ambitious PORT 2000 plan. Traditional southern European and Mediterranean liner ports never figured prominently as too many participants in too many countries were chasing too little trade. When, however, round-the-world, multi-ocean pendulum services and enlargement of scale drew traffic away from gateway ports to regional relay hubs, the latter experienced disproportionally rapid growth. Many were new creations at strategic sites, including Italy's Gioia Tauro, Spain's Algeciras (twentieth in 1998), and Malta's Marsaxlokk.

Container Ports and Terminals

Container ports of any significant size are highly specialised and purposeful creations. They must have terminals with huge slabs of open and well-founded space to park and arrange containers for shipment; appropriate equipment to move containers across the terminal; specialised container cranes; and, ideally, on-the-spot connections with rail, road and/or water transport facilities (the latter both inland and/or seaborne). Such space could hardly ever be made available in existing conventional port areas where docks, basins, finger piers, sheds, warehouses and godowns were almost immediately rendered obsolete. Following the example set from the early 1950s by bulk-handling facilities, container terminals were built at open spaces beyond existing facilities and often further out to sea. In their wake they often left the now-obsolete and soon-derelict inner-city facilities that once had been the heart of the liner trades of the world.

Sea-Land began its New York operations on an urban wasteland site, while London and Hamburg built their terminals to the seaward side of conventional facilities. Tilbury was a river terminal outside London's docklands; about twenty years later Antwerp's Europa-terminal was the first to be built "outside the gates." In Hong Kong the old port was left unchanged as Kwaichung terminal rested on material excavated from the tops of nearby mountains and dumped along the shoreline. Kobe's container terminals were built on an artificial island, while Rotterdam pushed its Maasvlakte ever further out into the North Sea. Sydney's Port Jackson, which had been a splendid harbour ever since 1788, could not cope with containerisation and by 1980 moved all operations to its second port, Botany Bay.[5] San Francisco was almost totally constrained by its topography and inner-city traffic congestion; as containerisation took off, its traffic moved to Oakland across the bay. Some ports had to build satellites. Marseilles located its container operations at the site of its bulk-shipping harbour, Fos. Bangkok's congestion problems were manifold, with both its river and the city almost choking with traffic so that Laem Prabang, a little over 100 kilometres to the southeast was built on a virgin site. In 1998, after a year of thirty-nine-percent growth, the satellite actually eclipsed its main port, 1.3 to 1.1 million TEU.[6]

Civil engineers, like their professional great-grandfathers during the first great wave of port and ship canal construction from the 1860s to the early twentieth century,[7] were able to build terminals at virtually any location chosen by port authorities, shipowners or other investors. Thus, while traditional ports – such as New York, Rotterdam, Hamburg, Antwerp, Hong Kong, Singapore, Yokohama, Kobe, Sydney, Los Angeles and, in due course, Shanghai – underwent the necessary expansion, ports that had never played a significant role in global trade could suddenly be turned into powerful challengers and participants. From the beginning this included British and European contenders, like Felixstowe, Southampton, Zeebrugge and La Spezia, but also many others elsewhere, especially in the fast-rising regions of the world economy. Oakland and Long Beach in California, Kaohsiung and Keelung on Taiwan, South Korea's Pusan, Dubai in the UAE, and Yantian in China are prime examples of such recent creations. In addition to these gateway ports with significant hinterlands, there are also others conceived as almost pure transshipment hubs on virgin sites, like Khor Fakkan, Fujairah and Salalah on the East Arabian coast, Algeciras, Gioia Tauro, Marsaxlokk and Damietta in the Mediterranean, or Freeport in the Bahamas.

The American and European containerisation pioneers built the first terminals. The work for Sea-Land's base facility at what became known as Elizabeth Marine Terminal began in 1958 with the dredging of some fourteen million cubic yards of mud from the riverbed to create deep-water wharfage; the terminal that at its opening in late 1963 covered ninety-two acres by 1980 had grown to 232 acres.[8] It was matched across the Atlantic at the most seaward site of the port of London, Tilbury, where the Port of London Authority, which had

---

[5]P.R. Proudfoot, "Sydney and its Two Seaports," *International Journal of Maritime History*, I, No. 2 (1989), 141-184.

[6]*Containerisation International* (March 1999), 95.

[7]Adrian Jarvis (ed.), *Port and Harbour Engineering* (Aldershot, 1998).

[8]Sea-Land, *Sea Notes*, Silver Anniversary Issue (1981), 4.

followed the construction of Elizabeth closely, developed two terminals.[9] One was for common users and in 1968 received its first ocean-going container vessel, US Lines' *Atlantic Lancer*. The other was built in cooperation with OCL and ACT for their exclusive use in the Australian trade. For reasons to be discussed in chapter 7, however, the two consortia were forced to initiate their service from Antwerp and could use Tilbury only from May 1970. Antwerp was available because of a scramble by port authorities in all four major trading regions to build container facilities that more than matched the frenetic pace with which liner companies embraced the new technology and accepted its ramifications.

Long-standing port rivalries were intensified in the wave of terminal construction that swept the world in the late 1960s and 1970s. As Sea-Land, for example, began its service with calls at Bremerhaven, Hamburg was initially at a disadvantage, exacerbated by the fact that its port counted a large number of individual stevedoring companies. Only in 1968 could it receive its first full-container ship – as at Tilbury, it was US Lines' *Atlantic Lancer*. But then the state-owned Hamburger Hafen- und Lagerhaus AG (HHLA) took the bit between its teeth and developed the Burchardkai into a fully-fledged terminal, capable of servicing the third-generation vessels of the TRIO Group with their maximum fourteen-metre drafts. As TRIO also called at Bremerhaven, very much the same demands were made there with regards to length of berth, depth alongside and stretch of the container cranes. The result was a neck-to-neck race in which Hamburg by 1976 had almost caught up with its rival: 433,000 against 466,000 TEU (1968: 37,000 against 70,000 TEU).[10] Around 1980, Hamburg took the lead, never to relinquish it again. The fall of the Berlin Wall and with it the Iron Curtain gave additional impetus, and in recent years its turnover has been about twice that of Bremerhaven. A contrasting example is that of the Dutch rivals, Amsterdam and Rotterdam. Within a few years, it was evident that problems of access and space had destroyed any chance for Amsterdam to play a role in the ballet of North Sea ports; its turnover in 1975 was a paltry 33,400 TEU, while Rotterdam had already passed the one million TEU mark.[11]

To keep pace with, or rather to anticipate, growth in ship's dimensions and trade volumes, and provide the ever-higher quality of service demanded by shipowners and shippers, neither port authorities nor container terminal operators could ever rest on their laurels. As traffic grew over time, the number and length

---

[9]R. Douglas Brown, *The Port of London* (London, 1978), chapters 7-8; and John Hovey, *A Tale of Two Ports. London and Southampton* (London, 1990), chapter 5.

[10]H.J. Witthöft, *Container. Transportrevolution unseres Jahrhunderts* (2nd ed., Hereford, 1978), 71-79.

[11]*Ibid.*, 30-31.

of berths increased; in many cases so did the number of terminals itself. In 1987, the Port of Singapore Authority's Tanjong Pagar Terminal comprised eight major and two feeder container berths;[12] twelve years later the PSA operated four terminals, totalling thirty-seven berths, with the potential for another twenty to be added if and when required.[13] Hong Kong added regularly to its first Kwai Chung terminal and by the end of the twentieth century began construction of CT9, which would add another six berths to come on stream in 2002. Rotterdam's ECT pushed out to sea with its Delta terminal. No port can afford to have ships queuing for berthing space because congestion incurs surcharges and customers move elsewhere; new ports include expansion plans as an integral part of the original project. Salalah was built in two stages, the first two berths opened in November 1998, and the next two were completed in November 1999, while the reclamation for yet another pair was then well under way.[14]

As important as adequate quayage is sufficient depth of water alongside and for access. Many port cities through the centuries were plagued, and in some cases destroyed, by silting rivers and sand bars, while others survived and thrived by constructing docks and dredging deep-water channels and harbours. As most leading ports were founded in the era of the sailing ship, their port authorities in the age of containerisation found themselves in the same position as their predecessors who had to cope with the rivalry of pre-1914 steam shipping companies, which led one port engineer to observe:[15]

A race between engineers: such might describe the condition of affairs in the maritime world of to-day in regard to two of the most important branches of engineering. On the one hand, we have the ship designers turning out larger and larger vessels; on the other is the harbour engineer, striving vainly to provide a sufficient depth of water in which to float these large steamships. The former has set the pace, and the latter finds it hot, so much so that he is hard put to it to keep on his rival's heels.

---

[12]*Lloyd's Asian Shipping Directory* (1987-1988), 156-157.

[13]*Fairplay*, 4 November 1999, 27.

[14]*Shipping Times Online*, 30 March 1999, quoting *Lloyd's List*.

[15]Fremantle Port Authority Library, H.D. Walsh, "Notes on Harbour Engineering." I am grateful to Malcolm Tull of Murdoch University for bringing this reference to my attention.

The increasing dimensions of container vessels, expanding in two decades from first-generation to post-Panamax, posed tremendous challenges. Evidently, in order to be included in main-line schedules, the largest class of vessel needs to be able to find accommodation. Yet with the rapid escalation of the largest ship's dimensions and draught, and expectations of further growth beyond 2000, the number of ports that can find the resources and are sufficiently centrally located to be able to load these commercial battle wagons is necessarily limited in number. One futuristic study even went so far as to envisage a fleet of 15,000-TEU vessels using a "necklace" of no more than four or five "mega-hubs."[16]

Leaving aside the value of such speculations, many ports indeed have to invest substantial resources in "keeping up to depth." During the mid-1990s, for example, over ninety percent of all US ports needed regular dredging; in the process they shifted some 400 million cubic yards of sediment.[17] Many container ports also handle bulk shipping and oil tankers, but that often only exacerbates the problems as access routes but not terminals are shared. Ironically, some ports with the densest hinterlands suffer from shallow access routes. Sydney's two container terminals, which now offer a maximum depth of 14.8 metres,[18] are located on the shores of Botany Bay, which in 1788 had been too shallow to receive the first fleet of sailing vessels carrying convicts. When Maersk in 1998 sent its first 6000-TEU carrier, *Regina Maersk*, around the North American coast, it did so at least partly to show US port authorities that this new class of ship would not remain restricted to the Europe-Asia trades and that local port authorities would have to be prepared to make heavy investments to handle Maersk's main-line business.

On the east coast of North America only Halifax, Nova Scotia, could receive the ship which, fully laden, draws fourteen metres. New York/New Jersey, Baltimore and all others fell far short of the required water depth. Their scramble for federal funding was made all the more urgent as Maersk/Sea-Land made it known that it was looking for one east coast port to become the centre of its operations. New York won, largely because of its location, hinterland and intermodal connections, as well as its promise to provide no less than US $1.7 billion for infrastructure projects over the duration of the twenty-eight-year lease, but it necessitated large-scale dredging of the entrance channels at both sides of Staten Island and in the container port itself at an expense of at least US $733

---

[16]Hoffmann, "Concentration in Liner Shipping," section II, D2.

[17]*Containerisation International* (May 1996), 45; and (December 1997), 87-95.

[18]*Australian Shipping Directory, 1999*, 87. Governor Phillip, the commander of that fleet, had the extraordinary luck that Port Jackson, which James Cook had missed during his exploration of the east coast in 1770, was just around the corner.

million.[19] The required depth is at least 13.7 metres and will have to be increased to 15.25 metres or even more, as by late 2000 more than seventy vessels will draw more than 13.7 metres.

Other east coast ports such as Baltimore and Savannah had to follow suit. West Coast ports were, of course, equally affected, and Oakland adopted a US $600 million expansion plan that included deepening the port from 12.8 to 15.25 metres.[20] Not surprisingly, US ports have tried hard, and with some success, to off-load the expenses involved onto the federal government; Washington will pay at least US $400 million of the deepening of the channel entrance of New York.[21] The unveiling of the world's latest mega-dredger, *Vasco da Gama*, with a record capacity seventy-percent larger than the previous biggest,[22] shows that the engineering limits of port construction and channel deepening have by no means been reached. This, however, may not be said of the capacity of all port authorities to carry the cost of such ventures.

On the other side of the world, Shanghai wrestled with physical problems of greater proportions. Although perfectly placed on the central Chinese coast with a dense and fast-growing hinterland, water depth on the Yangtze River sandbar is only seven metres at low tide.[23] In 1996 the port was accessible to 3000-TEU vessels which, when fully laden, required ten metres, which is just achieved at high tide. In February 1998 the first phase of a US $300 million project was approved to deepen the bar to 8.5 metres by late 1999 and 12.5 metres by 2010, allowing calls by 4000-TEU vessels.[24] *Regina Maersk* and other post-Panamax ships will have to wait until completion of the entire project in 2020. By that stage, it may be presumed, Shanghai may well and truly have been by-passed and/or replaced by new deep-water ports in the Yangtze River delta or Ningbo, with its 14.5 metre natural depth already regarded as its spillover port on the coast.[25] Shanghai, by the way, was by no means the only

---

[19]*Fairplay*, 5 August 1999, 20-24.

[20]*Containerisation International* (October 1998), 90-91.

[21]*Fairplay*, 24 October 1996, 12; and 19 February 1998, 44.

[22]*Ibid.*, 18 November 1999, 52.

[23]*Lloyd's Maritime Asia* (February 1992), 24; and (January 1994), 15, 17 and 37; and *Containerisation International* (October 1996), 53.

[24]"Striving to be a World Hub," *Shipping Times*, 24 February 1998.

[25]"Expansion Frenzy may be Over," *ibid.*, 29 May 1998; on Ningbo, see *Dock and Harbour Authority* (February 1991), 277.

port to look that far ahead; Rotterdam, for example, in 1999 released its report, "2020: Integrated Projections for Port and Industry," with the clear purpose of staying ahead of its European rivals. And in 1990 the neighbouring ports of Los Angeles and Long Beach, forced into extensive land reclamation schemes to cater for expansion without congestion, adopted a "2020 Project" which foresaw over 2500 acres of new land to be added to their San Pedro Bay sites.[26]

Ports have had to work as hard to stay abreast of developments on land as in the water. In the first instance, this involves the availability of ample storage space, sufficient gantry cranes of the latest generation, straddle carriers and the other physical equipment needed to handle boxes most expeditiously.[27] The maximum lift capacity of cranes was mostly determined by the greatest weight of two fully-laden FEUs, close to thirty tonnes, but some ports included more powerful cranes as well. Crucial for their capability to serve the largest carriers was the cranes' outreach, which determined the maximum number of box rows across the ship that could be handled. This vital statistic quickly rose from eight for first-generation North Atlantic carriers to thirteen for the third-generation TRIO vessels and US Lines' fourth-generation round-the-world econoliners (which were stretched to a nine-to-one length-beam ratio in order to remain Panamax at their much higher TEU capacity); ports wishing to be part of main-line services could not do with smaller equipment.

Post-Panamax dimensions, which pushed row numbers up to fifteen and higher (seventeen for the *Regina Maersk* class), set new standards for first-class ports. Salalah's first six cranes, bearing in mind the needs of its owners, Maersk/Sea-Land, were built for an eighteen-wide stow, or an effective outreach of forty-five metres, with the total length over the water extending to fifty-three metres.[28] Charleston, claiming to be the busiest container port on the US East and Gulf coasts behind New York, was equally not satisfied with standard sixteen-row post-Panamax cranes and went one better, ordering four cranes capable of handling nineteen boxes across, thus bringing its total post-Panamax fleet up to twenty-three.[29] The last word, at least for the moment, came when Yokohama issued its challenge to Tokyo in the form of an order for five new gantry cranes for its Maersk/Sea-Land terminal with an outreach of a record twenty-two rows

---

[26]*Fairplay*, 7 June 1990, 26.

[27]A useful overview can be found in *Containerisation International* (December 1997), supplement, "Ship-to-Shore Gantry Cranes."

[28]*World Cargo News* (December 1996), 53.

[29]*Fairplay*, 15 April 1999, 41.

across.[30] Partly related to the size, number and trolley operating speed of cranes, of course, is the question of port productivity in terms of TEUs lifted per crane per hour. In this respect Singapore and Hong Kong were the absolute leaders in their field (see table 15).

Table 15
Container Vessel Handling Rates, Selected Ports, 1997

Rank	Port	Containers/hour
1	Singapore	86
2	Hong Kong	74
3	Rotterdam	56
4	Tokyo	48
5	Bremerhaven	48
6	Kaohsiung	44
7	Port Kelang	41
8	Osaka	35

Source: *Containerisation International* (October 1997) 26.

Intermodalism in all its forms, but especially through integrated and dedicated railway services, made additional demands on ports and terminals. Although it was not unusual for conventional ports to have railway access to wharfside, there was nothing like a systematic provision of on-site transport. And only containerisation itself created a dynamic interface between shipping and road transport. Terminals needed to make full provision for both truck and train, and it is the failure to do so that hampered many ports in, for example, Australia and Latin America. Especially where competition was fierce, as in northern Europe, the USA and Japan, efficient connections with highway networks was of prime importance; one of the great advantages of Felixstowe and Southampton over Tilbury was the latter's inadequacy in that respect. Since then, especially in Europe, highway construction has very much included the consideration of port and hinterland access, as the network of motorways around Rotterdam and towards Germany demonstrates.

Intermodalism from the mid-1980s gave pre-eminence to railroad tracks and the direct transfer of containers between ship and train, but for a long time such facilities remained limited to North American ports, which vied with each other to offer the most up-to-date and efficient systems. Many of these provided common-user access, but the main effort was made by companies like APL, which controlled their own intermodal operations or entered into contractual services with individual companies. From the second half of the 1980s and throughout the 1990s, other leading American and Asian companies – such as

---

[30]*Ibid.*, 4 March 1999, 15.

Sea-Land, NYK, K-Line and Evergreen – followed APL's lead and concluded agreements with railroad companies to enable them to off-load containers in West Coast ports on dedicated double-stack trains scheduled to depart without delay to cities in the central and eastern states.

   As companies increasingly leased their own facilities (and in some cases also developed common-user terminals), many port authorities became landlords, facilitators, political lobbyists and, above all, developers. Instead of running ports and cargo-handling facilities, their main tasks became to make land available, provide infrastructure and continuously upgrade facilities to the requirements of the terminal operators. Long Beach, for example, from 1995 to 1998 spent over US $1 billion on terminal expansion and facility improvement.[31]

   Intermodalism, although nowhere imitated on the scale of the USA, created widespread interest in developing similar port-hinterland integration. Thailand's new container port, Laem Chabang, quickly adopted dedicated freight trains to help overcome the chronic congestion of Bangkok. By contrast, European intermodalism – despite the claim that it is environmentally friendly – has been slow to make substantial gains and to reverse the considerable decline of rail in intra-European freight movements. As table 16 shows, road transport in Europe since 1970 had made substantial gains at the expense of both inland waterways and rail in the volume of freight carried.

Table 16
Market Shares of Europe's Inland Freight Transport Modes

	1970	1980	1993
road	55%	66%	77%
rail	31%	23%	16%
water	14%	11%	7%

Source: *Containerisation International* (May 1995), 31; and (November 1997), 83.

   Intercontainer-Interfrigo, a twenty-nine-member international railway consortium, never achieved the real breakthrough and, once rail deregulation started, several of its partners entered into direct contract with either shipping or stevedoring companies. But Sea-Land's joint venture with the Netherlands and German national rail operators also failed. Among the positive signs is Hamburg's building up its rejuvenated transit trade to Central and Eastern Europe – rising on the ruins of former communist ports like Rostock and Gdynia – predominantly by rail.[32] Its leading container stevedores concluded intermodal

---

[31]*Containerisation International* (March 1999), 90.

[32]*Fairplay*, 8 October 1998.

joint ventures with Polish, Czech, Slovak and Hungarian railway authorities.[33] Another is the dynamism of the new Italian port Gioia Tauro, opened in 1995, which by 1998 boasted six tracks totalling 3000 metres on the wharfside.[34]

In addition to inland transport, it should be pointed out that in the USA, Asia and Europe short-sea shipping did not disappear. This is no surprise in the case of Asia, where long-distance highways and international rail connections are still rare; in fact, intra-Asian traffic is set to become the world's largest single trading region.[35] But the US coastal trade, still reserved by the 1920 Jones Act to US-flag carriers, fulfils important main-line and relay roles. Europe also still maintains a healthy and dense network of short-sea routes around its entire littoral, but especially in its two major basins, the North Sea and Baltic, and the Mediterranean-*cum*-Black Sea. The gradual re-establishment of peace in the Balkans has stimulated the opening of new lines by small operators, such as that of Coperman Shipping, linking Piraeus with Bar (Croatia) and Koper (Slovenia).[36] A new boost was given to Mediterranean short-sea shipping by fires in Alpine tunnels and congestion on many European arterial highways. This has meant that ports have also had to provide facilities for smaller container carriers; while the vessels of major lines are often handled at their own terminals, for others sufficient common-user berths must be available.

A final mode of onward transport that is bound to remain of limited significance but which can give a small number of ports an additional edge is that of sea-air transport. Designed to provide a fifty-fifty time-and-price compromise between airfreight and all-sea carriage, shipping-aviation intermodalism requires not just the right geographical location astride major trade routes but also consummate organisational and consolidating skills. Innovative Dubai, midway between East Asia and Europe, during the mid-1980s (when it also launched its Emirates Airline) was the pioneer in this field and established its sea/air transshipment system as the standard of the industry. By 1993, over 2500 TEUs per year were shipped in this way, mostly electronic goods but also an occasional garment shipment for Harrod's in London.[37] Dubai's initiative led to a more

---

[33]*Containerisation International* (March 1996), 37.

[34]*Ibid.* (August 1998), 32.

[35]*Ibid.* (October 1998), 55.

[36]Port of Koper, Port News, October 1999 (http://www.luka-kp.sl/eng/n10_99.html).

[37]See, for example, *Fairplay*, 20 November 1986, 34; *Containerisation International* (December 1994), Advertising section "Middle East," xiv; and (May 1996), 49; and *Cargo Today* (October 1997).

complex and efficient regional sea-air system as, on the one hand, neighbouring Sharjah Airport and, on the other, UAE East Coast hubs Khor Fakkan and Fujairah became involved.

One of the main issues of terminal productivity was, and still is, the positioning and repositioning of containers to maximise loading and discharging efficiency and storage management. To some extent this was a question of physical equipment, but even more so one of identification and information management, not dissimilar (although focussed on a much smaller area) to that faced by box owners tracking their property across the globe. In this respect ports were as market-driven as the shipowners providing just-in-time services to shippers and had to remain at the cutting edge of technology. From the beginning, computers were indispensable and ports worked hand-in-hand with experts to develop their speed and capacity; Felixstowe gained a reputation for its pioneering role.[38] As software programmes became ever-more sophisticated – like those aboard ship to ensure optimal loading[39] – new dimensions were added to electronic terminal management systems. These came in the mid-1990s to include the use of Differential Global Positioning Systems, satellite-based technology that allowed individual containers to be located with a tolerance of about half a metre, a practice pioneered by the Dubai Port Authority.[40]

Port Industrialisation

The most important impetus for individual and collective container port growth, was the demand of trade and shipping. But throughout the world from the 1950s onwards, beginning with Japan, ports were also increasingly seen as vital instruments for industrialisation and economic growth.[41] Although such development strategies mainly applied to bulk ports and the establishment of large-scale petrochemical and metallurgical plants, with the rise of

---

[38]*Dock and Harbour Authority* (June 1984), 33.

[39]See, for example, *Containerisation International* (July 1995), 74-75.

[40]*Cargo Systems* (November 1995) and (April 1996); and *Dock and Harbour Authority* (May 1996), 21-23. See also http://www.dpa.co.ae/taw.htm.

[41]W. Flüchter, *Neulandgewinnung und Industrieansiedlung vor den japanischen Küsten* (Paderborn, 1975); B.S. Hoyle and D.A. Pinder (eds.), *Cityport Industrialization and Regional Development* (Oxford, 1981); Ross Robinson, "The Foreign Buck: Aid-Reliant Investment Strategies in ASEAN Port Development," *Transportation Research Analysis*, XXIIIA, No. 6 (1989), 439-451; and Peter J. Rimmer and Toru Taniuchi, "Japan's Seaports and Regional Development during the Era of High-Speed Growth, 1960-75," in Frank Broeze (ed.), *Gateways of Asia* (London, 1998), 339-366.

containerisation the possibilities of more diversified production also became evident.[42] In combination with the establishment of Free Trade Zones in many port areas outside the high-cost industrialised countries and a certain fashion with international development banks and other investment fund providers, this gave a powerful push towards the building and expansion of container terminals. This strategy found its most widespread application in mainland China, where by the late 1980s a string of such port-based zones covered substantial parts of the republic's littoral.[43] Many of these in due course developed into full-fledged container ports, as table 17 shows.

Table 17
Top Ten Container Ports, China, 1998

Port	1998 Turnover		Growth 1997/1998
Shanghai	3066000	TEU	21.2%
Qingdao	1213000	TEU	17.7%
Yantian	1040000	TEU	63.0%
Tianjin	1018000	TEU	8.9%
Huangpu	848000	TEU	23.4%
Xiamen	654000	TEU	19.8%
Dalian	525000	TEU	15.4%
Shekou	463000	TEU	116.4%
Ningbo	353000	TEU	37.4%
Fuzhou	253000	TEU	12.4%
for comparison:			
Hong Kong	14529000	TEU	1.0%

Source: *Containerisation International* (April 1999), 39.

Originally linked by feeders to relay hubs such as Hong Kong and, to a much lesser extent, Tianjin, these ports rapidly aimed at establishing direct lines to overseas. Collectively, they were expected to achieve a turnover of twenty million TEU in 2000, thus overtaking Hong Kong's estimated eighteen million.[44] Their scramble for development was so fierce that authorities became seriously concerned about duplication, the wasting of resources and the collapse

---

[42]See, for example, D. Teurelincx, A. Verbeke and E. Declercq, *De economische betekenis van zeehavenprojecten: de economische evaluatie van de Containerkade-west Antwerpen* (Brussels, 1997).

[43]Y.C. Jao and C.K. Leung (eds.), *China's Special Economic Zones: Policies, Problems and Prospects* (New York, 1986).

[44]*Fairplay*, 21 September 2000, 50.

of freight rates from minor ports[45] – in other words, China had firmly joined the world of containerisation. But the explosion of port activity also stimulated the formation of China's second container operator, China Shipping (1997).[46]

Perhaps the most striking example of port industrialisation boosting container traffic across its quays was found in Dubai. Its 10,000-hectare Jebel Ali Free Zone, located around the world's largest man-made harbour, by 1999 had attracted over 1600 companies from eighty-five countries, including fifty-five of *Fortune's* top 500.[47] As a result, Dubai's container throughput was significantly boosted and became less dependent on transit traffic, with about half being generated from within the emirate. In 1999 Kuwait, the traditional hub of maritime activity in the Gulf, established its first free trade zone.[48]

Port Authorities and Terminal Operators

The need for dedicated terminals and the desirability of rapid turnaround of capital-intensive container vessels from the very beginning made container operators work closely together with port authorities, in which the legal constitution of the port authority mostly determined the form of cooperation that ensued. At that early stage, private interests owned very few ports; Felixstowe, of course, was the prime example of this exceptional situation. Broadly speaking, most liner ports were either owned by public authorities – state, provincial or local – or controlled by statutory bodies. Such port authorities were mostly found in Britain and former members of the British Empire, while Europe, Japan and the USA mainly favoured city-run administrative structures. While either of the two types precluded the outright sale of land, they mostly did embody, at least in principle, the possibility of short- or long-term leases of terminal space. There was nothing intrinsically new in this, as almost all conventional liner companies had leased wharves and warehouses from port authorities, but containerisation was to lead to considerable intensification and, ultimately, also globalisation of the container shipping industry as container companies invested heavily in providing the equipment and other facilities.

In addition, from the mid-1980s considerable organisational and structural alterations came to the port sector to give port managers greater

---

[45]"Free Fall in China Rates," *Shipping Times Online*, 29 December 1997, quoting *Lloyd's Shipping Maritime Asia*; and "Expansion Frenzy may be Over," *Shipping Times*, 29 May 1998.

[46]*Containerisation International* (August 1997), 11; and (February 1999), 11.

[47]Http://www.jafza.co.ae.

[48]*Fairplay Daily News*, 24 November 1999.

autonomy and improve port productivity and efficiency; commercialisation, corporatisation and privatisation became the most common of these.[49] These changes, which in many ports were to have far-reaching ramifications, were caused by complex sets of interactive forces generated within the port industry itself, pressures emanating from the shipping industry, and general shifts in political ideology and culture towards reducing the economic role of government and making public utilities perform on their own strength in the marketplace. Nevertheless, the extent of change should not be overestimated, as state, provincial and city authorities continue to subsidise port infrastructure investments.[50]

The direction was set as early as 1958, when Sea-Land began building its own Elizabeth Terminal on land leased from the Newark Port Authority (later merged into the Port of New York/New Jersey). Sea-Land, Matson and APL followed a systematic policy of using their own facilities wherever possible. Across the Atlantic, OCL designed and controlled its own terminals at Tilbury and Southampton, side-by-side to facilities owned by the existing London and Southampton port authorities.[51] In Europe, where as a rule city governments owned ports, private companies undertook stevedoring. In Rotterdam the introduction of container shipping led to a stormy process of amalgamation from which Europe Container Terminus emerged as the largest single terminal operator.[52]

Initially owned as a joint venture by a number of stevedoring companies, from 1970 two local shipping companies acquired minority shares to ensure privileged access. When Nedlloyd was formed, it became the largest minority shareholder. In Antwerp CMB was in a different position, as it already owned 50.1 percent in local stevedores Gylsen. It used this strategic investment to build a state-of-the-art terminal in the Churchill Dock. With its Dart partners and two other lines, it then built another terminal on land leased beside Sea-Land at

---

[49]For a good overview of the issues in a case study see M.T. Tull, *A Community Enterprise: The History of the Port of Fremantle, 1897 to 1997* (St. John's, 1997), chapter 7.

[50]See, for example, *Containerisation International* (May 1995), 39; and *Fairplay*, 21 May 1998, 20-22, reporting on the Barcelona conference on the future of European ports; and the references in this chapter to US federal funds for dredging.

[51]Hovey, *Tale of Two Ports*. Nedlloyd and CMB invested in large terminals (ECT and Gylsen) that also served other customers. The continuation of the trend was shown by CP Ships, which in the early 1990s acquired Montréal Terminals.

[52]H. van Driel, *Samenwerking in haven en vervoer in het containertijdperk* (Delft, 1990), chapter 6.

Elizabeth, New Jersey.[53] Similar practices were followed all over the world by companies ranging from NYK and MOL in Japan to ANL in Melbourne and CP Ships in Montréal.

In the first instance, vertical diversification into terminal investments was aimed at home and/or national ports, but it soon also extended to major overseas ports of call. The prime reason why shipowners increasingly became involved in controlling their own terminals was to ensure punctuality, speed and reliability, factors that in the 1980s and 1990s assumed ever-greater importance. The decisive step forward was made when OOCL in 1978 bought one of Felixstowe's two container terminals.[54] Similar arrangements were soon made in many ports all over the world, with the specific details depending on local conditions. In succession, two alternative yet often mutually-supportive strategies emerged. First, there was the increasingly frequent occurrence of land being leased to foreign operators. On the US West Coast, for example, each container port from San Diego to Seattle became involved in a bidding race which became all the sharper when it was evident that intermodalism would lock shipping companies more strongly than ever before to specific railroad companies and hence ports.

By the mid-1990s, all Japanese majors, Evergreen, Maersk, and several others were well ensconced on individual or joint concessions.[55] Alliance formation further intensified the movement and in its wake brought additional suitors. APL continued to set the standards with its two intermodal Global Gateways, South at Los Angeles and North at Seattle.[56] Hanjin in quick succession leased four US sites at New York, Long Beach, Seattle and Oakland.[57] The 900,000 TEU it put through Long Beach in 1998 was the largest contribution of any single company and propelled that port to a turnover of over four million

---

[53]G. Devos and G. Elewaut, *CMB 100. Een eeuw maritiem ondernemersschap 1895-1995* (Tielt, 1995), 173 and 210-211.

[54]J.H.W. Northfield, "Port Management and Operations at Felixstowe," in Institution of Civil Engineers (ed.), *Port Engineering and Operation* (London, 1985), 113-115.

[55]See the list of terminals at Los Angeles and Long Beach in *Containerisation International* (June 1996), 74.

[56]*Ibid.* (July 1997), 65-67; and *Fairplay*, 17 September 1998, 8.

[57]*Containerisation International* (December 1997), 31; and *Fairplay*, 28 October 1999, 12.

TEU.[58] Such figures also indicate the sheer size of the interests that are at stake for the port authorities involved in their intense rivalry to attract lines and alliances, and the pivotal role of intermodalism in their strategies. In 1997, Vancouver's new Deltaport entered the fray, capitalising on the huge networks of Canadian Pacific and Canadian National, both of which included Chicago. An acute case of "Sinophobia" in the US Congress, however, led to COSCO being refused a lease at Long Beach.[59]

Figure 18:   APL Global Gateway North, Seattle an intermodal terminal for rail and road, far away from Seattle's traditional waterfront.

Source: APL, Port of Seattle, advertising supplement with *Marine Digest* (August 1997).

---

[58]*Containerisation International* (February 1999), 28.

[59]*Fairplay*, 28 October 1999, 12. As a consequence, a Canadian parliamentary committee has started investigations into COSCO's deal with the Port of Vancouver – ironically at the same time that Canada helped to pave the way for China to become part of the World Trade Organisation.

On the other side of the Pacific, in October 1997 it was the same USA which after a sharp confrontation involving Japanese container ships being impounded in American ports forced the Japanese government to take the first steps on the way to fundamental port reform, designed to break the monopoly of the *yakuza*-dominated Japan Harbour Transport Association.[60] But it was not until February 2000 that the Japanese Cabinet approved a new port business law which would allow foreign companies (read Maersk, P&O Nedlloyd, etc.) to establish their own stevedoring operations in eleven main ports.[61] China had already opened its borders, and joint ventures with foreign companies became common-place;[62] Shekou Container Terminal's shareholders, for example, included both P&O and COSCO.[63]

Sealand, Maersk, Evergreen and Hanjin in particular built up networks of leases around the world, including both established and new ports. In 1995 Sea-Land operated terminals in seven US ports, five ports in East Asia (Hong Kong, Kobe, Yokohama, Kaohsiung, and Vostochny), Rotterdam, Algeciras and Adelaide.[64] Hanjin focussed on East Asia and the USA, with terminals in Busan and Kwangyang (Korea), Tokyo and Osaka, Kaohsiung, Long Beach, Seattle and New York.[65] OOCL, in a further demonstration of its close relations with China, invested in Qingdao.[66] Ports outside the main economic regions also attracted attention. P&O, for example, since the late 1980s had an interest in Colombo before it, with NYK, NOL and Evergreen, in July 1995 initiated a project, estimated to cost US $615 million to develop Colombo's container facility Queen Elizabeth Quay and boost its annual throughput from 230,000 to one million TEU.[67] Evergreen, in addition to its interests in the USA, East Asia and

---

[60]*Ibid.*, 30 October 1997, 11.

[61]*Fairplay Daily News*, 25 February 2000.

[62]*Lloyd's Maritime Asia* (January 1994), 15.

[63]*Fairplay*, 16 September 1999, 25.

[64]*Containerisation International* (July 1995), 60.

[65]*Ibid.* (January 1999), 32.

[66]*Ibid.* (December 1997), 31.

[67]*Fairplay*, 20 July 1995, 6.

Algeciras (Spain), in December 1997 signed a thirty-year lease at Taranto in southern Italy.[68]

Shipping companies played an active role in the creation of new ports. APL, for example, was the driving force behind both Cochin and Fujairah, and Evergreen at Manzanillo, its projected hub at the northern exit of the Panama Canal.[69]

The growing involvement of major operators in terminal operations gained a substantial stimulus from the late 1980s with the widespread corporatisation and privatisation of ports and port authorities which enabled them to act with greater autonomy than previously.[70] After a short interval, it also allowed the stronger corporations and companies to become global players.[71] The Port of Singapore Authority, which became PSA Corporation, and the ports of Kaohsiung and Rotterdam were corporatised, while Halifax, Montréal and Vancouver gained considerable autonomy.[72] The immediate result of the latter was that ECT gained permission to grant an exclusive lease to Maersk at its Maasvlakte Delta terminal; the contract was signed a year after Maersk/Sea-Land signed a similar agreement at Bremerhaven.[73] The trendsetter in port privatisation (and its sometimes companion, the liquidation of port unionism) was New Zealand.[74] Latin America also became prone to wholesale privatisation policies, although their implementation was spasmodic at best. In Italy the entire government-owned port sector was sold off with its shipping interests; few prospective domestic buyers were found and by September 1999 all major ports, most of them in far better shape than before, were under foreign control.[75]

---

[68]*Ibid.*, 1 January 1998, 8 and 46.

[69]APL believed that "Fujairah is ideally placed to take advantage of the potential new development in Pakistan, as well as markets in the Gulf, the Red Sea and East Africa" (*ibid.*, 28 September 1989). For Manzanillo, see *Asian Shipping* (August 1997), 32.

[70]For a global overview of port privatisation see *Containerisation International* (May 1998), 75 and 77; on British ports, see *ibid.* (June 1996), 69 and 71.

[71]*Ibid.* (May 1998), 39-43.

[72]*Fairplay*, 4 March 1999, 48.

[73]*Containerisation International* (August 1998), 27.

[74]*Ports and Harbors* (May-June 1991), 36-40.

[75]*Containerisation International* (November 1997), 99-101; and *Fairplay*, 30 September 1999, 21.

Curiously, two of the major countries that did not move in any significant way to corporatisation or privatisation were the USA and Japan.

The rise of corporate port authorities and terminal operators during the 1990s also led to the rise of a number of specialist firms which realised that they produced a packet of highly specialist transport services that could be applied profitably elsewhere. Previously, port authorities occasionally had provided consultancy services and even short-term management assistance to other port authorities, but now expertise in terminal operations became a marketable commodity and a source of profitable investment that could feed on the still-rapidly expanding volume of containerised trade.

In the USA, Stevedoring Services of America built up a portfolio of major terminals across the country, including Seattle's Terminal 18, which served the Global Alliance members as well as the COSCO-K-Line-Yang Ming consortium, Zim and FESCO.[76] In addition to the big container lines these firms constituted a second group of global port service providers, within which during the late 1990s the same tendency towards concentration emerged as in the shipping industry. In 1998, the main terminal operator at Bremen, BLG, merged with Hamburg's Eurokai, which since 1984 had held 33.4 percent in Italian terminal operator Contships. The new company Eurogate (a counter to Rotterdam's self-given soubriquet "Mainport Europe") became Europe's largest when it also took over Contship Italia's remaining 66.6 percent share in its terminals at La Spezia, Gioia Tauro and Lisbon.[77] As Eurokai president Eckelmann explained, a huge geo-economic pincer movement was the corner-stone of his expansionary strategy: "As market leaders in Germany and Italy, we can now concentrate all our cash resources on our connections with the Central European hinterland."[78]

From the early 1990s, indeed, major Hamburg terminal operators had been active in forging intermodal links with Central and East European railway companies as far afield as Croatia, Ukraine and Turkey; partly in consequence of these strategies, Hamburg's share of the traffic of the four major continental North Sea ports (Antwerp, Rotterdam, Bremerhaven and Hamburg) between 1985 and 1995 increased by 150 percent, against Rotterdam's "mere" eighty-percent rise.[79] Another aspect of Eurogate's new strategy appears from BLG's agreement with Maersk/Sea-Land to join in a new exclusive terminal in

---

[76]*Fairplay Daily News*, 1 December 1999.

[77]*Hamburger Abendblatt*, 16 September 1999.

[78]*Fairplay*, 21 May 1998, 52; *Fairplay Daily News*, 14 July 1999; and *Shipping Times*, 19 February 1998.

[79]*Containerisation International* (July 1996), 74-75.

Bremerhaven's most recent expansion, CT III.[80] Of more modest proportions was the equally international merger between the port authorities of Copenhagen and Malmö, prompted by the construction of the Oresund bridge.[81]

Figure 19:   The huge terminal at Bremerhaven, with a Maersk Sealand container in its latest livery. There is no person in sight.

Source: Courtesy Maersk Sealand.

Rapid expansion through foreign takeovers was the method of the other three major specialised international port operators. The most prominent of these was Hutchison Port Holdings (HPH), a subsidiary of the huge Hutchison Whampoa Group.[82] Owned by "Hong Kong's elusive billionaire," "Mr Money" Li Ka-shing, Hutchison Whampoa was the first western *hong* to fall under

---

[80]*Fairplay*, 22 April 1999, 29.

[81]*Fairplay Daily News*, 26 March 1999.

[82]*Fairplay*, 16 September 1999, 22-24.

Chinese control.[83] Already in 1979 Li was the largest private landlord in Hong Kong, and ten years later Hutchison Whampoa was the largest company on the island. Typical of the management discourse of the time, its internet advertisement claims it to be "the global leader in port development and operation."[84] Its flagship was, and has remained, Hong Kong International Terminals, which alone gave it control over about 7.5 percent of the world's turnover.[85]

In 1991, correctly believing that Hong Kong's growth potential was limited, HPH began a systematic policy of international expansion.[86] Its first purchase was P&O's seventy-five-percent share in Felixstowe (OOCL's remaining twenty-five percent followed in 1994), but at least equally important was its 1992 move into mainland China with investments at Shanghai and Yantian. Soon afterwards followed a network of smaller delta ports feeding into Hong Kong and Yantian; in all cases these were joint ventures with local authorities under HPH management.[87] In addition to terminals in Myanmar and Indonesia, HPH intensified its British involvement by buying Thamesport, Tilbury's most direct rival, and Harwich. In 1998, it crossed the North Sea to take a controlling forty-percent stake in Rotterdam's largest operator, ECT (annual throughput of about four million TEU).[88] In the Caribbean HPH was the moving force behind the Bahamas' Freeport and the Panama Ports Corporation at Cristobal and Balboa. Here it not only opposed Evergreen's double operation at Colon and Manzanilla but also provoked xenophobic right-wing US opinion which, already aghast at the imminent handover of the Panama Canal to Panama, viewed Hong Kong-based HPH as a Trojan horse aiming at grabbing control over the canal for China.[89] Needless to say, this episode told more about US politics than HPH's strategy.

---

[83]Anthony B. Chan, *Li Ka-shing. Hong Kong's Elusive Billionaire* (Hong Kong, 1996), especially 202-208.

[84]For example, on Fairplay's website: http:// www.fairplay.co.uk/home.hmtl.

[85]*Fairplay*, 13 February 1997, 6.

[86]*Lloyd's Maritime Asia* (July 1991), 3 and 6.

[87]*Containerisation International* (June 1995), 103 and 105.

[88]*Ibid.* (December 1998), 34. PSA and P&O Australia had both been interested, too, but had not been willing to accept the forty-percent maximum limit imposed on foreign buyers.

[89]*Fairplay*, 21 October 1999, 9 and 12; and "Hutchison Denies Controlling Panama Canal," *Shipping Times Online*, 16 August 1999.

No less dynamic than HPH were four other global operators, PSA Corporation, Dubai Port Authority, International Container Terminal Services Inc., and P&O Australia, the port operating subsidiary of P&O Nedlloyd. PSA, while at home leasing dedicated terminals to individual companies, developed a varied portfolio of investments in Asia and Europe on the basis of a new corporate vision expressed in modern terminology: "To move from being a world-class port operator to a world-class corporation with a network of ports, logistics and related businesses throughout the world, recognised everywhere for quality and value." Its strategy aimed at geographic expansion and output diversification into "logistics and marine related products."[90] Terminals were leased at Dalian (Maersk later joined the PSA) and Fuzhou in China, Tuticorin and Pipavav in India, Aden in Yemen, and a number of ports in Italy, including Leghorn, Genoa and Venice. One of its latest projects involved the green site of Sines, Portugal, designed to rival Algeciras as the leading Atlantic-Mediterranean hub.

On a smaller scale than the PSA, the Dubai Port Authority is spreading its wings with contracts for new terminals in Jiddah and Beirut.[91] ICTSI, which originated from Manila, simply declared its ambition to be "global."[92] The global spread of its interests lacked any geographic cohesion but were quite similar in kind as they all were leading ports in non-industrialised countries: Manila, Karachi, Dammam, Vera Cruz, and Buenos Aires.[93] P&O Ports, which in a 1996 corporate restructuring had taken over the long-standing terminal holdings of its parent company, became involved in significant investments and/or new projects in Britain, Australia, India, Pakistan, Argentina, China and several other countries.[94] In a major new departure, in June 1999 it gained a strategic presence in the USA by taking over a leading stevedoring company, International Terminal Operating, which had a presence in seventeen ports and handled some 800,000 containers and 650,000 vehicles.[95]

As port management and development was globalised by shipping companies and specialist port operators, it appears evident that the supply of

---

[90]*Fairplay*, 19 March 1998, 20.

[91]*Shipping Times Online*, 27 October 1998; and *Fairplay*, 27 May 1999, 15.

[92]*Fairplay*, 13 June 1996, 13.

[93]*Containerisation International* (January 1996), 76-77.

[94]*Fairplay*, 13 June 1996, 12-14, and *ibid.*, 27 February 1997, 42; and *Containerisation International* (February 1996), 34; and (March 1999), 98.

[95]*Fairplay*, 8 July 1999, 56.

container ports increased, competition sharpened and the port industry ran the risk of sliding into the same position of container shipping itself, with a chronic oversupply of capacity and ever-more desperate measures to cut costs and raise terminal handling charges. And although there was occasional talk about regional alliances of ports or some form of cooperation between, for example, Hong Kong and the new ports of southern China, it is difficult to see how enlargement of scale could lead to similar savings as those achieved by successful mergers and alliances in shipping – much of whose cost-cutting measures concerned rationalising services and, hence, port calls.

Container Networks and Regional Port Systems

As the examples of several new ports, such as Gioia Tauro, Algeciras, Fujairah and Manzanillo, may already have suggested, containerisation dramatically changed the network of the world's liner ports and the nature of port rivalry. Civil engineers could (and did) construct ports and container terminals at virtually any physical site. Naturally, all conventional ports wished to join the container revolution, but the entry of many newcomers over the forty years or so since 1960 thoroughly destabilised existing port systems. The aim of every port was to be included in as many high-quality services to as many overseas destinations as possible, and to enjoy the highest frequency of sailings, the lowest transit times, the largest choice of lines, and the best forward connections from overseas ports to the ultimate destination of the exports. As this was patently impossible, in most regions a certain hierarchy of ports had developed, with leading ports located on intercontinental and long-distance trunk lines and secondary ports providing feeder and distribution services as well as probably receiving a small number of main-line calls.

Shipowners had their own dilemmas. In order to keep capital-intensive and ever-larger container vessels moving profitably, they should be turned around as quickly as possible in as few ports as possible, but at the same time their load factors should also be as high as possible – in both directions. Moreover, in their choice of port shipping companies also had to consider issues of a semi-economic nature, such as integration of marine and rail facilities, the bureaucratic interface, rail height clearances, and the like.[96] Theoretically, revenue can be maximised by ships shuttling between two terminus ports. In reality, very few trade routes existed where this would be commercially possible, if only because most suffered from imbalances between traffic volumes in opposite directions. But such ferry operations were fundamentally unrealistic propositions in the deep-sea trades, where shipowners could not avoid serving a

---

[96]Richard Hill, president of APL's domestic transportation division, reported in *ibid.*, 4 December 1986, 23.

number of ports at either or both ends of long-distance services in order to achieve maximum load factors. Moreover, they found that any number of ports vied for their business, either in price or, more commonly, by generating sufficient trade volumes to warrant inclusion in main-line services. In consequence, and characteristic of the entire container industry, two contradictory tendencies have dominated the development of the world's container network: on the one hand, the concentration of traffic in a small number of global and/or regional primary ports against, on the other, the fragmentation caused by ever-more ports attempting to maintain or gain direct access to the ocean super-highway.[97] The latter tendency became all-the-more important as container ports became instruments of national development and industrialisation policies. In 1996, 163 ports turned over more than 100,000 TEU per annum, and these did not even include well-known traditional ports such as Kalkota (Calcutta), Philadelphia, Constantza and St. Petersburg, or fast-rising China ports such as Shekou and Yantian.[98]

From the viewpoint of the shipowner, the dilemma may be summarised as "To feed or not to feed,"[99] in which over time the length of relay lines rose significantly.[100] As larger vessels cascaded down from the main lines into secondary and north-south routes, hub formation was substantially encouraged. From the mid-1980s a second factor developed, which after 1990, with the flood of ever-larger post-Pamanax vessels, further stimulated the transformation of complex gateway-based networks into hub models.[101] Shipping companies began to aim at reducing sailing distances for their highly capital-intensive main-line vessels by the geographical straightening of east-west main lines and the adoption of single hubs in geographically-favourable locations. Mostly these were the "transit zones" of the east-west main lines (Mediterranean, Indian Ocean, Southeast Asia), but also in the main economic areas themselves a number of ports assumed significant relay hub functions. With the continued rise in capacity of the largest carriers, perhaps up to 12,500 TEU, the fight for hub status and transshipment business can only become more intense.

A crucial task of container ship operators became choosing the optimal geographic configuration of their liner networks. For analytical purposes any

---

[97]E. Ion, "Mutual Benefits," *Lloyd's Maritime Asia* (June 1996), 43-44 and 46.

[98]*Containerisation International Yearbook* (1998), 10.

[99]*Fairplay*, 3 February 1994, 33.

[100]See, for example, *ibid.*, 18 November 1999, 22-25, discussing the future of the Australia and New Zealand trades.

[101]See especially *Containerisation International* (June 1997), 43-47.

liner service may be seen as the combination of two or more of the following alternatives: terminuses[102] and hubs which represent concentration, and strings and loops which signify fragmentation. Four kinds of port calls can then be distinguished:

> - Terminus: the first and last port of a service. In round-the-world and multi-ocean pendulum voyages the home port of the shipping company involved may be presumed to serve as its terminus, but it may also be suggested that some services contain no terminus in the classical sense of the word, as the longer stay at the home port is replaced by an almost continuous movement through a string or loop of ports;

> - Hub: a port of which a significant proportion and/or volume of its trade is relayed by feeders to other ports in its region; it may be the first or last port of call in a service but more often is located *en route*;

> - String: a series of successive ports of call, roughly located in a straight geographic direction in a specifically defined region (e.g., US East Coast); and

> - Loop: a series of successive ports of call in a region, broadly characterised by a circular pattern; shipping enters and exits the area through the same strait (e.g., the "Havre-Hamburg range" of Channel and North Sea ports) or the same port.

This categorisation, of course, represents no more than a schematic representation of the reality of often-more complex service patterns, as loops and strings can be freely mixed and may, for example, include two calls at one particular port. Often, too, a company or alliance may serve a particular region with a number of services, with different sets of ports visited by each service – a strategy designed to increase the number of ports of call while, at the same time, lifting the frequency of calls at major ports. In their quest for maximum revenue, moreover, operators have also become adapt at continuously fine-tuning services, mixing changes in port patterns with the utilisation of vessels of varying capacity. The final section of this chapter will analyse how containerisation has affected the major port systems of the world and, more specifically, what new elements – and ports – have been introduced.

The interplay of the forces of concentration and fragmentation may, in the first instance, be illustrated by the development of the British container port

---

[102]I specifically use the term "terminus" and not terminal in order to avoid confusion with the term "terminal" as used in container terminal, which merely refers to a specialised port facility.

system. Broadly speaking, Britain's conventional trade had been carried by London and Liverpool, with minor shares going to Glasgow and Hull. Only a few years after containerisation began, however, Felixstowe, a private port that until then had never been served by long-distance liner traffic, had by far the largest turnover of containers in the country, by 1983 some 700,000 TEUs. Although the fact that it operated outside the system of state-owned British ports and their closed trade-union system was undoubtedly of great importance, Felixstowe's sudden rise to prominence was equally the result of its experimentation with roll-on roll-off traffic and its favourable location in relation to both its British hinterland and the countries on the opposite side of the North Sea that were served by short-sea feeders and ferries.[103] The trade which Felixstowe attracted, in the first instance, was taken from established ports. The British freight market was simply too small for the great consortia to call at more than one or, at the most, two ports. As containers could be easily moved by rail or road, the choice of a port for imports and/or exports was no longer determined by that port's situation in relation to a particular hinterland but rather by its situation in relation to the foreland. Thus, when OCL entered the Europe-East Asia trade as part of the giant TRIO group, neither London nor Liverpool were deemed adequate; instead, it chose Southampton, from where a net of motorways covered the whole length and breadth of the country.[104]

Once Britain became a one-port destination, the ports with traditional industrial relations and/or unfavourable location rapidly lost significance. Glasgow was annihilated, while Hull lost to newcomers like Immingham and Felixstowe. The most dramatic developments occurred in London and Liverpool. The latter, formerly the "Gateway of Empire,"[105] whose extensive global network of shipping lines as late as 1960 had been celebrated in George Chandler's review of the city's shipping industry,[106] was deserted as its companies were liquidated or submerged in consortia that directed their ships elsewhere. In the 1980s, Liverpool was a third-rate backwater with an annual turnover of only about 50,000 TEU before its fortune turned. The privately-owned Royal Seaforth Dock concentrated on trades in which Liverpool's location was of advantage: Canada, northern Russia and, reviving a traditional trade, the Mediterranean. Liverpool re-emerged as a modest participant and in 1993 achieved a record turnover of 385,000 TEUs, its new identity defined by its publicity brochure,

---

[103]Northfield, "Port Management and Operations at Felixstowe," 111-121.

[104]The highly interesting account by an insider of the genesis and first years of Southampton is Hovey, *A Tale of Two Ports*.

[105]Tony Lane, *Liverpool, Gateway of Empire* (London, 1987).

[106]George Chandler, *Liverpool Shipping* (London, 1960).

Liverpool – The UK HUB Port. London followed very much the same pattern, although OCL kept the Australian trade at Tilbury. It was only in the late 1980s, when P&O emerged as the strongest British operator, that Tilbury slowly advanced again. In 1994 Tilbury handled more than 369,000 TEUs, but by this stage Rotterdam and Hamburg had surpassed 4,500,000 and 2,700,000 TEUs per year, respectively.

In northwestern Europe the rivalry between traditional and new ports is sharper than ever because the entire region can be served from almost any location, including Antwerp, Zeebrugge and Bremerhaven.[107] Tilbury's rivals lie across the sea as well as in its own land and on its very doorstep: privately-owned Thamesport in 1997 handled some 385,000 TEUs, overtaking Tilbury and well on the way to attracting more majors, particularly after it was taken over by HPH.[108] Possessing "the kind of labour agreements that make unions wince and continental ports green with envy," HPH subsidiaries Thamesport and Felixstowe, and their south English rival Southampton, can be as much as a third cheaper than the ports across the Channel and North Sea.[109] It is no doubt figures like these that have motivated P&O Ports to commit itself by 2002 to build what is designed to become Britain's largest container port, on the site of the former Shell Haven oil refinery on the Thames.[110]

Significantly, no operator on an east-west main line has as yet dared to centralise all its container cargo in one northwest European port.[111] Despite the theoretical trend towards concentration, and the occasional revival of the "Falmouth myth," the ever-larger capacity of the individual ships and services

---

[107]The consequences of this bitter and expensive rivalry can be studied in Drewry Shipping Consultants, *North European Ports: A "US $2 Million Plus" Industry Adapts to Change* (London, 1999).

[108]*Containerisation International Yearbook* (1998), 9; and *Fairplay Daily News*, 8 March 1999.

[109]*Fairplay*, 26 November 1998, 3; see also *Containerisation International* (June 1998), 75 and 77.

[110]*Fairplay*, 7 September 2000, 5.

[111]According to OOCL (Europe) CEO Jim Poon, the size of 5000-TEU carriers certainly warranted major operators looking at reducing the number of calls to two or even one, but the efficiency of European railways, in comparison with those in North America, was too low to be able to cope with the cargo flows generated by such maritime rationalisation (*ibid.*, 16 January 1997, 9). The construction of the "Betuwelijn" from Rotterdam to the Ruhrgebiet may well be the decisive catalyst towards full-scale intermodalism in northern Europe.

can still only be met by multiple calls on a variety of loops, as is shown in table 18.

Table 18
Ports of Call in Northwest Europe,
Major Operators and Alliances, Europe-East Asia , 1996

Global Alliance:
> *Japan service:* Rotterdam, Hamburg, Southampton, Le Havre
> *China/Korea service:* Southampton, Le Havre, Bremerhaven, Rotterdam
> *China express:* Bremerhaven, Rotterdam, Southampton

Grand Alliance:
> *service >A<:* Hamburg, Rotterdam, Southampton
> *service >B<:* Antwerp, Hamburg, Le Havre, Malta
> *service >C<:* Le Havre, Hamburg, Rotterdam, Southampton
> *service >D<:* Rotterdam, Bremerhaven, Southampton

K-Line/Yang Ming:
> Japan service: Rotterdam, Hamburg, Felixstowe, Le Havre
> China service: Le Havre, Felixstowe, Hamburg, Antwerp

Maersk/Sea-Land:
> *Japan service:* Hamburg, Gothenburg, Rotterdam, Southampton,
> Algeciras *China/Korea service:* Hamburg, Felixstowe, Rotterdam,
> Le Havre, Algeciras

Tricon (DSR-Senator/Cho Yang):
> Le Havre, Rotterdam, Bremerhaven, Hamburg, Felixstowe, Antwerp

Hanjin:
> Rotterdam, Hamburg, Felixstowe, Le Havre

Hyandai/MSC/Norasia:
> Rotterdam, Felixstowe, Le Havre, Barcelona, Genoa, Malta

COSCO:
> Hamburg, Rotterdam, Felixstowe, Antwerp, Le Havre

Evergreen:
> Rotterdam, Hamburg, Thamesport, Zeebrugge, Le Havre
> *Mediterranean service:* Felixstowe, Bremerhaven, Antwerp, Gioia Tauro

Notes: The designation of the various services has been simplified. Note that on all services a call is made at Singapore for Southeast Asian destinations.

Source: Adapted from Michel Neumeister, "Extrême orient: l'axe majeur," *Journal de la marine marchande*, 11 October 1996, 2418-2424.

A rough "league table" of northern ports, based on the number of visits, shows the dynamic mix of concentration and fragmentation, and of traditional and new ports, characterising the trade. The ranking is Rotterdam, fourteen; Hamburg and Le Havre, twelve; Felixstowe, eight; Southampton, seven; Bremerhaven and Antwerp, five; and three ports (Thamesport, Zeebrugge and Maersk's "homeport" Gothenburg) with only one. It should also be noted that neither Liverpool nor London figured in the list. This table relates, of course, only to one particular main-line trade and reference should also be made to the throughput rankings given in table 13, but it clearly demonstrates the total dominance of loop services in the North Sea area. Confirmation of this pattern may be found in Sea-Land's loop Rotterdam-Bremerhaven-Felixstowe-Le Havre[112] and those of Hyundai's pioneer Atlantic services of 1996. Fully representative of those of all Asian newcomers, Hyundai sent its ships to northern US ports via Antwerp, Hamburg, Bremerhaven, Felixstowe and Le Havre; to southern and Gulf ports the loop was more simple: Antwerp, Bremerhaven and Felixstowe.[113]

Figure 20:   A green-site container port in the year 2000: Tanjung Pelapas (Malaysia) with S-class (6000 TEU) *Cornelius Maersk*. The port is intended to become a regional hub in direct competition to Singapore.

Source: Courtesy Maersk Sealand.

---

[112]Http://www.shipguide.com/maps/sealate_map.html [1999].

[113]*Containerisation International* (April 1996), 54.

A similar situation to that in northern Europe existed in East Asia, where loops including a variety of Japanese, Korean, Taiwanese and sometimes also other ports were part of all major services. The unprecedented economic growth of East Asia has made this region into the world's most dynamic centre for container shipping. During the 1980s, the transpacific trade overtook that on the Atlantic and became the driving force behind US intermodalism. No single dominant port arose in Northeast Asia, partly because too many states were pursuing fiercely nationalistic policies, partly also because the rivalry between Tokyo and Yokohama, as that between the Tokyo Bay ports and those of Osaka Bay,[114] was in every way as fierce as that between the ports of the Le Havre-Hamburg range. The unprecedented growth of China was accompanied by the inclusion of Shanghai and several other Chinese ports, especially by COSCO and OOCL. When American President Lines after forty-six years returned to China in 1995, it included the new southern ports of Yantian and Chiwan as well as Hong Kong.[115] The six transpacific services offered by the K-Line, Hyundai and Yang Ming consortium, all with a weekly frequency, were representative and vivid illustrations of the East Asia and US West Coast port systems with their strings and loops. With only few exceptions, all services included only the top twenty ports in East Asia. Evidently, most of these were gateways to major productive hinterlands as well as relay hubs pulling in huge volumes of trade through local and regional feeders. One important aspect in the continuous battle for market share in East Asia was the decline of Japan's ports, due to their being by-passed by many services originating in the arc stretching from Singapore to Korea, their high costs, and the many restrictive practices imposed by the Japan Harbour Transport Association.[116] It has been argued that this decline had serious consequences for Japanese exports.[117]

---

[114]The rivalry between Japanese ports is engagingly discussed by Francis E. Phillips in *ibid.* (October 1986), 59-65; and (November 1986), 62-67.

[115]*Fairplay*, 19 January 1995, 7. An interesting sketch of APL is "Oh, Lucky Man!," *Containerisation Annual* (July 1992), 29-37. A brief overview of the major US container partnerships and the types and number of their services is in *American Shipper* (August 1993). Yantian itself is becoming a "micro" container hub with feeders to be set up to Nanhai, Jiuzhou, Gaolan and Gaosha (*Fairplay*, 13 July 1995, 7).

[116]*Containerisation International* (August 1997), 31.

[117]H. Inamura, K. Ishiguro and M. Osman, "Asian Container Transportation Network and Its Effects on the Japanese Shipping Industry," *IATSS Research*, XXI, No. 2 (1997), 100-108.

Table 19
Loops and Strings in East Asia and the US West Coast, 1996:
Services of K-Line, Hyundai and Yang Ming

Service	Av. Size Vessels	Ports in East Asia, US West Coast and East Asia
PSW 1	3456 TEU	Hong Kong-Kobe-Nagoya-Shimizu-Tokyo-**Long Beach-Oakland**-Tokyo-Nagoya-Kobe-Hong Kong
PSW 2	2878 TEU	Singapore-Hong Kong-Kaohsiung-**Long Beach-Oakland**-Keelung-Hong Kong-Singapore
PSW 3	4440 TEU	Hong Kong-Kaohsiung-Busan-**Long Beach-Oakland-Seattle**-Busan-Hong Kong
PSW 4	3000 TEU	Kaohsiung-Hong Kong-Keelung-Busan-**Los Angeles-Oakland**-Tokyo-Kobe-Busan-Keelung-Kaohsiung
PNW 1	2250 TEU	Hong Kong-Kaohsiung-Kobe-Nagoya-Tokyo-**Tacoma-Portland**-Tokyo-Kobe-Hong Kong
PNW 2	2200 TEU	Hong Kong-Kaohsiung-Busan-**Seattle-Portland-Seattle**-Busan-Hong Kong

Source: See text.

In southern East Asia this tendency towards gateway-*cum*-hub development found its most important exponents. Uniquely, Hong Kong and Singapore became not just leading ports in their region but also grew into by far the largest two container ports in the world. Hong Kong, as a major producer, entrepot and gateway of southern China, in 1999 handled more than sixteen million TEU, and Singapore only slightly less. Third-placed Kaohsiung was far behind at seven million TEU.[118] There was no main-line service, round-the-world or otherwise, arriving from west or east, that did not include Singapore. Its location, continued programme of port expansion, repair and maintenance facilities, leadership as the worlds largest refuelling port,[119] established pattern of main-line and other container services, and a wealth of ancillary maritime services enabled it to build a role as a virtually unchallengeable regional and even hemispheric hub. It built up and maintained a stronghold over the secondary ports of a vast region stretching as far as Bangkok, Jakarta, Kuching, Ho Chi Minh City, Port Kelang, Fremantle and, further afield, to South Asia and the Australian East Coast.[120] In 1994, Singapore handled no less than thirty-five

---

[118]See table 13.

[119]*Lloyd's Maritime Asia* (April 1994), 6.

[120]For a general overview of Southeast Asia, see Keith Trace, "ASEAN Ports since 1945: Maritime Change and Port Rivalry," in Broeze (ed.), *Gateways of Asia*, 318-338. On Port Kelang, see, for example, *Fairplay*, 13 April 1995, 26; and *Asian Shipping*

percent of all ASEAN's seaborne trade and was a hub in a shipping network of 530 lines operating to over 700 ports worldwide. Every week nineteen container ships left for Rotterdam and eighteen for Hamburg.[121]

While both East Asia and northern Europe are characterised by loop services supplemented by regional feeders, the huge volume of the total trade of Singapore and Hong Kong and their supremacy as hubs created significant contrasts between the two port systems.[122] On the east coast of North America an altogether different configuration of ports and port rivalry came into existence, partly because New York in the 1950s had been far ahead of any other east coast port. In the first instance, containerisation focussed very much on New York. But soon, as in Europe, others saw a chance to capture a share of the trade, and by the 1980s Jacksonville, Savannah, Charleston, Norfolk and others became alternative gateways.[123] The dense network of interstate highways throughout the USA gave virtually every port direct access to a vast hinterland, and most also benefited from the rejuvenation of railroad networks.[124]

Instead of the shuttle services to individual North American ports that characterised conventional liner traffic, containerisation created loops and/or strings on all major types of services touching the US East Coast: transatlantic, Asia-US East Coast via Panama or Suez, round-the-world and South America-US East Coast. In September 1997, for example, Evergreen's east- and westbound round-the-world services called at Charleston, Baltimore and New York, and New York, Norfolk, Charleston, respectively. The OOCL/P&O Nedlloyd/Sea-Land consortium operated one loop and two string services: Halifax-New York-Charleston-Miami-Charleston-Baltimore-New York, Boston-

---

(August 1997), 38-39.

[121]*Fairplay*, 6 October 1994, 26.

[122]In 1984 Hong Kong and Singapore had still ranked third and sixth, respectively, with turnovers of 2.1 million and 1.6 million TEUs; the largest ports then had been Rotterdam (2.5 million) and New York (2.3 million) (*Fairplay Pacific*, 27 February 1986, xxv).

[123]The major ports of the North American East and Gulf coasts in 1994 were New York/New Jersey, two million TEU; Charleston, one million; Hampton Roads, 0.9 million; Montréal, 0.7 million; Houston, 0.6 million; Savannah, 0.6 million; Baltimore, 0.5 million; and Jacksonville, 0.5 million TEU (*Containerisation International*, XXX, No. 2 [Febraury 1997], 59); Philadelphia and Boston were well behind.

[124]Last of all, paradoxically (although, remembering the origins of Sea-Land, perhaps not), New York/New Jersey, after the takeover of Conrail by CSX Corporation and Norfolk Southern in 1997 (*Fairplay*, 19 June 1997, 44). In 1996 the Union Pacific and Southern Pacific had merged (*ibid.*, 22 August 1996, 11).

New York-Norfolk, and Charleston-Jacksonville-Port Everglades.[125] Montréal was situated too eccentrically to be included in any global or pendulum services, but as a terminus took full advantage of its inland location and rapidly-strengthening intermodal railroad connections with the Midwestern USA. Already by the mid-1990s its merger-happy CP Ships was the largest individual container carrier on the North Atlantic.[126]

The West Coast of North America offers a slightly different picture. In conventional days, San Francisco had been its undisputed regional leader but containerisation almost entirely killed off its port because its waterfront and transport infrastructure proved woefully inadequate.[127] Matson moved its operations to Oakland,[128] and soon ports within the entire range from Puget Sound to San Pedro Bay benefited from the exponential growth of transpacific trade. Seattle, Tacoma, Oakland and, especially, Los Angeles and Long Beach emerged strongly.[129] Crucial factors in the intense rivalry between adjacent ports were competitive pricing and the quality of intermodal sea-rail traffic to the population centres of the USA.[130] Despite the huge hinterland of each port, none has as yet developed into a single terminus gateway. As table 19 suggests, most services included at least two ports of call. The few exceptions included the round-the-world voyages of Evergreen, Wilhelmsen (RoRo), TriCon, and Zim; Los Angeles was the port of call for the former two, while TriCon and Zim opted for Long Beach.[131] The main advantage of the San Pedro Bay ports evidently was

---

[125]*Containerisation International* (October 1997), 41.

[126]*Ibid.* (December 1998), 46.

[127]In 1996, San Francisco hit rock bottom with a turnover of no more than 5500 TEU; *Fairplay*, 10 April 1997.

[128]William L. Worden, *Cargoes: Matson's First Century in the Pacific* (Honolulu, 1981), 155.

[129]The "league table" in 1994 was Long Beach, 2.6 million; Los Angeles, 2.5 million; Oakland, 1.5 million; Seattle, 1.4 million; Tacoma, one million; Vancouver, 0.5 million; and Portland, 0.3 million TEU (*Containerisation International*, XXX, No. 2 [February 1997], 59). As can be imagined, this pattern of transpacific maritime highways left no space for Honolulu to develop into a central oceanic hub (Edward D. Beechert, *Honolulu. Crossroads of the Pacific* [Columbia, SC, 1991], 168).

[130]See, e.g., *Fairplay*, 3 October 1996, 28, and 10 April 1997, 21-30.

[131]*Containerisation International* (October 1995), 64-65, gives a full overview of all transpacific services calling at US and Canadian West Coast ports.

the smaller deviation they required from the Panama-Japan route in comparison with ports to the north.

Deviation from main-line routes has become a major factor in the transformation of networks in the Mediterranean and Indian Ocean, both regions with three overlapping functions: internal trade, bilateral trade with other regions, and as thoroughfares for the Europe-East Asia trade. Due to its political fragmentation and geography, the Mediterranean has always had a vast number of rival ports, and containerisation initially brought little change. If anything, services between the Mediterranean and major overseas regions (e.g., North America or East Asia) became more international as the new operators and consortia transcended national markets to fill their ships. This is shown by the Mediterranean-East Asia services of the major players.

Table 20
Mediterranean Ports of Call of Main-line Operators,
Mediterranean-East Asia Services, 1996

Global Alliance:
  La Spezia, Barcelona, Fos, Damietta
Grand Alliance:
  northern European service >B<: Antwerp, Hamburg, Le Havre, Malta
Maersk/Sea-Land:
  Japan service: Hamburg, Gothenburg, Rotterdam, Southampton, Algeciras
  China/Korea service: Hamburg, Felixstowe, Rotterdam, Le Havre, Algeciras
  Mediterranean service (orig. from USA): Algeciras, Gioia Tauro
Tricon/Hanjin:
  Mediterranean: Cadiz, Valencia, La Spezia, Gioia Tauro
Hyandai/MSC/Norasia:
  Rotterdam, Felixstowe, Le Havre, Barcelona, Genoa, Malta
COSCO:
  Mediterranean: Limassol, Valencia, Barcelona, Fos, Genoa, Naples
Evergreen:
  Mediterranean: Larnaca, Piraeus, La Spezia, Fos, Barcelona, Valencia, Trieste
  combined Europe + Med.: Felixstowe, Bremerhaven, Antwerp, Gioia Tauro

Source: See table 18.

The Mediterranean possessed quite different characteristics again as table 20, listing calls in the Europe-East Asia trade, shows. Traffic was fragmented over many ports as Barcelona (four); and Algeciras, Valencia, Fos,

La Spezia,[132] and Gioia Tauro (three each) led a large pack of ports in the number of calls made by the great international alliances and companies.[133]

As the Mediterranean is both a terminus region and a thoroughfare, a number of global operators had both through- and terminal services. The result was that several different patterns became superimposed on each other. Services starting or ending in the Mediterranean used loops and strings, with calls at both traditional gateways (such as Barcelona and La Spezia/Genoa) and regional hubs, as the sequences of the Global Alliance (four calls) and Evergreen (six calls) showed. Hyundai's schedule included only three ports and used both Barcelona and Malta (Marsaxlokk) as hubs. For other operators even three calls was still too much. Maersk/Sea-Land's USA-Mediterranean-East Asia line, for example, only called at Algeciras and Gioia Tauro; Grand Alliance's "service B" only at Malta, and Evergreen's combined service only at Gioia Tauro. Of all Mediterranean ports, these three represented most perfectly the pure hub with their almost total dependence on relay trade. All three had been developed on green sites and were located close to the shortest route between the Atlantic and the Suez Canal. By 1994, before the opening of Gioia Tauro, the port system of the Mediterranean had been significantly altered by the growth of hub ports, as Table 21 shows.

The distinction between hub and general gateway ports rapidly sharpened after 1994. By June 1996 Gioia Tauro, which came on stream in late 1995, was used by Contship (its then-major shareholder), Evergreen, TriCon, and Maersk/Sea-Land, and sported a network of feeders linking it to all gateway ports in the western and eastern Mediterranean and the Black Sea.[134] Both Gioia Tauro and Algeciras, which from 1985 had been a Maersk strong point, in 1998 entered the top twenty of world container ports, with turnovers of 2.1 and 1.8 million TEU, respectively; at the same time Marsaxlokk (Malta) jumped over the one million TEU mark. All three ports increasingly attracted main lines and alliances by inducing them to change their regional networks into hub-and-spoke

---

[132]La Spezia's presence was entirely due to Genoa's long-standing failure to embrace containerisation due to strong restrictive work practices that for many years paralysed the port; these problems, however, were resolved in the early 1990s, and the short artificial summer of La Spezia ended as Genoa's superior situation can again be fully exploited; *Fairplay*, 22 May 1997, special supplement "Genoa;" and *ibid.*, 3 July 1997, 8.

[133]In 1994, the rank order in TEU turnover of Mediterranean ports was Algeciras, one million; La Spezia, 0.8 million; Barcelona, 0.6 million; Genoa, 0.5 million; and Fos, 0.4 millon TEU (*Containerisation International* (February 1997), 59).

[134]*Fairplay*, 20 June 1996, 16-17; and *Containerisation International* (June 1997), 44.

operations or by drawing them away from other ports; Evergreen, for example, in 1997 transferred its 100,000 TEUs per annum from Limassol to Gioia Tauro.[135] The economic effect of major hub formation was positive, as gateways and lower-ranking ports were stimulated by their feeder access to main-line high-quality services. By 1996, Genoa had advanced to 826,000, Barcelona to 767,000, and Marseilles to 544,000 TEU.[136] Two years later Piraeus missed the one million TEU by no more than a whisker.[137]

Table 21
Growth of Hub Ports in the Mediterranean, 1994

Rank	Port	Turnover (in TEU)	Relay Trade	Deviation from Direct Gibraltar-Suez Route	
				Miles	Hours
1	Algeciras	1004000	90%	0	9
2	La Spezia	823000	0%	298	28
3	Barcelona	605000	25%	209	22
4	Damietta	520000	95%	0	9
5	Piraeus	517000	20%	178	20
6	Genoa	512000	0%	352	31
7	Valencia	467000	9%	141	18
8	Marseilles	437000	8%	290	27
9	Malta	383000	90%	6	10
10	Leghorn	371000	0%	298	28

Source: See text.

Hub formation characterised the South Asia area of the Indian Ocean from the beginning. Traditionally, the major ports of this region were the linchpins of European colonialism, especially Mumbai, Chennai (Madras), Kalkota and Karachi, and the three coaling stations and entrepots of Aden, Colombo and Singapore.[138] When containerisation came to South Asia, however, India's ports were unable to respond to this challenge, and Sri Lanka's Colombo grew to be the regional hub where both its own country's and a large part of

---

[135]*Containerisation International* (November 1997), 37.

[136]*Containerisation International Yearbook* (1998), 9.

[137]*Independent*, 1 May 1999.

[138]See Frank Broeze, "The Ports and Port Systems of the Asian Seas: An Overview with Historical Perspective from c. 1750," in Agustín Guimerá and Dolores Romero (eds.), *Puertos y Sistemas Portuarios (Siglos XVI-XX)* (Madrid, 1996), 99-121.

India's container traffic became centralised.[139] In 1993, Colombo ranked sixteenth among all Asian ports, with Karachi the only other South Asian port among the top twenty, with just over 700,000 TEU; by 1998 it surpassed the 1,700,000 TEU mark.[140] By that time India finally had begun to grasp the nettle, and the intermodalist policy adopted in 1988 began bearing fruit.[141] Between 1990 and 1996 Mumbai (with Jawaharlal Nehru Port) increased turnover from 324,000 to just over 1,000,000 TEU, and Madras/Chennai from 109,000 to 256,000 TEU. But although the number of India's direct overseas services increased,[142] South Asia as a whole was still mainly served by feeders from Colombo, Singapore and the Middle East.

The Middle East developed a port system which superficially appeared to be quite similar to that of the Mediterranean, with which it shared the characteristic of being both terminus and port of call for ships sailing between the Atlantic and East Asia. During the boom time of the 1970s a rush of established companies and newcomers, often linked together in international consortia, flooded into Jiddah and a plethora of ports in the Gulf.[143] Operators, including local multinational UASC, at first continued traditional varieties of loops and strings along the multitude of ports that were the result of the political fragmentation and geographic configuration of the Gulf. The two Gulf Wars (1980-1988 and 1990-1991) and the trade crisis of the mid-1980s accelerated a hesitant trend towards concentration, as the western Gulf became a high-risk zone. Dubai rapidly gained dominance as a regional hub with an intensive network of short-sea feeders and rose to be among the top ten Asian container ports.[144] The

---

[139]*Fairplay*, 11 March 1993, 38. For an historical perspective see the article by K. Dharmasena, "Bombay and Colombo 1948-1984: A Study in Port Development with Special Reference to Containerization," *The Great Circle*, IX (1987), 119-133. See also K.V. Hariharan, *Containerisation Era in India. Prospects and Problems* (Bombay, 1995).

[140]*Containerisation International* (March 1999), 95; and *Fairplay*, 24 July 1997, 16.

[141]Hariharan, *Containerisation Era in India*, chapter 2; the port statistics are on 38.

[142]See, for example, *Fairplay*, 22 June 1995, 9.

[143]On the "supreme example of port disunity," the UAE, see *ibid.*, 29 August 1991, 44, but also earlier publications such as *Lloyd's Port Bulletin* (November 1986), 8-11.

[144]*Fairplay*, 21 November 1991; and 13 February 1992, 45-46; *Lloyd's Maritime Asia* (November 1993), 22; and (May 1994); and *Containerisation International* (February 1993), 85.

foundation for its rise was its long tradition as a maritime community, its strategic location in the eastern Gulf and the far-seeing and indubitably daring development policies of its ruler, Shaikh Rashid bin Sa'id.[145] He was the driving force behind the construction of Port Rashid and Jebel Ali, the largest man-made harbour in the world, and the creation of the highly successful Jebel Ali Free Zone. By 1985, Dubai was the largest port in the Gulf and since then has never looked back. When its two ports were administratively amalgamated in 1992 into the Dubai Ports Authority, turnover surpassed 1,400,000 TEU. Soon afterwards, Dubai entered the world's top twenty, reaching its as yet highest ranking (tenth) in 1997.

In contrast to the hub ports in the Mediterranean, Dubai's growth was increasingly achieved by other means than transshipment. Although relay trade was absolutely vital for its growth, especially during the period of take-off in the 1980s, by the late 1990s about half of its throughput was generated by local business.[146] The significance of this non-transshipment trade must be emphasised, since it is Dubai's hub function that has increasingly come under pressure from a large and varied series of rivals.

Some of these ports are gateways inside the Gulf, such as Bahrain, Kuwait and Bandar Abbas in Iran (the main point of entry for the central Asian republics of the former USSR), aiming at direct links with outside destinations. P&O Nedlloyd and NYK, for example, in 1999 included Bandar Abbas in their Singapore-Gulf service.[147] Others are primarily hubs located outside the Straits of Hormuz and much closer to the Europe-East Asia main line. The first two of these were entirely new ports built as early as the 1980s on UAE territory outside the Straits of Hormuz: Fujairah, in the emirate of the same name, and Khor Fakkan, a dependency of Sharjah. Both ports were connected with Dubai and Sharjah by highway but also functioned as relay hubs in the western Indian Ocean.[148] Benefiting from their location, which required less deviation from the Suez-Singapore main line than Dubai, their throughput rose rapidly. Already in 1993 Fujairah was the eighteenth-largest Asian container port with a throughput

---

[145]Frank Broeze, "Dubai: From Creek to Global Port City," in L.R. Fischer and A. Jarvis (eds.), *Harbours and Havens: Essays in Port History in Honour of Gordon Jackson* (St. John's, 1999), 159-190.

[146]"Dubai Ports Authority, Gulf Hub Sets Its Sights High," InforMare Press Review, 19 November 1998, quoting *Shipping Times*.

[147]*Containerisation International* (August 1999), 42-43.

[148]*Fairplay*, 13 February 1992, 46.

of 650,000 TEU.[149] With Khor Fakkan, which in 1993 ranked twentieth, and boasting a bonded "mini-landbridge" to Sharjah, Fujairah is the epitome of the new generation of regional hubs. It also regarded itself as a sea-air transshipment point, claiming that cargo discharged there is already on a plane at Dubai before the ship itself could have reached that port. Its "sexy" advertisements highlighted the "Ferrari red" of its cranes.[150] Khor Fakkan, a major port of call for APL and the New World Alliance, in June 1997 introduced the first Liebherr "super post-Panamax" gantry cranes capable of servicing ships with eighteen tiers of boxes.

The rise of Fujairah and Khor Fakkan inspired the creation of two more container ports in the region which in their historical significance for the liner trade could not have been more different. More important, both required even less deviation from the main-line route. The first was Salalah, or Port Raysut, in the extreme southwest corner of the Dhofar province of Oman, a small town with a long-standing indigenous fishing tradition. It had, however, never figured in any regional, let alone main-line, services until Maersk and Sea-Land selected it as the site for their Middle East/western Indian Ocean hub. Each company took fifteen percent of the US \$260 million investment capital, with Omani investors and the government of Oman supplying the remainder; the latter's main purpose was to use the port, as with Jebel Ali, as a stimulus to regional economic development.[151]

Designed for an annual throughput of about 900,000 TEU, Salalah was opened for service in November 1998. Its mission was to become the relay hub of the western Indian Ocean and Gulf, in direct competition with Dubai, Colombo and the smaller UAE ports. Initially, Salalah's only customers were its developers, who began using it to exchange boxes between the mother ships on their US East Coast-East Asia, Europe-Middle East and India, and two Europe-Africa lines, but the port is meant as a common-user facility as well. Salalah immediately diverted significant Maersk/Sea-Land box volumes from Dubai (where they accounted for 500,000 TEU per annum, almost twenty percent of the entire DPA throughput) and Colombo, causing both those ports to reconsider their positions.[152]

---

[149]*Ibid.*, 6 July 1995, 6.

[150]*Ibid.*, 29 August 1991, 52 and 54; 30 January 1992, 21; and 27 July 1995, 42.

[151]"New Terminals Upset Old Order," *Shipping Times Online*, 5 February 1998, quoting *Lloyd's List Maritime Asia*; and "Two Berths at Port Raysut Now Operational," *Shipping Times*, 3 December 1998.

[152]"Gulf Hub Sets Its Sights High," InforMare Press Review, 19 November 1998; "Shipping Giants Hold Future," *Shipping Times*, 30 March 1999.

The second port was Aden, which after the demise of the People's Democratic Republic of Yemen could emerge again from its Cold War isolation. Located on the crossroads of east-west and north-south routes, it had been a major coaling station and entrepot ever since steam shipping in the 1830s invaded the Indian Ocean. Various companies showed an interest in developing a large-scale container terminal, including, not surprisingly in view of the 150-odd year association of P&O with Aden, P&O Ports.[153] The winner of the contest for the lease was global port operator PSA, which opened its US $127 million facility in June 1999. Its first global customer was APL which until then had used Fujairah.[154] In short, in recent years the Gulf and western Indian Ocean had an influx of some of the most powerful private port developers and terminal operators. Dubai and Colombo will find it much harder to compete and – as also attested by the collapse of box rates to the Gulf – the entire region has become as explosive a "battlefield of ports" as the rest of the world.[155]

---

[153]See, e.g., *Fairplay*, 15 February 1996, 28-29, and 5 September 1996, 9; *Containerisation International*, January 1999, 62.

[154]*Containerisation International*, August 1999, 42.

[155]See also *Fairplay Daily News*, 26 November 1999, quoting Mr. David Young, president of Uniglory Marine Corp., regional subsidiary of Evergeen.

Chapter 7
Maritime Labour

[Quality] is also about a well-motivated crew.[1]

We cannot sit back as if life owed us a living.[2]

The human and social impact of containerisation was no less profound than its physical, commercial and structural effects on liner shipping and ports. On the waterfront, technological change revolutionised the nature of work and cut a swathe through the workforce. As terminals were constructed further out to sea or on green fields, ships, port workers and sailors alike vacated inner-city docks and harbours. Many previously-bustling maritime precincts became derelict zones. From the 1970s, waterfront redevelopment became one of the great challenges to urban planners; poignantly, a number of such projects – such as the Albert Dock in Liverpool and Darling Harbour in Sydney – included maritime museums chronicling the very world containerisation had destroyed.

Aboard ship great changes also took place as crew sizes were sharply reduced, almost irrespective of the tonnage of their vessels, and traditional job demarcations swept aside through multi-skilling. The 6000-TEU *Regina Maersk*-class ships sail with a crew of no more than fifteen, representing a ton/man ratio of 5000/1 and an investment per seafarer of roughly US $1.7 million.[3] With air-conditioned cabins requiring closed doors and port holes, social life aboard ground to an almost complete standstill; ashore very much the same was true as container ships, true to their financial mission, turned around rapidly at terminals often far removed from the former fleshpots of sailortown. But as the global number of seafarers declined through enlargement of scale of the individual ship, work restructuring and cost cutting, their ethnic composition was radically transformed, as seafarers from high-cost regions were increasingly replaced by

---

[1]Rev. Canon Glyn Jones, secretary general of the Missions to Seamen, quoted in *Fairplay*, 12 December 1996, 56.

[2]Tony Nunn, International Longshoremen's Association, January 1995, quoted in *ibid.*, 21/28 December 1995, 3.

[3]Jan Hoffmann, "Concentration in Liner Shipping: Its Causes and Impacts for Ports and Shipping Services in Developing Regions" (report prepared for the Economic Commission for Latin America and the Caribbean [1998] (http://www.eclac.cl/research/dcitf/lcg2027), section III, C4.

colleagues from countries with much lower living and wage standards; the same, albeit to a much lesser extent, applied from the 1980s to officers and masters.[4]

In discussing these changes it must be acknowledged that their causes did not always originate within the liner or container industry itself, and that they often were felt in other sectors of the shipping industry as well. The ramifications of economies of scale, for example, were already being felt aboard and in the handling of bulk carriers and bulk cargoes, while the meteoric rise of the modern flags of convenience after World War II had virtually nothing to do with liner shipping. The Liberian shipping register, largely as it is today, was created by attorneys of Standard Oil of New Jersey (now Exxon).[5]

When container companies adopted cheap flags in order to cut costs, they were following rather than leading global trends. National flag shipping, on the other hand, was (and still is) regarded in many countries, including the USA, as vital for national strategic or defence purposes. Similarly, shipbuilding was often considered an industry of national importance and the symbol of a modern diversified economy. The assigning of particular national significance to the maritime industries in turn often led to subsidy schemes of one kind or another which, mostly though not always, included an obligation to employ wholly or partly national crews. Opposing such protectionist or promotional policies, economic rationalists and Thatcherites refused to treat shipping in any other way than the rest of the economy in the conviction that the marketplace should be the arbiter of all things commercial (and, alas, many others, as well). The resulting political and industrial conflicts, of course, also involved seamen's and/or port workers' unions, whose members were vitally concerned about protecting their interests in times of rapid change and systematic downsizing.

Some issues also arose within the context of more general developments. Containerisation in several countries coincided with the process of decasualisation of dock labour and hence became subject to industrial and emotional forces that otherwise would have existed in different configurations or not at all. Crew-reduction programmes and the multi-skilling of seafarers, officers as well as ratings, applied as much to the bulk sector as to container shipping. Protests from maritime unions against job cuts, underpayment of crews, flagging out, or the privatisation of shipping and ports, more often than not related to the entire industry and not just the container sector. The same applied to offensives of big business and government against the trade-union movement in general and maritime unions in particular.

---

[4]In recent years the boom in cruise shipping created a swelling demand for service personnel, but most of these are not strictly speaking seafarers. They also generally hail from countries with low wage levels.

[5]Rodney P. Carlisle, *Sovereignty for Sale: The Origins and the Evolution of the Panamanian and Liberian Flags of Convenience* (Annapolis, 1981).

Ports often became focal points for national economic reform as well as the downsizing policies of terminal operators and hence were scenes of sharp conflicts between employers, occasionally supported by government, and the dockers and their unions. There are considerable parallels between the great era of steam navigation, c. 1870-1914, when maritime unions struggled to get established and recognised,[6] and that of containerisation, almost exactly a century later, when they had to fight for their very survival. It is more than a matter of fortuitous historical symmetry that the International Transport Workers' Federation, born in the crucible of the 1890s, would play an ever more important role in the 1990s. Yet, since it ultimately was technology that largely determined the possible level of employment, the waterfront also witnessed path-breaking agreements between unions and employers to regulate the reduction of the labour force in an orderly and fair manner. In recent years the contribution of the ITF and the leader of its Dockers Section, Kees Marges, was instrumental in building bridges with terminal operators and proposing ways to make dockers stakeholders in the future of the industry; this approach is also reflected in Tony Nunn's words introducing this chapter. Bearing in mind, however, that effective trade unions did not exist in all countries, it is evident that worldwide there were a tremendous variety of situations resulting from the intersection of containerisation with the forces of local traditions, history and the nature of employer-employee power relations.

Seafarers

It has been estimated that in 1995 the total number of commercial seafarers in the world was 1,234,000, made up of 409,000 officers and 825,000 ratings.[7] As table 22 shows, by far the largest individual national contingent was that of the Philippines. With the exception of Japan, Greece and Italy (the latter two still possessing sizeable domestic ferry fleets), all countries mentioned fell within the category of low-wage economies. Between the 1960s and 1990s, several major shifts took place in the supply of low-wage seamen. Filipinos came on the international labour market only from the early 1970s but established themselves quickly as the most numerous group. Their major rival during the late 1970s and 1980s, South Koreans, had virtually disappeared due to rapidly-rising wage levels in their homeland. They had been replaced by Indonesians and, to some extent, East Europeans, who only appeared after the fall of the Soviet Union and the

---

[6]Frank Broeze, "Militancy and Pragmatism. An International Perspective on Maritime Labour, 1870-1914," *International Review of Social History*, XXXVI (1991), 165-200.

[7]*ITF Seafarers Bulletin*, No. 11 (1997), 4, quoting a joint study of the International Shipowners Federation and the Baltic and International Maritime Council.

communist bloc. The use of Chinese crews on other than national vessels can also be expected to continue to rise, particularly as the country's important maritime sector has built up a vast reservoir of seafarers (estimated at c. 117,800 officers and 212,200 ratings, with 80,000 serving on deep-sea vessels) from which foreign agencies could draw.[8] Recruits may also be drawn from new sources, as Nepal's proposal for the establishment of a maritime training centre to find employment for ex-British army Ghurkas foreshadows.[9]

Table 22
Top Ten Nations Supplying Seafarers, 1995

Rank	Country	Officers		Ratings		Total
1	Philippines	49430	(12.1%)	195350	(23.7%)	244782
2	Indonesia	15500	(3.8%)	68000	(8.2%)	83500
3	Turkey	15000	(3.7%)	65000	(7.9%)	80000
4	China	29000	(7.1%)	47500	(5.8%)	76500
5	Russia	20100	(4.9%)	27600	(3.3%)	47700
6	India	12000	(2.9%)	31000	(3.8%)	43000
7	Japan	23800	(5.8%)	18750	(2.3%)	42550
8	Greece	22000	(5.4%)	18000	(2.2%)	40000
9	Ukraine	14000	(3.4%)	24000	(2.9%)	38000
10	Italy	14500	(3.5%)	17800	(2.2%)	32300

Source: *ITF Seafarers Bulletin*, No. 13 (1999), 28.

Historically, the practice of employing lower-paid foreign seamen was well established in the liner industry. Virtually all European companies operating East of Suez contracted indigenous seafarers, mostly Indians (the so-called "lascars," nowadays a pejorative term), Chinese, Arabs and Javanese. This applied especially to the engine room, as European stokers and trimmers were supposedly unable to withstand the additional burning heat resulting from the tropical sun beating down on steel decks, but also to the deck and cabin service. Large companies like P&O and the British India Steam Navigation Company could not have functioned without the tens of thousands of Indian seamen they hired. Dutch imperial shipping companies like the "Nederland" and Rotterdam Lloyd (all four companies mentioned were forerunners of present-day P&O Nedlloyd) and many others were equally dependent on Asian seafarers, who were available in abundant numbers. When the Hamburg-America Line by 1937 began suffering from a shortage of German seamen, many of whom were conscripted or otherwise recruited for Hitler's war machine, the company had no difficulty

---

[8]*Fairplay*, 21/28 December 1995, 13; and 2 December 1999, 38-39.

[9]*Fairplay Daily News*, 3 March 2000.

in recruiting Chinese stokers.[10] Although national seamen's unions occasionally protested against the presence of foreign crews on their nation's ships, before World War II the employment of the latter was never seriously contested except in the coastal trades of the United States and Australia which were reserved for nationals.

Flags of Convenience

One of the exceptions to the practice of hiring foreign crews was the USA. Since the first Registry Act of 1789, US-flagged ships had to be constructed in America and crewed by American officers and sailors. The Merchant Marine Act of 1936 introduced a "scientific" shipping policy, including the granting of both Construction Differential and Operation Differential Subsidies (CDS and ODS, respectively) to overcome the competitive weaknesses of high-cost US registration. As part of the measures to establish a balanced budget, however, ODS were not paid any more from 1997. The subsidies, however, were awarded exclusively to liner vessels plying a certain number of specific "strategic" routes; tramps and tankers did not qualify.

While US liner companies could maintain themselves, even after 1945, in the international arena through their subsidies – as is attested by the large number of American firms that participated in the early stages of international containerisation – this did not apply to the owners of bulk carriers and oil tankers. Without subsidies they would have stood little if any chance against lower-cost international competition in global markets where freight rates were determined by supply and demand. The only solution for these corporations was to flag out their ships to countries whose governments were sufficiently pliable and willing to enact registration legislation sympathetic to overseas interests. The example of Panama, used from the early 1920s by American shipping magnates to avoid the prohibition laws on their passenger vessels,[11] already existed when Exxon lawyers in 1947 put their minds to the task, but language problems and doubts about the efficiency of Panamanian authorities made them opt for another country. Their choice was Liberia, the English-speaking US-client state in West Africa. In return for the payment of a nominal registration fee, its government was willing to tolerate its register being operated from an office in New York rather than in its main port city, Monrovia, which would be the "official" home port painted on ship's sterns underneath the one-star-and-stripes of Liberia.

---

[10]Staatsarchiv Hamburg, Reederei Hapag, 4710, 4465, and 4418; also University of Warwick, Modern Records Office, International Transport Workers' Federation, 159/3/C/a/46, report, 16 June 1937.

[11]Lennart Johnsson, *Funny Flags. ITF's Campaign-Past, Present, Future* (Brevskolan, 1996), 15-16.

Figure 21:   Painting jobs are still performed by seafarers in port. The reputation of lines
                is also maintained by the appearance of the ships. But this photo tells
                another story. As the new home port (Douglas) of *Author* shows, its owner,
                Harrison of Liverpool, has just transferred its fleet to the Flag of Conve-
                nience of the Isle of Man.

Source: *ITF Seafarer's Bulletin*, No. 11 (1997).

The advantages of registration in Liberia, Panama or similar states were
numerous and financially significant.[12] A nominal registration tax bought
unparalleled fiscal freedoms, lack of US supervision, anonymity of beneficial
ownership if desired, less severe safety regulations, and a complete license with
regard to the nationality and payment of crews. While American corporations
like Exxon claimed Liberia was a "flag of necessity," other shipowners began
using it and other offshore registrations as "flags of convenience." (FOC). In
particular, Greek owners became keen FOC users,[13] and by the mid-1970s these
flags accounted for over twenty-seven percent of the world's fleet. The FOC

---

[12]For a general overview of the rise of the FOC, see Basil Metaxas, *Flags of
Convenience* (London, 1985). See also A. Verbeke and W. Winkelman, "The Strategic
Search for Sustainable Country Specific Advantage: The Case of the European Shipping
Industry," *International Journal of Transport Economics*, XVII (1990), 57-75; and
"European Community Shipping: Flying Whose Flag?," *100A1*, No. 1 (1990), 12-15.

[13]Gelina Harlaftis, *A History of Greek-Owned Shipping. The Making of an
International Tramp Fleet, 1830 to the Present* (London, 1996), 240-268.

share hovered around that mark until 1986. By then Cyprus had also become a sizeable FOC, partly through the influx of German management firms. From the second half of the 1980s, however, a new spurt brought the figure to well over forty percent by 1995,[14] and the number of FOC's increased rapidly, partly as a consequence of both Panama and Liberia experiencing severe political crises,[15] and partly as many other states recognised that the creation of an FOC registry might bring more revenue than printing postage stamps (which was also mostly done off-shore). Links with former colonial masters could be of assistance, as was shown by the Marshall Islands, a former US Trust Territory with limited sovereignty, which after its launch in 1988 rapidly became a popular choice for US owners – especially after USLICO, the private company operating the Liberian register, took over management of the Marshall Islands flag as well.[16]

It should be stressed that the strong rise of the FOCs did not go unopposed. In the first instance, this concerned national seamen's unions or the larger groups representing seamen, such as the All-Japan Seamen's Union, the German ÖTV (Öffentliche Dienste, Transport und Verkehr: public service, transport and traffic union) or the British Transport and General Workers Union. More important, in 1948 the International Transport Workers' Federation (ITF) began its campaign for the retention of the jobs of high-wage seafarers, protection of crews employed under FOCs, and the ultimate outlawing of the FOC system.[17] It established (and regularly updated) work and safety standards as well as minimum pay scales for FOC crews. The minimum wage for Able-bodied seamen (ABs), for example, was gradually lifted from US \$288 in 1972 to US \$785 in 1982, US\$1000 in 1990, and US\$1200 in 1998.[18] Through persuasion, industrial action and/or blacklisting, owners of FOC vessels were induced to adhere to these ITF standards. This could be affected particularly in

---

[14]Johnsson, *Funny Flags*, 93. See also A.D. Couper, *Voyages of Abuse. Seafarers, Human Rights and International Shipping* (London, 1999), 10-15.

[15]In Panama the cocaine-trading General Noriega was ousted by a classical US invasion ordered by President Bush, while the fall of the regime of former Sergeant Samuel Doe in Liberia ushered in one of the most brutal civil wars in recent African history.

[16]James Lawrence, "Flags of Necessity. Tumultuous Times for Open Registers," *Marine Log* (February 1991), 26-29.

[17]See, for example, Herbert R. Northrup and Richard L. Rowan, *The International Transport Workers' Federation and Flag of Convenience Shipping* (Philadelphia, 1983); Johnsson, *Funny Flags*; and Couper, *Voyages of Abuse*.

[18]Northrup and Rowan, *The International Transport Workers' Federation*, 123; and Johnsson, *Funny Flags*, 85 and 92.

the case of vessels trading to "ITF sensitive countries," such as Norway, Sweden, Australia and New Zealand.[19]

By the late 1990s some 5500 FOC vessels were covered by such ITF agreements, while the ITF represented 179 seafarers' unions with over 650,000 members.[20] When the United Nations Convention on the Law of the Sea (UNCLOS) in 1958 demanded that a "genuine link" exist between the flag state and the true owners of a ship, it appeared for a short while that the tide might be turned. UNCTAD became a strong opponent of FOCs, although not entirely for the same reasons as the ITF. While the latter tried to protect the jobs of European seafarers while also establishing workplace standards and minimum pay scales for all others, UNCTAD, with its strong membership of developing nations (the Group of 77) firmly, though wrongly, believed FOCs should be abolished as they prevented developing countries from becoming major participants in world shipping. But just as with its 1974 Code of Practice for Conferences, the forces of maritime capitalism swept aside any such international attempts to regulate the industry. UNCTAD's 1986 Convention on the Conditions for Registration of Vessels all but officially legalised the FOC regime.[21]

It was in the wake of UNCTAD's 1986 convention that a new element was introduced into the flagging issue when Norway, in addition to its existing national register, established a second register, the so-called Norwegian International Ship Registry (NIS). The NIS allowed Norwegian shipowners to use their own flag but largely on FOC conditions. Its creation decimated the country's seafaring profession. Overnight several thousand seamen lost their jobs, and by 1991 the NIS employed no more than 2100 Norwegians against about 10,000 Filipinos, 2000 Indians and 1000 Poles.[22] Denmark and Germany followed Norway's lead; the employment of national masters and officers

---

[19]William S. McCuskey, "Registries and Manning: How Some Compare," address given to the "Which Register, Which Flag...Now?" conference, New York, October 1988, 4.

[20]"New Joint Forum to Negotiate Seafarers' Employment Conditions," ITF press release, 22 November 1999 (http://www.itf.org.uk/SECTIONS/Mar/pr221199. html). This is not the place to discuss the problems arising from the fact that ITF wage standards in several Asian countries, including the Philippines, were higher than those local seafarers and their unions were willing to accept; see Northrup and Rowan, *International Transport Workers' Federation*, 96-102.

[21]George C. Kasoulides, "The 1986 United Nations Convention on the Conditions for Registration of Vessels and the Question of Open Registry," *Ocean Development and International Law*, XX (1989), 543-576.

[22]Johnsson, *Funny Flags*, 76-79.

remained obligatory but no further limitations existed on the nationality of crews. Britain adopted a different tactic by using the semi-autonomous Isle of Man to create a new flag – perhaps somewhat unnecessarily since a number of British colonial and former colonial areas, such as Bermuda, the Bahamas and Belize established their own FOCs. While Belgium ingeniously hoisted the Luxembourg tricolour as its cheap flag, France, to its embarrassment, discovered that its second register, rather ludicrously based on the barren waste of Kerguelen Island,[23] was illegal and had to be withdrawn.[24] Many of the new flags were run by American businessmen who saw a ship's registry as "another bauble to hang on the financial Christmas tree of their offshore haven" and as a strategy to draw ancillary business to their own firm and those of their associates.[25]

A number of high-cost countries preferred to avoid such complications and instead juggled tax and registration laws and attempted to negotiate agreements with national seamen's unions to keep vessels under, or lure them back to, the national flag.[26] With the backing of one such agreement, the Compagnie Maritime Belge from 1978 employed seamen from Zaire, paid according to their national wage standards. But the company still found the Belgian flag uncompetitive and began looking for ways to adopt a foreign flag.[27]

The difficulty of preventing a drain from the national fleet is best illustrated by the case of Japan. Since the 1950s, stated government policy was to import all strategic material on Japanese-flagged shipping, an increasingly difficult task since Japanese wages far exceeded those in Korea and Southeast Asia and, until 1982, it was not the flag but the nationality of the manning agency that, in combination with the closed shop of the All Japan Seamen's Union, determined that even foreign-flagged "tie-in," "charter-back" and "*maru*" ships had to sail with Japanese crews.[28] Yet by 1984 the total number of

---

[23]"Plan marine marchande. Le décret Kerguelen est paru," *Journal de la marine marchande*, 2 April 1987, 741-743.

[24]*Fairplay*, 16 November 1995, 8. The Kerguelen register had been set up in 1987 by a regulation that had no legal authority.

[25]John Guy, "Spoiled by Choice," *Fairplay*, 25 May 1989, 19.

[26]See, for example, *ITF Seafarer's Bulletin*, No. 5 (1990), 11-17.

[27]G. Devos and G. Elewaut, *CMB 100. Een eeuw maritiem ondernemersschap 1895-1995* (Tielt, 1995), 226.

[28]Shin Goto, "Globalization and International Competitiveness: The Experience of the Japanese Shipping Industry," in David J. Starkey and Gelina Harlaftis (eds.), *Global Markets: The Internationalization of the Sea Transport Industries since 1850* (St. John's,

seafarers had already been halved compared to the late 1960s.[29] The 1985 Plaza Accord, after which the yen appreciated from 254 to 185 (1986) and even 127 (1988) per US dollar, sharply exacerbated the financial woes of Japan's shipping companies and led to another massive outflow of tonnage. A study comparing wage costs to man one particular ship showed savings of US $2.3 million if, instead of twenty-four Japanese, the same number of Filipinos were recruited (US $2.65 million against US $0.3 million); even if the most extreme crew reduction was applied and the ship sailed with only eleven Japanese seamen, their annual costs would still amount to US $1.3 million. Even a mixed crew of nine Japanese and fifteen Filipinos was cheaper than the smallest Japanese crew.[30] The result of the massive and global flight to FOCs is summarised in table 23.

Table 23
Top Twenty Merchant Shipping Flags, 1997 (Ships over 100 grt)

Rank	Flag	Gross Tonnage
1.	Panama*	91,100,000
2.	Liberia*	60,100,000
3.	Bahamas*	25,500,000
4.	Greece	25,300,000
5.	Cyprus*	23,700,000
6.	Malta*	23,000,000
7.	Norway (2nd Register)*	19,800,000
8.	Singapore	18,900,000
9.	Japan	18,500,000
10.	China	16,300,000
11.	Russia	12,300,000
12.	United States	11,800,000
13.	Philippines	8,800,000
14.	St Vincent & Grenadines*	8,400,000
15.	South Korea	7,200,000
16.	Germany	6,900,000
17.	India	6,900,000
18.	Turkey	6,600,000
19.	Marshall Islands*	6,300,000
20.	Italy	6,200,000

Note: * Flag of Convenience

Source: *ITF Seafarer's Bulletin*, No. 13 (1999), 39.

1998), 355-383; see also *Fairplay*, 26 April 1979, 7.

[29][Mariko Tatsuki and Tsuyoshi Yamamoto], *The First Century of Misui O.S.K. Lines, Ltd.* (Osaka, 1984), appendix "Employees."

[30]Goto, "Globalization and International Competitiveness," 374.

The clear leaders were the two, by now "traditional" FOCs, Panama and Liberia. But other more recent creations figured prominently. The relatively strong showing of the USA is due to heavy subsidies and a considerable domestic trade. Notable absentees from this list were the United Kingdom and several other "traditional" maritime nations, such as the Netherlands, Sweden, Norway, Denmark, France and Spain, and powerful newcomers such as Taiwan and Hong Kong. With regards to other countries, notably Greece, Japan, the USA and Korea, their strength was vastly underestimated as a result of their FOC use. More enlightening on the real distribution of shipping power, according to the domicile of the parent company, is table 24.

Table 24
Top Twenty Shipowning Countries, 1996

Rank	% of World	Country	Total Fleet (in grt)	Foreign Flag (%)
1.	17.4	Greece	118,400,000	60.1
2.	12.8	Japan	87,300,000	74.7
3.	7.2	USA	49,100,000	73.2
4.	7.2	Norway	48,900,000	42.5
5.	5.3	China	36,300,000	36.1
6.	4.9	Hong Kong	33,500,000	83.9
7.	3.4	South Korea	23,100,000	55.7
8.	3.1	United Kingdom	21,100,000	75.1
9.	2.7	Germany	18,100,000	66.0
10.	2.6	Russia	17,300,000	29.5
11.	2.2	Taiwan	15,100,000	49.9
12.	2.1	Sweden	14,600,000	85.6
13.	2.1	Singapore	14,400,000	38.5
14.	1.9	Denmark	12,600,000	42.5
15.	1.8	India	12,400,000	10.1
16.	1.8	Italy	12,000,000	36.3
17.	1.6	Sa'udi Arabia	10,800,000	90.0
18.	1.4	Brazil	9,700,000	26.1
19.	1.3	Turkey	9,100,000	1.2
20.	1.1	France	7,800,000	44.4

Source: A.D. Couper, *Voyages of Abuse. Seafarers, Human Rights and International Shipping* (London, 1998) 13.

Although the use of foreign flags cannot be fully equated with purely FOC registration, it is evident that the major shipowning nations of the world, not excluding low-cost countries like China, Russia and even India, availed themselves abundantly of FOCs. By 1999, sixty-seven percent of all shipping owned by companies domiciled in OECD countries was flagged out to FOCs and the proportion was still rising.[31] As suggested before, many reasons could lead shipowners to register vessels under a foreign flag, including fiscal and commercial flexibility and freedom from domestic red tape. But overall, the freedom to employ cheap foreign crews under less stringent conditions than applied in their home states was the leading motive.

It must be stressed that FOCs for a long time were virtually unknown in the deep-sea liner sector. The major liner shipping companies were long-established traditional firms whose loyalty to their national flag was an important part of their marketing strategy, reputation and legitimacy as conference members. In addition, the economics of liner shipping and conference membership enabled companies with relatively high wage levels to co-exist and, when the crisis came in the 1960s, containerisation with its much more capital-intensive cost structure was a godsend. If Sea-Land with its US cost levels could exist without subsidies, European and East Asian owners should be all right as well. The problems of the Australian National Line were only to a small extent caused by its use of Australian crews. For the time being, with only very few exceptions, no major container operator did or, for his reputation, could afford to flag out. In 1986, the top ten flags for full container ships were the USA, West Germany, Panama, Japan, Taiwan, United Kingdom, Denmark, Singapore, South Korea, and only then Liberia.[32] None of the major operators from the USA, Europe or East Asia used a FOC, except for Taiwan's Evergreen and Wan Hai, both of which registered about half their fleet at home and half in Panama and Liberia, respectively.[33] Evergreen's policy was not due to the necessity of avoiding diplomatic problems but was based on adopting the Taiwanese flag for all its home-built vessels in recognition of the subventions granted by its government.

From 1987 onwards, however, the situation changed rapidly. As the overcapacity became a constant feature of life, profit margins contracted and competitive pressures increased, liner companies abandoned their reservations against cheap flags. Mitsui-OSK and OOCL chose Liberia for their latest acquisitions; other Japanese lines, like NYK, mainly preferred Panama.[34] Once the first companies had moved, many others followed. In November 1994, well over thirty-five percent of all container shipping was operated under FOCs, and

---

[31]"ITF Maritime Department" [1999] (http://www.itf.org.uk/SECTIONS/ MAR/ mar.htm).

[32]*Containerisation International* (February 1989), 25.

[33]*Fairplay Shipping Year Book* (1986).

[34]*Containerisation International* (February 1989), 27.

the top-ranking flag nations bore more resemblance to the situation in the general world's shipping industry (see table 25).

Table 25
Major Flags of Registry, Container Shipping, 1994

Rank	Country	Total TEU Capacity	% Growth Since 1988
1.	Panama	527,368	44.1
2.	Germany	385,820	83.6
3.	Liberia	294,791	130.5
4.	USA	230,553	2.0
5.	Bahamas	179,756	258.4
6.	Cyprus	165,248	91.6
7.	China	157,538	77.8
8.	Taiwan	152,114	(-0.4)
9.	Singapore	144,559	65.3
10.	Denmark	114,989	n.a.

Source: *Containerisation International* (March 1995), 53.

Taking into account that Germany's second place was largely (probably some eighty percent) the result of the introduction of its second register in 1989, FOCs clearly had established their supremacy. Their rapid expansion may be contrasted with the acute stagnation of the USA and Taiwan, Maersk's shift to the Danish second register and the absolute decline of Japan, from 110,946 in 1988 to 92,506 TEU six years later. Both NYK and MOL flagged out in Liberia, as did OOCL and Wan Hai. Panama benefited, above all, from Evergreen (about half its fleet, or 77,000 TEU) and the fast-rising Mediterranean Shipping Corporation (thirty-seven vessels, 40,710 TEU), but also retained much of the business of the traditional Japanese lines. Its future expansion was assured when Evergreen and COSCO used its flag for their next series of Panamax carriers, as did Yang Ming, when its expanding East Asian services incorporated mainland China.[35] US companies APL and Sea-Land in 1995 moved their ships off-shore to the Marshall Islands, out-sourcing their manning requirements to ship-management firms in Cyprus and Monaco.[36] A few years later, however, APL repatriated some of these ships and also registered a number of newbuildings and former Singapore-flagged NOL vessels under the US flag. Its main purpose in so doing was to qualify for the US Maritime Security Program and its financial

---

[35]*Ibid*. (May 1998), 8. For the flagging of Evergreen's fleet in 1999, see http://www.evergreen-america.com/Page7.htm.

[36]*Ibid*. (February 1995), 7; and (September 1995), 22; see also *Fairplay*, 7 May 1998, 22-23.

grants.[37] In 1998, after a massive exodus, Sweden's government reintroduced subsidies to keep ships under the national flag, but even so had to accept part-time employment by cheap crews.[38] But these moves had only marginal effects and, as Hapag-Lloyd abandoned the first German register, the trend toward FOCs shows no sign of abating.

A panoply of economic studies demonstrated the massive savings resulting from such substitutions.[39] "Every shipowner that [sic] uses a national flag is aware that his crewing costs could be reduced by up to 70 percent simply by changing flag."[40] Table 26 gives a representative indication of relative crew costs, depending on the nationality of the seamen.

Table 26
Crew Costs, Standard Container Ship, According to Nationality, 1983

Nationality	Annual Costs	Index	Company/Companies
USA	$3,400,000	100	APL, US Lines, Sea-Land
West Germany	1,474,000	43.4	Hapag-Lloyd
Denmark	1,307,000	38.4	Maersk
Norway	1,290,000	37.9	Knutsen, Barber Blue Sea
Japan	940,000	27.6	NYK, MOL, K-Line
Hong Kong	425,000	12.5	OOCL
Taiwan	425,000	12.5	Yang Ming, Evergreen
Philippines	390,000	11.5	various
Korea	280,000	8.2	KSC

Source: Ernst Gabriel Frankel, *The World Shipping Industry* (London, 1987), 176.

These figures reflected the extremely harsh reality faced by OECD seafarers and the companies employing them. Even if multi-skilling of high-cost seafarers could lead to significantly smaller crew sizes, the huge gap between American, European and Japanese crews, on the one hand, and cheap Asian crews, on the other, could never be bridged. Standards of training, specialisation, and perhaps even loyalty could play a role in a shipowner's decision regarding

---

[37]APL website, http://www.prnewswire.com/cgi-bin/micro_stories.pl?ACCT =107003&TICK=APL&STORY.

[38]*Fairplay Daily News*, 17 November 1998.

[39]See, for example, B.N. Metaxas, *The Economics of Tramp Shipping* (London, 1971), 166-174; Clinton H. Whitehurst, Jr., *The U.S. Merchant Marine* (Annapolis, 1983), chapter 15; Ernst Gabriel Frankel, *The World Shipping Industry* (London, 1987), 176; *Lloyd's Ship Manager* (April 1987), 7-13; and Niko Wijnolst and Tor Wergeland, *Shipping* (Delft, 1996), 209-213.

[40]McCuskey, "Registries and Manning," 1.

what nationality or mixture of nationalities of seamen to employ, but high-wage seamen, and to some extent also officers, were always on notice as long as such huge wage differentials existed. The British National Union of Seamen in the 1970s campaigned for wage equalisation on British ships but, as can be imagined, the shipowners were vehemently opposed.[41]

Table 27
Seamen in Japan's Deep-Sea Trades, 1975-1995

Year	Number	Yen/US dollar
1975	42,196	308
1980	30,776	242
1985	22,323	254
1990	5,508	150
1995	2,443	93

Source: Shin Goto, "Globalization and International Competitiveness: The Experience of the Japanese Shipping Industry," in David J. Starkey and Gelina Harlaftis (eds.), *Global Markets: The Internationalization of the Sea Transport Industries since 1850* (St. John's, 1998), 380-382.

Flagging out had catastrophic consequences for national seafarers who often were sacked overnight. (Such dramatic job reductions came on top of the more gradual downsizing of crews which will be discussed in a later section.) In the Netherlands fleet, as early as 1964-1974 the number of Dutch masters and officers declined from 11,560 to 6903, a fall of about forty percent, and ratings from 11,900 to 3020, or a plunge of approximately seventy-five percent.[42] Between 1979 and 1987, the number of ratings on the British Merchant Navy Establishment Register fell by forty-seven percent from almost 29,000 to 15,400, with many of the latter unemployed.[43] Altogether, Swedish Seafarers' Union leader Anders Lindström claimed, since the early 1980s close to 300,000 Western European seafarers lost their jobs, leaving their unions reduced to small and insignificant organisations.[44] In Japan the situation was no better. The number of seamen in the deep-sea trades remained relatively stable between 1965 and 1975 (41,101 and 42,196, respectively), but then the decline came hard and

---

[41]Arthur Marsh and Victoria Ryan, *The Seamen. A History of the National Union of Seamen* (Oxford, 1989), 217.

[42]G. Teitler, "Zeevarenden," in *Maritieme Geschiedenis der Nederlanden*, IV (1978), 101.

[43]Marsh and Ryan, *Seamen*, 222.

[44]Johnsson, *Funny Flags*, 310.

fast. Despite government intervention to place Japanese seamen on foreign ships with mixed crews,[45] it accelerated into freefall after the revaluation of the yen (see table 27).

The heavy slide during the first decade may largely be ascribed to reduced manning scales, but the real crunch came in the late 1980s, after mixed crews were introduced and the major liner companies began flagging out on a massive scale. In some countries foreign crews could be employed under existing national legislation, resulting in significant job losses. The French company CGM in 1994 switched over to Romanian crews, while in 1995 Hapag-Lloyd abandoned the first German register to save US $1.1 million per year per ship in manning costs.[46] When all the protests died down, its example was followed by Hamburg-Süd. Zim induced the Israel Transport Ministry to adopt new regulations which enabled it to replace its Israelis with Southeast Asian sailors.[47] P&O Nedlloyd in August 1998 inserted the thin end of the wedge when it "reluctantly" but determinedly replaced 330 British and New Zealand ratings with Filipinos; changes in British legislation had opened the door to this practice.[48]

The impact of such changes; the realisation that some FOCs were applying acceptable standards of pay, safety, training and certification of their crews; and finally, the belated acknowledgement that FOCs were here to stay induced the ITF in 1999 to begin cautiously shifting its previously uncompromising opposition to all FOCs. Instead, it considered (though still rejected) a distinction between good and bad FOCs, as well as the inclusion of some genuine national flags that did not meet ITF standards.[49] And for the first time, in November 1999 the ITF and the International Maritime Employers Committee agreed to meet and negotiate a model agreement, to be introduced in January 2001.[50] Its basis would be an acceptance of the ITF minimum standards and FOC

---

[45]*ITF Seafarers' Bulletin*, No. 5 (1990), 14-15.

[46]*Fairplay*, 3 February 1994, 9; and 16 November 1995, 9.

[47]*Ibid.*, 3 September 1998, 16.

[48]*Ibid.*, 20 August 1998, 6-7; and 10 September 1998, 4, an editorial which contrasts the sackings poignantly with the lavish naming ceremony of the *P&O Nedlloyd Southampton*. See also "Pragmatic Approach Needed to Flag of Convenience Debate," *Shipping Times*, 16 September 1998.

[49]*Fairplay*, 14 October 1999, 32.

[50]"New Joint Forum to Negotiate Seafarers' Employment Conditions," ITF press release, 22 November 1999 (http://www.itf.org.uk/SECTIONS/Mar/pr221199.html).

pay scales and the expansion of maritime trade unions into the FOC sector. As interest in seafaring careers in high-wage countries wanes, it is not improbable to suggest that by 2020 well over ninety percent of all seafarers may be employed under ITF conditions. This does not mean that the ITF in any way weakened its campaign against sub-standard shipping and rogue shipowners. In 1998 and 1999 it sent its ship, *Global Mariner*, to visit over seventy ports around the world and to carry its message through the medium of a powerful exhibition.[51]

Figure 22:   The post-Panamax P&O Nedlloyd *Southhampton* (6600 TEU). Ships of these huge dimensions are often crewed by no more than twenty men. In September 2000 the ship was a subject of dispute between P&O Nedlloyd and the ITF and British seamen's union about the replacement of British by cheap third-world ratings.

Source: *GL-Magazin*, No. 1 (1998).

Training

Three final but crucial points need to be considered concerning the seafaring side of container shipping: training, crew reduction and seamanship. In these contexts it is significant that among the thousands of actions undertaken by the ITF, virtually none have ever involved the fleets of the major container operators. At the quality end of the world's shipping industry there is no evidence of the abuses that have been so abundantly documented in the case of a company like Adriatic

---

[51]Its circumnavigation could be followed on http://www.itf-ship.org. Couper, *Voyages of Abuse*, in many ways constituted the academic counterpart of the *Global Mariner* project.

Tankers.[52] There have been no disputes about the underpayment of Asian and other crews or with the manning agencies supplying them. The risk of being boycotted and delayed in port is simply too great for companies that were increasingly run on just-in-time principles and for whom a good reputation was a vital ingredient of marketing strategy.[53]

In most cases foreign crews on deep-sea container vessels have met standards set in the 1978 International Convention on Standards of Training, Certification and Watchkeeping of the International Maritime Organisation and the alterations contained in the 1992 Associate Code. Although training schools and colleges are run according to the laws and regulations of individual countries, a number of major container shipping companies have played active roles in the establishment of new training centres. A consortium of German companies, including Hamburg-Süd, since the late 1960s have run a maritime training facility in the tiny Pacific state of Kiribati, offering much-needed employment to these natural seafarers; by the mid-1980s, about one thousand were employed, predominantly on German ships.[54] The operators of the Marshall Islands FOC register specifically aimed to provide local recruits to vessels under their flag. More substantial was the support given by Japanese lines, like NYK and K-Line, to training schools in the Philippines and, more recently, in China.[55]

Keen to increase the hard currency earned by its seafaring citizens, China helped COSCO to establish a maritime centre near Shanghai and its second container company China Shipping to join the world's largest shipping management company, Monaco-based V. Ships, in training and providing Chinese seamen to the world market.[56] V. Ships stands as another monument to the globalisation of the industry, with "recruiting centres worldwide, extensive in-house training" and a pool of 11,000 seamen, including Indians, Filipinos, and east and north Europeans.[57]

---

[52]See Couper, *Voyages of Abuse*, chapters 5-7.

[53]For the exceptional case of the ITF boycott of the Filipino-crewed *Maersk Oceania*, see *Fairplay Daily News*, 30 November 1999.

[54]*Fairplay*, 14 February 1985, 9; and 25 May 1995, 8.

[55]*Ibid.*, 14 December 1989, 6; *Lloyd's Maritime Asia* (June 1991), 32; and (July 1991), 19-21.

[56]*Shipping Times Online*, 22 July 1999, quoting Bernama-Xinhua.

[57]*Fairplay*, 11 March 1999, V. Ships-sponsored supplement, 19.

Down-sizing and Multi-skilling

Training became all-the-more important as ships became increasingly automated and computerised. Traditional work practices on board were swept away as shipowners pursued possibilities of reducing crew sizes through multi-skilling of officers and ratings. As early as the 1960s, experiments were made in Britain but with little success.[58] The first test in the Netherlands was made in the early 1970s, while the West German Shipowners' Association in 1973-1974 sent a container ship with an active crew of only twelve instead of thirty-two men on two voyages to East Asia.[59] But it was not until the depression of the late 1970s that crew downsizing became a matter of urgency in all major seafaring countries. What occurred in Japan was representative of global developments.

In 1979 Japan established the Committee for the Modernisation of the Seamen Working System to supervise the process – its administration was in hands of the Ministry of Transport.[60] Its purpose was to reduce the number of seamen on "modernised" ships in stages, predicated on and in tandem with authorised changes in ship's technology. One of the fundamental premises was that ships would be "machine-zero," i.e., without watchkeepers in the engine room, and equipped with the latest satellite navigation, auto-pilot and remote cargo-handling gear. New qualifications were introduced for ratings and officers with the purpose of first the former and gradually also the entire latter category gaining proficiency in navigation and engineering. But even with drastic crew reductions, from the twenty-four men of an "ordinary" vessel to the eleven of the "pioneer ship," or with the adoption of mixed Japanese-foreign crews, costs could not be depressed to the level of a totally foreign-manned vessel.

Although multi-skilling ultimately was a failure in that it could not prevent large-scale flagging out, it was adopted throughout the industry as a significant cost-cutting mechanism and stimulus to workplace reform in response to changing technology. Maritime unions, including those in Australia,[61] were unable to resist the push for ever-smaller crews. The All Japan Seamens' Union, for example, in 1982 vainly attempted to hold the line at twenty-two when

---

[58]Marsh and Ryan, *Seamen*, 204-205.

[59]*The Australian*, 1 February 1973 and 3 June 1974.

[60]Goto, "Globalization and International Competitiveness," 371-377; see also *Fairplay*, 21/28 December 1978, 6; and 26 June 1980, 24.

[61]Australian National Maritime Association, *Australian Shipping: Structure, History and Future* (Melbourne, 1989), 4-14.

NYK's highly-automated *Hakuba Maru* was designed for only eighteen men.[62] Sweden adopted a "core crew manning project" in a vain attempt to match the costs of Norway's International Register.[63] Nedlloyd in 1988 experimented with a fifteen-man crew on one of its container vessels.[64] As the size of the container ship was of little importance in determining crew size, it could thus become possible for Maersk to have its *Regina Maersk* manned by no more than fifteen officers and ratings. This was the most extreme case of downsizing, but other companies were not far away from that mark. Norasia's series of open-top (deckless) 2780-TEU vessels in 1996 were crewed by fifteen, Evergreen's 4173-TEU D-class by sixteen, and APL's six "Generation 6000" post-Panamax carriers (276.3 metres long, 4932 TEU), beginning with the *APL China*, by twenty-one people.[65]

Safety and Accidents at Sea

Not surprisingly, critics of downsizing emerged in the late 1980s, arguing that minimum manning might be safe under ordinary circumstances, but that there was no "defence in depth" in case of emergency. A particular case in point is the absence in many crews of a fully-professional electrician, but there are more general concerns as well. It was claimed that the small number of crew, especially as the vessels under their responsibility dramatically increased in dimensions, sapped their morale and will to overcome problems at sea.[66] Captain E.W.S. Gill, a veteran commander of large container ships, claimed that the essential requirement "that when crews are reduced, those who remain should be both more highly trained and motivated," had been neglected by many operators and that the "importance of team work, mental attitudes and co-operation" must be considered immediately.[67] Gill seriously questioned whether the newly-created General Purpose Seamen and the entire system of Interdepartmental Flexible Manning could properly function because many ratings and officers fulfilled dual roles but had been trained in, and were only paid for, one task. These dissenting

---

[62]*Fairplay*, 17 June 1982, 41.

[63]*Ibid.*, 16 June 1988, 16.

[64]*De Zee*, XVII, No. 6 (June 1988), 199 and 206.

[65]*Containerisation International* (August 1996), 59; *The Times*, 25 August 1999; and *Fairplay*, 19 October 1995, 6.

[66]*Fairplay*, 8 January 1987, 23.

[67]*Ibid.*, 27 August 1987, 23.

voices were all-the-more important as they addressed themselves not to the bottom end of the FOC industry but to the high-quality container sector. Practical problems of considerable magnitude also arose from recent international mergers of container operators, such as P&O Nedlloyd, since the professional accreditation in each of the states could differ markedly.[68]

It was no coincidence that from now on container operators in East Asia became more closely involved in the running of training centres in, for example, the Philippines and China. Yet, however well trained a crew may be, the sheer workload and exhaustion resulting from crew downsizing and lack of time to recuperate has become a major source of concern. Especially fast port turn-arounds (on average down from 198 hours in 1970 to just sixteen hours in 1998) have been blamed for a recent rise in the incidence of death and injury among seamen.[69] Chilling evidence was produced of excessive overtime, long periods of work without rest and the resulting fatigue, depression, stress and trauma after accidents "waiting to happen."[70] A chaplain offered this brief explanation of why seamen took their risks: "In order to keep up with the schedule, because otherwise they were penalised. The charterer would penalise the owner, who would probably take it out of their wages." It was also stressed that reduced manning scales were based on tasks to be performed at sea, not taking into account the considerable work still to be done in port and the lack of shore leave and rest. It is unlikely that a European Union directive, following ILO guidelines, establishing maximum working time per day (fourteen hours) and per week (seventy-two hours)[71] will find acceptance in Asia.

Fortuitously, with the exception of the sinkings of *München* and *MSC Carla*, no container ships have been lost at sea, in contrast to numerous sinkings and wreckings of what in Australian parlance became known as "Ships of Shame," mostly bulk carriers and tankers under FOCs. But with increasing ship sizes and higher and wider deck loads, the proper lashing of the top tiers of boxes became a contentious issue. Often held only by their twistlocks, containers have been shaken loose by vessels rolling in heavy-weather crossings. *Hyundai Seattle* in December 1994 lost forty-nine containers on the North Pacific *en route*

---

[68]*Ibid.*, 27 January 2000, 21.

[69]*Ibid.*, 11 November 1999, 31, discussing a study by Dr. Erol Kahveci of the Seafarers International Research Centre in Cardiff.

[70]Another recent study of Indian seamen found alarming evidence about their high rate of serious disease and early death (*ibid.*, 5 November 1998, 15). It should be stressed, however, that this predominantly concerned other than container vessels.

[71]*Fairplay Daily News*, 20 November 1998.

to the USA.[72] In another Pacific storm the deck cargo of four carriers was badly mauled, including the post-Panamax *APL China*, which lost almost 400 boxes and suffered damage to many more.[73] In November 1997 MSC's high-age *MSC Carla* broke in two and lost its forward half; later the stern half sank as well.

The causes of these accidents were addressed by the German classification society, Germanische Lloyd (GL). The latest newbuildings for P&O Nedlloyd, which proudly claimed that it had never lost a container,[74] sported a comparatively straight and significantly-strengthened stem instead of the flare that had become fashionable in the mid-1990s. Clearly referring to the above incidents, GL explained succinctly that "The design change has been made for a very good reason. Ships' officers have been driving vessels too hard in bad weather, causing damage on numerous occasions in recent years."[75] The two main causes of these ships being driven too fast through dangerous conditions appear to be the commercial imperative not to lose time on the one hand, and the isolation of officers, often with no other experience than service on large ships, from the elements outside and contact with colleagues, on the other.

Although it is yet too early to reach any firm conclusions about the 24 August 1999 collision in the North Sea, on a calm day with a clear sky, between Evergreen's 4192-TEU *Ever Decent, en route* from Thamesport to Zeebrugge, and the almost equally large cruise ship *Norwegian Star*, the "lack of defence in depth" on the latter evidently was one of the major factors.[76] The same factor may also lie at the bottom of the finding of "crew negligence" in the case of the collision in March 1999 between the Panama-registered *Hyundai Duke* and a smaller conventional cargo-ship in the Indian Ocean after neither vessel had kept a proper watch.[77] From the recent spate of incidents and accidents it appears evident that the heady combination of just-in-time scheduling, crew reductions, and isolation from the elements through air conditioning and push-button ship handling has made many ships, including the largest container carriers, into potential *Titanics*.

---

[72]*National Geographic* (October 2000), 93.

[73]*Fairplay*, 15 July 1999, 22-23.

[74]*Ibid.*, 24.

[75]"Weather Damage to Container Ships Can Be Costly for Owners," *Shipping Times*, 17 November 1999.

[76]*Fairplay*, 8 June 2000, 22-24, "Norwegian Nightmare."

[77]*Fairplay Daily News*, 7 February 2000.

Port Workers

> Modern stevedoring is as much about machines as it is about men.[78]

> All of us working in the port are at the mercy of these modern innovations.[79]

As the world political economy evolved since the introduction of containerisation in the late 1950s, its three main agents of change have been modernisation, globalisation and privatisation.[80] The effect of these forces on dockers,[81] although as profound as that on seafarers, differed in a number of important aspects. Since container terminals needed only a fraction of the men employed in conventional shipping to handle higher tonnages in much less time, the number of port labourers was reduced much more sharply than that of seafarers. One estimate in the mid-1960s showed that two small gangs could move 6000 tons per shift while fifteen to twenty men shifted no more than 500 tons of conventional goods.[82] Another showed that productivity per man-hour increased from 1.67 tons in conventional shipping to 4.5 tons if pallets were used, and thirty tons for containers;[83] containerisation, in other words, would ultimately make about

---

[78]*Fairplay*, 4 June 1992, 39.

[79]John Kiernan, chairman of the London Port Employers, quoted in David F. Wilson, *Dockers. The Impact of Industrial Change* (London, 1972), 278.

[80]"Globalisation, Privatisation and Modernisation: Effects on Port Labour," address by Kees Marges, secretary of the ITF Dockers' Section, to the World Bank Transport Expo, Washington DC, April 1999 (http://www.itf.org.uk/SECTIONS/dockers/Wash120499.htm).

[81]For convenience I shall use this term throughout, although it is a prime example of "English English." In the USA the equivalent is longshoreman, in Australia and New Zealand waterside worker or "wharfie." The naming of the Australian Rules football club Fremantle Dockers is a classical case of a publicity agency attempting artificially to create historical tradition and warm community feeling but totally failing to do its homework properly. In Fremantle, by the way, dockers were traditionally known as "lumpers."

[82]Malcolm Tull, *A Community Enterprise. The History of the Port of Fremantle, 1897 to 1987* (St John's, 1997), 210; for a comparable calculation see H.J. Witthöft, *Container. Transportrevolution unseres Jahrhunderts* (2nd ed., Herford, 1977) 68.

[83]Peter Turnbull, Charles Woolfson and John Kelly, *Dock Strike: Conflict and Restructuring in Britain's Ports* (Aldershot, 1992), 60, quoting a 1970 UNCTAD study.

nineteen in every twenty men redundant. In the course of time domestic and regional competition between ports, privatisation and the emergence of global terminal operators ensured that the quest for further productivity gains, lowering of costs and downsizing of workforces never abated.

Figure 23:   Even the loading of containers is largely mechanised and hardly requires labour. A Polish Ocean Lines box in Hamburg.

Source: Barbara Thode, *Das Hafen-Buch* (Hamburg, 1984).

        Port productivity and competitive pricing were vital marketing assets for the ports but could also significantly affect the absolute and relative export performance of their hinterlands, an issue that assumed ever-greater importance as national economies from the 1980s were opened to the forces of globalisation. Moreover, an additional competitive dimension existed because port or terminal efficiency could be measured through the adoption of the "pure," though often misleading, yardstick of the counting of box movements per crane per hour. Especially in Australia, where waterfront reform at times assumed a prominent place in national politics, crane rates per hour were often used to "prove" the low productivity of local ports. Australian crane rates, of 12.8 per hour, were contrasted unfavourably with those prevailing in the UK (18.1), Singapore (25.7), Northern Europe (27.5) and North America (32.0).[84] A recent study by London consultants Drewry, however, demonstrated conclusively that crane rates

---

[84]Peter Stubbs, *Australia and the Maritime Industries* (Melbourne, 1981), 187.

were the product of many port-specific factors, including the percentage of cargo lifted and the place of the port in the total number of ports visited. Its conclusion was that Australian crane productivity in the 1990s was perfectly comparable with overseas benchmarks.[85] On the other hand, as container terminals are land-based within national boundaries, the impact of international competition was never felt as immediately as aboard ship where, ultimately, no seafarer was assured of not being replaced by a cheaper colleague from abroad. As yet, with the exception of the Middle East, no terminal operators have introduced foreign labour, but many attempted, with greater or lesser success, to smash or by-pass unions in order to obtain cheaper and smaller national workforces.

Decimation of the Work Force

Worldwide port employment numbers plummeted from the 1960s. No global figures are available, but some examples may illustrate the magnitude of the job losses. On the US East Coast the number of registered longshoremen dropped from 51,000 in 1952 to 15,000 in 1972.[86] In Britain, dockers' numbers fell from over 70,000 in the early 1960s to under 10,000 in the late 1980s.[87] On Merseyside there were 17,000 dockers in 1957; by November 1995 500 were left.[88] Cape Town stevedores were downsized from about 2000 in the mid-1970s to 540 by 1987.[89] Waterside workers in Australia in the 1950s numbered over 30,000 men; by 1990 there were about 5000 left.[90] The newly-established Waterfront Industry Reform Authority believed that up to 3000 of these had to go to make Australian ports internationally competitive. This sharp reduction was achieved in the aftermath of the bitter dock dispute of 1998. In France, where

---

[85]Clive Hamilton, "The Drewry Formula," *Maritime Workers' Journal* (April-June 1998), 22-24.

[86]André Vigarié, *Ports de commerce et vie littorale* (Paris, 1979), 455.

[87]Turnbull, Woolfson and Kelly, *Dock Strike*, 48.

[88]"Liverpool Dockers Have Been Locked Out by the Mersey Docks and Harbour Company" (http://www.labournet.org.uk/docks2/9511/article.htm).

[89]Anon., *Organising at the Cape Town Docks* (Cape Town, 1987), 40.

[90]Malcolm Tull and James Reveley, "Microeconomic Reform and the Economic Performance of Ports: A Comparative Study of Australian and New Zealand Seaports" (unpublished paper, 1999), 23.

reforms lagged behind those elsewhere, the 1992 port reform cut jobs in a few years from 8000 to 4000.[91]

Social Consequences of Containerisation

Port workers and their communities have always been more visible and audible to society at large, in their living and work conditions as well as in their numerous conflicts and strikes, than seafarers. Researchers of all persuasions appear to have felt more comfortable with their feet ashore (even when perched high in the cabin of a gantry crane) than on the deck of a deep-sea vessel. As a result, a rich literature has emerged on the waterfront and its industrial and social aspects. It has been said that "class war was seen at its most ferocious on the waterfront,"[92] and the discourse of class struggle runs through much of that literature.

Many authors have investigated the dock scene as a *prima facie* case of the destruction by rampant capitalism of traditional working-class skills and autonomous work practices – and dock-worker communities with their deep-rooted and particular sub-cultures[93] – in often-bitter struggles with dockers' unions.[94] Others have contended that skills changed rather than disappeared and that technology may even have created a brave new world in which the back-breaking and highly dangerous work of dockers handling conventional cargo

---

[91]*Fairplay*, 23 March 1995, 43; see also International Labour Organization, Press Release, 20 May 1996, "ILO Meeting Focuses on Social and Labour Problems in Ports" (http://www.ilo.org/public/english/bureau/inf/pr/96-14.htm).

[92]W. Lowenstein and T. Hills, *Under the Hook. Melbourne Waterside Workers Remember: 1900-1980* (Melbourne, 1986), 6.

[93]R.C. Miller, "The Dockworker Subculture and Some Problems in Cross-Cultural and Cross-Time Generalizations," *Comparative Studies in Society and History*, XI (1969), 302-314.

[94]See, for example, M. Beasley, *Wharfies. A History of the Waterside Workers' Federation of Australia* (Rushcutter's Bay, 1996); Turnbull, Woolfson and Kelly, *Dock Strike*; David Wellman, *The Union Makes Us Strong: Radical Unionism on the San Francisco Waterfront* (Cambridge, 1995); Herb Mills and David Wellman, "Contractually Sanctioned Job Action and Workers' Control: The Case of San Francisco Longshoremen," *Labor History*, XXVIII (1987), 167-195; Reg Theriault, *Longshoring on the San Francisco Waterfront* (San Pedro, 1980); Herb Mills, *The San Francisco Waterfront. Labor/Management Relations: On the Ships and Docks. Part 2: Modern Longshore Operations* (Berkeley, 1979), and Mills, "The San Francisco Waterfront: The Social Consequences of Industrial Modernization," in Andrew Zimbalist (ed.), *Case Studies on the Labor Process* (New York, 1979), 127-155.

carriers was replaced by cleaner and safer jobs that demanded "more modern" skills relating to placing containers quickly and accurately on trailers or train cars and handling computer printouts or screen displays.[95] The process of dramatic workplace change even contained the potential for class attitudes and differences to be overcome successfully, especially as dockers' weekly wages rose considerably; in Britain, for example, from c. £50 in the early 1970s to well over £300 by the late 1980s.[96] Experienced crane drivers in the tight labour markets of Singapore and Hong Kong in the mid-1990s were able to command wages that compared well with those of skilled manual labour.[97] Australian wharfies by then averaged AUS $70,000 (US $51,800) a year.[98]

Inexorably linked with the debate over the "quality" of change is that of quantity: the meaning of the devastating loss of employment, comparable with that suffered by many high-cost seafaring nations but carrying far greater social consequences, as entire dockers' communities were gutted and those that remained were regarded with antagonism by real estate developers. The few dockers still employed were often "atomised," physically as well as psychologically isolated in their air-conditioned jobs on cranes or in straddle carriers, sometimes without a union and employed on individual workplace agreements. Yet, after a traumatic transitional phase and over a longer period of time, as redundant workers found other jobs and those who remained often settled away from the ports in more attractive locations, many integrated into the general community as any other specialists worker in other service industries. The greatest tragedy, of course, concerned those who were too old or otherwise not able or willing to move from areas that were soon characterised by material dereliction and social isolation. In the final assessment of the social impact of containerisation, the impossibility of reaching an impartial judgement is probably the only consensus that can ever be achieved.[99]

---

[95]See, for example, William Finlay, *Work on the Waterfront. Worker Power and Technological Change in a West Coast Port* (Philadelphia, 1988); and ILO, "ILO Meeting Focuses on Social and Labour Problems in Ports" (1996).

[96]Turnbull, Woolfson and Kelly, *Dock Strike*, 23.

[97]*Fairplay*, 23 March 1995, 41.

[98]*Ibid.*, 23 March 1995, 44.

[99]For a similar formulation see, John Hovey, *A Tale of Two Ports. London and Southampton* (London, 1990), 155.

Industrial Conflicts and Port Workers' Unions

From an historical viewpoint it is highly significant that containerisation came when dockers' unions worldwide were in a stronger position than they probably had ever been. They had survived the ravages of the Great Depression and had been able to utilise World War II, postwar reconstruction and the economic boom of the 1950s, when unemployment fell to unprecedentedly low levels and the volume of world trade rose rapidly, to entrench their power. Not hesitating to exploit their strategic economic position and to call strikes to further their cause, many unions had been able to gain a monopoly on the supply of dock labour and to introduce work practices that in later times would be fiercely attacked by employers and others as wasteful, capricious and downright bloody-minded. It must, however, always be remembered that the unions in their triumph not only obtained the fulfilment of pent-up demands for improvements in working conditions but a certain measure of retribution for decades of inhuman and humiliating treatment tolerated and even enforced by employers. The 1947 introduction of the National Dock Labour Scheme in Britain, the 1948 settlement between the International Longshoremen's and Warehousemen's Union and the Waterfront Employers' Organization on the US West Coast, and the operations of the 1949 Australian Stevedoring Industry Board, sarcastically described by one of its opponents as "a workers 'benefit society,'"[100] all stand as testimony to newly-gained union power.

Traditionally militant and still very conscious of standing at the "cutting edge" of the class struggle, the men of the waterfront throughout the world would respond with hostility to containerisation. The very first international container service was scuttled by the dockers of La Guayra, Venezuela, who, fearing for their jobs, in 1960 boycotted the vessels of Grace Lines – thus setting back containerisation on that continent by several years.[101] In many developing and developed countries dockers and their unions would react in similar ways but with far less success. Still, in several instances change was brought about through negotiations between terminal operators and unions, sometimes assisted by government mediation. In Australia, for example, the government in 1965 established the National Stevedoring Industry Conference to achieve the transformation from the casual system of waterside employment to permanency with guaranteed minimum wages. This was achieved in 1967, after the introduction of containers in coastal shipping but well before the first British

---

[100]Turnbull, Woolfson and Kelly, *Dock Strike*, chapter 1; Wilson, *Dockers*, chapter 5; Finlay, *Work on the Waterfront*, 48-50; and Tull, *Port of Fremantle*, 230, quoting Frank Tydeman, General Manager of the Fremantle Port Authority.

[101]Witthöft, *Container*, 14.

vessels of OCL and ACT reached Australian ports and the Australian National Line entered the overseas trade.[102]

In principle, as a seminal International Labour Organization report in 1969 succinctly stated, the introduction of containerisation had to be met by socio-industrial policies aimed at compensating for the inevitable job losses by the adoption of both job and income security:[103]

> One of the essential features of any attempt to meet the situation arising from the introduction of new methods of cargo handling is either the provision of full-time regular employment or a scheme for the registration and allocation of dockers so designed as to provide adequate guarantees of employment or income. Little progress can be made in securing the workers' consent to new methods, and therefore in making the best use of them, if some such guarantees are not offered against possible redundancy.

To this must be added a third equally indispensable requirement: that the massive redundancies should be made attractive enough to constitute a genuine option for both older and younger dockers. To satisfy these conditions was more easily said than done, however, and in many countries and ports major conflicts could not be avoided.

In practice, five major issues had to be addressed in the transformation of dock work from largely manual methods to highly mechanised and computerised operations: the need for the introduction of permanent employment through decasualisation; the sharp reduction in the workforce and hence the prime importance of job protection and the adoption of regular wages and redundancy payments; the demarcation of the area within which dockers could work; the control over work practices; and the role – and sometimes also the survival – of dock unions. None of these issues, in principle, stood alone, but in practice they were often dealt with separately and successively in negotiations between employers and unions. The industrial scene, moreover, was often further complicated by sharp differences of outlook between union leadership and rank-and-file members, on the one hand, and great differences in the nature of the employer, on the other. Among the latter, from the beginning a new element emerged in the form of specialised terminal operators – initially mostly hard-

---

[102]S. Deery, "The Impact of the National Stevedoring Industry Conference (1965-67) on Industrial Relations on the Australian Waterfront," *Journal of Industrial Relations*, XX (1978), 202-222.

[103]A.A. Evans, *Technical and Social Changes in the World's Ports* (Geneva, 1969), 41.

nosed shipowners but later also specialist operators – who naturally were intent on making as clean a break with the past as possible. In that context, it is important to realise that containerisation came to the waterfront during a period in which in many ports a process of change had already, albeit hesitatingly, been started.

Since World War II, productivity in the handling of liner cargoes had slowly improved through the widespread introduction of forklift trucks and pallets, but the effects of these gains were largely offset by rising wages and the unwillingness of the unions to change their work practices. The expansion of world trade in the 1950s helped to some extent overshadow problems on the waterfront. In Fremantle, for example, the number of registered waterside workers increased from 1298 in 1950 to a peak of 1973 in 1956 and still stood at 1712 in 1965. Productivity, in tonnes per worker per year, fell from 976 in 1950 to a low of 590 in 1956 and then steadily increased but only surpassed the 1950 mark in 1964.[104] Productivity on the US West Coast did not increase in the 1950s, and maritime employers felt caught in a trap from which only radical action could liberate them.[105] As Matson's director of research, Foster Weldon, wrote, the cost of cargo handling "has steadily increased...and will continue to do so as long as the operation remains a manual one. There is certainly no indication of change in the current trend of spiralling longshore wages with no corresponding increase in labour productivity."[106]

It was, of course, exactly these circumstances that led to the introduction and rapid diffusion of containerisation, but the quest for waterfront reform had its beginnings in traditional break-bulk handling. The breakthrough came first on the US West Coast in 1959, when the International Longshoremen's and Warehousemen's Union (ILWU) and the employers' organisation, Pacific Maritime Association (PMA), concluded a first agreement under which a US $1.5 million Mechanization and Modernization Fund (the M&M Fund) was established, and the union accepted the cessation of certain work practices and the introduction of certain labour-saving equipment against guarantees of guaranteed income and generous redundancy payments. This was followed in 1961 by a comprehensive agreement, under which employers set aside the huge sum of US $27,500,000 for the next five and one-half years to enable early retirement and voluntary redundancies to be paid in a systematic policy so that the number of longshoremen could be reduced to the requirements of the

---

[104]Tull, *Port of Fremantle*, 299.

[105]Finlay, *Work on the Waterfront*, 52-57.

[106]Quoted in *ibid.*, 56. See also William L. Worden, *Cargoes: Matson's First Century in the Pacific* (Honolulu, 1981), 144.

employers. Radically new technology could now be introduced, including the gantry cranes and straddle carriers of containerisation.

The second M&M agreement of 1966 confirmed the shift of control over longshore work from the men to the employers, but the latter committed themselves to guarantee ILWU members a job for life or, alternatively, generous retirement packages.[107] A corollary of the package deal was that longshoremen's wages could rise with port productivity, and by the late 1970s many had grown easily into middle-class lifestyles, even if they had not entirely lost their industrial militancy or their commitment to political protest. With the explosive growth of the transpacific trade, job losses were less than might have been expected: the number of ILWU workers declined from 14,500 in 1960 to 12,600 in 1970; 8400 in 1980; and 7443 in 1986. Local 13, covering the San Pedro Bay boom ports Los Angeles and Long Beach, actually experienced an increase from its low point of 2200 in 1977 to 2700 in 1986.[108]

The ILWU accepted the M&M agreements for a mixture of reasons. Perhaps the most important, both for the ILWU itself and as a realisation of the situation in which dockers worldwide found themselves, was the acknowledgement that rapid technological change was inevitable and that the union should attempt to share in the fruits of rising productivity. At the same time the ILWU insisted that the interests of all members could be protected if changes in work practices were accepted. That the ILWU adopted this position was all the more remarkable given that the radical Australian-born Harry Bridges led it. But Bridges firmly believed that his was the only course to be followed, and he forced acceptance of the agreements on opposing local leaders and the rank-and-file. The ballot on the first M&M agreement was won with the ample margin of 7882 against 3695, but Los Angeles-Long Beach voted 1864 to 1065 against.[109] The latter result, more understandable perhaps than Bridges' overall success, had considerable tinges of irony, as it was those two ports that benefited more than any other from California's economic growth, while the ILWU stronghold San Francisco itself was almost totally obliterated by containerisation. The second agreement was accepted by the smaller margin of 6448 to 3985, with now also Portland and Seattle against. The growing opposition mostly concerned the vital issue of who was responsible for the packing and unpacking of containers outside the immediate dock areas. Traditionally, workers and their unions had moved with the work, but that appeared not only unrealistic but also immediately involved the Teamsters' Union, which claimed rights on the waterfront itself.

---

[107]Wellman, *The Union Makes Us Strong*, 201-203.

[108]Finlay, *Work on the Waterfront*, 64.

[109]Lincoln Fairley, *Facing Mechanization: The West Coast Longshore Plan* (Los Angeles, 1979), 166.

Bridges later admitted that he and the ILWU had been caught off-guard by the rapid rise of the box.[110] Even after the first great post-containerisation strike of the ILWU in 1971-1972, the issue was not determined *de jure*, but *de facto* west coast longshoremen had lost the battle.

On the US East Coast, the International Longshoremen's Association (ILA), by contrast to the ILWU, did not have control over the supply of dock labour. Work had remained largely casual, corruption was rife and diverse conditions applied in different ports. But in its fight for uniform agreements, standard wages, permanency and minimum hours along the entire coastline the ILA early on had the foresight, or good luck, to include containers. Assisted in its campaign by its good relations with organised crime, in 1959 a levy of US $1.00 was placed on each container, and three years later the ILA gained the right to consolidate container loads away from the wharves up to a distance of fifty miles.[111] This did not impinge on manufacturers stuffing full loads into their containers but, with many ports at small intervals on the east coast, established the right of ILA members to work in an almost continuous band from New England to Florida. A major strike in 1968-1969 confirmed that right. Although ILA's conflict with east coast port authorities continued throughout the 1970s, the net effect was that many freight forwarders and others packed their containers at the waterfront.

An important factor in understanding the power wielded by both the ILWU and ILA was that they had used their monopoly strength earlier to terminate the casual employment of the longshoremen and to introduce permanent systems of employment with minimum hours of pay per year, irrespective of the availability of work. But while the essence of the west coast M&M agreements was to provide generous payments to induce longshoremen to leave the industry and to provide real work to those who remained, on the east coast all stayed on the active payroll, while only a fraction actually worked. This situation was only changed after a number of legal challenges in the 1980s.[112]

When containerisation came to Britain, the situation in three respects differed dramatically from that in the US. In the early 1960s, most British ports, including London and Liverpool, were part of the 1947 National Dock Labour Scheme under which only registered dockers could obtain work; decasualisation was only just beginning, after the publication of the Rochdale and Devlin reports (1962 and 1964); and the relationship between the dockers and their employers was generally characterised by a century or more of distrust and often acute

---

[110]Bridges in 1970, quoted in Finlay, *Work on the Waterfront*, 65.

[111]Wilson, *Dockers*, 143; see also Turnbull, Woolfson and Kelly, *Dock Strike*, 46.

[112]Whitehurst, *U.S. Merchant Marine*, 194-195.

antagonism. The casualness of work opportunities and work itself had bred a casual attitude among the workers, who were rarely united in their views or in their loyalty to the union leadership.[113]

The task of transforming a conservative industry in the face of impinging modernisation and containerisation proved to be more traumatic in Britain than in most other countries. As both the big shipowners and unions were divided on how to structure the wages of the newly decasualised dockers, the largest union involved, the Transport and General Workers' Union (TGWU), in January 1968 imposed a total ban on new container handling, which would not be lifted until April 1970. Even if the breakdown in wage negotiations had been the occasion for the strike, its root causes lay in the massive job losses that resulted from the packing and unpacking of containers outside port areas as well as the unwillingness of the employers to introduce roster systems of employment as existed in the USA and elsewhere. The effects of the strike were immediate and profound, especially at Britain's premier port, Tilbury. One container berth had been completed and was assigned to US Lines, but the other three, still under construction for OCL and ACT, were closed just before their Australian services were to commence. Until the ban was lifted both consortia were forced to use Antwerp as their temporary "home" port. Many other services that could have used London by-passed it in favour of continental ports or, even more to the detriment of London, Felixstowe. Dockers there had not joined the national strike because Felixstowe was privately owned and employed no union men.

It took more than two years before employers and dockers could sign an agreement which incorporated several major changes, such as the replacement of piecework by shift work and the adoption of a standard weekly wage, abolition of manning scales for individual gangs, and the principle that a man could only be paid if he actually worked. Rather astoundingly in view of the situation in the USA and in most other countries in the world, it took several years' more after the lifting of the container-handling ban in April 1970 until permanency of employment was complemented with rotational systems of work distribution. The only major exception to that rule was Southampton, which already had a long (and strong) tradition of job sharing. Ironically, it was this circumstance which was the main cause of John Hovey, executive director of OCL's new terminal operations (Solent Container Services), being unable to make his firm independent from the local port authority in the recruitment of its dockers. Instead of the specialised operators that containerisation required, until the late 1980s virtually the entire Southampton workforce rotated through SCS's terminal – which, one should remember, handled all the East Asian business of the TRIO group as well as the South African trade of OCL - thus maintaining the system preferred by the local leaders of the TWGU and defeating the shipowners' purpose of taking full

---

[113]Still the most comprehensive overview of this period from the dockers' viewpoint is Wilson, *Dockers*, but see also Hovey, *Tale of Two Ports*.

control of the terminal's manpower and establishing employer-employee relations on a permanent basis.

When change finally came to Southampton it was under dramatically different circumstances than those of the early 1970s. Margaret Thatcher had come to power with the avowed aim of breaking Britain's unions and privatising its public utilities, including the British Transport Docks Board. On its part, P&O in 1986-1987 took control of OCL and bought the terminals at Tilbury and Felixstowe. In January 1987, a new firm, Southampton Container Terminal Ltd., was formed to take over all container operations and downsize its work force to its requirements. Against the prolonged resistance of the TGWU it took until July 1988 for the new privatised order to be introduced. A majority share in SCT was sold to P&O and Ben Line, which now turned Southampton into a privately-owned independent terminal with a much reduced and flexible workforce. Although the men who remained were assured of permanent and regular employment, their wages and other conditions fell far short of what their colleagues across the North Sea, under protection from their unions, had been able to gain. Ironically, the roll-on roll-off, passenger and non-containerised part of Southampton became the ideological counterpart of SCT, as privatisation was achieved through a takeover by a workers' cooperative; but significantly, they also had to accept flexibility and interchangeability of almost all staff.[114]

Mrs. Thatcher's programme was completed in 1989 when the National Dock Labour Scheme was terminated.[115] The shipowners had been pressing for several years for this opening of the dock labour market. Again, the TWGU proved powerless to protect the interests of its members against the powerful alliance of government and big business, partly because of doubts whether the interests of a small and dwindling section of its membership could or should jeopardise the existence of the union itself, and partly because political strikes had been outlawed in 1982.[116] Moreover, as the big stick was combined with a carrot of £35,000 redundancy pay for each docker with fifteen or more years of registration, the TWGU's support from within was severely eroded.

Liverpool was one of the last ports to resume work, but its final stance was representative of the country as a whole.[117] On the day the redundancy offer expired, 400 men accepted employment on the new conditions and 289 took the money. As another once-powerful group of workers lost their industrial power,

---

[114]Hovey, *Tale of Two Ports*, 159-160.

[115]For an extensive discussion of the events of 1989 see Turnbull, Woolfson and Kelly, *Dock Strike*, chapters 3-6.

[116]See "Postscript by Keith Harper," in Hovey, *Tale of Two Ports*, 161-168.

[117]*Fairplay*, 3 August 1989, 5.

shipowners gained the right to employ on their own terms. The dockers, downsized from 9400 to just over 6000, now faced the full impact of the free labour market, with loss of permanency and re-introduction of casual and part-time work. Significantly, neither the ITF nor any of its affiliates had been able to provide any effective assistance to the TGWU.

In the wake of the national dock strike, Felixstowe – where the National Dock Labour Scheme had never applied – was also shaken by a brief strike after management imposed new conditions. Here the dockers also lost, and they had to accept an agreement in which they became "berth operators." Also, fixed manning scales were abolished and complete labour flexibility established, and a thirteen-week probation period was used to get rid of incapable or unwilling workers. As Felixstowe could now operate its new Trinity II terminal without additional labour, it gained a massive boost in productivity.[118] Cost levels in English ports had now dropped considerably below those of their rivals on the continent, but this had been achieved by destroying the very basis of the labour system created twenty years' earlier: job permanency, security and specialisation, and replacing it with a return to casual labour.

Although containerisation posed the same challenges the world over, developments in the USA and Britain demonstrated that great variations existed in the responses of dockers to rapid technological change. The same applied throughout the world, although much depended on the relative strength of unions and dock operators and the specific historical and cultural circumstances of each port, region or nation. France, running counter to what was becoming the mainstream, only decasualised its docks in the Le Drian plan of May 1992. Against the strong, but ineffective, opposition of the unions, dockers had to accept that they had become direct employees of the private terminal operators.[119] In Japan, to take an extreme case, the National Council of Dockworkers' Unions of Japan strongly resisted the Japan Harbour Transportation Association, in which the major shipowners had joined forces and which had used the *yakuza* to break strikes in the 1960s.[120] As late as 1995, Japan stood out "as the bastion of restrictive practices and union power;"[121] work on Sundays, for example, was only accepted in the late 1980s under very restrictive conditions.[122] The NCDUJ,

---

[118]Turnbull, Woolfson and Kelly, *Dock Strike*, 196-197.

[119]*Fairplay*, 4 June 1992, 38, and 23 March 1995, 43.

[120]"Home Truths on Japan Ports," *Shipping Times Online*, 4 November 1997, quoting the *Journal of Commerce*.

[121]*Fairplay*, 23 March 1995, 41.

[122]*Lloyd's Maritime Asia*, August 1989, 44; *Fairplay*, 23 March 1995, 42.

moreover, had never lost its monopoly on the supply of dock labour, and in March 1997 still counted 56,000 members. But France and Japan were exceptional cases. As the 1990s unfolded, the pattern of events in Britain became both the dominant model for continued changes in dockers' employment and the catalyst for significant developments in dockers' trade unionism.

Three main reasons determined the success of the British model: privatisation, globalisation and the weakness of the union movement. Privatisation was not an entirely new phenomenon, as a few ports, like Felixstowe, had always been privately-owned, and shipping companies had already during the first stages of containerisation begun operating their own terminals. But from the mid-1980s such vertical diversification became a central part of the expansion strategy of most leading shipowners, including the US majors, Evergreen and P&O. The globalisation of their shore operations was matched by the expansion of "pure" terminal operators, either private corporations such as Hutchison or commercialised traditional port authorities, such as the Port of Singapore Authority, which from 1996 was known as the PSA Corporation. Late in the 1980s, a third kind of commercialised port emerged through the privatisation of individual ports. In addition to Britain, New Zealand was the most notable pioneer in this radical programme of micro-economic reform. New Zealand, ironically, was a country that in the late nineteenth century had been in the vanguard of social reform.[123] Its Port Companies Act of 1988 reconstituted port authorities as commercial companies, whose principal objective was designated to be "to operate as a successful business."[124] A nationwide dock strike was unable to amend or stop the act's enforcement, by contrast to the strike by 3000 Thai dockers which, at least for the moment, prevented Laem Chabang from being established as a privately-owned port.[125]

In line with developments in many other sectors of the economy and public sector, privatisation and globalisation strengthened the hands of those whose attitudes to terminal management were not satisfied by cooperative agreements with unions and permanency for the workforce. Unions were targeted again as terminal operators sought to obtain workplace flexibility; further downsizing through re-casualisation; and the introduction of part-time labour hired through global employment agencies like Drake International. Overtime, traditionally a strong component of the docker's income, was reduced and

---

[123]James Reveley, "Waterfront Labour Reform in New Zealand: Pressures, Processes and Outcomes," *Journal of Industrial Relations*, XXXIX, No. 3 (1997), 369-387.

[124]Tull and Reveley, "Microeconomic Reform," 15.

[125]Turnbull, Woolfson and Kelly, *Dock Strike*, 5; and *Lloyd's Maritime Asia* (April 1990), 41.

replaced by the short-term hiring of outsiders. The men themselves came under increasing pressure to accept individual work contracts and significant erosions of their conditions. South Korea, long a Japan-like example of cosy industrial relations, in 1994 began deregulating its port sector and allowing the private sector to take over terminal operations. Almost overnight a flexible twenty-four-hours per day, 365-days per year service was introduced.[126]

The rapidly-increasing pressures of privatisation and globalisation provoked considerable resistance and strikes in which the eroded power of the unions was severely tested. Probably the most important industrial conflict was the strike that broke out in Liverpool in September 1995 after the privatised Mersey Docks and Harbour Company sacked 500 dockers for refusing to accept the re-casualisation of port labour. It became an international rallying point for unions and unionists around the world. Support for the Liverpool men came from the ILWU and ILA, the Maritime Union of Australia, and many European unionists who felt that the Liverpool dockers were also fighting for them.[127] Abandoned by their own TGWU but buoyed by international solidarity, the striking men maintained their picket for over two years until January 1998 before bowing to the inevitable, when it became painfully evident that the newly-elected Labour government of Tony Blair was unwilling to mediate.[128] The TGWU had failed to provide any effective assistance because it was unwilling to take the risks resulting from Thatcher's labour laws for what had become a very small section of its overall membership. Without its support – but probably also with it – the dockers stood no chance to be reinstated.

For some British observers the meaning of the Liverpool strike transcended its immediate dockside environment, as they identified the issues involved in more general terms: everywhere employers are introducing casual labour and individual contracts; they want to cut their costs through flexible labour; they want workers at their beck and call to be brought to work or discarded at will; nearly half the labour in Britain today is casual and part-time; and in education, services, industry, banking and other clerical work there is a

---

[126]*Fairplay*, 11 August 1994, 39.

[127]"The World is Our Picket Line," website www.labournet.org/dock/9601/front.htm.

[128]See websites www.labournet.net/docks/other/dockhome.htm, and www.labournet.org.uk/docks2/9511/article.htm. See also the BBC Channel 4 drama *Dockers*, written by Irvine Welsh, Jimmy McGovern, and the Dockers Writers Workshop (London, 1999), and the review of the film by John Henry Bohanna, 26 July 1999, website www.labournet.net/docks2/9907/film.htm.

rash of individual short-term contracts.[129] Unfortunately for them, no support or even any significant sympathy came forth from those sectors. Other observers saw the Liverpool conflict as a battle in the "global war" waged by transnational companies on the dockers unions.[130] They found grounds for these claims in the great Australian crisis of 1998 and the imminence of similar attacks on workers' rights in the USA. Even at Felixstowe no stability existed. In December 1998 its new owners, Hutchison Port Holdings, proposed to slash workers' rights, rearrange shifts and premiums, reduce sickness and accident benefits, and hire new personnel on inferior terms than those for existing employees.[131] In June 1999 the dockers had to accept defeat; it meant the end of the last dockers' collective agreement in England. While privatisation of ports and container handling led to English ports regaining their momentum, there can be no doubt that the cost in human terms has been huge. As one of the Liverpool picketers, Mick, expressed it:

> See they didn't just sack the men and we all lost our jobs. They broke up a community. It wasn't just the job. Most people in this room started on the dock as young men. You grew up together, you knew the families, you knew how many kids and how many grandkids, you'd probably been to weddings or communions or whatever. We've lost a community.[132]

Only a short time after the Liverpool strike ended, serious industrial trouble began in Australia. After a few smaller skirmishes, one of the country's two main stevedoring companies, Patrick, overnight sacked its entire nationwide, 1400-strong MUA workforce. Armed guards with balaclavas and dogs took control. An extremely bitter conflict ensued in which it soon became evident that ministers in the anti-unionist conservative government had conspired with

---

[129]"Liverpool dockers have been locked out by the Mersey Docks and Harbour Company," website www.labournet.org.uk/docks2/9511/article.htm.

[130]"International unionism challenges the global economy on the docks," radio commentary by David Bacon, website www.labournet.net/docks2/9812/bacon.htm.

[131]*Lloyd's List*, 5 December 1998.

[132]Dockers group interview, 17 February 1998 (http://www.labournet.net/docks2/9807/kilculgp.htm).

Patrick.[133] The latter's campaign to engage non-unionised men, steeped in deception and controversy,[134] was foiled in most ports by pickets reinforced by unionists from all sectors, including the National Tertiary Education Union. Ultimately, as Patrick was forced by a court order to take back its workers and recognise the MUA as the sole supplier of dock labour, the situation returned to where it had been before the midnight sacking, that is, at the negotiating table. Job reductions were inevitable and encouraged by the government making available AUS $250 million (c. US $160 million) for redundancies. Over forty percent of Patrick's pre-lockout workforce of 1400 chose to go.[135] After the conflict Patrick sacked its strikebreakers who cruelly discovered the *raison d'être* of unions. Some time after the agreement with Patrick the MUA signed a similar contract with P&O. In both it had to accept retrenchments of around forty percent. Ultimately, as the union itself acknowledged, this outcome was inescapable, but the high emotions that had been whipped up during the lockout profoundly embittered relations between the MUA and especially Patrick. But significantly for the shift in the balance of power, when Patrick recently sacked one of the strike leaders, the MUA did not even protest.[136]

Britain and Australia were not the only places with serious disputes on the docks in the late 1990s. Privatisation provoked strikes in countries strewn around the world, such as Chile and Brazil, India and Bangladesh, Italy and Greece. Chile, in 1998 and 1999, despite the distance between its democratic government and the previous Pinochet regime, was the scene of especially violent

---

[133]See, especially, *The Weekend Australian* and *The Australian Magazine*, both of 11-12 April 1998; for a detailed account of the strike see Helen Trinca and Anne Davies, *Waterfront: The Battle that Changed Australia* (Sydney, 2000); and G. Griffin and S. Svensen, "Industrial Relations Implications of the Australian Waterside Dispute," *Australian Bulletin of Labour*, XXIV (1998), 194-206. Compulsory reading is also Christopher Sheil (ed.), *War on the Wharves. A Cartoon History* (Sydney, 1988).

[134]One of Patrick's first moves had been to send a party of serving and retired soldiers to Dubai to be trained for waterside work. A threat by the ITF to boycott all shipping calling at Dubai immediately had an effect as the Dubai government withdrew its permission and sent the men home. Somewhat surprisingly, Patrick's CEO, Chris Corrigan, in July 2000 said "sorry" for the tactics he had used (*Fairplay*, 20 July 2000, 16).

[135]*Ibid.*, 10 September 1998, 7.

[136]"Feathers Unruffled over Dock Sacking," *The Sydney Morning Herald*, 5 November 1999.

confrontations, often provoked by a seemingly unreconstructed police force.[137] In 1998 a wildcat strike hit New York, as ILA members reacted angrily at the prospect of non-union men being hired after Sea-Land's takeover by Maersk.[138] In France the question of job demarcation in port-related industrial zones, which elsewhere had been decided many years previously, erupted into a full-blown strike. In all cases the unions lost. At the eve of the new millennium dockers the world over were faced with the same dilemma, militancy or pragmatism, that had characterised the first stage of unionism in the pre-1914 era. But by now their membership had dwindled to a few thousand at best, while the march of container technology remained unstoppable. Strikes and boycotts had proven increasingly ineffective and divisive. An American longshoreman in 1995 accepted the inevitable: "We cannot sit back as if life owed us a living."[139]

The International Transport Workers' Federation

While many national unions were pushed hard to survive, the International Transport Workers' Federation in 1996 made a historic shift in its position.[140] The leader of its Dockers' Section, Kees Marges, declared that the ITF gave up its opposition in principle to privatisation – just like the ITF's Seafarers Section soon afterwards qualified its opposition against flags of convenience. No doubt inspired by the ILO report of that year on docks, and the negotiations that had preceded it,[141] Marges adopted a realistic position. He began a concerted campaign to convince his own constituents as well as employers and other stakeholders in the efficient functioning of ports that unions still had a vital role to play in the globalised world of shipping and ports. In many speeches he hammered the point that port reform needed to be based on joint planning, cooperation and partnership; essentially, ports were social as well as economic

---

[137]*Fairplay*, 3 June 1999, 3; see also "Chilean Dockers under Attack," 31 January 1998 (http://w1.874.telia.com/ ~ u87402827/text/dn/chile.htm).

[138]*Journal of Commerce*, 23 December 1998.

[139]Tony Nunn, International Longshoremen's Association, January 1995, quoted in *Fairplay*, 21/28 December 1995, 3.

[140]*Containerisation International* (May 1998), 75.

[141]ILO, "ILO Meeting Focuses on Social and Labour Problems in Ports."

organisations in which dockworkers must be accepted as stakeholders.[142] At the same time, it should be stressed, the ITF continued its support for member unions, such as the ILWU, the Busan Port and Transport Workers' Union, and the Dockers Union of Russia.[143]

It is still much too early to be able to judge whether, and to what extent, the ITF's new cooperative policy has been successful in restoring a modicum of influence to the dockers and their unions. But there are many signs that the failure of the Liverpool strike, the recent lack of industrial success, the increasing power of the shipowners in US ports, and the adoption of more pragmatic attitudes and policies deeply disillusioned part of the ITF's constituency. During May 1999 a meeting with representatives of dockers' unions from eleven countries in Europe and North America was held at Gothenburg to discuss "the problems and threats, more or less urgent, to which dock worker unions over the world are forced to respond."[144] While Felixstowe's collective agreement was on the point of being swept aside, dockers' unions in Mexico, Brazil and Chile had been "knocked out" by legislation. The ITF was severely criticised for its inefficiency, lack of active involvement, and the distance between its bureaucracy and the membership. Several delegations, including those from France and Spain, demanded that a new international association of dockers be established to which non-ITF members could also belong. A follow-up steering group meeting took place in October 1999 in Liverpool, hosted by Jim Nolan and a number of other leaders of the 1995-1998 strike, with representatives from the ILWU, ILA, Swedish, French and Spanish unions, and preparations were made to constitute an International Dockworkers Committee.[145]

---

[142]See, for example, his speeches to the Container Handling Automation and Technologies Conference, London, 22 February 1999; the World Bank Transport Expo, Washington, DC, 12 April 1999; and the first meeting of the Inter-American Committee on Ports, Guatemala, 12 October 1999 (http://www.itf.org.uk/SECTIONS/dockers/ratify137.htm).

[143]*Ibid.*; and ITF, press release, 29 January 1999 (http://www.labournet.net/docks2/9901/kalinin.htm).

[144]Press release from Swedish Dockworkers Union, 16 June 1999 (http:// home. swipnet.se/hamn/akt/prconf.htm).

[145]Greg Dropkin, "International Dockworkers Committee," 8 October 1999 (http://www.labournet.net/docks2/9910/conf1.htm). With the MUA and NCDUJ, these five unions had been the main supporters of the Liverpool strikers.

Resurgent Militancy and Political Protest

While the ITF and its followers adopted a realistic and pragmatic line, the militant tendency in dockers' unionism evidently has re-emerged with a vengeance; whether the more activist approach will be able to produce better results for the dockers, however, remains a moot point. But what is important is that both the pragmatic and militant sections of the maritime trade-union movement remained committed to social and political causes, as they had been before containerisation. This was evident in the Liverpool dockers' stand against the introduction of casual labour in most sectors of the economy and other methods to create a "flexible" workforce as much as in the ITF support for ILO calls for cooperation between unions and private enterprise, both to lessen the backlash against globalisation and to protect the unions against attacks from economic rationalists and transnational corporations.[146] How strong the dockers' ideological commitment to social justice and fairness has remained was demonstrated by their widespread support for the campaign to free black journalist Mumia Abu-Jamal from death row and the ILWU's protests at the 1999 conference of the World Trade Organization in Seattle.[147] The dockers, with many others around the world, viewed the WTO as the instrument of the unbridled forces of transnational corporations. They argued that its policies had been purely based on the pursuit of short-term economic advantage. Instead of alleviating the scourge of poverty, the WTO had sharpened the distinctions between rich and poor, within individual societies and across the globe. World leaders were called upon "to acknowledge that economics should be the servant of social policy and social justice – not the other way round."[148]

The strong presence of the ILWU at the Seattle protests demonstrated that, as had been the case so many times in the past, dockers' unionism still represented the ideological cutting-edge not just of radical social protest but also

---

[146]ILO, press releases, 8 November 1996 and 4 November 1997 (http:// www. ilo.org/public/english/bureau/inf/pr/96-37.htm, and /1997/28.htm#N_1_).

[147]See "International Labour Solidarity Web Site" (http://www.labournet.org); and "Docks Update" (http://www.labournet.net/docks2/other/update.htm#WTO). The ILWU was visible enough to be mentioned in general reports on the WTO in magazines such as *Time*, 29 November 1999, 36.

[148]The literature critiquing globalisation has itself become a global industry. For a good variety of the genre see, for example, Thomas Friedman, *The Lexus and the Olive Tree* (New York, 1999); *Foreign Policy* (Spring 2000); Hugh Mackay, "The Real Meaning of Seattle," *The West Australian*, 14 December 1999, 17; and *The Economist*, 11 December 1999, 13 and 17-19.

of the concerns of the community at large. Historians – as maritime journalists[149] – may well find that the protests against the WTO conference marked a turning point in world history in that the expansion of transnational business power was halted and the pursuit of social values once again was given top priority. Ironically, the implication of many anti-WTO protests, that engagement with the forces of transnational capitalism is necessary in order to tame its excesses and help ensure that further advances in maritime and information technology are managed fairly and justly, was also the crux of the newly-found reformism and pragmatism of the ITF. As the clock cannot be turned back, the task at hand is now to humanise the trinity of modernisation, globalisation and privatisation. That applies as much to the world in general as to its ports.

---

[149]*Fairplay*, 14 December 1999, 22-24.

Chapter 8
Culture, the Environment and Recycling

Economy vs Ecology. This is what it all boils down to.[1]

What has been the influence of containerisation beyond its economic function as the world's maritime and intermodal infrastructure system carrying the predominant share, in value, of the plethora of goods and commodities produced and consumed within the global village? This final chapter will explore the wider implications of the box and its still rapidly growing numbers as well as the alternative uses to which it has been put over the years. As in the previous chapter, several issues are highly box-specific while others (particularly in the environmental arena) transcend the boundaries of container transport and, sometimes, that of the shipping industry in general.

The greatest direct impact containerisation has made on the people of the world is cultural, i.e., the container has become an integral part of the view people hold of the meaning of their world. In the pluralist and global village the exchange of commodities and the intertwining of centres of production and consumption is one of the essential aspects of understanding globalisation. As the ECT video clip suggested, containers connect humanity. The box is carried by sea and on land. Panamax and post-Panamax carriers are as indispensable as modest short-sea and feeder vessels. Semi-trailers and trucks haul it from the remotest producers and penetrate into the furthest nooks for house-to-house delivery. It is a common sight on the highways and byways of all continents.

Intermodalism put the box on transcontinental and international freight trains crossing North America and, to a lesser extent, Europe, Asia and Australasia. Container depots surround port areas, and distribution centres have sprung up beside strategically-located nodal points of motorway and railway networks. When TV news bulletins require illustrations or graphics to accompany stories relating to issues like overseas commerce, the balance of trade, tariff negotiations or the WTO, in most cases container vessels and/or terminals feature in one virtual way or another. By contrast, the box has as yet made no impact on literature or the film industry. *The Greek Tycoon* was about Aristotle Onassis, not a scheming container operator. But what could be achieved in police dramas by replacing the traditional scrap yard with a container terminal was demonstrated in the Austrian series *Kommissar Rex*. The episode "Tödliche Leidenschaft" was

---

[1]*Containerisation International* (May 1996), 43.

located in the terminal of Vienna's river port, with Romanian boxes playing a significant part and one detective being crushed by a falling forty-foot container.

The box is always physically present in industrial areas and also near wholesalers, department stores, electrical and a myriad of other traders. Antique dealers and furniture warehouses, in almost nineteenth-century fashion, advertise the arrival of their latest container. In its utilitarian ubiquity the container has become an integral part of modern land- and city-scape, society and culture. Global performers, like Michael Jackson, the Rolling Stones, the Circle du Soleil or the Kirov Ballet move their equipment in containers, as do the support crews of Whitbread and Volvo round-the-world racing yachts. The travelling show of Disneyland needs no fewer than ninety-nine FEUs to carry its show tent, equipment, costumes and props.[2] The British equestrian team for the Seoul Olympics (1988) shipped its horses in containers laid out with real English turf.[3] The containers themselves were the show when they formed the pieces in the APL-sponsored "World's Largest Chess Game" during Rotterdam's 1997 "World Port Festival."[4]

Drugs are often shipped by container, between cladding and skin, in double bottoms, in frozen cargoes or simply under false labelling.[5] In recent years, the box has also acquired notoriety as the number of illegal immigrants carried on container vessels has risen sharply. From the early 1990s, especially from Latin America to the USA and Canada, and from West and North Africa and a number of the successor republics of the former Soviet Union and Yugoslavia to southern and Western Europe, a passenger traffic of some density developed. In 1995, it was estimated that about three-quarters of all stowaways travelled in boxes on container or RoRo vessels, costing the industry in the USA some US $8 million in extra expenses.[6] Most of the stowaways are young men between fifteen and thirty years, keen to leave their country of origin, well-organised and equipped to break into locked containers. One set of Romanian stowaways was discovered in Antwerp through the presence of two air holes in the top of the container; they had made a good choice for their temporary abode

---

[2]*Ibid.* (November 1997), 23.

[3]Sam Ignarski (ed.), *The Box. An Anthology Celebrating 25 Years of Containerisation and the TT Club* (London, 1996), 141.

[4]APL website (http://www.apl.com/content/about/chess.html).

[5]Ignarski (ed.), *The Box*, 158-160.

[6]*Containerisation International* (November 1995), 70-71. In the USA carriers are liable for the keep of illegal immigrants until the day of their deportation or acceptance as genuine refugees.

for its cargo was a large consignment of beer. In another case, on an Atlantic voyage a container was discovered to house fifteen stowaways who, with the vessel's crew also totalling fifteen, caused considerable anxiety to the latter. In the West African-Europe trade occasionally even larger numbers hide aboard, but according to one source, "stowaways are usually non-belligerent."[7] Nevertheless, Linea Messina, which sails between West Africa and Italy and, despite preventative measures, continued to find stowaways on board, claimed that their presence could be "a real danger to safe navigation and operational activity."[8]

Political dictatorships in the Less-Developed World and the failure in many countries of the fight against poverty, which was so strongly emphasised in the protests against the WTO meeting at Seattle, continue to fuel the flows of unofficial migrants. Through 1999 the Republic of Ireland received about a thousand or so illegal immigrants by sea, predominantly in containers, from countries like Romania, Lithuania and Morocco. On arrival, to prevent both accidents and incidents, containers are inspected for air holes, and occasionally thermal scanners are used to check for the presence of warm human bodies.[9] A containerised stowaway of a different kind was a forty-three-year-old Mrs. Harper, who in 1988 travelled with her household goods in a container from the USA to South Africa. On arrival, however, she was refused entrance and deported by the local authorities, making the return trip in a more conventional manner.[10]

Illegal immigration by sea container went trans-Pacific in the second half of the 1990s. The first Chinese stowaways were discovered in 1998 at the terminal in Tacoma. Since then, many hundreds more were tracked down by immigration and customs inspectors in that port, as well as in Vancouver, Seattle, Long Beach and Los Angeles; how many slipped through the net can only be guessed. In most cases illegal crime syndicates were responsible for organising the migrants' illegal passage, at costs of up to US $60,000 per head, and smuggling them in containers aboard vessels bound for the Canadian and US West Coasts. Although they constitute only a minute part of overall Chinese emigration, which may total as many as one million people per year, and also of the number of illegal Chinese entrants into the USA, some 5000 annually, the arrivals in containers have gained a high media profile. Profits made by the smuggling syndicates, which are known as "snakeheads," have been estimated to amount to as much as US $1 billion per year, and it is evident that a good deal

---

[7]*Ibid.*, 71.

[8]*Fairplay*, 2 September 1999, 20.

[9]Informant on ABC (Australia) radio, station 6WF, 12 November 1999.

[10]Ignarski (ed.), *The Box*, 164.

of exploitation and hardship, both during the passage and also after landing, is involved. Of the illegals who were captured, many were in a poor condition, but none more so than those on board *Cape May*. On landing at Seattle in January 2000 one container was found to have turned into a floating steel coffin. Of the eighteen Chinese who had boarded at Hong Kong, three had died at sea. Their corpses had travelled with the fifteen survivors who themselves were in a terrible state of malnourishment and dehydration.

Although some containers appear to be well fitted for the voyage, even with sanitary facilities, most snakeheads did not bother too much about comfort, as the demand for emigration to the USA and Canada, especially from seafaring Fujian province, remained high. With heavy fines imposed on their vessels (Canada, for example, demanded that NYK pay US $15,000 for each of the twenty-five stowaways discovered on its *California Jupiter* before it was allowed to leave Vancouver for Seattle), container operators like OOCL and Zim took measures to screen soft-top containers in particular for stowaways. Similarly, both the Hong Kong Shipowners Association and the Hong Kong Container Terminal Operators Association in January 2000 adopted measures to fight the illegal traffic, while Hong Kong, and later also Shenzhen, customs authorities introduced a "mega X-ray scanner" when local snakeheads switched their operations from soft-top to all-steel containers.[11] In addition, in a frank acknowledgement of social realities inside the People's Republic, Beijing itself has warned overseas countries not to grant asylum to container stowaways in order to prevent a "tidal wave" of illegal emigration from China.[12]

Australia is the objective of a smaller stream of illegal "boat people," formerly mostly from China, Vietnam and Cambodia, most recently predominantly Afghans, Iranians and Kurds. Their voyages are commonly made via Indonesia, where they board the fishing vessels and other small craft carrying them across the Timor Sea and, occasionally, even through Torres Strait. Although inbound containers are popular with smugglers, there has as yet been no case of successful "box-hiking." The only recorded attempt cannot fail to have a deterrent effect.[13] In late 1999, the badly decomposed body of a man was found in an otherwise empty container that had arrived from Africa at the Patrick terminal in Adelaide. Reconstructing the previous moves of the box, it appeared

---

[11]*Los Angeles Times*, 30 December 1999; and 11, 12 and 17 January 2000; *Seattle Times*, 12, 16 and 23 January 2000; "HK Bids to Curb Illicit Trade. Grisly Finds on US-bound Ships Raise the Question of How Many Other Illegal Migrants are Packed into Containers" (http://PD > 19990118?AND?@PD < 20000125)' + 1 + 1 + '-PD,HDA,CO, PHA'); and *Fairplay Daily News*, 21 February 2000.

[12]*Fairplay Daily News*, 14 January 2000.

[13]*Ibid.*, 2 November 1999.

that it had three weeks earlier been loaded aboard a Mediterranean Shipping Co. ship at Dar-es-Salaam (Tanzania) for Fremantle, from where it had been railed east without having been opened and/or inspected.

In addition to the box having become an integral part of the world sea- and landscape, the branding of containers with the owner's name and logo has given it a remarkable specificity. None, probably, would give a greater brand recognition than Maersk's white-on-light-blue stars or Evergreen's all-green boxes, but many others stand out with bold colours, creative logos and strong lettering. Some designs are purely functional; others by contrast suggest that, as the box itself has no aesthetic values to offer, the markings on its sides have artistic as well as marketing purposes. This may not be as far-fetched an idea as it appears at first sight. Container shipping itself is hardly visible to the community, as the ships rush in and out again at remote terminals. And who, apart from people in the business, still reads the shipping news? The box-like designs of container carriers, moreover, seem to have extinguished the genuine interest that the community at large in many countries felt for its merchant fleet. Like the equally utilitarian and even more uniform tankers and bulk carriers, container ships hardly raise the heartbeat of even the most fervent ship lover; the only ships that appear to be of interest to lay persons are cruise liners and fast ferries. Among the magazines and journals carried by general news agencies are few ship lover's publications, in contrast to the vast number of aviation and boating periodicals. Container vessels have made little or no impact on the artistic scene, even after the establishment of the ACTA, later P&O, Maritime Art Awards in Australia.[14]

The same lack of public interest applies to their interior design ("What interior design?" I hear you ask.). In earlier days, merchant ships, especially passenger and mixed-cargo liners, were counted among the expressions of the artistic creativity and accomplishment of nations, but container vessels are as prosaic as the balance sheets by which they are propelled. Moreover, as the ships increasingly originated in Japan and Korea, the people of other countries, especially those that regarded themselves as "traditional maritime nations" and saw their established shipbuilding industries decline, lost their close ties with the liner-shipping industry. As well, the headquarters of most modern container lines have long ago lost the traditional concern for style and the representation of national architectural accomplishment; Hapag-Lloyd is one of the few still resident in its 1900 Hamburg *kontorstil* building on the Ballindamm. Instead, they express global functionalism with few variations of note. Perhaps the best known worldwide is the Nedlloyd office block in Rotterdam, as its roof and sloping glass facade featured prominently in Jackie Chan's film *Who Am I?*

---

[14]Frank Broeze, *Island Nation. A History of Australians and the Sea* (Sydney, 1998), 232.

Figure 24:   The box travels everywhere: (a) across the Andes; and   (b) inland in
                 Southeast Asia.

Sources: Compañia Sud Americana de Vapores, "125 Years Serving South America
                 and the World, 1872-1997," special advertising supplement, *Containerisa-
                 tion International* (October 1997); and Hapag-Lloyd, *Annual Report* (1998).

Figure 25:   The box is visible in the inner city of New York.

Sources: Courtesy Maersk Sealand; and Hapag-Lloyd, *Annual Report* (1998).

Figure 26:   The style of the headquarters of container operators reflects their utilitarian and cost-aware outlook: (a) Maersk headquarters in Copenhagen; and (b) UASC headquarters at Dubai.

Sources: Courtesy Maersk Sealand; and http://www.uasc-sag.com.

The intensity of the cultural imprint of the box increases near terminals, where they are stacked in huge quantities at depots and other operations areas. The trip between Kowloon and Hong Kong's new airport is probably the nearest one can come to container saturation. But also when viewed from a greater distance, terminals have changed the skylines with their huge gantry cranes, symbolising technological prowess and linkage with the wider world. Also in the striking colours of the cranes is a concern for modernity, publicity and cultural awareness. Gone are the sombre greys and blacks of the era of steam and conventional shipping in which brightness and cleanliness were regarded as a luxury workers did not need or deserve. Instead, individual ports and terminals have adopted their own favourite colours, ranging from the somewhat unimaginative white of Rotterdam's ECT to the sexy "Ferrari red" of Fujairah, with many others in between. Red comes in a full range of shades, pure or chequered with white. Exceptional and sophisticated are the green of Voltri Terminal at Genoa and the racy yellow of Laem Chabang. Blue comes in all hues and variations, from the Maersk-like ultramarine at Yantian through Manzanilla's medium blue to Thamesport's navy blue.

But if containerisation through the box and its facilities has made a deep impression on the modern community's cultural mind, shipping in general is known foremost through its disasters and their environmental impact. *Torrey Canyon*, *Amoco Cadiz*, *Exxon Valdez* and *Erika* are just a few of the ships whose names conjure up the ecological disasters connected with vast oil spills, environmentally unfriendly cargoes and occasionally also drunkenness at the rudder. *Titanic*'s cinematographic appeal will always remind the public of the ultimate vulnerability of all ships. Container carriers have not been associated with such disasters, although in 1999 two container ships developed fires in containers laden with toxic chemicals that mobilised considerable public concern.[15] *MSC Carla* went down in mid-ocean and scarcely caused a ripple in the media, nor did the knowledge that in recent years an increasing number of containers were washed overboard and became risks to shipping. Environmental issues relate to containers, too. Over the years, water-borne paints were developed to replace solvent-borne coatings, and in the case of refrigerated units CFC coolants were phased out. In the flooring of boxes, tropical hardwood was replaced by more easily-renewable sources of timber.[16] Needless to say, in countries with strict quarantine regimes the timber cladding of containers occasionally concerned inspectors; in one bizarre case, the Kirov Ballet had to

---

[15]These were *CMA Jakarta* and *Ever Decent*, both in the summer of 1999; the fire aboard the latter was reported on the front page of *The Times* under the headline "Toxic Blaze in the Channel" (25 August 1999). The effects of this fire could have been much worse, as nearby containers with cyanide remained unaffected.

[16]*Containerisation International* (May 1996), 3.

cancel the first performance of an Australian tour when the container with its props and costumes was held up for fumigation.[17]

Container ships themselves have recently also become entangled in environmental and conservation issues when their scrapping propelled them into the media's attention. Many vessels of the early days reached the end of their physical lives during the 1990s, when it had become a matter of general concern that they had been built with copious quantities of asbestos and contained many other poisonous materials, including the anti-fouling agent tributyltin (TBT). Shipowners showed little or no concern since scrapping moved to yards and beaches in China, and then to poorer nations like Pakistan, Bangladesh and India,[18] when in Western countries the industry had come under stringent environmental controls. International environmental groups like Greenpeace, however, alerted world opinion to the dangers to which the workers in the scrap yards were exposed; it was estimated that no fewer than twenty-five percent of all 80,000 or so workers in the industry did or would develop cancer.[19] An inspection team of the International Metalworkers' Federation in 1999 slammed the safety and working conditions at all three Indian scrapping beaches in Gujarat state as "inadequate."[20]

As part of their struggle against the export of polluting technology, Greenpeace mounted campaigns against companies like P&O Nedlloyd, Hapag-Lloyd and Hamburg-Süd.[21] P&O Nedlloyd scrapped ten vessels in 1998 alone, and its *Encounter Bay*, one of the veterans of 1969, became the subject of a demonstration in Singapore harbour.[22] Greenpeace Nederland in December 1999 identified no fewer than sixty toxic ships at Alang beach, India, alone.[23] Although the export of ships containing toxic materials was banned in the Basel Convention

---

[17]*The West Australian*, 18 November 1999.

[18]*Fairplay*, 23 April 1998, 20-21.

[19]Greenpeace Nederland, press release, 11 January 1999 (http://www. greenpeace.org/ ~ nl/persberichten/99/0111a.html).

[20]*Fairplay Daily News*, 23 December 1999.

[21]*Ibid.*, 24 November 1998; Greenpeace Nederland, "Giftige Stoffen," and press releases, 12 May and 9 November 1999 (http://www.greenpeace.org/ ~ nl/gif/ 09exporttechno.shtml); www.greenpeace.org/ ~ nl/persberichten/99/0512a.html; and /1109a.html.

[22]*The West Australian*, 12 January 1999.

[23]*Fairplay Daily News*, 15 December 1999.

on the disposal of dangerous waste, which came into force on 1 January 1998, owners claimed that scrapping was not covered and refused to decontaminate their ships in appropriate facilities before their last voyage to the knacker's yard. Interestingly, in view of the ever-more elaborate mission and strategy statements of the major carriers, is that NYK in its "New Millennium Declaration" included a commitment to "helping to protect [the] environment."[24] A recent radical proposal that new shipbuilding contracts should contain a clause committing the same yard to scrap the vessel at the end of its life probably contains more problems than its would solve.[25]

Another problem is that in active service ships can release toxic material, such as TBT, and thus add to the pollution of water and harbour sediments. The clean-up of the Miami River alone is estimated to cost US $80 million.[26] Sediment pollution, in fact, constitutes one of the major environmental problems of ports because of the disposal of mud raised through dredging which in many cases is already severely contaminated by industrial waste. In 1995 a survey by the American Association of Port Authorities identified dredging and the disposal of dredged material as the most pressing environmental concern.[27] With the continued growth of the largest class of container ships (but, of course, also tankers and bulk carriers) hardly any port in the world can avoid deepening its access routes, basins and wharfside berths. In the USA alone, the 1995 survey showed that ninety percent of ports need to dredge regularly and that annually some 4000 million cubic yards of mud was being moved.

Perhaps the most environmentally-conscious authority has become the European Commission – cynics would contend that this is in order to interfere in even more issues – but the real strength of the EU position is the support of all Western European countries, with the exception of the United Kingdom. But legislation does not immediately signify implementation, and environmentalists have remained alert as economic pressures too often induce local authorities and/or port operators to cut corners. In November 1998 the European Commission stepped in after environmentalists complained that massive dredging of the River Elbe had started before the finalisation of environmental assessments. The Hamburg city government claimed it ordered the work to begin, as it was "vital to retain the port's competitiveness and secure huge numbers of jobs."[28]

---

[24]Http://www.nyk.com/nyk21/profit/index.htm.

[25]*Fairplay*, 16 December 1999, 5.

[26]*Fairplay Daily News*, 15 March 2000.

[27]*Containerisation International* (May 1996), 45.

[28]*Fairplay Daily News*, 18 November 1998.

Greenpeace Nederland was sufficiently provoked by the disposal policies of the Rotterdam municipal port authority to dump toxic mud on its doorstep.[29]

In addition to dredging, the most important environmental issue confronting ports relates to their expansion since this more often than not involves the invasion and transformation of adjacent nature reserves. In an ironical reverse of priorities in comparison with the reckless abandon with which such green fields in the 1960s and 1970s had been used for port construction, the 1980s and especially the 1990s became the decades of the fight for green ports.

From the early 1980s, national and international environmental organisations like Friends of the Earth and Greenpeace raised awareness of the importance of maintaining and respecting the world's eco-structure. Ecology became the subject of "green policies" in many, especially developed, countries and raised environmental concerns. No longer was it acceptable to destroy natural habitats, wetland or dune landscapes in the name of economic progress. The expansion of ports like Rotterdam, Hamburg and lately even Hong Kong has become a closely-guarded process in which great care is taken to maintain natural corridors and reserves.[30] Portland, Oregon, initiated the preparation of an environmental impact study and an endangered species assessment before it began construction of its new Hayden Island site.[31] Felixstowe's Trinity III terminal, completed in 1996 after initial permission was given in 1988, included the creation of a similar nature reserve, but as the project had started before EU regulations came into force, the balance of the development was still tilted toward economics rather than ecology. The adoption of the Natura 2000 schedule means that such procedures can never be repeated. It is unlikely that Hong Kong today would be able, as in the 1970s, to level mountains and create its terminals with the material. The state of Maine in 1996 gave up a project to build an entirely new hub port halfway between New York and Halifax as the cost of meeting environmental requirements would have wiped out any advantages gained by its location; the configuration of Sears Island, moreover, prevented the most efficient lay-out of its terminal.[32] In the case of Vadhavan, "the finest site in western India" according to one local official, it was a coalition of local environmentalists which forced the abandonment of the construction of a new

---

[29]Greenpeace Nederland, press release, 13 September 1999 (http://www. greenpeace.org./ ~ nl/persberichten/99/0913a.html).

[30]*Fairplay*, 14 October 1999, 12; and *Fairplay Daily News*, 20 September and 9 October 2000.

[31]*Containerisation International* (December 1997), 32.

[32]*Ibid.* (May 1996), 44-45.

container port, although P&O Ports and the government of Maharashtra state had already agreed on its construction.[33]

The proposed management of the expansion of Khor Fakkan in 1996 raised the question of economics versus environment (and culture) in a poignant manner that illustrated the extremely complex issues at stake. In order to create space for the additional berths, four small mountains were to be raised and a fifth terraced to obtain the material to fill part of the bay, thus destroying habitats for turtles and sharks. The mountains were sold to the Oman Mining Company which used their high-quality granite for the construction of seawalls and other projects in the Gulf region. Noise levels, vibration and air quality were constantly monitored. The maritime life of one part of the bay was already affected by the construction of a wharf; more water space was to be filled in during a later stage of the project. The bay is the breeding ground of turtles, for which no alternative exists. While the mountains do not contain any flora or wildlife, a number of 3000-year-old graves were uncovered during excavation activities. It may well be that, with the subsequent opening of Salalah and Aden, Khor Fakkan's expansion will be less than was foreseen in 1996, but that would hardly solve its dilemmas. And although it appears that engineers and port operators generally have become "greener" themselves, in many countries less stringent or no environmental controls have been put in place. As one port manager put it, "we still have to compete and your competitors will always cut corners."[34] As the example of Hamburg showed, when it comes to the crunch, environmental safeguards may not always be enforced.

The grave environmental problems relating to oil spills, accidents at sea and port expansion stand, ironically, in contrast to the "green" character of shipping in general. In comparison with road and rail traffic, shipping is "notably environment friendly."[35] It is by far the most efficient form of transport in terms of energy spent to move a given volume of cargo. Since the 1980s national and international regulations on the reduction of diesel-engine emissions and volatile compounds from tank venting, and the replacements of CFCs in refrigeration, have considerably cleaned up the industry. Coastal shipping is increasingly seen and promoted as the green alternative to road and rail transport, especially in European waters from the North Sea to the Mediterranean and Black Sea, and on the North American West Coast. Motorway congestion, moreover, in many areas has taken on such proportions that the diversion of freight to shipping, including the combination of short-sea and inland transport, is becoming an integral part

---

[33]*The Australian*, 12 October 1998.

[34]Derek Harrington, managing director of Felixstowe, quoted in *Containerisation International* (May 1996), 44-45.

[35]*Lloyd's Maritime Asia* (January 1991), 11.

of long-term traffic planning.[36] The council of EU transport ministers was urged to take "rapid and effective" action on measures to promote short-sea shipping, but as in the USA, it may take a great effort to move bureaucracy and lure shippers away from the road.[37] A similar environmental anti-road transport campaign, of course, was and still is waged by railway and intermodal companies. APL, with its energetic and innovative publicity machine, was particularly active in promoting the many green qualities of its railroad operations.[38]

A particular problem is posed by the need to dispose of used containers after they complete their working lives of about ten to fifteen years. Estimating the total of TEUs in service in 1999 at c. 13,000,000,[39] each year about one million are ready for disposal. In addition, there are thousands of boxes that are lost, abandoned or stolen. With regard to the latter, firms exist that specialise in the recovery of stolen containers and, if a shipping company working with leased containers goes bankrupt, a retrieval team is sent out immediately. Datatracer's record includes the recovery of containers lost in post-1991 Russia, which is no mean feat.[40] By far the larger part of used containers is disposed of by scrapping. The Rotterdam firm CETEM, according to its advertising sign outside the local maritime museum "Prins Hendrik," keenly trades in second-hand containers, and so does Black Wolf, which claims to be the biggest container lease-and-sale company in Australia. Worldwide, there are many more businesses like these. Zim Israel is the first major which has offered its used containers for sale on the internet. For good measure, it also is "interested in purchasing your used, second-hand containers if they are still seaworthy and w/w/t condition."[41] If the container already shows an extraordinary flexibility in its normal commercial use by its ability to carry virtually any kind of cargo from any place on earth to any other, it is outside the industry that the full potential of its mobility, shape and

---

[36]Athanasios A. Pallis, "Towards a Common Ports Policy? EU Proposals and the Port Industry's Perceptions," *Maritime Policy and Management*, XXIV (1997), 365-380. See also, for example, *Containerisation International* (June 1995), 73.

[37]*Fairplay*, 16 December 1999, 17.

[38]APL, *The Green Alternative: A Transportation Assessment* (Oakland, 1995).

[39]*Fairplay*, 16 September 1999, 5. The box-repair industry alone is estimated to be worth about US $1 billion per year (*Containerisation International* [June 1995], 3).

[40]See, for example, Ignarski (ed.), *The Box*, 149-150.

[41]Http://www.zim.co.il/used_cont.htm.

adaptability are achieved. As Zim put it, "The possibilities are unlimited and restricted only by the imagination."

Over the years people all over the world have indeed used ingenuity and, occasionally, perversity in developing new purposes for the recycled standard box. The key to their success is their functional form, cheapness, transportability and easy convertibility. Floor and walls are strong and durable, yet it is easy to cut extra doors and windows. No foundations are needed. They can conveniently and rapidly be furnished and stripped, thus providing accommodation for both short- and long-term purposes. With both ends already fitted with doors for access, they are ready-made for the storage of building materials, equipment or plain rubbish. Construction sites around the world abound with containers, often still identifiable through their registration. Denser concentrations can be found in the vicinity of major ports and huge development or redevelopment projects, such as the centre of Berlin or the industrial zones of Shanghai. With a few windows cut into a side, the container is easily made into a canteen, which can be equipped with any standard of comfort and, following jobs and workers, can easily be moved from site to site. The container that provided shelter to the owners and staff of the Whim Creek Hotel, in the north of Western Australia, during 1999 Cyclone John, was firmly chained to three concrete-filled and buried barrels.[42] Around the same time Evergreen donated containers for earthquake relief in Taiwan, an example followed by Hamburg-Süd in Turkey.[43] At the other end of the climatic spectrum, containers provide storage space at Australia's Antarctic base, Casey.

More important, containers have also been used to provide more permanent accommodation, both for business and residential purposes. At least one group of right-wing Jews, in their campaign to "create facts," used a container to stake a claim to land on the West Bank.[44] As far back as 1967 a prominent German exporter suggested that containers would form ideal homes in what then were called Third-World countries,[45] and a few years later the British firm Nickson and Borys and Partners spent £150,000 developing the idea of using containers as the "building blocks" for larger structures that could be erected anywhere in the world in a fraction of the time needed for conventional

---

[42]*The West Australian*, 16 December 1999.

[43]Http://www.fairplay.co.uk/showarticle.asp?artnum=dn0019991001013507; and *Fairplay*, 13 January 2000, 4.

[44]*Time*, 1 November 1999, 50.

[45]H.J. Witthöft, *Container. Transportrevolution unseres Jahrhunderts* (2nd ed., Herford, 1977), 16.

construction.[46] The Borys system was not widely adopted but, in more informal ways (sometimes, it appears, literally by "falling off the back of a truck"), many boxes found their way to such destinations in Africa, Asia and Latin America.

In 1991 the South African container operator Safmarine, realising the tremendous potential of the container for housing and other purposes, launched "Containers-in-the-Community" as "the flagship of our social investment programme."[47] During the 1990s, over 5000 containers were made available for housing projects and a large number of other community projects. Even taking into account an average conversion cost of about US $2000, the containers provided cheap and, above all, extremely versatile solutions to South Africa's appalling shortage of facilities in the black and coloured townships created by the former white Apartheid regime. The ingenuity used in Safmarine's programme is astounding. Following community opinion, the vast majority of the boxes are used for public projects. As one respondent said, "If you use the containers for basic housing, only one family will benefit from one container. If used for community projects, many more people will benefit."[48] With the removal of one or more walls, it was found that the potential of the container was unlimited. Containers could be used individually or for more complex multi-story structures and also as corner walls and roof support at a fraction of the cost of conventional building materials and with immediate application. A hostel at Simon's Town was constructed with well over fifty boxes. In cooperation with the African Council for Hawkers and Informal Business, individual boxes were located in densely-populated areas to serve as banks providing daily working capital to the still-predominant street hawkers. Other projects included community halls, hairdressing saloons, restaurants, schools, pharmacies, shops and health-care centres.[49] Safmarine's social programme, maintained after its takeover by hard-nosed Maersk, stands as a shining example to companies elsewhere, but until now there appear to be no successors.

Safmarine's container project to some extent may be seen as a microcosm of the recycled container world, but elsewhere many other purposes have been pursued, some of which one could hardly categorise as falling under "social responsibility." One of these is prostitution, the second oldest and probably the most mobile of all professions. Containers share that quality and

---

[46]Ignarski (ed.), *The Box*, 44-45; see also http://www.zim.co.il/used_cont.htm.

[47]Safmarine, "Social Responsibility" (http://www.safmarine.co.za/social.html).

[48]*Fairplay*, 2 September 1999, 27, "The Ultimate Box Recycling. Shipping Company with a Conscience."

[49]Ignarski, *The Box*, 205-208 (originally an article by Bob Jacques in *Seatrade Review* [1995]).

have been rumoured to be used as brothels in locations as far apart as New York, the former East Germany and Dili on East Timor. Deeper into the interior of East Timor, television journalists showed the stronghold of one militia force built around two forty-foot containers, one clearly sporting the name of its former owner, Matson – forty years after that company pioneered containerisation in the Pacific. Western Australia attempted to solve the accommodation problems resulting from its excessively high incarceration rate by converting containers into a low-security gaol; the conversions, allegedly, are decidedly comfortable. On a loftier and more cultural level, recycled boxes are pressed into service for community fairs and temporary exhibitions. Most poignantly, the entrance "gate" and souvenir shop of the International Transport Workers' Federation's ill-fated anti-FOC campaign ship *Global Mariner* were cut from the same cloth. The future of the recycled box appears to have as much space for expansion as the container itself.

Conclusion

We say "The World is Square" – because global trade as we
know it would not exist without the square container.[1]

Containerisation provides a prime example of revolutionary economic and social
change caused by the introduction of a new technology. Like a juggernaut carried
forward by its own momentum, it moved inexorably through the liner industry
and the adjacent links in the total transport system between the places of
production and final destination. Its ultimate creation was the first-ever integrated
global logistics system. The truly amazing aspect of this revolution is that its
technological foundation was utterly simple in concept, design and construction.
By comparison, for example, to the computer chip, jet engine and atomic reactor,
the box was one of the least complicated technological achievements of the post-
World War II world. But the true innovation which created containerisation
resided not only in the box itself but also in the entrepreneurial flash which
understood how it should be used.

Containerisation not only gave liner shipping a new lease of life through
its revolution in technology and organisation but also dramatically changed the
character of the industry. Long-standing attitudes and practices had to be
abandoned in the scramble to be part of the brave new world of container
shipping. Productivity increases were so prodigious that traditional rivals were
forced to team up with each other in national and international consortia. At first
these joint ventures only comprised operators located within a particular region,
but soon companies from both ends of major trade routes joined forces. Partly
through the concentration of power and resources resulting from the consortium
system, but also partly through the entry and rapid rise of powerful newcomers,
containerisation gained and maintained an extraordinary entrepreneurial
momentum. This dynamism showed the way out of the severe crisis of the early
1980s in the form of the second revolution in which the leading firms established
round-the-world services and global networks, on the one hand, and
intermodalism, on the other. As they increasingly catered for the needs of
transnational customers with global manufacturing and/or distribution interests,
the major container companies adopted global identities through alliances and
mergers. Characterised by its worldwide seaborne operations and agency
networks, an advanced state of diversification into adjacent transport facilities
and, above all, a global outlook in vision and employment policies, the container

---

[1]C. C. Tung, quoted in Fiona Gilmore (ed.), *Brand Warriors. Corporate Leaders
Share Their Winning Strategies* (London, 1997), 80.

industry in the 1990s became one of the pillars of globalisation in the world economy. In the process of making their own operations transnational, their leaders adopted the fashionable outlook, jargon, vision and mission statements of mega-management prevalent in sectors that had already reached the stage of globalisation. Ironically, at the same moment as such mission statements proclaimed the commitment of the container shipping companies to the welfare of their customers, national and continental shippers' organisations combined in global associations to press for a thorough reform of the systematic collusion and restrictive practices characteristic of the liner freight market.

Globalisation, however, did not bring stability to the container business. This, of course, is no exceptional situation, since as of this writing another wave of mergers is hitting the North American railroad system, and around the globe many other sectors are undergoing similar phenomena, including civil aviation, automobile manufacturing, banking and media/information technology. Hundreds of thousands of workers are faced with dismissal as their corporations desperately seek additional synergies and cost savings. As container freight rates continue to decline as a result of both supply and demand factors – increased productivity, economies of scale resulting from sustained strong growth in turnover, sharp competition and chronic overcapacity – cost-cutting will likely continue to dominate the industry for at least the next decade or so. Despite widespread orders for post-Panamax carriers, more mergers may be expected until the number of major players in container shipping is reduced from about twenty to fifteen or even twelve. At the same time, the leading transnational port operators will continue to expand rapidly into new areas, while traditional port authorities become little more than rent-seeking landlords. The container may be expected to mop up most of the last remaining pockets of conventional freight and increase its share of neo-bulk and specialised cargoes, such as fully-built cars.

How much further the transition from loops, strings and other more traditional forms of liner networks to hub-and-spokes models will go will depend very much on the trading characteristics and geographic configuration of each particular region. It is as yet inconceivable that one company or alliance would dare concentrate all its main-line traffic in northwest Europe or East Asia in one port. As long as ports are regarded as agents of economic growth and development, the twin patterns of concentration and diffusion will continue to operate in tandem. The Mediterranean, for example, will be bustling with a large number of competing hubs, as will the Caribbean. In the Middle East and the Gulf, the struggle between Dubai and its many rivals will never abate.

In human terms, the management of the container industry will become increasingly global, though for entirely different reasons than those that led to the internationalisation of ship's crews. And in national and ethnic composition there will be even less symmetry between employers and employees, thus adding to the distance – even alienation – felt by the latter. With regard to the down-sizing and multi-skilling of crews, it appears impossible to achieve any further productivity increases (or sackings, depending on what perspective one takes), especially as professional opinion holds that present crew sizes are perilously close to safety limits. But seafarers, and even officers, from high-cost countries will truly become endangered species, as shipowners use their industrial and political power to gain greater access to cheaper foreign crews; from the perspective of the latter and their governments, maritime employment is a most welcome source of income and foreign exchange. With regard to container terminals, the processes of automation and privatisation have by no means run their course, and severe job losses can be forecast to occur in most ports around the globe. Especially in countries with volatile industrial and political relations, strong resistance on the part of maritime workers and their unions may lead to considerable strike activity. At the same time, there is the likelihood of confrontations with conservation activists and their rapidly-growing number of allies in the community and political circles. These are likely to be triggered by environmental problems resulting especially from the push toward ever larger and deeper ports. The ultimate meaning of containerisation must therefore be seen not only in its remarkable contribution to the growth of the world economy and to globalisation but also in its role in the creation of the forces that are rising in sharp opposition to these very phenomena.

Select Bibliography

Frequently Used Periodicals

American Shipper
Annual Report, various shipping companies
Australasian Ships and Ports
Australian
Containerisation International
Containerisation International Yearbook
Dagblad voor de scheepvaart
Fairplay International Shipping Weekly
International Transport Workers' Federation Seafarers Bulletin
Lloyd's List
Lloyd's Maritime Asia
Lloyd's Shipping Economist
OECD Maritime Transport
Shipping Times (Singapore)

Frequently Used E-mail and Internet News Sites

Fairplay Daily News (London) (http://www.fairplay.co.uk)
InforMARE (Genoa) (http://www.informare.it/news/review/)
Shipping Times Online (Singapore) (http://www.business-times.asia1.com.sg/shippingtimes/)

Websites of Companies and Organisations

American President Lines (http://www.apl.com)
Canadian Pacific (CP Ships) (http://www.cp.ca)
Compañía SudAmericana de Vapores (CSAV) (http://www.csav.cl)
Dubai Port Authority (http://www.dpa.co.ae)
Evergreen Marine Corp. (http://www.evergreen-america.com; pdx.rpnet.com/dontim)
Far Eastern Shipping Co. (Vladivostok) (http://www.fesco.com)
Farrell Lines (http://www.farrell-lines.com)
Greenpeace Nederland (http://greenpeace.org/~nl/)
Hutchison International Port Holdings (http://www.hph.com.hk)
Inchcape Group (http://www.inchcape-shipping.com)

International Labour Organisation (http://www.ilo.org)
International Labour Solidarity (http://www.labournet.org)
International Transport Workers' Organisation (http://www.itf.org.uk)
Jebel Ali Free Trade Zone (http://www.jaf.za.co.ae)
K-Line (http://www.k-line.com)
Kanoo Group (http://www.kanooshipping.com)
Maersk (http://www.maerskline.com)
Mitsui OSK Lines (http://www.mol.co.jp)
Nippon Yusen Kaisha (NYK) (http://www.nyk.com)
Orient Overseas Container Lines (http://www.oocl.com)
P&O Nedlloyd (http://www.ponl.com)
Safmarine (http://www.safmarine.com.za)
United Arab Shipping Co. (http://www.uasc-sag.com)
Wilhelmsen Lines (http://www.wlines.com)
Zim Israel (http://www.zim.co.il)

Company Histories

Anon. *All Ways Zim. 50 Anniversary Album 1945-1995*. Tel Aviv, 1995.

Burrell, David. *Furness Withy 1891-1991*. Kendal, 1992.

Chan, Anthony B. *Li Ka-shing. Hong Kong's Elusive Billionaire*. Hong Kong, 1996.

Dalkmann, H.A. and Schoonderbeek, A.J. *125 Years of Holland-America Line*. Edinburgh, 1998.

De Boer, G.J. and Mulder, A.J.J. *Nedlloyd, 25 Jaar Maritiem*. Alkmaar, 1995.

Devos, Greta and Elewaut, Guy. *CMB 100. Een eeuw maritiem ondernemersschap 1895-1995*. Tielt, 1995.

Dick, H.W. and Kentwell, S.A. *Beancaker to Boxboat. Steamship Companies in Chinese Waters*. Canberra, 1988.

Fritz, Martin and Olsson, Kent. "Twentieth-Century Shipping Strategies: Broström and Transatlantic, Gothenburg's Leading Shipping Companies." In Ville, Simon P. and Williams, David M. (eds.). *Management, Finance and Industrial Relations: Essays in International Maritime and Business History*. St John's, 1994, pp. 91-109.

Hornby, Ove. *"With Constant Care..." A. P Møller: Shipowner 1876-1965*. [Copenhagen], 1988.

Johnson, Howard. *The Cunard Story*. London, 1987.

Korver, H.J., *Koninklijke Boot. Beeld van een amsterdamse scheepvaartonderneming 1856-1981*. Amsterdam, 1981.

MacGregor, David R. *The China Bird. A History of Captain Killick, and the Firm He Founded: Killick Martin and Company*. 2nd ed., London, 1986.

Neptune Orient Lines. Special 30th Anniversary Edition. Lloyd's List, December 1998.

Niven, John, *The American President Lines and Its Forebears, 1848-1984*. Newark, DE, 1986.

Prager, Hans Georg. *DDG Hansa. Vom Liniendienst zur Spezialschiffahrt*. Herford, 1976.

Rabson, Stephen and O'Donoghue, Kevin. *P&O. A Fleet History*. Kendal, 1988.

Skipp, Robert J. (ed.). *Sea Notes: Twenty-five Years of Container Shipping, 1956-1981*. Iselin, NJ, 1981.

[Tatsuki, Mariko and Yamamoto, Tsuyoshi]. *The First Century of Mitsui O.S.K. Lines, Ltd*. Osaka, 1984.

Taylor, James. *Ellermans. A Wealth of Shipping*. London, 1976.

Van Driel, H. *Een verenigde nederlandse scheepvaart. De fusie tussen Nedlloyd en KNSM, 1980-81*. Rotterdam, 1988.

Wiborg, Susanne and Wiborg, Klaus. *The World is Our Oyster. 150 Years of Hapag-Lloyd 1847-1997*. Hamburg, 1997.

Worden, William L. *Cargoes: Matson's First Century in the Pacific*. Honolulu, 1981.

General Works

Abraham, Claude. "Lignes tour du monde: viable ou non, pas de miracle." *Transports* (January 1987), pp. 35-37.

Al-Abdul Razzak, Fatimah H.Y. *Marine Resources of Kuwait*. London, 1984.

Australian National Maritime Association. *Australian Shipping: Structure, History and Future*. Melbourne, 1989.

Bach, John. *A Maritime History of Australia*. West Melbourne, 1976.

Beechert, Edward D. *Honolulu: Crossroads of the Pacific*. Columbia, SC, 1991.

Beth, Hans Ludwig; Hader, Arnulf; and Kappel, Robert. *25 Years of World Shipping*. London, 1984.

Bird, J.H. *Seaports and Seaport Terminals*. London, 1971.

Boyce, Gordon. *Information, Mediation and Institutional Development. The Rise of Large-Scale Enterprise in British Shipping, 1870-1919*. Manchester, 1995.

Broeze, Frank. "Rederij." In Baetens, R.; Bosscher, Ph.M.; and Reuchline, J.H. (eds.). *Maritieme Geschiedenis der Nederlanden*, IV, Bussum, 1978, pp. 158-222.

_____. "The Ports and Port Systems of the Asian Seas: An Overview with Historical Perspective from c. 1750." Guimerá, Augustín and Romero, Dolores (eds.). *Puertos y Sistemas Portuarios (Siglos XVI-XX)*. Madrid, 1996, pp. 99-121.

_____. "Containerization and the Globalization of Liner Shipping." In Starkey, David J. and Harlaftis, Gelina (eds.). *Global Markets: The Internationalization of the Maritime Industries.* St. John's, 1998, pp. 385-423.

_____. *Island Nation. A History of Australians and the Sea.* Sydney, 1998.

_____. "Dubai: From Creek to Global Port City." In Fischer, L.R. and Jarvis, A. (eds.). *Harbours and Havens: Essays in Port History in Honour of Gordon Jackson.* St. John's, 1999, pp. 159-190.

Brooks, Mary R. "International Competitiveness – Assessing and Exploring Competitive Advantage by Ocean Container Carriers." *Logistics and Transportation Review,* XXIX, No. 3 (1993).

Carlisle, Rodney P., *Sovereignty for Sale. The Origins and Evolution of the Panamanian and Liberian Flags of Convenience.* Annapolis, MD, 1981.

Couper, A.D. *The Geography of Sea Transport.* London, 1972.

_____. *Voyages of Abuse. Seafarers, Human Rights and International Shipping.* London, 1998.

Chrzanowski, I. *Concentration and Centralisation of Capital in Shipping.* Westmead, 1975.

Dagnino González, Tomás A. "El Contenedor: ¿Una Revolucion en el Transporte?" *Revista de Marina* [Chile], IV (1985), pp. 476-480.

Davies, J.E. "Competition, Contestability and the Liner Shipping Industry." *Journal of Transport Economics and Policy,* XX (September 1986), pp. 299-312.

Dharmasena, K. *The Port of Colombo 1860-1939.* Colombo, 1980.

_____. *The Port of Colombo. Vol. II, 1940-1995.* Tokyo, 1998.

_____. "Bombay and Colombo 1948-1984: A Study in Port Development with Special Reference to Containerization." *The Great Circle,* IX (1987), pp. 119-133.

Fairplay. *Centenary.* London, 1983.

_____. *Container Operators Directory 1996.* London, 1996.

Finlay, William. *Work on the Waterfront. Worker Power and Technological Change in a West Coast Port.* Philadelphia, 1988.

Frankel, Ernst Gabriel. *The World Shipping Industry.* London, 1987.

Gilmore, Fiona (ed.). *Brand Warriors. Corporate Leaders Share Their Winning Strategies.* London, 1997.

Goto, Shin. "Globalization and International Competitiveness: The Experience of the Japanese Shipping Industry." In Starkey, David J. and Harlaftis, Gelina (eds.). *Global Markets: The Internationalization of the Sea Transport Industries since 1850.* St. John's, 1998, pp. 355-384.

Griffin, G. and Svensen, S. "Industrial Relations Implications of the Australian Waterside Dispute." *Australian Bulletin of Labour,* XXIV (1998), pp. 194-206.

Harlaftis, Gelina. *A History of Greek-Owned Shipping. The Making of an International Tramp Fleet, 1830 to the Present.* London, 1996.

Hariharan, K.V. *Containerisation Era in India. Prospects and Problems.* Bombay, 1995.

Heideloff, C.; Lemper, B.; and Zachcial, M. "Changing Times Ahead?" *Hansa,* CXXXV, No. 9 (September 1998), pp. 12-19.

Hoffmann Jan. "Concentration in Liner Shipping: Its Causes and Impacts for Ports and Shipping Services in Developing Regions." Report prepared for the Economic Commission for Latin America and the Caribbean [1998] (http://www.eclac.cl/research/dcitf/lcg2027).

Hovey, John. *A Tale of Two Ports. London and Southampton.* London, 1990.

Hoyle, B.S. and Pinder, D.A. (eds.). *Cityport Industrialization and Regional Development.* Oxford, 1981.

Ignarski, Sam (ed.). *The Box. An Anthology Celebrating 25 Years of Containerisation and the TT Club.* London, 1996.

Jao, Y.C. and Leung, C.K. (eds.). *China's Special Economic Zones: Policies, Problems and Prospects.* New York, 1986.

Jennings, Eric. *Cargoes. A Centenary Story of the Far Eastern Freight Conference.* Singapore, 1980.

Johnsson, Lennart. *Funny Flags. ITF's Campaign – Past, Present and Future.* Brevskolan, 1996.

Kasoulides, George C. "The 1986 United Nations Convention on the Conditions for Registration of Vessels and the Question of Open Registry." *Ocean Development and International Law,* XX (1989), pp. 543-576.

Labaree, Benjamin W., *et al. America and the Sea: A Maritime History.* Mystic, CT, 1998.

Kutze, Wolfgang. "Containerkonsortien der führenden Linienreedereien aus west-europäischen Ländern und Regulierung des wissenschaftlich-technischen Fortschritts im Linienkodex." *Wissenschaftliche Zeitschrift der Wilhwlm-Pieck Universität* (Rostock), XXXIII (1984).

Marsh, Arthur and Ryan, Victoria. *The Seamen. A History of the National Union of Seamen.* Oxford, 1989.

Metaxas, B.N. *Flags of Convenience.* London, 1985.

Mitsui-OSK Lines. "The Present Situation of Liner Shipping 1997/98." [Tokyo, 1998] (http://www.mol.co.jp/JE3/e3/nenpo/frame.html).

Neumeister, Michel. "Extrême orient: l'axe majeur." *Journal de la marine marchande,* XI (October 1996).

Nijhof, Erik. *"Gezien de dreigende onrust in de haven..." De ontwikkeling van de arbeidsverhoudingen in de Rotterdamse haven 1945-1965.* Amsterdam, 1988.

Nippon Yusen Kaisha. Research Chamber. *World's Containership Fleet and Its Operations.* Tokyo, 1988.

Northfield, J.H.W. "Port Management and Operations at Felixstowe." In Institution of Civil Engineers (ed.). *Port Engineering and Operation.* London, 1985, pp. 111-121.

Pallis, Athanasios A. "Towards a Common Port Policy? EU-Proposals and the Port Industry's Perceptions." *Maritime Management and Policy*, XXIV, (1997), pp. 365-380.

Pearson, R. *Container Ships and Shipping*. London, 1988.

_____ and Fossey, J. *World Deep-Sea Container Shipping*. Aldershot, 1983.

Proudfoot, P.R. "Sydney and Its Two Seaports." *International Journal of Maritime History*, I (1989), pp. 141-184.

Randier, Jean. *Histoire de la marine marchande française des premiers vapeurs à nos jours*. Paris, 1980.

Reveley, James. "Waterfront Labour Reform in New Zealand: Pressures, Processes and Outcomes." *Journal of Industrial Relations*, XXXIX, No. 3 (1997), pp. 369-387.

Schreiber, Hermann. *Verkehr, Schienenbahnen, Schiffahrt, Luftfahrt*. Darmstadt, 1972.

Salack, Brian; Comtois, Claude; and Sletmo, Gunnar. "Shipping Lines as Agents of Change." *Maritime Management and Policy*, XXIII (1996), pp. 289-300.

Stubbs, Peter. *Australia and the Maritime Industries*. Melbourne, 1981.

Sturmey, S.G. *British Shipping and World Competition*. London, 1962.

Suykens, F., *et al. Antwerp. A Port for All Seasons*. Antwerp, 1986.

Tabak, Herman D. *Cargo Containers. Their Stowage, Handling and Movement*. Cambridge, MD, 1970.

Thanopoulou, H.A. "From Internationalisation to Globalisation: Trends in Modern Shipping." *Journal of Maritime Research* (electronic) (February 2000).

_____; Ryoo, Dong-Keun; and Lee, Tae-Woo. "Korean Shipping in the Era of Global Alliances." Unpublished conference paper, 1997.

Trace, Keith. "Shipping Links between Australia and Japan: An Analysis of Current Problems and an Agenda for Further Research." Unpublished paper, Melbourne, 1977.

_____. "ASEAN Ports since 1945: Maritime Change and Port Rivalry." In Broeze, Frank (ed.). *Gateways of Asia. Port Cities of Asia from the 14th to 20th Centuries*. London, 1997, pp. 318-338.

_____. "For 'Tyranny of Distance' Read 'Tyranny of Scale:' Australia and the Global Container Market." Unpublished paper, Australian Association for Maritime History, Vaughan Evans Memorial Lecture, Wellington, NZ, 1998.

Trinca, Helen and Davies, Anne. *Waterfront. The Battle that Changed Australia*. Sydney, 2000.

Tull, M.T., "American Technology and the Mechanisation of Australian Ports 1942 to 1958." *Journal of Transport History*, VI (1985), pp. 79-90.

_____. *A Community Enterprise: The History of the Port of Fremantle, 1897 to 1997*. St. John's, 1997.

Turnbull, Peter; Woolfson, Charles; and Kelly, John. *Dock Strike: Conflict and Restructuring in Britain's Ports*. Aldershot, 1992.

Van den Burg, G. *Containerisation and Other Unit Transport*. London, 1975.

Van Driel, Hugo. *Een verenigde nederlandse scheepvaart.De fusie tussen Nedlloyd en KNSM in 1980-1981*. Delft, 1988.

_____. *Samenwerking in haven en vervoer in het containertijdperk*. Delft, 1990.

_____. "Collusion in Transport: Group Effects in a Historical Perspective." *Journal of Economic Behavior and Organization*, XLI (2000), pp. 385-404.

Wallace, G.J. "Felixstowe: Britain's Little Big Port." *Geography*, LX (1975), pp. 209-213.

Wellman, David. *The Union Makes Us Strong. Radical Unionism on the San Francisco Waterfront*. Cambridge, 1995.

Whitehurst, Clinton H., Jr. *The U.S. Merchant Marine*. Annapolis, MD, 1983.

Wijnolst, Niko and Wergeland, Tor. *Shipping*. Delft, 1996.

Wilson, David F. *Dockers. The Impact of Industrial Change*. London, 1972.

Witthöft, Hans Jürgen. *Container. Transportrevolution unseres Jahrhunderts*. 2nd ed., Herford, 1977.

Woods, James R. "The Container Revolution." *Journal of World Trade Law*, VI (1972), pp. 661-692.

Printed and bound by CPI Group (UK) Ltd, Croydon, CR0 4YY